Emerging Markets and Sovereign Risk

Also by Nigel Finch

BEST PRACTICES IN MANAGEMENT ACCOUNTING (*with G. N. Gregoriou*)

CONTEMPORARY ISSUES IN MINING: LEADING PRACTICE IN AUSTRALIA

FUNDAMENTALS OF CORPORATE FINANCE (*with J. Berk, P. DeMarzo, J. Harford, and G. Ford*)

Emerging Markets and Sovereign Risk

Edited by

Nigel Finch
Associate Professor, The University of Sydney, Australia

palgrave
macmillan

Softcover reprint of the hardcover 1st edition 2015 978-1-137-45065-4

First published 2015 by
PALGRAVE MACMILLAN

Palgrave Macmillan in the UK is an imprint of Macmillan Publishers Limited, registered in England, company number785998, of Houndmills, Basingstoke, Hampshire RG21 6XS.

Palgrave Macmillan in the US is a division of St Martin's Press LLC, 175 Fifth Avenue, New York, NY 10010.

Palgrave Macmillan is the global academic imprint of the above companies and has companies and representatives throughout the world.

Palgrave® and Macmillan® are registered trademarks in the United States, the United Kingdom, Europe, and other countries.

ISBN 978-1-349-49703-4 ISBN 978-1-137-45066-1 (eBook)
DOI 10.1057/9781137450661

This book is printed on paper suitable for recycling and made from fully managed and sustained forest sources. Logging, pulping, and manufacturing processes are expected to conform to the environmental regulations of the country of origin.

A catalogue record for this book is available from the British Library.

A catalog record for this book is available from the Library of Congress.

Contents

Part III Management of Sovereign Risk and Ratings

List of Figures

List of Tables

Acknowledgements

I would like to thank Aimee Dibbens at Palgrave Macmillan for guiding me through the project. I would also like to thank Siew-Ching Lim for the excellent work in editing this manuscript. Thanks also to the anonymous referees who assisted in the selection of chapters for this book and to each of the authors for their generous contribution of time, knowledge, and expertise. While all care has been taken, neither the publisher nor the editor is responsible for the accuracy of each chapter written by the contributors.

Notes on Contributors

David E. Allen is Adjunct Professor of Finance in the Centre for Applied Financial Studies at the University of South Australia, Adelaide, and a Visiting Professor in the School of Mathematics and Statistics at the University of Sydney, NSW. He is the author of three monographs and over 80 refereed publications on a diverse range of topics covering corporate financial policy decisions, asset pricing, business economics, funds management and performance bench-marking, volatility modelling and hedging, and market microstructure and liquidity.

Astrid Ayala is a professor at the School of Business of Universidad Francisco Marroquín. She has a PhD degree in Economics from Universidad de Navarra, Spain. She teaches several courses of finance and economics at Universidad Francisco Marroquín. Her articles have been published in *Economic Systems, Journal of Applied Economics, Applied Economics, Applied Economics Letters*, and *Applied Financial Economics.*

Banita Bissoondoyal-Bheenick is a senior lecturer in the Department of Accounting and Finance. Banita's research interest is mainly in asset pricing, stock market volatility, stock markets analysis, mostly related to credit ratings – analysing the determinants of credit ratings, stock market impact and rating changes, structured finance products ratings and the Global Financial Crisis, and corporate ratings.

Robert Brooks is a professor in the Department of Econometrics and Business Statistics and Deputy Dean, Education in the Faculty of Business and Economics. His primary area of research interest is in financial econometrics, with a particular focus on beta risk estimation, volatility modelling, and the analysis of the impacts of sovereign credit rating changes on financial markets.

Szabolcs Blazsek is a professor at the School of Business of Universidad Francisco Marroquín. He has a PhD degree in Economics from Universidad Carlos III de Madrid, Spain. He teaches several courses of finance and econometrics at Universidad Francisco Marroquín. His articles have been published in *Journal of Econometrics, The European Journal of Finance, Applied Financial Economics, Applied Economics, Applied Economics Letters,* and *Economic Systems.*

Marie Cavanaugh worked for Standard & Poor's Rating Services for 30 years through early 2014. She participated in many committees determining global sovereign ratings, was a key point-person for external and internal inquiries on a range of analytical and procedural issues, and served as Chief Global Sovereign Criteria Officer and Chief Global Sovereign Quality Officer. Marie has a Master's in Public Policy from Harvard University's Kennedy School of Government.

David Chaikin is an associate professor at the University of Sydney Business School. Prior to his academic appointment he was a practising lawyer specialising in multi-jurisdictional investigations, transnational commercial and criminal litigation as well as offshore corporate and banking law. He has held appointments as Senior Assistant Secretary of the Australian Attorney-General's Department and Senior Legal Officer of the London-based intergovernmental body, the Commonwealth Secretariat, and has worked as a consultant to the United Nations, the OECD-based Financial Action Task Force, and the Asia/Pacific Group on Money Laundering. David teaches in the areas of banking and finance law, corporate and commercial law, and asset protection/management of wealth risks. He has previously been a tenured lecturer at the London School of Economics and Political Science and a lecturer at Kings College, University of London. David's research expertise is in comparative corporate law, financial crime, tax evasion and money laundering, financial services law and regulation, offshore finance, private banking, and wealth management. He is a recipient of an ARC Discovery Grant and has been a lead consultant on major international research projects in Europe, the Americas, and Asia.

John B. Chambers is the Chair of the Sovereign Rating Committee, which makes all of Standard & Poor's sovereign rating decisions. He publishes and speaks regularly on a variety of issues involving sovereign creditworthiness around the globe. He has also worked in the Financial Institutions Group and as a private sector banker. John is a CFA and has a Master's in English from Columbia University.

Serge Darolles is Professor of Finance at Université Paris Dauphine where he has taught financial econometrics since 2012. Prior to joining Dauphine, he worked for Lyxor between 2000 and 2012, where he developed mathematical models for various investment strategies. He also held consultant roles at Caisse des Dépôts et Consignations, Banque Paribas, and the French Atomic energy Agency. Darolles specializes in financial econometrics and has written numerous articles which have been published in academic journals. He holds a PhD in Applied Mathematics from the University of Toulouse and a postgraduate degree from ENSAE, Paris.

Jérémy Dudek is a PhD candidate at CREST (Centre de Recherche en Economie et Statistique) and Paris Dauphine. He did a master's in econometrics at Université d'Orléans. In 2012 he visited New York University-STERN School of Business, where he was sponsored by Professor Viral Acharya. His research interests are in financial econometrics. His recent researches have included liquidity and contagion measurement in order to propose tools for fund managers, especially in the case of emerging markets but also market liquidity and systemic risk measurement.

Nigel Finch is Associate Dean (Undergraduate) at the University of Sydney Business School. His academic qualifications include degrees in accounting, business, and law, and a doctorate in business law. His professional qualifications include membership of CPA Australia and the Institute of Chartered Accountants in Australia. He is also a fellow of the Financial Services Institute of Australasia, the Taxation Institute of Australia, the Australian Institute of Company Directors, and CPA Australia, and Associate Professor in Accounting at the University of Sydney Business School. His principal areas of research and teaching include financial reporting, financial performance measurement, and the valuation and impairment of assets. He is the editor of the *Journal of Applied Research in Accounting and Finance* and a member of the editorial board of the *Journal of Intellectual Capital* and *Managerial Finance*. Dr Nigel Finch is a Certified Practising Accountant, a Chartered Accountant, a Chartered Tax Adviser, and an adviser to several businesses and industry groups in Australia and Asia. He is a member of the Business Council of Mongolia, a founding director of Australia Mongolia Business Council Limited, and a member of CPA Australia's International Advisory Committee.

Anna M. Fisher is currently Project Manager at BAEconomics Pty Ltd. She was previously with the infrastructure advisory firm Evans & Peck in project management and commercial services. She holds a Bachelor's of Project Engineering and Management (Civil) and a Bachelor of Arts (Spanish) from the University of Sydney.

Brian S. Fisher is currently the Chairman and Managing Director of BAEconomics Pty Ltd. He was previously the Executive Director of the Australian Bureau of Agricultural and Resource Economics (ABARE), the Professor of Agricultural Economics, and the Dean of the Faculty of

Agriculture at the University of Sydney. He holds a PhD in agricultural economics and a DScAgr (University of Sydney).

Anna Golab is the Faculty of Business and Law's Research Consultant and lecturer at Edith Cowan University, where she has recently completed her PhD in the research field of European emerging markets and economies. Her research adopted a time series framework and extensive econometrics analysis.

Raúl B. González de Paz is technical adviser at the Financial Area of Banco de Guatemala (Central Bank of Guatemala). He has a doctorate in Mathematics from Université de Montpellier II, France. He works on quantitative modelling and risk analysis at Banco de Guatemala. He teaches Investment Theory, Quantitative Methods for Finance, and Fixed Income Analysis at Universidad Francisco Marroquín. He has published research articles on financial derivatives applied to central banking risk management and monetary policy.

Sean Hinton is the founder of Terbish Partners and advises on cross-border transactions in the energy and minerals sector in China, Mongolia, and Africa focusing on the social and economic impact of large-scale investment projects. Hinton was a consultant at McKinsey & Company from 1995 to 2000 and studied at GSMD (London), University of Cambridge, and MIT Sloan School of Management.

Gaëlle Le Fol is Full Professor of Finance at Paris Dauphine and Research Fellow at the CREST. She is the scientific director of the QMI (Quantitative Management Initiative). She holds a PhD in Economics from University Paris 1 Panthéon – Sorbonne. Before joining Paris Dauphine, Gaëlle Le Fol was Professor of Economics at the University of Evry. She has also been Professor of Economics at the University of Angers and Assistant Professor at University Paris 1 Panthéon – Sorbonne. Her research interests are in financial market microstructure and financial econometrics.

Max McGraw provides data and other support to analysts in the Sovereign Group, helping to prepare documents critical for rating committees and for special studies. He is responsible for several regular publications on sovereign rating and transfer and convertibility assessment histories, as well as ratings above the sovereign. Max has a BA in Economics from Vassar College.

Jeffrey Manns is an Associate Professor of Law at George Washington University. He serves as the Executive Director of the Center for Law,

Economics, and Finance, as well as the Co-Director of the Business and Finance Law LLM program. He was consulted as an expert on credit rating agencies for the Securities & Exchange Commission's and Government Accountability Office's studies on the implementation of the Dodd-Frank Act. Professor Manns is widely cited for his rating agency expertise and has authored several law review articles on rating agencies, as well as op-eds in the *New York Times* and *Bloomberg*. He received his JD degree from Yale Law School and his D.Phil. from Oxford University.

R. McFall Lamm, Jr. is chief investment officer at Stelac Advisory Services LLC, an investment management boutique. He was previously chief global strategist at Deutsche Bank and Bankers Trust Company. Lamm has received several awards for outstanding research, published numerous articles appearing in professional journals, and written dozens of book chapters appearing in edited works. He is well-known for proficiency in managing global portfolios, asset allocation, and expertise in alternative investments.

Lebogang Mateane is a graduate student at the New School University and a research assistant at the Schwartz Center for Economic Policy Analysis.

Mauro Megliani is senior research fellow in international law at the Catholic University of Milan where he is also adjunct professor of law and member of the board of the PhD School 'Istituzioni e Politiche'. He is a qualified lawyer and member of the editorial board of the journal *Diritto del commercio internazionale*. He has received the degree of Magister Juris in European and Comparative Law from the University of Oxford.

Albert Metz is the Managing Director of Credit Policy Research at Moody's Investors Service. He also works as Director of Default Research, related to both fundamental and structured finance instruments. Metz maintains Moody's patented corporate default and rating transition forecast models. Metz joined Moody's in December 2003. Prior to that, he was an economist in the Microeconomic and Financial Studies division of the Congressional Budget Office. He also worked as Chief Economist of Security Capital Group. Metz holds a PhD in Economics from the University of Chicago.

Robert Powell has 20 years' banking experience in South Africa, New Zealand, and Australia. He has been involved in the development and implementation of several credit and financial analysis models in banks. He has a PhD from Edith Cowan University, where he currently works as an Associate Professor, teaching and researching in banking and finance.

Willi Semmler is the Henry Arnhold Professor of Economics, Department of Economics at The New School, New York. He is author or co-author of more than 85 articles in international journals and is author or co-author of 11 books, among them books on industrial organization, economic growth, growth, resources and the environment, macroeconomics, and the European macroeconomy. His recent book is *Asset Prices, Booms and Recessions* (2011). He has taught at the American University, Washington, DC; Bielefeld University; and UNAM, Mexico City; and at various French universities. He is a regular evaluator of EU research projects. He was visiting scholar at Columbia University; Stanford University; Humboldt University, Berlin; and Fulbright Professor at the University of Economics and Business, Austria. He is Research associate at the SCEPA, New School University.

Prakash Kumar Shrestha is Deputy Director, Nepal Rastra Bank, Kathmandu. He holds a PhD in Economics from The New School for Social Research, New York, USA.

Lúcio Vinhas de Souza is the Sovereign Chief Economist of Moody's Investor Services. Before that, he coordinated the analysis and forecasting for developed economies and the ECA region at the World Bank's Development Prospects Group. Prior to that, he was Head of the Russia/Belarus Desk at the DG-ECFIN of the European Commission. He is widely published in several languages. Vinhas de Souza holds a PhD in Economics from the Erasmus University Rotterdam.

Merxe Tudela is a Senior Analyst in Credit Policy Research at Moody's Investors Service covering Sovereign and Sub-sovereign credit risk. She is the author of Moody's default studies for the sovereign, sub-sovereign, U.S. public finance and infrastructure sectors. Merxe joined Moody's in 2011 and prior to that, she was a Senior Economist at the Bank of England. She holds a PhD in Economics from the London School of Economics.

Part I

Risk and Emerging Market Investment

1
Economic Growth vs. Equity Returns in Emerging Markets

R. McFall Lamm, Jr.

1 Background

An important controversy in modern finance is the conclusion by some researchers that countries with high economic growth rates do not deliver superior equity returns versus nations growing slowly. The absence of a positive growth-return correlation was first suggested by Siegel (1998). In a comprehensive and influential study covering 16 countries and using a century of history extending back to 1900, Dimson, Marsh, and Staunton (henceforth DMS) (2002) found that the growth-return correlation was actually negative. Ritter (2005) employed somewhat different sources and reported that the growth-return correlation was zero for 19 developed markets from 1970 to 2002 and negligible for 13 emerging markets using data from 1988 to 2002. DMS (2010) updated their original work and confirmed that for 44 countries, there was no statistically significant relationship between growth and returns.

The implications of these findings are far-reaching. For example, if equity returns are no greater from investing in high-growth emerging markets, then there is little reason for international capital to flow in their direction, presuming that equity market performance parallels capital returns. There could be portfolio diversification benefits, of course, but this rarely serves as the primary motivation for investing in emerging markets. DMS and Ritter argue that committing funds outside one's own country is essentially pointless from a return perspective, a counter-intuitive proposition.

Most economists believe that the free flow of international capital to high-growth countries rewards investors with superior returns while simultaneously allowing recipients to grow faster than if they had relied solely on internally generated financing. Nonetheless, the DMS and

Ritter conclusions have been accepted by a broad swath of the investment world. For example, Saldanha (2010) concurs with DMS and Ritter, arguing that strong economic growth by itself is not likely to produce superior equity market performance. Davis, Aliaga-Diaz, Cole, and Shanahan (2010) replicate DMS and Ritter's results, and caution against emerging market investment in anticipation that more rapid economic growth will lead to higher returns. Barra Research (2010) also confirms the DMS and Ritter findings, and contends that a zero growth-return correlation is justified due to earnings dilution and the fact that high growth is already reflected in current stock prices.

A few investment professionals have challenged DMS and Ritter. O'Neill, Stupnytska, and Wrisdale (2011) argue that the link between GDP growth and equity returns is in fact very strong – as long as growth expectations are taken into account. Anderson (2011) makes the case that returns in one's home currency from investing in high-growth markets are in fact correlated with macro outcomes, although no proof is presented.

In this chapter, I consider the growth-return puzzle from a global investor's perspective and concur with those who dispute DMS and Ritter. I specifically argue that DMS and Ritter focus on the wrong metric – country growth versus local equity returns rather than growth versus the equity return that an international investor would receive. When one looks at the world from this latter perspective, I demonstrate that the growth-return correlation is positive and statistically significant. This conclusion holds for a variety of different countries and time periods.

2 What does intuition tell us?

There is a strong foundation for presuming that the growth-return relationship should be positive. On a simple accounting basis, GDP equals the sum of wages, profits, rents, and other factor returns. If the profit share of GDP is relatively constant, as it is for many countries, then more rapid economic growth should produce a proportionately high rate of profit growth in a closed economy. Equity returns should rise in parallel as long as valuations (price-to-earnings ratios) are stable.

For sure, there are extraneous factors that might distort a positive growth-return correlation. For example, most economies are open and the dominant companies in any market may be global firms that earn virtually all of their profits offshore. One would expect a very weak or no relationship between stock returns and GDP growth in such a situation.

The Swiss market is a good illustration where Nestle, Novartis, Roche, UBS, and Credit Suisse account for 70% of the Swiss Market Index. Switzerland's economic growth is largely irrelevant to the earnings of these multinational firms and their stock returns.

Another mitigating influence that might alter the growth-return relationship is the time horizon considered. For example, examining growth versus returns for Japan over a few years before or after 1989 would be very misleading – the period encompasses the build-up and bursting of the greatest equity bubble ever with valuations surging to extraordinary levels.

Supporters of DMS and Ritter suggest other reasons for an absence of any relationship between growth and returns. Market participants may have already bid up stock prices in high-growth countries; political developments could fundamentally shift the profit share of the economy; or firms may not pass through total earnings growth to investors because of share dilution. These possibilities are credible and could neutralise a positive growth-return relationship. It is thus perhaps not surprising that many people accept the DMS and Ritter thesis as unadulterated fact.

Nonetheless, there is a flipside to these arguments, and it is not clear why the growth-return relationship should be zero. Most companies in major equity markets do have strong home country exposure.[1] Furthermore, if stock prices are already bid up to reflect expected growth, then early arrivers should benefit; bubbles contained in any sample can be addressed by lengthening the time horizon considered; and share dilution is in reality not excessive in most markets. In addition, among others, Fama (1981) and Bakaert and Harvey (2000) point to theoretical reasons why the relationship between growth and equity returns should be positive, although the interaction is complex and involves factors such as economic structure and currency volatility.

3 Relevant growth-return metrics

Of critical importance is the way the growth-return relationship is measured. In a world of international capital mobility where investors constantly scour the globe searching for higher stock returns than are available domestically, it seems rational to expect that a country growing 10% annually would offer more than a stagnant economy. However, the comparison needs to be made in the global investor's home currency since changes in foreign exchange values could offset gains or accentuate losses.

DMS and Ritter compare economic growth to equity returns for their sample countries on a local currency basis. While this is appropriate for residents, it is irrelevant to external investors – DMS and Ritter neglect currency translation, which ultimately determines the returns that outsiders receive. To argue that there is no relationship between local returns and growth does not matter to the international investor who cares only whether there is a relationship between local growth and the realized return denominated in their home currency.

In a world of permanently fixed exchange rates, this would not matter. But the reality is that currency values fluctuate, rising or falling over the long run depending on relative fiscal and monetary policy as well as structural changes such as privatisations and other political reforms. There is no reason to believe that changes in currency values will exactly offset equity gains or losses for investors who purchase foreign stocks.

Supporters of DMS and Ritter will no doubt argue that the local growth-return relationship is pertinent because an outside investor can hedge away currency exposure and thereby reap the same equity return as a local investor. However, hedging is often very expensive and needs to be explicitly taken into account, which DSM and Ritter do not.

4 A case study of the US and UK growth-return relationship

The US and UK offer an excellent starting point for examining the issue – available data for these two countries are the most comprehensive available over a long period of time. I take UK real GDP, inflation, and sterling/dollar rates from Thomas, Hills, and Dimsdale (2010, updated) and UK equity returns from DMS.[2] For the US, I use real GDP data from Balke and Gordon (1986) up to 1928 and from the US Dept. of Commerce thereafter. US equity returns are from Shiller (2005, updated). Results for this sample, which covers 112 years from 1900 to 2012, are summarised in Table 1.1.

My conclusions are the following. First, nominal equity returns are almost exactly the same in the UK and US, averaging 9.4% and 9.5% per year, respectively. However, real equity returns in the US are 1.1% higher due to UK inflation averaging close to 1% more annually. Over the sample period, real GDP in the US grew 1.3% faster in aggregate and 0.5% more per capita annually than in the UK. US domestic investors experienced higher real equity returns compared with their UK counterparts.

Second, US investors were well advised to stay at home in their own high-growth market, while UK investors should have invested abroad

Table 1.1 Equity returns vs. economic growth for the US and UK – 112 years from 1900 to 2012

Metric	UK	US
Average annual growth in local currency		
Real GDP	1.9%	3.2%
Real GDP per capita	1.5%	2.0%
Nominal stock return	9.4%	9.5%
Inflation	3.9%	3.0%
Real stock return	5.2%	6.3%
Sterling	–	–1.0%
Dollar	1.0%	–
US investor's return ($)	**Nominal**	**Real**
On US equities	9.5%	6.3%
On UK equities	8.3%	5.1%
UK investor return (£)		
On US equities	10.6%	6.4%
On UK equities	9.4%	5.2%

Note: all entries are geometric means.

in the higher-growth US. In fact, US investors would have underperformed by 1.2% annually in real terms on funds invested in the UK, while UK investors would have gained a similar amount each year by investing in the US. This differential approximates the 1% fall in sterling vs. the dollar and compounds to a huge cumulative outperformance over time.

There are extended periods within the sample where the performance difference is muted. This is why Ritter shows UK vs. US real returns of 4.8% and 5.2% from 1970 to 2002 compared with GDP per capita growth of 2.1% vs. 1.9%. Over Ritter's 33-year window, there is no growth-return correlation.[3] It appears that sometimes a long investment horizon is necessary for the growth-return relationship to fully reveal itself. Regardless, the very long-run US-UK growth-return relationship is positive on a local currency basis, in dollars or in sterling.

The analysis is revealing in another way – the growth-return differential is stronger for aggregate GDP growth than on a per capita basis. The US economy expanded more than 1% faster annually than the UK, which aligns nicely with the real return differential of 1.2%. However, on a per capita basis, the growth differential is only 0.5%, which is not a lot. This raises the question of why one should focus on per capita rather than aggregate growth. The latter seems preferable since the investor should be indifferent as to whether equity returns arise from market growth due to population expansion or as a result of productivity gains.

5 Emerging markets vs. developed economies

Moving beyond a simple two-country comparison, I turn to emerging versus developed markets as represented by broad indices. Reliable equity return data for emerging markets begin in 1987, so this limits the sample to 25 years from 1988 to 2012. I use MSCI dollar returns for both developed and emerging markets deflated by the US consumer price index. For real GDP growth, I take reported World Bank growth rates for two groups: 'low- and middle-income' countries, a proxy for emerging markets; and the bank's 'high-income' category to represent developed economies. This not an exact one-for-one match because the growth and return series have different country weights; therefore, the comparison is proximate.

Table 1.2 shows the results. In sum, real economic growth in low- and middle-income countries (emerging markets) averaged 4.8% over the past quarter century. This was more than twice that of high-income countries where real growth averaged 2.3%. At the same time, real equity returns for emerging markets averaged 9.7% versus 4.3% for developed markets. This is much as one would expect – a positive growth-return relationship – and it is difficult to argue that the outcome is spurious. Interestingly, emerging markets' currencies fell 16% versus the dollar over the 1988–2012 period. Very high nominal equity returns in emerging markets more than compensated for weak currency performance.

As in the US–UK comparison, a substantial amount of time was necessary for the growth-return relationship to become evident. For example, emerging market equity returns were negative for nearly a decade from 1994 to 2003, heavily influenced by the 'bubble burst' after NAFTA

Table 1.2 Equity returns vs. economic growth for emerging vs. developed markets – 1988 through 2012

Metric	Developed economies	Emerging markets
Real GDP (local)	2.3%	4.8%
Real equity return ($)	4.3%	9.7%
Currency (vs. $)	–	–16.4%
Time series growth/ return correlation	0.76	0.56

euphoria in 1993 and the Asia currency crisis that began with the Thai baht crash in 1997. Indeed, in 1999, one might have argued that there was no growth-return correlation whatsoever since both emerging and developed markets posted essentially the same real returns over the prior ten years. One needed to know that the business cycles were out of sync – in 1999, emerging markets were in recession while developed markets were still experiencing a robust expansion. In the following decade, emerging market growth rose substantially above that of developed markets and equities outperformed strongly.

Besides the top-line growth-return comparison, I also regressed real equity returns on real growth for developed economies and emerging markets separately, finding the growth-return correlations to be 0.76 and 0.56, respectively.[4] This confirms the existence of a highly significant positive time-series relationship for both developed and emerging markets.

6 Individual country comparisons over a long horizon

MSCI reports equity returns in dollars for 18 countries beginning in 1971. Table 1.3 displays average real returns for each over the 43-year period 1971 to 2012 (in dollars, deflated by the US CPI), as well as average real GDP growth per capita from the World Bank. I include both the geometric mean return, which reflects the actual return that investors receive, as well as the arithmetic return, which captures return volatility and serves as input for higher moments used in forecasting applications. In the case of real GDP growth, geometric and arithmetic values are virtually identical, so I report only the former.

I use MSCI stock return data because they are transparent and readily obtainable.[5] Furthermore, MSCI indices are the dominant worldwide benchmark used by professional investors and the basis for most equity market ETFs (Exchange Traded Funds). MSCI statistics are the public domain flagship. In contrast, DMS data are available on a fee basis and are qualitatively difficult to evaluate.

For the 18 countries considered in Table 1.3, the geometric growth-return correlation is 0.37 while the arithmetic growth-return correlation is 0.72. The former is statistically different from zero with 87% confidence while the latter is significant with 99% confidence off standard tests. Within the sample, Denmark is the major outlier; dropping it from the analysis raises the growth-return correlations to 0.44 for geometric and 0.77 for arithmetic returns, respectively.

Table 1.3 Economic growth vs. stock returns for 18 countries, 1971–2012

Country	Geometric real equity return ($)	Arithmetic real equity return ($)	Geometric real GDP growth (per capita, local)	Temporal growth-return correlation	Currency return
Hong Kong	10.5%	18.5%	4.4%	0.63	–0.8%
Sweden	9.1%	13.1%	1.8%	0.59	–0.5%
Denmark	8.5%	11.9%	1.5%	0.46	0.7%
Netherlands	7.5%	9.6%	1.8%	0.65	1.8%
Singapore	7.1%	14.3%	5.0%	0.56	2.2%
Norway	7.0%	13.8%	2.4%	0.20	0.6%
Switzerland	7.0%	9.3%	1.1%	0.23	3.7%
Belgium	6.9%	10.7%	2.0%	0.47	1.1%
UK	5.8%	9.2%	2.0%	0.38	-0.9%
Canada	5.5%	7.7%	1.7%	0.43	0.2%
France	5.5%	8.8%	1.8%	0.35	0.3%
Germany	5.4%	9.0%	2.0%	0.36	2.2%
Australia	5.1%	8.4%	1.8%	0.51	-0.2%
US	5.1%	6.7%	1.8%	0.60	–
Japan	4.6%	8.8%	2.0%	0.56	3.4%
Spain	4.5%	8.6%	1.9%	0.50	-1.3%
Austria	4.0%	9.2%	2.2%	0.29	2.1%
Italy	1.0%	5.7%	1.6%	0.31	-2.0%

A closer examination of the information in the table reveals that the sample is characterised by clustering with many countries averaging close to 2% in real growth and exhibiting similar equity returns. However, Hong Kong and Singapore lie far outside the cluster in the northeast growth-return quadrant and heavily influence the results. Moreover, several small countries – Sweden, Denmark, the Netherlands, and Switzerland – have higher returns while being low-growth countries. This anomaly likely reflects the sizeable offshore exposure of domestic firms and suggests that weighting small countries equally with far larger markets may be misleading.

Using arithmetic averages corrects the clustering problem to some extent by broadening the return dispersion but does not address the relative size issue. As a crude remedy, I arbitrarily assign large, medium, and small markets scale coefficients of 3, 2, and 1, respectively. The recomputed geometric growth-return correlation rises to 0.85. Weighting the observations by pure market capitalisation takes the growth-return correlation to over 0.90.

The next to last column of the table shows the time series growth-return correlation for each country. As in the previous section, the results are based on a regression of current returns on the subsequent year's real growth to reflect the fact that equity prices are anticipatory. All of the growth-return correlations are statistically different from zero with more than 95% confidence with the exception of Austria, Norway, and Switzerland. The lack of a strong growth-return correlation for these markets could be due to the fact that companies in these small countries are largely international. Otherwise, fairly strong return-growth temporal correlations validate the cross-section results.

My sample is similar to Ritter's. However, I use dollar returns and a longer horizon (43 versus 33 years). Also, my 18 countries include Hong Kong while excluding Ireland and South Africa. The exclusion of Hong Kong from Ritter's 19-country analysis is quite important because it is a high-growth, high-return entry far from the cluster centre. As for Ireland and South Africa, MSCI does not report returns for these countries prior to 1987, and I therefore omit them.

To recap, I find a positive and statistically significant relationship between growth and returns – both for geometric and arithmetic returns, both cross-sectionally on a time-series basis. The positive cross-section correlation is largely attributable to Singapore and Hong Kong, which lie outside the traditional developed markets sphere. Investors living at the beginning of the sample in 1970 might have regarded these two countries as the emerging markets of the day. It is reassuring to discover that they delivered substantially greater equity returns, as would be expected. In addition, adjusting country weights used in the analysis to reflect market size yields an even stronger growth-return relationship.[6]

7 More countries, a shorter horizon

The 43-year sample should be long enough to capture the basic relationship between average growth and returns. After all, the 1970–2012 period includes a half-dozen global business cycles, and averaging over four decades mitigates the possibility of distortion due to an errant starting or ending point at a valuation extreme. Even so, 12 of the 18 countries are in Europe. Greater regional diversification would more strongly support the positive growth-return hypothesis.

In 1988, MSCI began disseminating returns for 17 additional countries – mostly emerging markets. One's first impulse might be to include the newcomers to produce a broad universe of 35 countries covering 25 years. But this would be naïve – many of the added countries were experiencing extreme inflation at the time. In fact, as late as 1993, more than a dozen of the new MSCI countries reported double-digit inflation. This makes the corresponding real GDP data subject to potentially serious measurement error, and the reported growth rates are therefore questionable.

Even reported MSCI returns should be treated with some scepticism. For example, offshore investors were unlikely to have realised the 731% one-year dollar return reported by MSCI for Poland in 1993, nor the 243%, 390%, and 238% returns reported for Indonesia, Argentina, and Russia in 1988, 1991, and 1998, respectively. While the MSCI methodology may be technically correct, equity return reality may be altogether different.

Rather than use possibly corrupt information and risk error, one option is to focus on more recent statistics that are significantly improved. Acknowledging the limitations of employing a short horizon to broaden country coverage, I arbitrarily take the past 10 years for a quick snapshot.[7] Table 1.4 presents average real returns versus real GDP growth for a 48-country sample. Returns cover the years from 2002 to 2011 while growth is over the 2003 to 2012 period to reflect lead-lag growth-return dynamics. The growth-return correlation is 0.56, which is highly significant statistically.[8] If one utilises the 3, 2, 1 weighting scheme previously discussed, the growth-return correlation rises to 0.61 and to 0.91 off pure market capitalisation weighting.

I also report currency returns for each market over the sample. In contrast to the cases examined earlier in this chapter, changes in currency values are larger and play a greater role in determining investment returns. Currency appreciation or depreciation appears to be especially germane for short horizons.

An advantage of using a more contemporary sample is that metrics such as price-to-earnings ratios are available, which allow an assessment of whether the results are sensitive to starting valuations. I include earning yields (the inverse of the P/E ratio from MSCI) as of December 2002 as a relative value indicator. The results of regressing real returns on earnings yield and economic growth for each country are presented in Table 1.5. Both are highly significant statistically, and the addition of earnings yield drives up the joint correlation with returns to 0.68. The positive growth-return relationship is confirmed yet again, as is the critical importance of starting valuation.

Table 1.4 Ten years of growth vs. returns for 48 countries, ranked from highest to lowest

Country	Return	GDP (t+1)	FX	Start E/P	Country	Return	GDP (t+1)	FX	Start E/P
	--------	%	--------			-------	%	-------	
Colombia	34.5	4.7	5.0	12.9	Denmark	8.7	0.6	2.3	5.3
Indonesia	29.8	5.7	–0.7	16.6	Arg.	7.6	7.1	–1.1	5.0
Peru	26.9	6.5	0.8	14.4	Poland	7.4	4.3	2.2	0.4
Czech Rep.	22.1	2.9	4.7	11.0	Hungary	7.0	1.1	0.2	10.2
Egypt	20.9	4.6	–3.1	18.4	Sweden	7.0	2.2	3.0	1.1
Thailand	19.7	4.2	3.5	5.2	HK	6.0	4.5	0.1	7.4
Brazil	18.6	3.6	5.6	7.9	Switz.	5.1	1.9	4.2	2.8
Pakistan	16.1	4.7	5.1	7.9	Spain	5.1	1.3	2.3	3.9
S. Africa	15.8	3.5	0.1	5.6	Jordan	4.0	5.7	–2.1	0.0
Chile	15.0	4.4	4.2	3.4	Israel	3.8	4.0	2.1	2.3
India	13.4	7.6	–1.3	7.7	Austria	3.7	1.6	2.3	6.4
China	12.3	10.4	0.1	9.5	Germany	2.6	1.2	2.3	1.2
Mexico	12.2	2.5	–2.1	7.5	Taiwan	2.3	4.1	1.8	2.5
Morocco	12.0	4.6	1.8	0.4	UK	2.3	1.4	0.1	1.4
Philippines	11.9	5.2	2.7	5.0	Neth.	1.2	1.2	2.3	1.7
Russia	11.4	4.6	0.5	12.6	France	1.0	1.0	2.3	0.0
Korea	11.3	3.6	1.0	12.2	Portugal	0.7	–0.1	2.3	4.6
Australia	11.0	3.1	6.3	5.0	Japan	0.6	0.8	3.2	0.0
Malaysia	11.0	5.1	2.2	6.1	US	0.5	1.6	–	5.2
Norway	11.0	1.6	2.2	6.3	Belgium	–0.4	1.3	2.3	7.0
Turkey	9.3	5.0	–0.7	11.0	Italy	–1.3	–0.1	2.3	2.2
Canada	9.0	1.8	4.7	5.4	Finland	–4.3	1.6	2.3	4.9
N. Zealand	8.9	1.9	4.7	0.2	Ireland	–8.5	1.8	2.3	7.9
Singapore	8.8	6.0	3.6	5.2	Greece	–12.4	–0.1	2.3	8.6

Table 1.5 Real returns regressed on earnings yield and real GDP growth for 48 countries

	Real GDP	E/P	Intercept	r	R^2
Estimate	1.65	0.85	–0.02	0.68	0.462
Std. error	(0.47)	(0.24)	(0.02)		
T statistic	3.51	3.56	–0.90		
Estimate	2.25		0.01	0.56	0.311
Std. error	(0.49)		(0.02)		
T statistic	4.56		0.72		
Estimate		1.14	0.02	0.56	0.315
Std. error		(0.25)	(0.02)		
T statistic		4.60	1.02		

Note: average real returns in dollars regressed on starting earnings yield and average real GDP growth.

8 Caveats

The evidence presented here strongly supports the proposition that high-growth countries deliver better equity returns to investors in their home currency, which I take to be the US dollar. Indeed, I cannot find any hard evidence to refute a positive growth-return correlation. This explicitly contradicts DMS and Ritter who view equity returns abstractly from a local currency perspective.[9]

My major qualifications are that: (1) the relationship is weaker for small countries with markets dominated by multinational firms; (2) the return-growth correlation is time variant, and a number of years may be necessary for it to fully show itself; and (3) starting valuations are important, especially for short horizons such as a decade.

One might logically inquire why, if high-growth countries in fact provide superior equity returns, has the phenomenon not been arbitraged away? The obvious response is that it is not common knowledge – as illustrated by DMS and Ritter who maintain that the relationship does not even exist. Furthermore, simply knowing the existence of the relationship does not guarantee that one can successfully exploit it – one must be able to forecast which countries will experience high growth in the future. Carelessly selecting any emerging market may not work since there are examples in recent years where growth in some countries such as Brazil and China has not met expectations. Even if one can guess which emerging markets will deliver higher growth, it may be necessary to hold the exposure for a long time to collect the pay-off. While institutions may have the necessary wherewithal to persevere, most private investors and hedge funds do not.

Another reason why market participants may not have fully exploited positive growth-return correlation is the persistence of home-country bias. Studies have long demonstrated that investors overweight domestic markets and underweight others in their portfolios. While this may be no more than natural risk aversion, if home-country bias diminishes in the future, the growth-return relationship should be there since developed-market investors generally underweight emerging markets.

A more sophisticated approach to capture the growth-return link might be to weight emerging markets proportionate to size rather than equally as suggested by correlation analysis (for example, China has more than 20 times the market capitalisation of some small emerging markets). However, it is not clear what alternative weighting scheme is best. Order of magnitude (1, 2, 3 scaling) or market capitalisation are options, but why not use GDP weighting? Alternative weighting schemes can yield significantly different outcomes as demonstrated by Lamm (2011).

9 Conclusion

The generic DMS and Ritter assertion that there is no correlation between real economic growth and equity returns appears fallacious when viewed on a common currency basis. Over more than a century, US real growth outpaced the UK, and so did real equity returns. Investors in either country profited more by investing in the high-growth US. Investing in high-growth countries also paid off over the past four decades for the 18 countries examined, over the past quarter of a century if one bought the MSCI emerging markets basket versus developed markets, and even over the past decade for 48 countries considered. The growth-return relationship appears undeniably positive.

This conclusion implies that capital flows to high-growth countries are in fact defensible and investors should ultimately reap higher returns from buying stocks in these markets accordingly. In addition, researchers such as Cornell (2010), Lamm (2010), and others who previously argued the virtues of investing in high-growth emerging markets appear fully justified in doing so. For sure, investors may have to be patient awaiting the pay-off, and they need to make sure that valuations are not excessive when capital is committed. However, these considerations are also integral to investing in home markets where valuations are sometimes too high and equity market performance can sometimes languish for years.

The alternative to accepting a positive growth-return relationship is to embrace the DMS and Ritter argument. This means believing that capital flows to high-growth markets make little sense and one is just as well off investing 100% at home. No doubt, if you reside in a high-growth market or one where most companies have external exposure to other high-growth markets, staying at home might work. Otherwise, if you're like the majority of investors, then emerging markets beckon.

Notes

1. For example, national income data show that only 20% of US corporate profits come from offshore, and Huizinga and Laeven (2006) report that foreign sales account for only 23% of total revenue for European companies with offshore subsidiaries.

2. The one exception I make is to use Morgan Stanley Capital International (MSCI) data for the UK after 1970. My reason is that DSM report average returns that exceed those of MSCI by more than 1% annually over the overlap period. MSCI data appear to be more conservative.
3. US growth was unusually sluggish over these years and the UK's above its long-term average. Above trend UK growth was likely due to the Thatcher revolution, which included the privatisation of state-owned companies that had spillover effects into the 1990s, and windfall economic benefits from the exploitation of huge North Sea oil deposits.
4. I actually use the one-period ahead real economic growth rate because equity prices are based on expected growth, not the concurrent rate of expansion. Using next-period growth presumes perfect foresight, and one would prefer to use actual expectations, which unfortunately are unobservable.
5. MSCI provides month-by-month stock price and total return indices for all countries on its website.
6. I also note that currency returns (displayed in the last column of the table) are generally small, which indicates that currency fluctuation played a limited role in influencing the results.
7. This may not be as restrictive as it looks – this period starts at a neutral point and incorporates a full global business cycle through the Great Recession and beyond to several years later.
8. Normally one can disregard the lead-lag dynamic between returns and growth since rates converge over long horizons. However, for a ten-year period, the differential can be substantial.
9. The conclusion that growth and returns are positively correlated is equally valid for an investor using any base currency, subject to a linear transform foreign exchange adjustment.

References

Anderson, J (2011), 'Explaining the Equity-Growth Puzzle in Emerging Markets', *UBS Macro Keys*, 8 June.

Barra Research (2010), 'Is There a Link between GDP Growth and Equity Returns?', *MSCI/Barra Research Bulletin*, May.

Balke, N & Gordon, R J (1986), 'Historical Data' in Robert J Gordon (ed.), *The American Business Cycle*, National Bureau of Economic Research, University of Chicago Press.

Bakaert, G & Harvey, C R (2000), 'Foreign Speculators and Emerging Market Equities', *Journal of Finance*, vol. 55, no. 2, pp. 565–613.

Cornell, B. (2010), 'Economic Growth and Equity Investing', *Financial Analysts Journal*, vol. 66, no. 1, pp. 54–64.

Davis, J H, Aliaga-Diaz, R, Cole, C W & Shanahan, J (2010), 'Investing in Emerging Markets: Evaluating the Allure of Rapid Economic Growth', Vanguard Investment Consulting & Research, The Vanguard Group, April 2010.

Dimson, E, Marsh, P & Staunton, M (2002), *Triumph of the Optimists*, Princeton University Press, Princeton, New Jersey.

Dimson, E, Marsh, P & Staunton, M (2010), 'Economic Growth', *Credit Suisse Global Investment Returns Yearbook*, Credit Suisse Research Institute, 13–19 February.

Fama, E F (1981), 'Stock Returns, Real Activity, Inflation and Money', *American Economic Review*, vol. 71, no. 4, pp. 545–565.

Huizinga, H & Laeven, L (2006), 'International Profit Sharing within Multinationals: A Multi-Country Perspective', European Commission Directorate-General for Economic and Financial Affairs Economic Papers, no. 260, December 2006.

Lamm, R M (2010), 'Equity Returns in Emerging Markets: Prospects for the BRICs' in G N Gregoriou (ed.), *Emerging Markets: Performance, Analysis and Innovation*, Chapman-Hall/Taylor and Francis, London.

Lamm, R M (2011), 'Improving Emerging Market Equity Performance through Equal-Weight Country Indexing', *The Journal of Index Investing*, Spring, vol. 1, no. 4, pp. 18–30.

O'Neill, J, Stupnytska, A & Wrisdale, J (2011), 'Linking GDP Growth and Equity Market Returns', Goldman Sachs Asset Management, *Monthly Insights*, May 2011.

Ritter, J R (2005), 'Economic Growth and Equity Returns', *Pacific-Basin Finance Journal*, vol. 13, no. 5, pp. 489–503.

Saldanha, C (2010), 'Does Economic Growth in Emerging Markets Drive Equity Returns?' Neuberger Berman Research Report, August 2010.

Siegel, J (1998), *Stocks for the Long Run*, McGraw Hill, New York.

Shiller, R J (2005), *Irrational Exuberance*, Princeton University Press, Princeton, New Jersey.

Thomas, R, Hills, S & Dimsdale, N (2010), 'The UK Recession in Context – What Do Three Centuries of Data Tell Us?', *Bank of England Quarterly Bulletin 2010 Q4*, December 26.

2
Default Risk of Sovereign Debt in Central America

Astrid Ayala, Szabolcs Blazsek, and Raúl B. González de Paz

1 Introduction

This chapter analyses the drivers of sovereign debt default risk for the following Central American countries: Belize, Costa Rica, Guatemala, Honduras, Panama, and El Salvador. Table 2.1 presents the long-term credit ratings of government bonds for these countries by Moody's, Standard & Poor's, and Fitch. We use daily data on the yield spread of bonds issued by the governments of these states. Spreads are computed with respect to the fixed income instruments issued by the United States (US) Treasury. We are motivated to use the yield spread variable since it reflects investors' evaluation about the default probability of sovereign debt. We measure the sensitivity of yield spreads to several global, regional, and country-specific factors. The dynamic econometric models applied in this chapter are new in the literature of default risk analysis. In particular, we use the recent beta-t-EGARCH dynamic volatility model of Harvey and Chakravarty (2008) and Harvey (2013a) combined with the autoregressive (AR) model, to specify the conditional volatility and mean of yield spreads. Moreover, we use a Markov regime switching AR model for the yield spread that identifies high- and low-volatility sub-periods and involves time-dependent effects of default risk factors. To the best of our knowledge, this study is the first in the literature about the determinants of sovereign bond default risk in Central America. This may be explained by the fact that it is relatively difficult to obtain data on sovereign yields and country-specific variables for these countries. The results reported in this chapter may be interesting for practitioners since the econometric methods suggested can be applied to determine the drivers of Central American sovereign default risk. Moreover, the techniques applied here can be implemented for the default risk analysis for other emerging markets as well.

Table 2.1 Credit ratings of Central American long-term sovereign bonds in November 2013

Rating description	Moody's		Standard & Poor's		Fitch	
Low investment grade	Baa1		BBB+		BBB+	
	Baa2	Panama	BBB	Panama	BBB	Panama
	Baa3	Costa Rica	BBB–		BBB–	
Non-investment grade	Ba1	Guatemala	BB+		BB+	Costa Rica, Guatemala
	Ba2		BB	Costa Rica, Guatemala	BB	
	Ba3	El Salvador	BB–	El Salvador	BB–	El Salvador
Highly speculative	B1		B+		B+	
	B2	Honduras	B	Honduras	B	
	B3		B–	Belize	B–	
Substantial risk	Caa1		CCC+		CCC	
	Caa2	Belize	CCC		CCC	
	Caa3		CCC–		CCC	

The remaining part of this chapter is organised as follows. In Section 2, we present why the yield spread between Central American and US government bonds represents investors' evaluation about the default probability of sovereign bonds. In Section 3, the measurement of Central American yield spreads is summarised. In Section 4, we present the measurement of global, emerging market, and country-specific factors of default risk. In Section 5, we discuss the single-regime dynamic models of conditional mean and volatility, applied to estimate the effects of default risk factors. In Section 6, we present the empirical results of these dynamic models for each Central American state. In Section 7, we use an extended regime-switching dynamic model that identifies high- and low-volatility sub-periods of sovereign yield spread and estimates differential effects of global, regional, and country-specific variables in these periods. In Section 8, we conclude.

2 Default risk of sovereign bonds

In the existing literature, there are different approaches for the measurement of default risk of government bonds. Several works focus on the spread computed between the yields of a sovereign bond with default risk and a benchmark government bond with negligible default risk (e.g., Cantor & Packer, 1996; Codogno, Favero, & Missale, 2003; Duffie, Pedersen, & Singleton, 2003; Diaz Weigel & Gemmill, 2006; Hilscher & Nosbusch, 2010; Vrugt, 2011; Bernoth, von Hagen & Schuknecht, 2012). Other studies analyse the price difference of credit default swaps written on default risky and default risk-free government bonds (e.g., Remolona, Scatigna, & Wu, 2007; Pan & Singleton 2008; Longstaff, Pan, Pedersen, & Singleton, 2011; Ang & Longstaff, 2013; Arce, Mayordomo, & Peña, 2013). In this chapter, we use the first approach and approximate the default risk of Central American sovereign bonds by the yield spread between the Central American government and US Treasury bonds. Our methodology assumes that US bonds have non-significant default risk; in other words, they are risk-free investments. We use this assumption since all Central American sovereign bonds analysed in this chapter are US dollar (USD) denominated and the bonds emitted by the US Treasury are safe benchmarks for Central America.

The yield spread based method for default risk measurement can be summarised as follows. Consider two zero coupon bonds with unit face value paid on the same future date T. Suppose that the first bond has default risk and on date t it is traded at price D_t. Moreover, suppose that the second bond is default risk-free and on date t it is valued at price B_t. These bond prices are related according to the following equation:

$$D_t = B_t \Pr(T < \tau | t < \tau) + R_t B_t \Pr(T \geq \tau | t < \tau) \tag{2.1}$$

where τ denotes the random date of default of the risky bond that may occur before or after the maturity date, T. The two terms of this equation capture the value of the risky bond as the sum of the value in the case of no default, and in the case of default, both multiplied by the corresponding probabilities. The first term is the value of the risk-free bond weighted by the probability of no default before T. The second term is the value of the risk-free bond multiplied by the recovery rate, R_t, weighted by the probability of default before T. The recovery rate is interpreted as the percentage of the bond value recovered in the case of default. We assume that in the case of default, the recovery rate of a Central American bond is zero. Although there are works in the literature where the recovery rate is estimated, we use this assumption since there have been relatively few default events for Central American sovereign bonds and the proper measurement of the country-specific recovery rate in this region is difficult. Due to this assumption, our estimates provide an upper boundary for true default probabilities. Given that $R_t = 0$ for all t, the value of the default risky bond can be expressed as follows:

$$D_t = B_t[1 - \Pr(T \geq \tau | t < \tau)] = B_t(1 - p_t) \tag{2.2}$$

where p_t is the time-dependent default probability of the Central American sovereign bond. In order to relate the default probability with the yield spread, we write the prices of the unit face value default risky and default risk-free bonds by the corresponding discount factors as follows:

$$D_t = \exp[-(T - t)r_t] \tag{2.3}$$

$$B_t = \exp[-(T - t)r_{f,t}] \tag{2.4}$$

where r_t and $r_{f,t}$ denote the annual log yield to maturity of default risky and default risk-free bonds, respectively. From Equations (2.3) and (2.4) we can derive that

$$D_t = B_t \exp[-(T - t)(r_t - r_{f,t})] = B_t \exp[-(T - t)s_t] \tag{2.5}$$

where s_t is the log yield spread between the Central American and US bonds. Combining Equations (2.2) and (2.5), we can express the default probability as a function of the log yield spread:

$$p_t = 1 - \exp[-(T - t)s_t] \tag{2.6}$$

This equation provides the basis for the market analysis of the log yield spread to approximate the default risk of Central American sovereign fixed income securities. In our empirical analysis, we use as dependent variable the yield spread to find the determinants of sovereign bond default risk in Central America.

3 Measurement of yield spread

Perhaps the most difficult issue related to the proper analysis of default risk of Central American bonds is the availability of sovereign bond price data. We collected daily mid-yield to maturity of all Central American USD-denominated sovereign bonds available in Bloomberg. Our focus on the dollar bonds is justified by the fact that most foreign investors include bonds with USD cash flows in their portfolios to avoid exchange rate risk. We obtained bond yield data for Belize (2 bonds), Costa Rica (22 bonds), Guatemala (8 bonds), Honduras (2 bonds), Panama (21 bonds), and El Salvador (4 bonds). We could not get sovereign bond price data for Nicaragua. Therefore, in this chapter, we do not analyse the default risk of bonds issued by this state.

Most econometric methods measuring the determinants of default risk proposed in this chapter require large sample size. For several bonds, the sample size is too small to estimate the global, emerging market, and country-specific effects with dynamic models. Therefore, we focus on a smaller set of sovereign bonds to analyse the drivers of sovereign default risk. The Ticker CA column of Table 2.2 shows the Bloomberg code for the 23 Central American sovereign bonds considered.

To compute the yield spread between Central American and US fixed income instruments, we obtained from Bloomberg the US Treasury note and bond daily mid-yields to maturity. In total, we obtained yield data on 370 US Treasury bonds. From these assets, we excluded the inflation indexed Treasury bonds since the face value of the Central American bonds analysed is not influenced by the evolution of the consumer price index. We match the US bonds with the Central American ones according to the maturity date. When there are several US bonds available with the same date of maturity, we choose the US fixed income asset allowing the largest sample size for the yield spread. The Ticker US column of Table 2.2 shows the Bloomberg code for the US sovereign bonds matched.

As the Bloomberg annual yield data downloaded are not log yields, we convert both Central American and US yields to annual log yields to maturity by the formula $r_t = \ln(1+R_t)$. Then, we take the difference between these series to compute the log yield spread, s_t, between Central America and the US. Table 2.2 shows the bond maturity dates, the data period, and some descriptive statistics for each spread. Moreover, the last column of Table 2.2 presents the average default probability computed based on Equation (2.6) for each Central American sovereign bond. Notice in Table 2.2 that the average default probability is relatively high for bonds with maturity date further ahead. This motivates the use of time to maturity as a control variable in the yield spread equations.

Table 2.2 Descriptive statistics

Spread	Ticker CA	Ticker US	Maturity CA	Maturity US	Start	End	Max	Mean	Min	SD	Mean Pr
B1	EJ603369	912810PW	20-Feb-2038	15-Feb-2038	25-Mar-2013	11-Jun-2013	6.380	6.048	5.816	0.125	78%
B2	EJ603299	912810PW	20-Feb-2038	15-Feb-2038	20-Mar-2013	11-Jun-2013	6.355	5.975	3.041	0.415	77%
C1	ED288664	912828CA	20-Mar-2014	15-Feb-2014	16-Feb-2004	11-Jun-2013	6.760	2.388	0.862	0.935	12%
C2	ED288660	912828CA	20-Mar-2014	15-Feb-2014	29-Sep-2008	11-Jun-2013	6.774	2.640	0.866	1.217	8%
C3	EC276712	912810EG	1-Aug-2020	15-Aug-2020	9-Nov-2000	11-Jun-2013	5.641	2.579	0.923	0.815	26%
C4	EC276706	912810EG	1-Aug-2020	15-Aug-2020	29-Sep-2008	11-Jun-2013	5.708	2.820	1.467	0.829	23%
G1	ED084583	912828BH	1-Aug-2013	15-Aug-2013	11-Dec-2003	11-Jun-2013	8.367	2.412	0.349	1.160	10%
G2	ED634027	912810FT	6-Oct-2034	15-Feb-2036	29-Sep-2008	11-Jun-2013	6.172	2.775	1.232	0.915	48%
G3	ED634011	912810FT	6-Oct-2034	15-Feb-2036	29-Sep-2008	11-Jun-2013	6.161	2.756	1.232	0.894	48%
H1	EJ591651	912810EQ	15-Mar-2024	15-Aug-2023	12-Mar-2013	11-Jun-2013	5.496	5.232	4.952	0.155	43%
H2	EJ586293	912810EQ	15-Mar-2024	15-Aug-2023	13-Mar-2013	11-Jun-2013	5.500	5.243	4.924	0.166	43%
P1	ED700117	912828MW	15-Mar-2015	31-Mar-2015	24-Mar-2010	11-Jun-2013	2.289	1.259	0.572	0.329	4%
P2	EI049103	912828MP	30-Jan-2020	15-Feb-2020	11-Feb-2010	11-Jun-2013	2.297	1.267	0.687	0.275	10%
P3	EC272015	912810EF	15-May-2020	15-May-2020	29-Sep-2008	11-Jun-2013	5.411	2.449	0.787	0.938	20%
P4	EC771369	912810EP	16-Jan-2023	15-Feb-2023	29-Sep-2008	11-Jun-2013	5.970	2.529	1.164	0.958	26%
P5	EF178776	912810EW	29-Jan-2026	15-Feb-2026	21-Nov-2005	11-Jun-2013	5.397	1.723	0.784	0.741	24%
P6	TT333942	912810FA	30-Sep-2027	15-Aug-2027	19-Sep-1997	11-Jun-2013	6.167	2.712	0.989	1.118	44%
P7	EC118120	912810FG	1-Apr-2029	15-Feb-2029	26-Mar-1999	11-Jun-2013	5.737	2.451	0.991	0.894	42%
P8	ED302136	912810FP	28-Apr-2034	15-Feb-2031	23-Jan-2004	10-Jun-2013	5.678	2.313	1.023	0.767	42%
P9	EF250094	912810FT	26-Jan-2036	15-Feb-2036	7-Feb-2006	11-Jun-2013	5.681	1.799	0.888	0.752	37%
S1	EG945370	912828EW	20-Jan-2016	15-Feb-2016	29-Sep-2008	11-Jun-2013	17.510	3.950	1.978	2.030	16%
S2	EG945394	912828HR	18-Jan-2018	15-Feb-2018	29-Sep-2008	11-Jun-2013	17.918	4.175	1.818	1.977	23%
S3	EI057773	912828LY	1-Dec-2019	15-Nov-2019	23-Nov-2009	11-Jun-2013	4.752	3.316	1.895	0.669	23%

Notes: Central America (CA); United States (US); Maximum (Max); Minimum (Min); Standard Deviation (SD); mean default probability (mean Pr). The maturity columns present the date of maturity for each bond. The Start and End columns show the first and last dates of observations, respectively.

4 Measurement of default risk factors

The econometric methods measuring the determinants of the government bond yield spread involve a number of explanatory variables. We classify these variables to three groups: (a) global factors, (b) emerging market factors, (c) country-specific factors. Compared to existing studies, we consider a large number of factors as possible determinants of default risk in order to avoid the problem of omitted variables in the econometric models. The global and emerging market factors are common to all Central American sovereign bonds, while the country-specific factors are common to all bonds from the same country. In this section, we motivate the selection of these factors by the existing literature on the credit risk of Latin American sovereign bonds and present how we measure the global, emerging market, and country-specific factors.

First, in the existing literature, several authors use global factors to explain the default risk of Latin American government bonds. Ferucci (2003) employs a panel of 23 emerging market countries, including Argentina, Brazil, Colombia, Ecuador, Mexico, Panama, Peru, and Venezuela, over the period 1992–1998. This author considers global risk aversion measured by the yield spread between low- and high-rating US corporate bonds and the Standard & Poor's 500 (S&P500) equity index among the global determinants of sovereign bond default risk. García-Herrero and Ortíz (2005) study the determinants of yield spread of government bonds of Argentina, Brazil, Chile, Mexico, Venezuela, Panama, Ecuador, Peru, and Colombia over the period 1994–2003. As global determinants of sovereign bond spreads, they consider the global risk aversion measured by the US Baa rating corporate high yield spread, the Organisation of Economic Co-operation and Development (OECD) leading indicator, and the Federal Fund rate. Diaz Weigel and Gemmill (2006) use data on Argentina, Brazil, Mexico, and Venezuela over the period 1994–2001. They consider the S&P 500 index and oil price as global determinants of credit risk for Latin American government bonds. Grandes (2007) analyses default risk in Argentina, Brazil, and Mexico over the period 1993 to 2001. This author explains default risk by global risk aversion measured by the US BB rating Merrill Lynch high yield spread.

Motivated by these works, we consider the following five global factors obtained from Bloomberg: (a1) global risk aversion index, measured by the yield spread between the US corporate bond index with Baa rating and the 10-year-maturity US Treasury bond (ticker: BICLB10Y INDEX); (a2) global indicator of economic activity, measured by the OECD composite leading indicator of economic activity (ticker: OLEDUSA INDEX); (a3) US Federal Fund effective rate (ticker: FEDL01 INDEX); (a4) US stock market return, measured by the log return on the S&P500 index (ticker: SPX INDEX); (a5) return on the oil price, measured by the log return on the Brent Crude Index (ticker: COY COMDTY).

Second, motivated by Diaz Weigel and Gemmill (2006), we use the following two variables obtained from Bloomberg to approximate emerging market factors: (b1) emerging market equity investment performance, measured by the log return on the Morgan Stanley Capital International (MSCI) Emerging Markets Equity Index (ticker: MXEF INDEX); (b2) emerging market fixed income investment performance, measured by the log return on the JP Morgan EMBI Global Total Return Index (ticker: JPEIGLBL INDEX). We use global emerging market indices for equity and fixed income investment performance instead of Central American regional indices to avoid potential endogeneity of these variables in the econometric models.

Third, several authors use data on country-specific explanatory variables of sovereign default risk in Latin America. Ferucci (2003) considers external government debt to GDP, government deficit to GDP, trade openness, trade balance to GDP, inflation, current account to GDP, international reserves to GDP, and real exchange rate change. Diaz Weigel and Gemmill (2006) apply the international reserves and inflation rate variables. Grandes (2007) uses real GDP growth and current account to GDP as country-specific determinants of sovereign default risk.

We consider the following nine country-specific drivers of default risk: (c1) external debt to GDP (*sources*: Bloomberg for Belize and Panama; Consejo Monetario Centroamericano, CMC henceforth, for Costa Rica, Guatemala, Honduras, and El Salvador); (c2) total government deficit to GDP (*source*: IMF); (c3) trade openness to GDP, where trade openness is measured as the sum of the exports and imports of goods and services (*source*: Penn World Table from the Center for International Comparisons of Production, Income and Prices, University of Pennsylvania); (c4) trade balance to GDP, where trade balance is measured as the difference between exports and imports of goods and services (*sources*: IMF for Belize and Panama; CMC for Costa Rica, Guatemala, Honduras, and El Salvador); (c5) inflation rate, measured by log change in the consumer price index (*sources*: World Bank for Belize; CMC for Costa Rica, Guatemala, Honduras, and El Salvador; Bloomberg for Panama); (c6) current account to GDP (*sources*: IMF for Belize and Panama; CMC for Costa Rica, Honduras, and El Salvador; Bloomberg for Guatemala); (c7) international reserves to GDP (*sources*: Bloomberg for Belize and

Panama; CMC for Costa Rica, Guatemala, Honduras, and El Salvador); (c8) real exchange rate change, measured by the log change in the real exchange rate index (*sources*: Penn World Table for Belize and Panama; CMC for Costa Rica, Guatemala, Honduras, and El Salvador); (c9) real GDP growth (*sources*: IMF for Belize and Panama; Total Economy Database of the Groningen Growth and Development Centre, University of Groningen, for Costa Rica and Guatemala; Bloomberg for Honduras and El Salvador).

5 Single-regime dynamic models of yield spread

In the existing literature of the default risk of Latin American sovereign bonds, several papers apply linear regression or linear panel data models to measure the impact of default risk factors on the yield spread. These models are restrictive since the dynamics of the conditional expectation and volatility of the yield spread are not modelled properly. This may cause inconsistent parameter estimates for the default risk factors. In this chapter, we extend the econometric methods applied in the literature employing dynamic models for both the conditional mean and volatility for Central American bond spreads. Some of these models are new in this literature and they may provide additional insights about the effects of default risk factors for practitioners. We are motivated to use these models for Central American data since preliminary data analysis suggests that both the conditional mean and variance exhibit significant serial correlation. Moreover, the Central American yield spreads exhibit large shifts in the mean and volatility, motivating the application of sophisticated dynamic econometric models.

In the following, we present the formulation of the econometric models estimated. Practitioners may replicate the models proposed for other emerging-market bond yield spreads to analyse their determinants and to forecast sovereign default risk. The conditional expectation of the yield spread is modelled according to the following first-order autoregressive, AR(1) equation with exogenous explanatory variables:

$$s_t = X_t\beta + \phi s_{t-1} + \varepsilon_t \qquad (2.7)$$

where X_t is a vector including the default risk factors. The first element of X_t is one for the constant parameter and we also consider in X_t the years to maturity, $T-t$, as a control variable motivated by Equation (2.6) and Table 2.2. The AR(1) model is covariance stationary when $|\phi|<1$. For the countries of Belize and Honduras, the number of observations is too small to estimate dynamic models of volatility. Therefore, for the bonds issued by these states, we suppose that the variance of the error term is constant, that is, Var(ε_t)=σ^2. For Costa Rica, Guatemala, Panama, and El Salvador there are more observations. Therefore, for these states, we model the error term, ε_t, by two competing Generalised Autoregressive Conditional Heteroscedasticity (GARCH) type volatility equations. First, we estimate the t-GARCH (1,1) model of Bollerslev (1986) and Taylor (1986), parameterised as follows:

$$\varepsilon_t = \sigma_t u_t \quad \text{where } u_t \sim t(v) \text{ i.i.d.} \tag{2.8}$$

$$\sigma_t^2 = \alpha_0 + \alpha_1 \varepsilon_{t-1}^2 + \beta_1 \sigma_{t-1}^2 \tag{2.9}$$

The parameters of the AR(1)-t-GARCH (1,1) model are estimated jointly by the maximum likelihood method. The error term of Equation (2.8) is assumed to have t distribution with v degrees of freedom. Under this assumption, the model may capture large innovations in Central American yield spreads. The GARCH (1,1) model is covariance stationary when $\alpha_1 + \beta_1 < 1$. In the case of a non-stationary GARCH model, we replace Equation (2.9) by the Integrated-GARCH, IGARCH (1,1) equation:

$$\sigma_t^2 = \alpha_0 + (1 - \lambda)\varepsilon_{t-1}^2 + \lambda\sigma_{t-1}^2 \tag{2.10}$$

where $0 < \lambda < 1$. Second, we apply the beta-t-Exponential-GARCH (beta-t-EGARCH) model of Harvey (2013a):

$$\varepsilon_t = \exp(\lambda_t/2)u_t \quad \text{where } u_t \sim t(\text{v}) \text{ i.i.d.} \tag{2.11}$$

$$\lambda_t = \alpha_0 + \alpha_1\, e_{t-1} + \beta_1\, \lambda_{-1} \tag{2.12}$$

$$e_t = (v + 1)b_t - 1 \tag{2.13}$$

$$b_t = [\varepsilon_t^2 / v\exp(\lambda_t)]/[1 + \varepsilon_t^2 / v\exp(\lambda_t)] \tag{2.14}$$

We are motivated to use this model since according to Harvey (2013b), the beta-t-EGARCH (1,1) model may capture volatility dynamics better than the traditional t-GARCH model. The parameters of the AR(1)-beta-t-EGARCH (1,1) are estimated by the maximum likelihood method. The log likelihood maximisation procedure is very fast for this model, and it gives precise estimates of the parameters and their standard errors. This volatility model is covariance stationary when $|\beta_1| < 1$. In the case of non-stationarity, we use the beta-t-E-Integrated-GARCH (beta-t-EI-GARCH) specification of Harvey (2013a: 114), where $\beta_1=1$ in Equation (2.12).

We compare the competing econometric models by using the following likelihood-based model performance metrics: (a) Log Likelihood (LL) and (b) Bayesian Information Criterion, BIC=$K\ln(T)$–2LL, where K is the number of parameters estimated and T is the sample size. Higher LL and lower BIC suggest better model performance.

6 Empirical results for single-regime models

In this section, we present the estimation results for each Central American country. Before interpreting the results for each country, we summarise some general empirical evidence and model diagnostic results from Tables 2.3–2.7.

We find that the conditional mean equation is always covariance stationary. This result supports modelling the spread variable and not its first difference. The t-GARCH volatility model is non-stationary for one bond from Costa Rica (C1), two bonds from Guatemala (G1 and G3), and two bonds from El Salvador (S1 and S2). However, for these bonds, we find that the beta-t-EGARCH model is covariance stationary. Therefore, in these cases, we interpret the beta-t-EGARCH estimates. This result supports the application of the beta-t-EGARCH model for Central American yield spreads. Furthermore, both the t-GARCH and beta-t-EGARCH models fail the covariance stationarity condition for one bond from Guatemala (G2) and two bonds from Panama (P5 and P9). For these bonds, we report the estimation results for the AR-t-IGARCH and AR-beta-t-EIGARCH models. For four bonds from Panama (P1, P2, P3, and P4) we could not estimate the AR-t-GARCH model due to numerical problems, related to the incorrect GARCH specification for conditional volatility. In these cases, we only report the AR-beta-t-EGARCH estimates. The beta-t-EGARCH model is estimated without problems for these spreads, which also supports the application of the beta-t-EGARCH formulation for Central American yield spread volatility. For the bonds from Belize and Honduras we could not collect data on country-specific factors. For these states, we estimated the models only with global and emerging market factors. For some bonds of Costa Rica, Guatemala, Panama, and El Salvador, we could not obtain the trade openness to GDP and real exchange rate variables. Therefore, we estimated the restricted models for these countries. For 10 Central American bonds (C2 to C4, G2, P5 to P9, and S3), both dynamic volatility specifications satisfy the underlying model assumptions. The results for these specifications are robust since the sign of most significant parameter estimates coincide for both models. Finally, the degrees of freedom, v, parameter estimates justify the selection of the t distribution for the error term since for 21 of the 23 spreads we have degrees of freedom estimates less than 10. Therefore, the t distribution estimated for most error terms is different from the standard normal one.

6.1 Belize

Table 2.3 shows the parameter estimates for two bonds of Belize (B1 and B2). Due to the small sample size, we had numerical problems with the estimation of both GARCH-type models. Therefore, the parameter estimates of Table 2.3 correspond to the AR(1) model with constant volatility. The equation includes all global and regional factors. We could not obtain data on country-specific risk factors for Belize. The results are robust since all parameter estimates have the same sign for both B1 and B2. From the global determinants of default risk, the most significant positive effect is found for the global risk aversion index.

Table 2.3 Parameter estimates for Belize and Honduras

	B1	B2		H1	H2
constant	38.022***	142.874***	constant	16.536**	15.959*
T-t	-1.307**	-5.657**	*T–t*	-1.134	-1.116
GRA	0.399***	1.446	GRA	0.549***	0.508***
OECD	-3.228	-6.855	OECD	-3.131	-1.126
FED	0.102	6.930	FED	-1.140	-0.696
S&P500	-0.007	-0.040	S&P500	0.014**	-0.009
OIL	-0.013*	0.000	OIL	-0.010*	-0.003
EE	-0.010	0.016	EE	-0.026***	-0.006
EB	0.058	0.135	EB	0.042*	0.016
CPI	NA	NA	CPI	-0.137	-0.034
RER	NA	NA	RER	-0.045	-0.029
ϕ	0.748***	0.200	ϕ	0.905***	0.889***
LL	72	-22	LL	100	87
BIC	-101	-88	BIC	-146	-120
T	49	58	*T*	64	63

Notes: years to maturity (*T–t*); Global Risk Aversion index (GRA); global indicator of economic activity (OECD); Federal Fund effective rate (FED); US stock market return (S&P500); oil price return (OIL); emerging market equity investment performance (EE); emerging market fixed income investment performance (EB); inflation rate (CPI); Real Exchange Rate log change (RER); Log Likelihood (LL); Bayesian Information Criterion (BIC); number of observations (*T*). *, **, and *** denote parameter significance at the 10%, 5%, and 1% levels, respectively.

This index captures the risk premium associated with unexpected losses from defaults in risky fixed income markets. The effect of global risk aversion on emerging sovereign yield spreads depends on whether they are viewed by investors as complements or substitutes to the US high-yield corporate bonds. The positive global risk aversion coefficient of Belize signals that fixed income investors view the government bonds of Belize as complementary assets. To anticipate further results, we note that significant positive global risk aversion effect is estimated for all Central American yield spreads analysed in this chapter. We also find that emerging market factors have non-significant impact on the yield spreads of Belize.

6.2 Costa Rica

Table 2.4 presents the parameter estimates for both dynamic volatility models for four bonds from Costa Rica (C1–C4). The results are robust for these bonds since all significant estimates have the same sign and also most non-significant ones have identical parameter signs. From the global factors, the global risk aversion index has a significant positive effect on the yield spread and the US stock market return has a significant negative influence on the default risk of the Costa Rica bonds. The negative effect of the US stock market return can be explained as follows. If the US equity market performance increases, then there will probably be less demand for US Treasury securities. As a consequence, the price of US sovereign bonds will fall and their yield will increase. This diminishes the yield spread between Costa Rica and the US. Anticipating further results, we find the same negative effect of the US stock market return on the sovereign default risk for all Central American countries. For the emerging market factors, we find that both variables are highly significant. The emerging market equity investment performance has a significant negative effect, while the emerging market fixed income investment performance has a significant positive effect on default risk. The negative effect of the emerging market equity investment performance variable can be explained in a similar way as that of the US stock market return variable. The positive effect of the emerging market fixed income investment performance represents the global evaluation of investors about the performance of emerging market bonds, including the Costa Rica sovereign bonds. To anticipate further results, we find that the effects of both emerging market factors estimated for Costa Rica are robust for all Central American countries. Regarding the country-specific drivers of the yield spread, we find that higher government external debt to GDP significantly increases the default probability. Moreover,

Table 2.4 Parameter estimates for Costa Rica

	C1(a)	C1(b)	C2(a)	C2(b)		C3(a)	C3(b)	C4(a)	C4(b)
constant	−0.001	−0.013	0.090**	0.092***	constant	0.076	0.071	0.192***	0.198***
$T-t$	−0.004	−0.004	0.000	−0.001	$T-t$	−0.008***	−0.008***	−0.013***	−0.013
GRA	0.017***	0.015**	0.008	0.010	GRA	0.014***	0.015***	0.034***	0.032
OECD	−0.009	−0.008	0.007	0.010	OECD	−0.001	−0.003	0.023**	0.023
FED	0.004	0.003	0.010	0.049*	FED	0.001	0.001	−0.010	0.025
S&P500	−0.020***	−0.019***	−0.013***	−0.012	S&P500	−0.026***	−0.025***	−0.027***	−0.027
OIL	−0.001	0.000	−0.001	−0.001	OIL	0.000	0.000	0.000	0.000
EE	−0.009***	−0.009***	−0.003	−0.003	EE	−0.006***	−0.005***	−0.004**	−0.003
EB	0.057***	0.060***	0.001	−0.001	EB	0.047***	0.048***	0.012**	0.011
debt/GDP	0.003**	0.003*	0.004	0.003	debt/GDP	0.005***	0.006***	0.005*	0.005
TD/GDP	−0.001	−0.001	−0.011***	−0.013	TD/GDP	−0.001	−0.001	−0.004	−0.006
TO/GDP	0.000	0.001	NA	NA	TO/GDP	0.000	0.001	NA	NA
TB/GDP	0.001	0.002	0.019*	0.017	TB/GDP	0.008	0.008	0.014	0.016
CPI	0.000	0.000	−0.001	0.000	CPI	−0.003	−0.004	−0.003	−0.003
CA/GDP	−0.001	−0.001	−0.008*	−0.006	CA/GDP	−0.004**	−0.004*	−0.006	−0.007
IR/GDP	−0.005***	−0.004**	−0.006	−0.005	IR/GDP	−0.006***	−0.007***	−0.009***	−0.009
RER	−0.003*	−0.003*	−0.002	−0.003	RER	−0.001	−0.001	−0.002	−0.002
GDP	−0.003	−0.003	0.002	0.002	GDP	−0.001	−0.001	−0.001	−0.001
ϕ	0.980***	0.980***	0.987***	0.986***	ϕ	0.981***	0.980***	0.965***	0.966***
α_0	0.001***	−0.233***	0.000***	−0.239***	α_0	0.000***	−0.131***	0.000***	−0.090***
α_1	**0.459*****	0.303***	0.171***	0.132***	α_1	0.063***	0.104***	0.091***	0.055**
β_1	**0.576*****	0.956***	0.781***	0.959***	β_1	0.901***	0.979***	0.887***	0.986***
v	3.224***	3.140***	5.309***	5.149***	v	3.653***	3.553***	5.266***	5.854***
LL	2231	2198	1496	1490	LL	3229	3229	1657	1664
BIC	**−4284**	−4211	**−2836**	−2816	BIC	**−6279**	−6271	−3157	**−3164**
T	2284	2284	1215	1215	T	2384	2384	1214	1214

Notes: (a) AR(1)-t-GARCH (1,1) model; (b) AR(1)-beta-t-EGARCH (1,1) model; years to maturity ($T-t$); Global Risk Aversion index (GRA); global indicator of economic activity (OECD); Federal Fund effective rate (FED); US stock market return (S&P500); oil price return (OIL); emerging market equity investment performance (EE); emerging market fixed income investment performance (EB); government external debt to GDP (debt/GDP); government total deficit to GDP (deficit/GDP); Trade Openness to GDP (TO/GDP); Trade Balance to GDP (TB/GDP); inflation rate (CPI); Current Account to GDP (CA/GDP); International Reserves to GDP (IR/GDP); Real Exchange Rate log change (RER); real GDP growth (GDP); Log Likelihood (LL); Bayesian Information Criterion (BIC); number of observations (T). The bold numbers indicate that the covariance stationarity condition is not satisfied and lower BIC value. *, **, and *** denote parameter significance at the 10%, 5%, and 1% levels, respectively.

both current account to GDP and international reserves to GDP have significant inverse relation with the yield spread in Costa Rica.

6.3 Guatemala

Table 2.5 shows the estimation results for both dynamic models of volatility for three bonds from Guatemala (G1–G3). We find that the global risk aversion index has significant positive effect and the US stock market return has significant negative effect on the default probability of Guatemalan bonds. For the emerging market variables, the results evidence significant negative impact of the equity investment performance and positive impact of the fixed income investment performance on Guatemalan yield spread. For the country-specific determinants, surprisingly, we find that debt to GDP has negative and international reserves to GDP has positive relation with yield spread for two bonds. This can be explained by the sample period of observations for G2 and G3; see Table 2.2. Reviewing the debt to GDP parameter estimates for other Central American states in Tables 2.4–2.7, we can see that for the bonds with observation periods starting during the 1990s, the debt to GDP has positive impact and international reserves to GDP has negative impact on the yield spread. However, for several bonds with shorter observation period starting in the 2000s and in several cases after the 2008 US financial crisis, we evidence the opposite effects. This finding suggests a possible time variation in the debt to GDP and international reserves to GDP parameters. In Section 7, we investigate this hypothesis by implementing a Markov regime-switching model (e.g., Kim & Nelson, 1999) for Central American sovereign yield spreads.

6.4 Honduras

In Table 2.3, we report the parameter estimates of the AR-constant volatility model for two bonds of Honduras (H1 and H2). The results are robust since the sign of all estimates coincide for both bonds. The only significant factor for both assets is the global risk aversion index with highly significant positive effect on sovereign bond yield spread in Honduras. Furthermore, for the H1 spread we find that the emerging market equity investment performance has significant negative effect and the emerging market fixed income investment performance has significant positive impact on default risk.

6.5 Panama

Table 2.6 shows the results of both dynamic volatility models for nine bonds from Panama (P1–P9). From the global factors, the global risk

Table 2.5 Parameter estimates for Guatemala

	G1(a)	G1(b)		G2(a*)		G2(b*)		G3(a)	G3(b)
constant	0.016	−0.033	constant	0.883***	constant	0.229***	constant	−0.336	−0.405
T–t	0.010***	0.010***	*T–t*	0.185***	*T–t*	0.036	*T–t*	0.000	0.001
GRA	0.015*	0.016*	GRA	0.062***	GRA	0.028	GRA	0.032***	0.033***
OECD	−0.002	−0.001	OECD	0.013	OECD	0.027	OECD	0.032**	0.036**
FED	−0.008**	−0.009**	FED	−0.004	FED	0.001	FED	−0.032	−0.012
S&P500	−0.017***	−0.016***	S&P500	−0.024***	S&P500	−0.022	S&P500	−0.030***	−0.030***
OIL	−0.001	−0.001	OIL	−0.002	OIL	0.001	OIL	−0.001	−0.001
EE	−0.008***	−0.009***	EE	−0.010***	EE	−0.006	EE	−0.007***	−0.007***
EB	0.084***	0.085***	EB	0.071***	EB	0.031	EB	0.035***	0.031***
debt/GDP	−0.009**	−0.009**	debt/GDP	−0.020	debt/GDP	−0.092***	debt/GDP	−0.014*	−0.014
TD/GDP	−0.003	−0.002	TD/GDP	0.008	TD/GDP	0.014	TD/GDP	−0.001	−0.005
TO/GDP	−0.001	0.000	TO/GDP	−0.103***	TO/GDP	−0.020	TO/GDP	0.005**	0.005**
TB/GDP	−0.005	−0.007	TB/GDP	−0.042***	TB/GDP	−0.019	TB/GDP	0.001	0.000
CPI	−0.001	−0.002	CPI	−0.013	CPI	0.006	CPI	−0.014**	−0.015***
CA/GDP	−0.003	−0.001	CA/GDP	−0.045***	CA/GDP	−0.021	CA/GDP	−0.002	−0.002
IR/GDP	0.006	0.006	IR/GDP	0.028*	IR/GDP	0.077**	IR/GDP	0.014**	0.016**
RER	0.000	−0.001	RER	0.008	RER	0.003	RER	0.000	−0.001
GDP	0.005	0.006	GDP	0.224***	GDP	0.048*	GDP	0.000	0.001
ϕ	0.983***	0.982***	ϕ	0.899***	ϕ	0.954***	ϕ	0.967***	0.968***
α_0	0.001***	−0.096***	α_0	0.001***	α_0	−0.008	α_0	0.000***	−0.070**
α_1	**0.429*****	0.290***	$1-\lambda$	0.894***	α_1	0.433***	α_1	**0.079*****	0.131***
β_1	**0.678*****	0.981***	λ	0.106***	β_1	NA	β_1	**0.916*****	0.988***
v	2.881***	2.896***	v	2.877***	v	1.188***	v	3.567***	3.580***
LL	1712	1699	LL	−1521	LL	−1542	LL	1632	1626
BIC	**−3250**	−3215	BIC	−3206	BIC	**−3247**	BIC	**−3101**	−3083
T	1954	1954	*T*	1218	*T*	1218	*T*	1211	1211

Notes: (a) AR(1)-t-GARCH (1,1) model; (b) AR(1)-beta-t-EGARCH (1,1) model; (a*) AR(1)-t-IGARCH (1,1) model; (b*) AR(1)-beta-t-EIGARCH (1,1) model; years to maturity (*T–t*); Global Risk Aversion index (GRA); global indicator of economic activity (OECD); Federal Fund effective rate (FED); US stock market return (S&P500); oil price return (OIL); emerging market equity investment performance (EE); emerging market fixed income investment performance (EB); government external debt to GDP (debt/GDP); government total deficit to GDP (deficit/GDP); Trade Openness to GDP (TO/GDP); Trade Balance to GDP (TB/GDP); inflation rate (CPI); Current Account to GDP (CA/GDP); International Reserves to GDP (IR/GDP); Real Exchange Rate log change (RER); real GDP growth (GDP); Log Likelihood (LL); Bayesian Information Criterion (BIC); number of observations (*T*); Not Available (NA). The bold numbers indicate that the covariance stationarity condition is not satisfied and lower BIC value. *, **, and *** denote parameter significance at the 10%, 5%, and 1% levels, respectively.

Table 2.6 (part 1) Parameter estimates for Panama

	P1(b)	**P2(b)**	**P3(b)**	**P4(b)**		**P5(a*)**		**P5(b*)**
constant	−0.016	−0.036	−0.019	0.169***	constant	1.827***	constant	0.800***
$T-t$	0.010	0.030	0.004	0.011	$T-t$	0.006	$T-t$	0.004
GRA	0.046*	0.097***	0.012	0.038	GRA	0.036*	GRA	0.033*
OECD	0.013	0.015	0.014	0.017	OECD	0.000	OECD	−0.003
FED	−0.127***	−0.160***	0.049*	0.001	FED	0.002	FED	0.003
S&P500	−0.011	−0.026	−0.025	−0.025	S&P500	−0.023	S&P500	−0.023
OIL	0.002	0.000	0.000	−0.001	OIL	−0.001	OIL	−0.001
EE	0.002	−0.002	−0.004	−0.006	EE	−0.006	EE	−0.006
EB	−0.044	−0.034	NA	0.008	EB	−0.008	EB	−0.007
debt/GDP	0.005	0.004	0.027	−0.014	debt/GDP	−0.053***	debt/GDP	−0.027
TD/GDP	−0.045*	0.148***	0.021	−0.008	TD/GDP	−0.089***	TD/GDP	−0.048**
TO/GDP	NA	NA	NA	NA	TO/GDP	0.023	TO/GDP	0.013*
TB/GDP	−0.003	−0.009	−0.011	0.002	TB/GDP	−0.041**	TB/GDP	−0.023
CPI	−0.007	−0.013	−0.002	−0.001	CPI	−0.003	CPI	−0.005
CA/GDP	0.019	0.024	0.027	0.009	CA/GDP	0.083***	CA/GDP	0.043**
IR/GDP	−0.019	0.029	−0.038	0.008	IR/GDP	−0.131***	IR/GDP	−0.070***
RER	NA	NA	0.036	NA	RER	0.043**	RER	0.022
GDP	0.012	−0.040	−0.056*	0.025	GDP	−0.130***	GDP	−0.072***
ϕ	0.961***	0.927***	0.989***	0.969***	ϕ	0.958***	ϕ	0.960***
α_0	−0.123***	−0.107***	−0.137***	−0.135***	α_0	0.000	α_0	−0.048***
α_1	0.120***	0.094***	0.161***	0.174***	$1-\lambda$	0.172	α_1	0.079***
β_1	0.981***	0.984***	0.978***	0.977***	λ	0.828***	β_1	NA
ν	5.927***	4.863***	1.984***	2.455***	ν	11.190***	ν	5.628***
LL	1356	1420	1342	1278	LL	2899	LL	2967
BIC	−2563	−2692	−2529	−2401	BIC	−5623	BIC	**−5759**
T	838	867	1218	1213	T	1969	T	1969

Table 2.6 (part 2) Parameter estimates for Panama

	P6(a)	P6(b)	P7(a)	P7(b)	P8(a)	P8(b)		P9(a*)		P9(b*)
constant	−0.062*	−0.065*	−0.037	−0.051	0.409	0.350	constant	0.437***	constant	0.348***
$T-t$	0.003**	0.003**	0.002	0.002	0.013***	0.013***	$T-t$	0.002	$T-t$	0.005
GRA	0.023***	0.023***	0.020***	0.022***	0.047***	0.048***	GRA	0.030	GRA	0.035*
OECD	−0.006	−0.007	−0.004	−0.004	−0.030***	−0.030***	OECD	−0.004	OECD	−0.003
FED	0.000	0.001	−0.001	−0.001	−0.004	−0.004	FED	0.003	FED	0.002
S&P500	−0.018***	−0.018***	−0.016***	−0.016***	−0.018***	−0.018***	S&P500	−0.022	S&P500	−0.023
OIL	−0.001	−0.001	0.000	0.000	−0.001	−0.001	OIL	0.000	OIL	0.000
EE	−0.009***	−0.009***	−0.008***	−0.008***	−0.008***	−0.008***	EE	−0.007	EE	−0.007
EB	0.004	0.004	0.007***	0.007***	0.028***	0.030***	EB	−0.024	EB	−0.025
debt/GDP	0.001**	0.001**	0.002***	0.002***	−0.007**	−0.006*	debt/GDP	−0.018	debt/GDP	−0.017
TD/GDP	−0.002*	−0.002	−0.003*	−0.004*	−0.011**	−0.011**	TD/GDP	−0.028	TD/GDP	−0.023
TO/GDP	0.000	0.000	0.000	0.000	0.001	0.001	TO/GDP	0.009	TO/GDP	0.009
TB/GDP	0.000	0.000	0.000	0.000	−0.002	−0.002	TB/GDP	−0.015	TB/GDP	−0.014
CPI	−0.004***	−0.004***	−0.003**	−0.003***	−0.007***	−0.008***	CPI	−0.004	CPI	−0.004
CA/GDP	−0.004***	−0.004***	−0.003***	−0.004***	0.006*	0.005	CA/GDP	0.032	CA/GDP	0.032*
IR/GDP	−0.003**	−0.003**	−0.002*	−0.002*	−0.035***	−0.035***	IR/GDP	−0.045**	IR/GDP	−0.041**
RER	0.000	0.000	0.000	0.000	0.005***	0.005***	RER	0.017	RER	0.017
GDP	−0.004***	−0.004***	−0.003	−0.003**	−0.017***	−0.017***	GDP	−0.046**	GDP	−0.042**
ϕ	0.971***	0.972***	0.971***	0.971***	0.937***	0.937***	ϕ	0.965***	ϕ	0.959***
α_0	0.000***	−0.116***	0.000***	−0.068***	0.000***	−0.091***	α_0	0.000	α_0	−0.043**
α_1	0.080***	0.114***	0.051***	0.070***	0.089***	0.127***	$1-\lambda$	0.214***	α_1	0.074***
β_1	0.903***	0.980***	0.935***	0.989***	0.896***	0.985***	λ	0.786***	β_1	NA
v	4.984***	4.876***	7.125***	6.099***	4.257***	3.942	v	20.158***	v	6.502***
LL	5504	5477	5440	5415	3192	3180	LL	2848	LL	2911
BIC	**−10816**	−10754	**−10690**	−10634	**−6204**	−6173	BIC	−5522	BIC	**−5648**
T	4030	4030	3659	3659	2374	2374	T	1909	T	1909

Notes: (a) AR(1)-t-GARCH (1,1) model; (b) AR(1)-beta-t-EGARCH (1,1) model; (a*) AR(1)-t-IGARCH (1,1) model; (b*) AR(1)-beta-t-EIGARCH (1,1) model; years to maturity ($T-t$); Global Risk Aversion index (GRA); global indicator of economic activity (OECD); Federal Fund effective rate (FED); US stock market return (S&P500); oil price return (OIL); emerging market equity investment performance (EE); emerging market fixed income investment performance (EB); government external debt to GDP (debt/GDP); government total deficit to GDP (deficit/GDP); Trade Openness to GDP (TO/GDP); Trade Balance to GDP (TB/GDP); inflation rate (CPI); Current Account to GDP (CA/GDP); International Reserves to GDP (IR/GDP); Real Exchange Rate log change (RER); real GDP growth (GDP); Log Likelihood (LL); Bayesian Information Criterion (BIC); number of observations (T); Not Available (NA). The bold numbers indicate lower BIC value. *, **, and *** denote parameter significance at the 10%, 5%, and 1% levels, respectively.

aversion index has positive effect and the S&P 500 index return has negative impact on the yield spread of all bonds from Panama. When the emerging market factors are significant, we find negative impact of emerging market equity investment performance and positive impact of emerging market fixed income investment performance. For the country-dependent default risk factors, we find significant negative impact of real GDP growth, the inflation rate, and international reserves to GDP for all bonds. These results show that improving economic activity and price level in Panama decreases the default risk evaluated by the market and that the higher level of international reserves decrease the yield spread. Furthermore, we find that total deficit to GDP has inverse relation with the default risk of Panama. For the external debt to GDP and current account to GDP variables, the results depend on the specific bond. Following the discussion about the country-specific variables of Guatemala, these mixed results may be related to the time variation of parameters investigated in Section 7.

6.6 El Salvador

Table 2.7 presents the parameter estimates of both dynamic volatility models for three bonds of El Salvador (S1–S3). For the global factors, we find significant positive effect of the global risk aversion index and significant negative impact of the US stock market return on El Salvador yield spreads. Moreover, the table shows significant negative impact of the US Federal Fund effective rate on the default risk of all sovereign bonds from El Salvador. This can be explained as follows. When the Federal Fund rate increases, the yield of US Treasury bonds probably will also increase. This implies a reduction in the spread between El Salvador and the US. We also find negative effects of the emerging market equity investment performance and positive influence of the emerging market fixed income investment performance on El Salvador sovereign yield spreads. The country-specific effects are not clear for El Salvador since in the AR-beta-t-EGARCH model these parameters are not significant, and the t-GARCH model for S1 and S2 is non-stationary (see Table 2.7).

7 Regime-switching dynamic model of yield spread

The GARCH-type dynamic volatility models estimated for different sample periods provide mixed results for some country-specific factors for the Central American countries. As discussed for Guatemala and Panama, this may be a sign of time-dependent parameters of default risk

Table 2.7 Parameter estimates for El Salvador

	S1(a)	S1(b)		S2(a)	S2(b)		S3(a)	S3(b)
Constant	0.127	0.195***	constant	0.548***	0.627***	constant	0.252**	0.247***
$T-t$	−0.026***	−0.027	$T-t$	−0.046***	−0.049	$T-t$	−0.034***	−0.035
GRA	0.113***	0.128**	GRA	0.152***	0.177***	GRA	0.126***	0.123***
OECD	0.048	0.068*	OECD	0.057	0.055	OECD	0.036**	0.025
FED	−0.259***	−0.308***	FED	−0.347***	−0.395***	FED	−0.247***	−0.246***
S&P500	−0.014***	−0.013	S&P500	−0.018***	−0.017	S&P500	−0.024***	−0.025
OIL	−0.003***	−0.004	OIL	−0.002	−0.002	OIL	−0.002*	−0.002
EE	−0.004**	−0.005	EE	−0.004**	−0.004	EE	−0.007***	−0.007
EB	0.012*	0.013	EB	0.010	0.010	EB	−0.010	−0.008
debt/GDP	−0.022***	−0.027	debt/GDP	−0.037***	−0.043	debt/GDP	−0.013***	−0.013
TD/GDP	0.042***	0.040	TD/GDP	0.053***	0.053	TD/GDP	0.034***	0.034
TO/GDP	NA	NA	TO/GDP	NA	NA	TO/GDP	NA	NA
TB/GDP	−0.006	−0.006	TB/GDP	−0.003	−0.001	TB/GDP	−0.005	−0.002
CPI	−0.011*	−0.012	CPI	−0.018***	−0.023	CPI	−0.007	−0.004
CA/GDP	−0.003	−0.002	CA/GDP	0.003	0.002	CA/GDP	0.024***	0.025
IR/GDP	0.029***	0.034	IR/GDP	0.045***	0.052	IR/GDP	0.013***	0.012
RER	−0.028***	−0.031	RER	−0.042***	−0.053	RER	−0.011*	−0.010
GDP	0.016***	0.011	GDP	0.024***	0.026	GDP	0.010***	0.008
ϕ	0.939***	0.938*	Φ	0.912***	0.901***	Φ	0.942***	0.944***
α_0	0.001*	−0.124***	α_0	0.004	−0.136***	α_0	0.000**	−1.086***
α_1	**1.655****	0.406***	α_1	**4.252*****	0.579***	α_1	0.097***	0.235***
β_1	**0.375*****	0.981***	β_1	**0.338*****	0.976***	β_1	0.883***	0.827***
v	2.355***	2.283***	N	2.121***	1.945***	N	5.036***	4.920***
LL	633	633	LL	614	597	LL	1324	1308
BIC	**−1125**	−1118	BIC	**−1087**	−1046	BIC	**−2498**	−2461
T	606	606	T	597	606	T	876	876

Notes: (a) AR(1)-t-GARCH (1,1) model; (b) AR(1)-beta-t-EGARCH (1,1) model; years to maturity ($T-t$); Global Risk Aversion index (GRA); global indicator of economic activity (OECD); Federal Fund effective rate (FED); US stock market return (S&P500); oil price return (OIL); emerging market equity investment performance (EE); emerging market fixed income investment performance (EB); government external debt to GDP (debt/GDP); government total deficit to GDP (deficit/GDP); Trade Openness to GDP (TO/GDP); Trade Balance to GDP (TB/GDP); inflation rate (CPI); Current Account to GDP (CA/GDP); International Reserves to GDP (IR/GDP); Real Exchange Rate log change (RER); real GDP growth (GDP); Log Likelihood (LL); Bayesian Information Criterion (BIC); number of observations (T); Not Available (NA). The bold numbers indicate that the covariance stationarity condition is not satisfied and lower BIC value. *, **, and *** denote parameter significance at the 10%, 5%, and 1% levels, respectively.

factors. In this section, we investigate this hypothesis by employing the following Markov regime switching AR (MS-AR, henceforth) model:

$$s_t = X_t \beta(z_t) + \varphi(z_t) s_{t-1} + \sigma(z_t)\varepsilon_t \quad \text{with } \varepsilon_t \sim t[\nu(z_t)] \quad \text{and} \quad z_t \in \{1,2\} \tag{2.15}$$

All parameters are driven by the regime or state variable, z_t. The transition probabilities of this underlying variable are parameterised as follows: $\Pr(z_t = 1|z_{t-1} = 1) = p$ and $\Pr(z_t = 2|z_{t-1} = 2) = q$. Time-varying effects of global, emerging market, and country-specific factors are measured by the vector $\beta(z_t)$. Furthermore, time-dependent volatility is captured by the regime-dependent scaling parameter $\sigma(z_t)$ and the degrees of freedom parameter $\nu(z_t)$. We estimate the MS-AR model by the maximum likelihood method; see Kim and Nelson (1999). According to Francq and Zakoian (2001), the MS-AR(1) model is covariance stationary when

$$W = \sum_{i=1}^{2} \pi_i \log\left[|\varphi(i)|\right] < 0 \quad \text{where} \quad \pi_1 = (1-q)/(2-p-q) \quad \text{and} \quad \pi_2 = (1-p)/(2-p-q) \tag{2.16}$$

We estimate the MS-AR model for all Central American bonds presented in Table 2.2. For most yield spreads, the Markov switching specification is not appropriate due to the small sample size. However, we find significant regime-switching dynamics for the spreads G1 and P6 from Guatemala and Panama, respectively. These are the bonds with the highest number of observations for both countries. In the following, we interpret the estimation results for these yield spreads; presented in Table 2.8 and Figures 2.1 and 2.2. Although these results refer only to two bonds from Central America, we present them since they may be interesting for practitioners focusing on the determinants of sovereign debt default risk in Central America.

The regime-switching volatility scaling parameter, $\sigma(z_t)$, is about two times higher in regime one than in regime two; see Table 2.8. Therefore, we call state one the 'high-volatility regime' and state two the 'low-volatility regime'. Figures 2.1 and 2.2 present for G1 and P6, respectively, the evolution of the filtered probability of the high-volatility regime, $\Pr(z_t=1|s_1,\ldots,s_{t-1})$, and the default probability computed by Equation (2.6). These figures present the sub-periods when the yield spread is in the high-volatility regime. We can see from these figures that the high-volatility sub-periods of G1 and P6, in most cases, coincide with

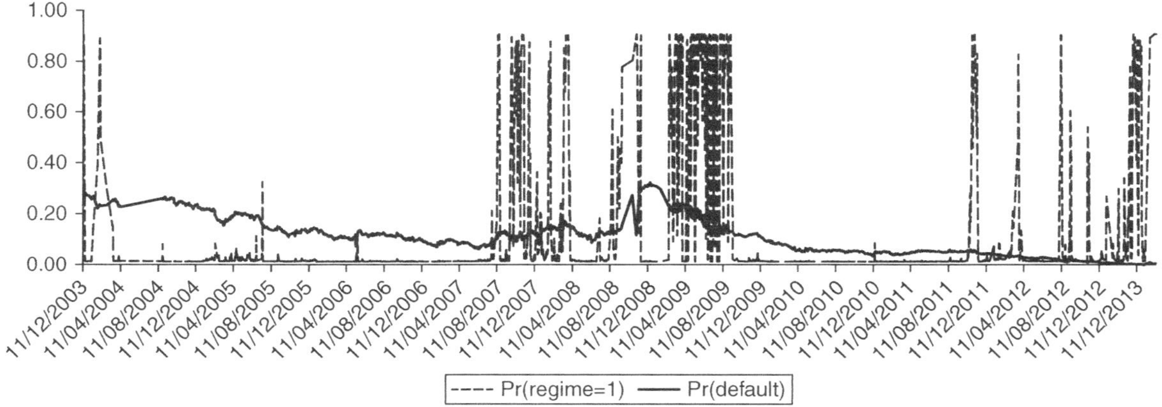

Figure 2.1 Probability of the high-volatility regime and default probability for G1

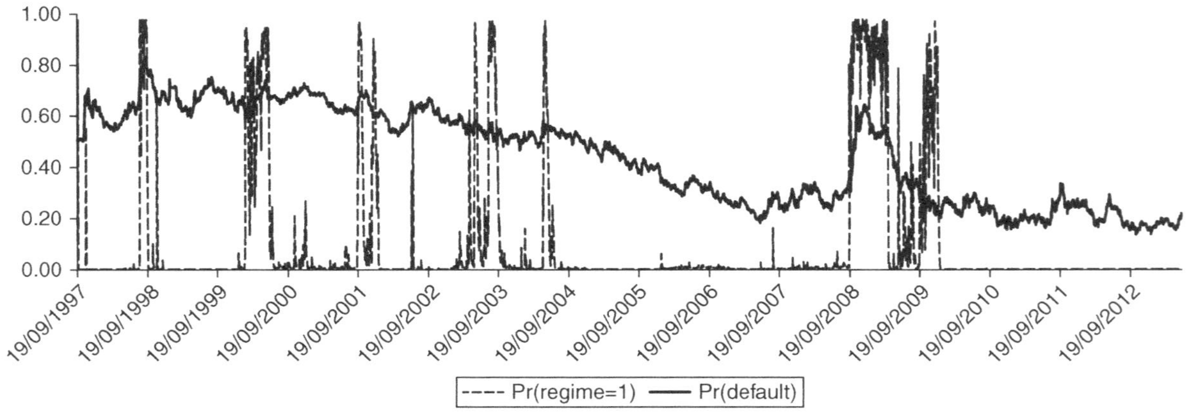

Figure 2.2 Probability of the high-volatility regime and default probability for P6

increased volatility or financial crisis periods of global financial markets. This suggests that switching from the low- to the high-volatility state is mostly driven by global factors. On Figures 2.1 and 2.2 we can also see that switches to the high-volatility regime many times coincide with jumps in the yield spread.

Table 2.8 shows that from the global default risk factors, the global risk aversion index has significant positive impact on the yield spreads, both in the high- and low-volatility states. Moreover, the US stock market return has significant negative impact on the default probability of these bonds in the low-volatility regime. The most important

Table 2.8 Estimation results for the regime switching model for G1 and P6

	G1(z_t=1)		G1(z_t=2)		P6(z_t=1)		P6(z_t=2)
Constant	3.154***	constant	0.011***	constant	0.153***	constant	-0.032**
T–t	0.544***	*T–t*	0.010	*T–t*	-0.008	*T–t*	0.004
GRA	0.408***	GRA	0.014**	GRA	0.200***	GRA	0.015*
OECD	0.024	OECD	0.014	OECD	0.060***	OECD	-0.004
FED	-0.279***	FED	-0.010	FED	0.080***	FED	0.000
S&P500	-0.007	S&P500	-0.017*	S&P500	-0.011	S&P500	-0.019*
OIL	-0.008	OIL	-0.002	OIL	0.003	OIL	-0.001
EE	-0.010	EE	-0.008	EE	-0.009	EE	-0.009
EB	-0.140***	EB	0.068**	EB	-0.003	EB	0.003
debt/GDP	-0.427***	debt/ GDP	-0.010	debt/GDP	-0.046***	debt/ GDP	0.001
TD/GDP	1.580***	TD/GDP	-0.002	TD/GDP	0.297***	TD/GDP	-0.002
TO/GDP	-0.045***	TO/GDP	-0.001	TO/GDP	0.017	TO/GDP	0.000
TB/GDP	-0.281***	TB/GDP	-0.009	TB/GDP	-0.114***	TB/GDP	0.000
CPI	0.199***	CPI	0.000	CPI	-0.029**	CPI	-0.003
CA/GDP	-0.018*	CA/GDP	-0.003	CA/GDP	0.223***	CA/GDP	-0.003
IR/GDP	-0.010	IR/GDP	0.008	IR/GDP	0.213***	IR/GDP	-0.004
RER	0.122***	RER	0.001	RER	0.096***	RER	0.000
GDP	0.271***	GDP	0.011	GDP	0.129***	GDP	-0.004
$\phi(1)$	0.032***	$\phi(2)$	0.992***	$\phi(1)$	0.850***	$\phi(2)$	0.973***
$\sigma(1)$	0.119***	$\sigma(2)$	0.053***	$\sigma(1)$	0.084***	$\sigma(2)$	0.044***
p	0.986***	q	0.906***	p	0.997***	q	0.977***
$v(1)$	0.996***	$v(2)$	2.726***	$v(1)$	3.101***	$v(2)$	3.914***
W (stationarity)	-3.006			*W* (stationarity)	-0.147		
LL	1703			LL	5376		
BIC	-3073			BIC	-10386		
T	1954			*T*	4030		

Notes: years to maturity (*T–t*); Global Risk Aversion index (GRA); global indicator of economic activity (OECD); Federal Fund effective rate (FED); US stock market return (S&P500); oil price return (OIL); emerging market equity investment performance (EE); emerging market fixed income investment performance (EB); government external debt to GDP (debt/GDP); government total deficit to GDP (deficit/GDP); Trade Openness to GDP (TO/GDP); Trade Balance to GDP (TB/GDP); inflation rate (CPI); Current Account to GDP (CA/GDP); International Reserves to GDP (IR/GDP); Real Exchange Rate log change (RER); real GDP growth (GDP). *, **, and *** denote parameter significance at the 10%, 5%, and 1% levels, respectively.

finding of Table 2.8 is that the country-specific factors are only significant in the high-volatility regime. This result suggests that in the low-volatility regime, the default risk evaluation of the market about these Central American bonds is only influenced by global and emerging market factors. However, when the yield spread switches to the high-volatility state, then global, regional, and country-specific determinants are considered by the market to re-evaluate Central American default probability.

8 Conclusions

In this chapter, we analyse the determinants of sovereign debt default probability for six Central American countries: Belize, Costa Rica, Guatemala, Honduras, Panama, and El Salvador. We study the yield spread of sovereign bonds issued by the governments of these countries. Fixed income spreads are computed with respect to the benchmark yield to maturity offered by US Treasury bonds. We measure the sensitivity of Central American sovereign yield spreads to several global, regional, and country-specific factors by using different dynamic specifications of conditional mean and volatility. These dynamic models are new in the literature of Latin American sovereign default risk analysis.

We find robust effects of global and emerging market factors on Central American sovereign yield spreads for all countries. The global risk aversion index has positive effect, while the US stock market return has negative effect, on sovereign default risk in all countries. Furthermore, emerging market equity investment performance has negative, while emerging market fixed income investment performance has positive, impact on sovereign yield spread in all countries. As results for some of the country-specific factors are mixed among the Central American countries and they may be explained by time-varying effects for different sample sub-periods, we estimated a regime-switching dynamic model to test this hypothesis. For two bonds from Guatemala and Panama, we find switching dynamics driven by a latent state variable switching between high- and low-volatility regimes. We find that the high-volatility sub-periods in most cases coincide with volatile and crisis periods of global financial markets. Moreover, we also find that the market incorporates information from country-specific factors in the sovereign yield spread only within the high-volatility sub-periods. During the low-volatility sub-periods that represent the major part of the total data period, investors employ only global and emerging market factors in their default probability evaluation for Central American sovereign bonds.

The results reported in this chapter may be interesting for practitioners, since the econometric methods suggested can be applied in practice to determine the main drivers of Central American sovereign default risk. Moreover, the techniques applied here can be implemented for the default probability evaluation and prediction of sovereign bonds issued in other emerging markets as well.

References

Ang, A & Longstaff, F (2013), 'Systemic Sovereign Credit Risk: Lessons from the US and Europe', *Journal of Monetary Economics*, vol. 60, no. 5, pp. 493–510.

Arce, O, Mayordomo, S & Peña, J I (2013), 'Credit-Risk Valuation in the Sovereign CDS and Bonds Markets: Evidence from the Euro Area Crisis', *Journal of International Money and Finance*, vol. 35, pp. 124–145.

Bernoth, K, von Hagen, J & Schuknecht, L (2012), 'Sovereign Risk Premiums in the European Government Bond Market', *Journal of International Money and Finance*, vol. 31, no. 5, pp. 975–995.

Bollerslev, T (1986), 'Generalised Autoregressive Conditional Heteroskedasticity', *Journal of Econometrics*, vol. 31, no. 3, pp. 307–327.

Cantor, R & Packer, F (1996), 'Determinants and Impact of Sovereign Credit Ratings', *Economic Policy Review*, Federal Reserve Bank of New York, October, pp. 37–53.

Codogno, L, Favero, C & Missale, A (2003), 'Yield Spreads on EMU Government Bonds', *Economic Policy*, vol. 18, no. 37, pp. 503–532.

Diaz Weigel, D & Gemmill, G (2006), 'What Drives Credit Risk in Emerging Markets? The Roles of Country Fundamentals and Market Co-Movements', *Journal of International Money and Finance*, vol. 25, no. 3, pp. 476–502.

Duffie, D, Pedersen, L H & Singleton K J (2003), 'Modeling Sovereign Yield Spreads: A Case Study of Russian Debt', *The Journal of Finance*, vol. 58, no. 1, pp. 119–159.

Ferrucci, G (2003), 'Empirical Determinants of Emerging Market Economies' Sovereign Bond Spreads', Working Paper No. 205, Bank of England.

Francq, C & Zakoian, J M (2001), 'Stationarity of Multivariate Markov-Switching ARMA Models', *Journal of Econometrics*, vol. 102, no. 2, pp. 339–364.

García-Herrero, A & Ortíz, A (2005), 'The Role of Global Risk Aversion in Explaining Latin American Sovereign Spreads', Documentos de Trabajo No. 505, Banco de España.

Grandes, M (2007), 'The Determinants of Sovereign Bond Spreads: Theory and Facts from Latin America', *Cuadernos de Economía*, vol. 44, no. 130, pp. 151–181.

Harvey, A C, & Chakravarty, T (2008),'Beta-t-(E)GARCH', Cambridge Working Papers in Economics 0840, Faculty of Economics, University of Cambridge.

Harvey, A C (2013a), *Dynamic Models for Volatility and Heavy Tails: With Applications to Financial and Economic Time Series*, Cambridge University Press, New York.

Harvey, A C (2013b), *Time Series Modelling and Analysis*, Econometrics Course taught by A C Harvey and organized by Timberlake Consultants, 23–25 July 2013, University of Cambridge, Cambridge, UK.

Hilscher, J & Nosbusch, Y (2010), 'Determinants of Sovereign Risk: Macroeconomic Fundamentals and the Pricing of Sovereign Debt', *Review of Finance*, vol. 14, no. 2, pp. 235–262.

Kim, C J & Nelson, C R (1999), *State-Space Models with Regime Switching*, The MIT Press, Cambridge, MA.

Longstaff, F A, Pan, J, Pedersen, L H & Singleton, K J (2011), 'How Sovereign Is Sovereign Credit Risk?', *American Economic Journal: Macroeconomics*, vol. 3, no. 2, pp. 75–103.

Pan, J & Singleton, K J (2008), 'Default and Recovery Implicit in the Term Structure of Sovereign CDS Spreads', *The Journal of Finance*, vol. 63, no. 5, pp. 2345–2384.

Remolona, E M, Scatigna, M & Wu, E (2007), 'Interpreting Sovereign Spreads', *BIS Quarterly Review*, March, pp. 27–39.

Taylor, S (1986), *Modelling Financial Time Series*, Wiley, Chichester.

Vrugt, E (2011), 'Estimating Implied Default Probabilities and Recovery Values from Sovereign Bond Prices', *The Journal of Fixed Income*, vol. 21, no. 2, pp. 5–14.

3

Contagion in Emerging Markets

Serge Darolles, Jérémy Dudek, and Gaëlle Le Fol

1 Introduction

Emerging markets (EM) are experiencing continued high economic growth that accompanies strong corporate earnings growth, usually associated with large financial assets returns. Moreover, this class of assets is offering a broader diversification to international portfolios by usually being only weakly correlated with the assets of developed countries. These particular features have greatly enhanced the attractiveness of EM to the financial industry, scientific community, and other stakeholders. Sullivan (2008) even advises developed-world investors to allocate more capital to those countries, if that is indeed the case.

However, this needs to be tempered. First, EM growth seems to be slackening, and the IMF said that growth rates in China, India, Brazil, and other developing countries are projected to decelerate in 2014.

Moreover, economic growth and financial asset returns are sometimes at odds with each other (see Henry and Kannan, 2008; Davis, Aliagia-Diaz, Cole, & Shanahan, 2010, for examples). For Davis et al. (2010), the high returns are the result of the low equity valuation in the early 2000s, coupled with higher-than-expected economic growth, rather than the high economic growth per se. The actual period seems to be quite different, and the link could be weaker and even disappearing.

Moreover, Conover (2011) reports the decline of the international diversification benefits due to the rise in correlations over time. Several authors are pointing out this increase in the correlations between developed and emerging countries (see, for example, Goetzmann, Li, & Rouwenhorst, 2005). More recently, Christoffersen, Errunza, Jacobs, & Langlois (2012) analysed these correlations and their evolutions between 1973 and 2009. They use new measures of dynamic diversification benefits that take into account higher-order moments and non-linear dependence. They show that correlations have increased in both developed and emerging markets, but they are much lower in the latter than in the former. They also show that tail dependence has also increased, but remains rather low in EM. Like Eun and Lee (2010), they conclude that EM are still offering significant diversification benefits for global investors.

Finally, investing in emerging countries involves greater risk than investing in developed countries because of political, currency, liquidity, extremes returns, contagion, and even systemic risks. The past 20 years have witnessed numerous financial crises that have had a major impact on emerging country economies.

The Mexican crisis (1994–1995), also called *Tequila crisis* or *el error de diciembre*, is one example. The peso devaluation sparked off a flight of capital. The magnitude of the capital outflow and the panic that started in financial markets led to that financial crisis. First, the impact on the Mexican real economy has been devastating before spreading out to the rest of the world. For the first time, the term 'financial contagion' is used to describe this rapid risk propagation from one geographic region to another. The Asian crisis, a few years later, also pointed out some local and worldwide contagion phenomena. It affected many Asian countries before contaminating Russia in 1998. On November 1998, one could read in the *Wall Street Journal*:

> Earlier this year, so many families living in the fashionable suburb of San Peddro Garza Garcia invested in Russian bonds that it became known as San Pedroburgo. Now this wealthy enclave feels more like Stalingrad...

This Russian crisis would see the collapse of the *hedge fund* LTCM (*Long Term Capital Management*) and the rise of systemic risk around the world. The Brazilian (1999), Turkish (2001), and Argentinian (2002) crises were also characterised with large-scale contagion phenomena, not to mention the *subprime crisis* of 2007–2008.

In all cases, even if the source of the crisis might have changed (see Bekaert and Harvey, 2003; Boyer, Kumagai, & Yuan, 2006), the consequences have been similar: sudden stop of capital in-flow followed by an economic crunch. The global downturn of 2008–2009 is no exception even if it started in developed economies (Ozkan and Unsal, 2012).

Most of the emerging countries have weathered the crisis of 2007–2008 and proved resilient even if some emerging economies (East-Europe EM) have turned to the IMF and the European Union for financial support to avoid default. Because financial institutions have received rescue capital from their governments since the last debt crisis (2009), they are more sensitive to their governments' health so that the sensitivity of the financial institution's default risk to the sovereign default risk has increased. Government debt can provide a good overview of the overall sovereign risk. In fact, sovereign debt is issued or guaranteed by a sovereign issuer. As a consequence, the risk premium associated with this debt reflects the country's default risk, and the analysis of sovereign debt becomes key to controlling and regulating the sovereign risk that EM are facing.

Overall, fundamentals have improved, but past recession and expansion cycles are likely to continue in the future just as contagion episodes. Moreover, the reduction of the 'quantitative easing', also called 'tapering', by the Fed in May 2013 and postponed in September 2013, revived the threats of 'assets spirals' in emerging markets.

Which emerging economies are at greatest risk of overheating is obviously an important issue, but understanding the dynamic of contagion appears to be even more important. Indeed, contagion mechanisms can enable the international financial system to prevent a crisis that can turn violent quickly and spur a systemic crisis.

The aim of this chapter is threefold. First, we review the literature and propose a definition of financial contagion. Second, we detail the econometric-based procedure to detect contagion phenomena. Third, we apply this methodology to emerging markets and particularly to their sovereign debt. We show that emerging sovereign debt markets exhibit contagion phenomena.

2 Literature review

If the literature on contagion goes back to the work of Sir Ronald Ross (1911) in epidemiology, economists' interest on this topic increased particularly during the second half of the 1990s, when financial crises spread across emerging countries, affecting countries with apparently low correlated fundamentals (Masson, 1999a, 1999b; Edwards, 2000). However, there is still no consensus on what constitutes contagion and how it should be defined (Forbes & Rigobon, 2002; see also Bekaert, Harvey, & Ng, 2005). We review in this section the main empirical works on this topic and introduce the statistical approach of contagion phenomena we use in the empirical application.

2.1 Contagion and interdependence

Correlation shift is the criterion generally chosen in this literature to separate 'normal' from contagious periods (see, for example, Corsetti, Percolo, & Sbracia 2001, 2005; Forbes & Rigobon, 2002). This shift is economically justified by the transmission of exogenous idiosyncratic shocks across countries or markets during these contagious periods. Of course, the shift depends on the endogenous level of correlation, or interdependence, between countries or markets. A rigorous computation of the reference value for the shift measurement requires a good evaluation of the correlations during calm periods. Following Dungey, Fry, Gonzalez-Hermosillo, & Martin (2005), the model of interdependence of asset markets during non-crisis periods can be specified as a latent factor model. This model basically distinguishes two risks in the asset returns: the non-diversifiable risk (i.e., the common exogenous factors) and the diversifiable risk (i.e., the idiosyncratic uncorrelated factors) (see Sharpe, 1964; Solnik, 1974). On the one hand, common factors capture all the dependence across assets. This corresponds to the fundamental dependence, or interdependence. These common factors may or may not be observed. Dungey et al. (2005) assume, for example, a unique common factor following a latent stochastic process with zero mean and unit variance. But this common factor can also capture richer dynamics including both heteroscedasticity and auto-correlation. On the other hand, a shock on any idiosyncratic factor only impacts the corresponding asset, and then idiosyncratic shocks only contribute to the volatility of asset returns through individual loadings.

During contagious periods, local idiosyncratic shocks observed on a specific country or market may be transmitted to another country or market after controlling for the interdependence level prevailing during normal periods, that is, via the exposures to common factors. The consequence is an increase in correlation during periods of crisis due to the dependence structure now allowed between idiosyncratic factors. In other words, we observe a change in the factor structure, and a fraction of the diversifiable risk – that is, one or several idiosyncratic factors – becomes non-diversifiable during crisis periods. The aim of empirical models of contagion is then to test the statistical significance of the parameters capturing this additional dependence (see Dungey, Fry, Gonzalez-Hermosillo, & Martin, 2002, 2003, 2006).

2.2 Heteroscedasticity

An important stylised fact of financial returns during crisis is that they exhibit high volatility. Hence, models ignoring or not allowing the change in volatility are potentially misspecified. Forbes and Rigobon (2002) observe that correlations are a positive function of volatility. They adjust their test procedure of contagion to take into account the change in volatilities and so the change in correlations during crisis periods. Without this adjustment, an observed correlation shift could only come from an increase in volatility and not from a conditional dependence between idiosyncratic factors. This in turn could cause the detection of spurious contagion phenomena (see Boyer, Gibson, & Loretan, 1999; Loretan & English, 2000; Corsetti, Percolo, & Sbracia, 2005).

The factor model framework used to discriminate between interdependence and contagion can be extended to include such dynamic features. These extensions can concern both the common and idiosyncratic terms, or the mean (see Mody & Taylor, 2003; Darolles, Dubecq, & Gourieroux, 2013; Darolles, Gagliardini, & Gourieroux, 2013) and the variance of asset returns (see Dungey et al., 2003, 2006; Dungey & Martin, 2004; Bekaert et al., 2005). In the latter case, a GARCH structure is generally imposed to the common factors only (see Diebold & Nerlove, 1989) and not to the idiosyncratic ones. This provides a parsimonious multivariate GARCH model based for example on the BEKK specification (Engle & Kroner, 1995). Finally, contagion in GARCH factor models causes a shift during crisis periods not in the marginal measure of dependence but in the conditional one. This result can be directly used to build a test of contagion (Dungey, Martin, & Pagan, 2000).

However, some parsimonious multivariate GARCH approach exists. For example, Engle (2002) introduces the dynamic conditional correlations (DCC-GARCH) model, now widely used for contagion analysis (see, e.g., Wang & Nguyen Thi, 2007; Chiang, Jeon, & Li, 2007; Naoui, Liouane, & Brahim, 2010; Gardini & De Angelis, 2012). In a first step, this model allows a flexible modelling of the idiosyncratic factors in line with the heterogeneity of dynamics observed between markets. In a second step, the dynamic correlation structure can be described using a limited number of parameters. Kenourgios, Samitas, and Paltalidis (2011) extend this framework by considering asymmetries in the correlations dynamics. Finally, we use an alternative approach: the regime switching dynamic correlation (RSDC-GARCH) model introduced by Pelletier (2006).

2.3 Definition of Crisis Periods

The identification of the contagion parameters in such a factor model scheme depends on both normal as well as crisis periods' returns. The choice of the length of the time window during the turmoil period might be a problem for some markets (see, e.g., Boyer et al., 1999; Billio & Pellizon, 2003). The definition of sub-sample periods is also an arbitrary process subjected to a selection bias. Moreover, a change in the inception date of the crisis period can lead to very different results. Therefore, the use of a state-space model with an endogenous definition of crisis periods is a much better choice. Billio and Caporin (2005), for example, propose a DCC-GARCH model including a switching regime component that automatically defines these crisis periods (see, e.g., Jeanne & Masson, 2000). Several other papers use the same approach to filter crisis periods (see, e.g., Ramchand & Susmel, 1998; Chesnay & Jondeau, 2001; Ang & Bekaert, 2002) and address both the heteroscedasticity and the definition of crisis periods issues. Finally, Dungey et al. (2012) introduce a smooth transition structural GARCH and show that a dependence structure, modified by the crisis period, does not return to the initial configuration when the crisis ends. Nevertheless, all these approaches consider pairwise correlations and do not allow a full modelling of the correlation matrix dynamics. This can, for example, be problematic when we are interested in portfolio applications.

2.4 Our Approach of Contagion Modelling

The regime-switching dynamic correlation (RSDC-GARCH) model (Pelletier, 2006) is an alternative to the DCC-GARCH approach. First, it provides a multivariate framework to model individual returns conditional heteroscedasticity with few parameters. Second, the correlation matrix is time varying, and correlations can instantaneously switch between normal and crisis periods.

Let us consider K asset returns, defined by:

$$r_t = H_t^{1/2} U_t,$$

where $U_t|\Phi_t \sim iid(0,I_K)U_t$ is the $T \times K$ innovation vector and Φ_t is the information available up to time t. The conditional covariance matrix H_t can be decomposed into (see, e.g., Bollerslev, 1990; or Engle, 2002):

$$H_t = S_t \Gamma_t S_t$$

where S_t is a diagonal matrix composed of the standard deviation, $\sigma_{k,t}$,k=1,...,K, and Γ_t is the $K \times K$ correlation matrix. Both matrices are time varying. We assume in a first step that the individual conditional variance follows a TGARCH (1,1) such that:

$$\sigma_{k,t} = w_k + \alpha_k^- \min\left(r_{k,t-1}, 0\right) + \alpha_k^+ \max\left(r_{k,t-1}, 0\right) + \beta_k \sigma_{k,t-}$$

hence, $\sigma_{k,t}$ would be interpreted as the conditional standard deviation of $r_{k,t}$. The parameters in each univariate TGARCH model are estimated with maximum likelihood under the assumption $U_t \sim N(0,1)$. The filtered volatility $\hat{\sigma}_{k,t}$ are immediately obtained from the previous equation. Finally, we can easily get the standardised returns, noted $\widetilde{\mathrm{r}_{k,t}}$.

$$\widetilde{\mathrm{r}_{k,t}} = \frac{\mathrm{r}_{k,t}}{\hat{\sigma}_{k,t}}$$

for k=1,...,K, which is used in a second step to estimate the correlation dynamics. In line with most common definition of contagion, that is, correlation shift, we introduce a regime-switching process that defines at each time t in which correlation regime we are. The correlation matrix is defined as:

$$\Gamma_t = \sum_{n=0}^{1} 1_{(\Delta_t = n)} \Gamma_n$$

where **1** is the indicator function, Δ_t is an unobserved Markov chain process independent from U_t with 2 possible values; (Δ_t =0,1) and Γ_n are correlation matrices. Regime switches are then governed by a transition probability matrix $\Pi = (\pi_{i,j})$with:

$$\Pr\left(\Delta_t = j | \Delta_{t-1} = i\right) = \pi_{i,j} \qquad \forall i, j = 0,1$$

This matrix gives the probability to stay in the same regime or switch in another regime, conditional on the initial regime. The correlation matrices and probabilities to be in state n, $n = 0,1$, are estimated by an EM algorithm (Dempster, Laird, & Rubin, 1977). This two-step approach is more tractable than the direct maximum likelihood approach when the number of observed series is important. Indeed, the number of parameters could become very large, and the one-step likelihood maximisation could become intractable.

3 Empirical application

We focus in this empirical application on the sovereign debt issued in local currencies by emerging market countries, studying both bond yields and the associated 5-year sovereign CDS premiums.

3.1 Data

We study the sovereign bond yields with a 5-year maturity and the 5-year CDS premiums written on these underlyings. We also use foreign exchange rates between the US dollar and the currencies for each of the following nine countries: Brazil, Chile, Hungary, Mexico, Poland, Russia, South Africa, Thailand, and Turkey. Our sample ranges from January 2007 to December 2011, allowing the analysis of the behaviour of the sovereign risk of emerging markets during the last sub-prime crisis and the next few years. We use as a risk-free rate, the five-year US Swap rate. All the data is derived from the Bloomberg database.

3.2 Empirical results and sovereign risk

As we have already seen, detecting a contagion event means spotting a shift in terms of correlations. In other words, we want to know whether there exists a change in the dependence structure of the studied time series.

Our specification of the RSDC model is a multivariate model that distinguishes only two states: (i) the state 0 for which the correlations are low and (ii) the state 1 for which the correlations are high. As a consequence, we only study the behaviour of the probability to be in state 1. This probability reflects the dynamic of the time, which should increase greatly in the case of a contagion.

In order to focus on contagion, we filter interdependence by measuring correlations during calm periods (i.e., state 0). A contagion event occurs when correlations suddenly increase, that is, when we switch to state 1. The natural measure of contagion is then the probability to be in state 1. Considering that the main channel of the shock propagation is the price, we simultaneously study whether bonds prices and CDS premiums experience contagion phenomena during our sample period.

Figure 3.1 presents the probability to be in state 1 at each date for the sovereign bond markets. We see, from January 2007 to December

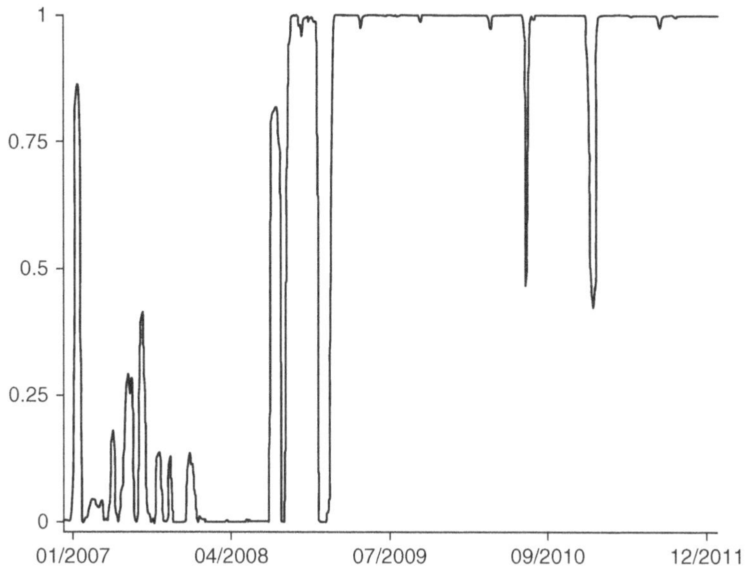

Figure 3.1 Probability to be in the state of high correlations: sovereign bonds

2011, the low volatility of this probability. It stays close to zero between January 2007 and September 2011, then goes and stays close to one between this date and December 2011. This plot also shows us that state 1 is more stable than state 0. This result also appears through the probability to stay in state 1 during two periods, consecutively. This latter is, in the case of sovereign bonds, equal to 0.9995 while the same probability concerning state 2 falls to 0.92. However, the main feature of this graph is that only one significant switch between state 0 and state 1 occurs during 2008. There is no come back to state 0 after this event for this market.

The results on the CDS market are not the same. In fact, the dynamic of the probability in this case is quite different from the one observed for the sovereign bonds. If the most important regime switching also occurs at the end of 2008, we see on Figure 3.2 that the volatility of the probability is much higher in the case of CDS market. The decrease of the probability to continue in state 2 between two consecutive dates is a confirmation of this fact. Indeed, the probability to stay into the state of high correlations is equal to 0.9966, but it drops to 0.9410 when the continuing date is in the state of low correlations. Nevertheless, we

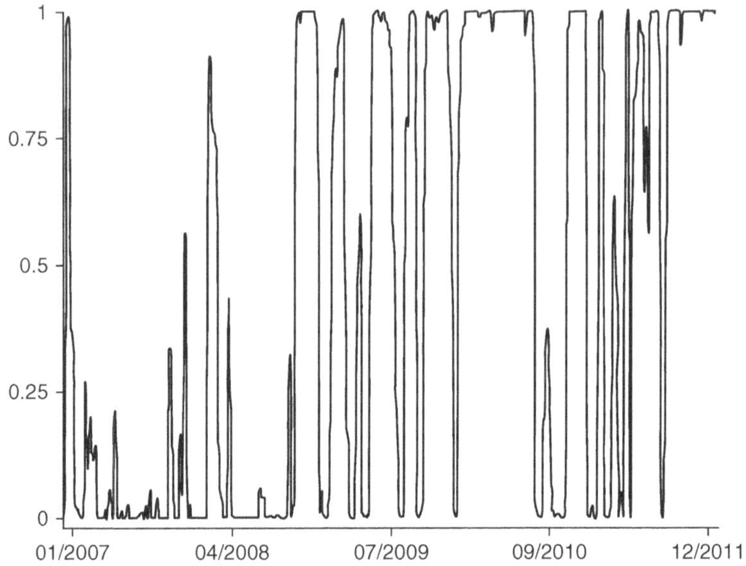

Figure 3.2 Probability to be in the state of high correlations: CDS premiums

find in both cases the same shift of probability, splitting our sample into two sub-periods, before the crisis and after the Lehman Brothers collapse.

The most important point when one seeks for detecting a contagion phenomenon is to distinguish different states of the correlation matrix. We present the results in Tables 3.1 and 3.2: the lower part of the tables gives the correlations in state 0 while the upper part corresponds to the correlations in state 1.

First, all the correlations are increasing between state 0 and state 1 except for the Polish-Russian pair in Table 3.1 and the Brazilian-Turkish as well as the Mexican-Turkish pairs in Table 3.2. This increase is ranging from –15% (Poland-Russia pair) to 104545% (Hungary-Thai pair) with a median of 59% for the sovereign bond yields and from –5% (Mexican-Turkish pair) to 83% (Polish-Turkish pair) with a median of 29% for the CDS premium.

For the sovereign bond, Thailand is the country that most features contagion phenomenon with a rise in correlation beyond 151% in all cases. As of the CDS premium case, Poland is dominating with a lowest increase of 14% but an average of 55% and a median above 60%.

Table 3.1 Correlation matrix, sovereign bond yields

	Brazil	Chile	Hungary	Mexico	Poland	Russia	South Africa	Thailand	Turkey
Brazil		0.32	0.57	0.58	0.61	0.38	0.61	0.21	0.59
Chile	0.26		0.39	0.37	0.39	0.36	0.37	0.18	0.39
Hungary	0.41	0.29		0.58	0.87	0.55	0.68	0.27	0.70
Mexico	0.49	0.26	0.35		0.64	0.40	0.63	0.24	0.61
Poland	0.30	0.35	0.66	0.23		0.53	0.71	0.27	0.71
Russia	0.20	0.22	0.53	0.10	0.62		0.48	0.24	0.49
Sth Afr.	0.43	0.31	0.52	0.45	0.36	0.23		0.26	0.69
Thailand	0.01	0.07	0.00	0.03	0.08	0.09	0.03		0.30
Turkey	0.39	0.32	0.47	0.34	0.41	0.27	0.52	0.04	

Table 3.2 Correlation matrix, CDS premiums

	Brazil	Chile	Hungary	Mexico	Poland	Russia	South Africa	Thailand	Turkey
Brazil		0.62	0.52	0.95	0.55	0.62	0.60	0.40	0.66
Chile	0.42		0.43	0.65	0.43	0.51	0.53	0.34	0.53
Hungary	0.37	0.32		0.54	0.77	0.75	0.74	0.43	0.74
Mexico	0.87	0.45	0.42		0.55	0.62	0.60	0.39	0.64
Poland	0.31	0.30	0.59	0.33		0.73	0.73	0.42	0.74
Russia	0.61	0.38	0.54	0.63	0.44		0.88	0.50	0.91
Sth Afr.	0.52	0.35	0.57	0.54	0.47	0.74		0.48	0.89
Thailand	0.31	0.34	0.34	0.33	0.37	0.44	0.39		0.50
Turkey	0.68	0.36	0.50	0.67	0.40	0.80	0.71	0.40	

Moreover, the difference between the likelihood of the RSDC model with two states and a CCC model (for Constant Conditional Correlations) corresponding to a RSDC model with only one state is so large that we are sure that the difference between the two correlation matrices is statistically significant. All these results are clearly pointing out the existence of contagion phenomena in emerging markets.

4 Concluding remarks

We have shown that the plots of the dynamics of the probabilities for both bonds and CDS markets are quite similar. They both exhibit a strong increase of the probability to be in state 1 at the end of September 2008. Indeed, we are able to distinguish two sub-periods over our sample.

Before the end of 2008, the correlation matrix is mainly in the state of low correlations while after the Lehman Brothers collapse, this matrix spent the most of time in state 1, of high correlations. In addition, we show a median increase of 59% and 29% of the correlations between state 0 and state 1 for sovereign bonds and CDS premium, respectively. These results confirm that there exists a contagion phenomenon following the bankruptcy of Lehman Brothers. Moreover, the results shed light on the fact that there is no return to a normal (pre-crisis) state. Indeed, correlations are still high at the end of 2011, far from their level prevailing before the crisis.

References

Ang, A & Bekaert, G (2002), 'International Asset Allocation with Regime Shifts', *Review of Financial Studies*, vol. 15, no. 4, p. 1137.

Bekaert, G & Harvey, C (2003), 'Emerging Markets Finance', *Journal of Empirical Finance*, vol. 10, no. 1–2, pp. 3–56.

Bekaert, G, Harvey, C & Ng, A (2005), 'A Market Integration and Cointegration', *Journal of Business*, vol. 78, pp. 39–69.

Billio, M & Caporin, M (2005), 'Multivariate Markov Switching Dynamic Conditional Correlation GARCH Representations for Contagion Analysis', *Statistical Methods and Applications*, vol. 14, no. 2, pp. 145–161.

Billio M & Pellizon, L (2003), 'Volatility and Shocks Spillover Before and After EMU in European Stock Markets', *Journal of Multinational Financial Management*, vol. 13, no. 4–5, pp. 323–340.

Bollerslev, T (1990), 'Modelling the Coherence in Short-Run Nominal Exchange Rates: A Multivariate Generalized Arch Model', *The Review of Economics and Statistics*, vol. 72, no. 3, pp. 498–505.

Boyer, B, Gibson, M & Loretan, M (1999), 'Pitfalls in Tests for Changes in Correlations', Federal Reserve Board, IFS Discussion Paper No. 597R.

Boyer, B, Kumagai, T & Yuan, K (2006), 'How Do Crises Spread? Evidence from Accessible and Inaccessible Stock Indices', *The Journal of Finance*, vol. 61, no. 2, pp. 957–1003.

Chesnay, F & Jondeau, E (2001), 'Does Correlation Between Stock Returns Really Increase During Turbulent Periods?', *Economic Notes*, vol. 30, no. 1, pp. 53–80.

Chiang, T, Jeon, B & Li, H (2007), 'Dynamic Correlation Analysis of Financial Contagion: Evidence from Asian Markets', *Journal of International Money and Finance*, vol. 26, no. 7, pp. 1206–1228.

Christoffersen, P, Errunza, V, Jacobs, K & Langlois, H (2012), 'Is the Potential for International Diversification Disappearing? A Dynamic Copula', *Review of Financial Studies*, vol. 25, no. 12, pp. 3711–3751.

Conover, C M (2011), 'Investment Issues in Emerging Markets: A Review', *The Research Foundation of CFA Institute Literature Review*, vol. 6, no. 1, pp. 1–27.

Corsetti, G, Percolo, M & Sbracia, M (2001), 'Correlation Analysis of Financial Contagion: What One Should Know Before Running a Test'. Mimeo, University of Rome.

Corsetti, G, Percolo, M & Sbracia, M (2005), 'Some Contagion, Some Interdependence: More Pitfalls in Tests of Financial Contagion', *Journal of International Money and Finance,* vol. 24, no. 8, pp. 1177–1199.

Darolles, S, Dubecq, J & Gourieroux, C (2013), 'Contagion Analysis in the Banking Sector', Mimeo, CREST.

Darolles, S, Gagliardini, P & Gourieroux, C (2013), 'Hedge Funds Survival: Between Frailty and Contagion', Mimeo, CREST.

Davis J H, Aliagia-Diaz, R, Cole, C W & Shanahan, J (2010), 'Investing in Emerging Markets: Evaluating the Allure of Rapid Economic Growth', Vanguard Research, Working Paper.

Dempster, A, Laird, N & Rubin, D (1977), 'Maximum Likelihood from Incomplete Data via the EM Algorithm, *Journal of the Royal Statistical Society Series B (Methodological),* vol. 39, no. 1, *pp. 1–38.*

Diebold, F & Nerlove, M (1989), 'The Dynamics of Exchange Rate Volatility: A Multivariate Latent-Factor ARCH Model', *Journal of Applied Econometrics,* vol. 4, no. 1, pp. 1–21.

Dungey, M, Martin, V & Pagan, A (2000), 'A Multivariate Latent Factor Decomposition of International Bond Yield Spreads', *Journal of Applied Econometrics,* vol. 15, no. 6, pp. 697–715.

Dungey, M, Fry, R, Gonzalez-Hermosillo, B & Martin, V (2002), 'The Transmission of Contagion in Developed and Developing International Bond Markets' in Committee on the Global Financial System (ed.), *Risk Measurement and Systemic Risk, Proceeding of the Third Joint Central Bank Research Conference,* Bank for International Settlements, pp. 61–74.

Dungey, M, Fry, R, Gonzalez-Hermosillo, B & Martin, V (2003), 'Unanticipated Shocks and Systemic Influences: The Impact on Contagion in Global Equity Markets in 1998', Working Paper, International Monetary Fund (IMF), WP/03/84.

Dungey, M & Martin, V (2004), 'A Multifactor Model of Exchange Rates with Unanticipated Shocks: Measuring Contagion in the East Asian Crisis', *Journal of Emerging Market Finance,* vol. 3, no. 3, pp. 305–330.

Dungey, M, Fry, R, Gonzalez-Hermosillo, B & Martin, V (2005), 'Empirical Modelling of Contagion: A Review of Methodologies', *Quantitative Finance,* vol. 5, no. 1, pp. 9–24.

Dungey, M, Fry, R, Gonzalez-Hermosillo, B & Martin, V (2006), 'International Contagion Effect from the Russian Crisis and the LTCM Near-Collapse', *Journal of Financial Stability,* vol. 2, no. 1, pp. 1–27.

Dungey, M, Milunovich, G, Thorp, S & Yang, M (2012), 'Endogenous Crisis Dating and Contagion Using Smooth Transition Structural GARCH', Mimeo, UTAS.

Edwards, S & Susmel, R (2001), 'Volatility Dependence and Contagion in Emerging Equity Markets', *Journal of Development Economics,* vol. 66, no. 2, pp. 505–532.

Engle, R (2002), 'Dynamic Conditional Correlation', *Journal of Business and Economic Statistics,* vol. 20, no. 3, pp. 339–350.

Engle, R & Kroner, K (1995), 'Multivariate Simultaneous Generalized ARCH', *Econometric Theory,* vol. 11, no. 1, pp. 122–150.

Eun, C S & Lee, J (2010), 'Mean–Variance Convergence Around the World', *Journal of Banking & Finance,* vol. 34, no. 4, pp. 856–870.

Forbes, K J & Rigobon, R (2002), 'No Contagion, Only Interdependence: Measuring Stock Market Comovements', *Journal of Finance,* vol. 57, no. 5, pp. 2223–2261.

Gardini, A & De Angelis, L (2012), 'A Statistical Procedure for Testing Financial Contagion', *Statistica*, vol. 1, pp. 37–61.

Goetzmann, W N, Li, L & Rouwenhorst, K G (2005), 'Long-Term Global Market Correlations', *Journal of Business*, vol. 78, no. 1, pp. 1–38.

Henry, P B & Kannan, P (2008), 'Growth and Returns in Emerging Markets', in Ito, E and Rose, A K (eds), *International Financial Issues in the Pacific Rim: Global Imbalances, Financial Liberalization and Exchange Rate Policy*, National Bureau of Economic Research, vol. 17, pp. 241–265.

Jeanne, O & Masson, P (2000), 'Currency Crises, Sunspots and Markov-Switching Regimes', *Journal of International Economics*, vol. 50, no. 2, pp. 327–350.

Kenourgios, D, Samitas, A & Paltalidis, N (2011), 'Financial Crises and Stock Market Contagion in a Multivariate Time-Varying Asymmetric Framework', *Journal of International Financial Markets, Institutions and Money*, vol. 21, no. 1, pp. 92–106.

Loretan, M & English, W (2000), 'Evaluating "Correlation Breakdowns" During Periods of Market Volatility', Federal Reserve Board, International Finance Discussion Paper No. 658.

Masson, P (1999a), 'Contagion: Macroeconomic Models with Multiple Equilibria', *Journal of International Money and Finance*, vol. 18, pp. 587–602.

Masson, P (1999b), 'Contagion: Monsoonal Effects, Spillovers, and Jumps Between Multiple Equilibria' in Agenor, P R, Miller, M, Vines, D & Weber, A (eds), *The Asian Financial Crisis: Causes, Contagion and Consequences*, Cambridge University Press, Cambridge.

Mody, A & Taylor, M (2003), 'Common Vulnerabilities', Discussion Paper, Centre for Economic Policy Research, London.

Naoui, K, Liouane, N & Brahim, S (2010), 'A Dynamic Conditional Correlation Analysis of Financial Contagion: The Case of the Subprime Credit Crisis', *International Journal of Economics and Finance*, vol. 2, no. 3, pp. 85–96.

Ozkan, F G & Unsal, D F (2012), 'Global Financial Crisis, Financial Contagion, and Emerging Markets', Working Paper, International Monetary Fund.

Pelletier, D (2006), 'Regime Switching for Dynamic Correlations', *Journal of Econometrics*, vol. 131, no. 1–2, pp. 445–473.

Ramchand, L & Susmel, R (1998), 'Volatility and Cross Correlation Across Major Stock Markets', *Journal of Empirical Finance*, vol. 5, no. 4, pp. 397–416.

Ross, R (1911), *The Prevention of Malaria*, John Murray, London.

Sharpe, W (1964), 'Capital Asset Prices: A Theory of Market Equilibrium Under Conditions of Risk', *Journal of Finance*, vol. 19, no. 3, pp. 425–442.

Sullivan, R (2008), 'Taming Global Village Risk', *Journal of Portfolio Management*, vol. 34, no. 4, pp. 58–67.

Solnik, B (1974), 'The International Pricing of Risk: An Empirical Investigation of the World Capital Market Structure', *Journal of Finance*, vol. 29, no. 2, pp. 365–378.

Wang, K & Nguyen Thi, T (2007), 'Testing for Contagion Under Asymmetric Dynamics: Evidence from the Stock markets Between US and Taiwan', *Physica A: Statistical Mechanics and Its Applications*, vol. 376 (C), pp. 422–432.

4 Aspects of Volatility and Correlations in European Emerging Economies

Anna Golab, David E. Allen, and Robert Powell

1 Introduction

This chapter examines the implications for European investors of the recent European Union (EU) expansion to encompass former Eastern bloc economies. It is questionable whether the formation of the European Monetary Union (EMU) within the EU has increased the correlation of national assets. This clearly has important implications for investors wishing to diversify across national markets, such as the implications of growing asset correlations, if they are displayed, and whether investors should diversify outside the Central and Eastern European (CEE) countries. It could be argued that the former Eastern bloc economies constitute emerging markets which typically offer attractive risk-adjusted returns for international investors. Therefore, this chapter explores a number of important aspects of portfolio selection and investment opportunities and their implications for CEE-based investors, culminating in a Markowitz efficient frontier analysis of these markets pre- and post-EU expansion.

It could be argued that the CEE economies form a unique emerging markets structure, which typically offers attractive risk-adjusted returns for international investors. Besides, both theoretical models and practical concerns motivate researchers towards focusing on the relationship between stock market index return volatility. This chapter includes a discussion of the volatility process of stock market indices as well as their individual pair-wise correlation coefficients to test the temporal stability of the co-movements between returns. An accurate characterisation of volatility and correlation has direct implications for portfolio management and asset allocation.

The results show growing investment potential in these emerging equity markets, with a lowering of average risk post-joining EU. This provides good opportunities for European investors as well as important indications for economic stability, growth, and integration of these markets in the post-EU period.

This chapter is structured as follows. Section 2 reviews the literature. Section 3 explains the data used in the empirical analysis and presents some summary statistics. Section 4 describes the methodology used in the study. The empirical results are analysed in Section 5 followed by concluding remarks in Section 6.

2 Literature review

The transmission of volatility between markets and the co-movements of stock markets have been extensively investigated in recent years. Globalisation has brought about market integration, especially in stock markets, a fact which attracted the researchers' interest regarding the transmission of volatility among markets.

The investigation of the determinants of cross-country financial interdependence has been studied in a large empirical literature aimed at identifying the role of a set of factors of influence, such as trade intensity (Forbes & Chinn, 2004), financial development (Dellas & Hess, 2005), and business cycle synchronisation (Walti, 2005). All of these papers concentrate on similar topics; however, their results and conclusions are slightly different. These concerns might be partly explained by the nature of the econometric approaches (cross-section vs. time-series), the measurement of market co-movement, and the nature and the measurement of explanatory factors.

Volatility modelling has been one of the most active and successful areas of research in time series econometrics and economic forecasting in recent decades. The modelling of the risk-expected return relationship is of central importance in modern financial theory and of key practical importance to investors. Risk is typically characterised by uncertainty and measures such as the variance or volatility of a time series. Since 1982 when Engle introduced the Autoregressive Conditional Heteroscedasticity (ARCH) model, variants and developments from this model have been effectively applied to numerous economic and financial datasets in the modelling of financial time series. The original ARCH model generated a huge family of direct descendants in univariate and multivariate models' categories. This includes Bollerslev's (1986) model of generalised ARCH (GARCH), which is currently the most popular and successful time series model. This chapter examines a GARCH (1,1) volatility model for the pre- and post-EU period in the context of the previously mentioned economies with a view to analysing the impact of EU membership on the behaviour of financial assets in these economies.

During the past few years, a few empirical studies have been undertaken on four of the 12 mentioned CEE emerging markets: the Czech Republic, Hungry, Poland, and Slovakia. These studies mainly examine correlations in stock returns and their volatility in the Polish and Slovakian stock markets (Hranaiova, 1999), time varying co-movements while applying Engle's (2002) GARCH models between developed economies, such as France, Germany, and the UK, and emerging ones; Czech Republic, Hungry, and Poland (Scheicher, 2001; Egert & Kocenda, 2007; Samitas & Kenourgios, 2011). Worthington and Higgs (2004) analysed market efficiency using methods applying the serial correlation coefficient, ADF (Augmented Dickey-Fuller), PP (Phillips-Perron), and KPSS (Kwiatkowski, Phillips, Schmidt, and Shin) unit root tests and MVR (multiple variance ration) tests. Another study constructed in a random walk framework is the paper by Cuaresma and Hlouskova (2005). An alternative issue to market efficiency is the issue of the degree of financial integration amongst the stock exchange markets in the Czech Republic, Hungry, Poland, and Slovakia in comparison with the euro zone market (Babetski, Komárek, & Komárková, 2007). The EMU equity market's volatility and correlation vs. US ones is also the subject of a study by Kearney and Poti (2008) and for global markets that of Capiello, Engle, and Sheppard (2006). Another approach, adopted by Bruggemann and Trenkler (2007) discusses the catching-up process in the Czech Republic, Hungry, and Poland by investigating GDP behaviour. The spill-over effects of emerging markets had been presented by Harrison and Moore (2009) and the co-movements and volatility of 10 Eastern European countries have been discussed. Some other studies focussed on stock market co-movements in Central Europe (Hanousek & Kocenda, 2011; Kocenda & Egert, 2011), but yet again the studies have been limited to a few main countries.

Overall, the majority of past studies of stock market co-movements and integration have concentrated mainly on mature developed markets or advanced emerging markets such as the Czech Republic, Hungary, and Poland whilst the behaviour and inter-relationship of all others has been neglected. Little attention is given to the investment potential in CEE equity markets only. Thus the literature lacks a model which analyses the interaction and integration of these markets at a regional and global level. The purpose of this study is an attempt to fill this gap.

3 Data

The statistical data in this study consists of the daily stock market indices in the 12 CEE stock markets[1] (Bulgaria, Czech Republic, Cyprus, Estonia, Hungary, Latvia, Lithuania, Malta, Poland, Romania, Slovakia, and Slovenia). The data is obtained for the period from January 1995 to September 2009. The 12 countries joined the EU during the latest two enlargements which took place on 1 May 2004 for the Czech Republic, Cyprus, Estonia, Hungary, Latvia, Lithuania, Malta, Poland, Slovakia, and Slovenia and 1 January 2007 for Bulgaria and Romania. Based on those two accession dates, the sample period is divided into two phases: pre-EU period (January 1995–April 2004) and post-EU (May 2004–September 2009). One common currency, the euro, is used to express stock market prices in order to provide comparable findings (after Scheicher, 2001; Syriopoulos, 2007). The common currency is assumed for a euro-based investor, who does not hedge currency risk.

4 Empirical methodology

This chapter uses several methods to test the behaviour of the return series of the 12 CEE markets. Firstly, the hypothesis of unit roots occurrence in the series is tested; then the correlation coefficients are analysed. The applied methodology is analysed for two specified periods: the pre-EU and post-EU phases as explained previously.

4.1 Non-stationarity of time series

There are a number of tests for non-stationarity of time series data. This chapter adopts two of them: the Augmented Dickey-Fuller (ADF) test (Dickey & Fuller, 1981) and Phillips-Perron (PP) non-parametric test (Phillips & Perron, 1988). If a series is defined as stationary, the mean and auto-covariance of the data series do not depend on time. The results are shown in Table 4.2. The fact that the price series are non-stationary is consistent with market efficiency and a reasonable level of competition in these markets. For example, if prices were trending and predictable, this would have strong implications for market efficiency and be evidence of a lack of competitiveness.

4.2 Pairwise correlation

Correlation is a measure of co-movements between two return series. Strong positive correlation indicates that upward movements in one return series tend to be accompanied by upward movements in the others and vice-versa for negative correlation. The pairwise correlation of the selected 12 European emerging markets is computed as below:

$$corr(x, y) = \frac{\text{cov}(x, y)}{\sigma_x \sigma_y} \tag{4.1}$$

where the covariance between two variables x and y is defined as the expected value of the product $(x - \mu_x)(y - \mu_y)$ and given as:

$$\text{cov}(x,y) = \text{E}[(x - \mu_x)(y - \mu_y)]. \tag{4.2}$$

4.3 Volatility measure

The GARCH class of models has proven to be particularly suited for modelling the behaviour of financial time series. These models are capable of capturing the three most common empirical observations in daily return data, including fat tails due to time-varying volatility, skewness resulting from mean non-stationarity, and volatility clustering.

GARCH models can provide a parsimonious parameterisation of a high-order ARCH process. Moreover, the model performs much better than the ARCH model due to more sensible constraints on coefficients and fewer parameters (Ling & McAleer, 2002). GARCH (1,1) model is equivalent to an infinite ARCH model with exponentially declining weight and takes the form of

$$h_t = \omega + \sum_{i=1}^{p} \alpha_i \varepsilon_{t-1}^2 + \sum_{i=1}^{q} \beta_i h_{t-1} \tag{4.3}$$

where for the GARCH process to exist, $\omega > 0$, α and $\beta \geq 0$ are sufficient conditions for the conditional variances to be positive. The conditional variance depends on constant value of ω, the error/reaction coefficient α, and lag/persistence coefficient β. ε_{t-1}^2 is the ARCH term and represents news about volatility from the previous period and h_{t-1}, the GARCH term, which is the last period's forecast variance. Both parameters (α and β) are sensitive to the historical data used. The size of the parameters α and β determine the short-run dynamic of the resulting volatility time series. A large GARCH lag coefficient β indicates that shocks to conditional variance take a long time to die out, so volatility is 'persistent'. A large ARCH error coefficient α means that volatility reacts quite intensively to market movements and so if α is relatively high and β is relatively low then volatility tends to be more 'spiky'. In practice, numerous studies have demonstrated that a GARCH (1,1) specification is often most appropriate. The coefficients of the model are easily interpreted, with the estimate of α_1 showing the impact of current news on the conditional variance process and the estimate of β_1 the persistence of volatility to a shock or, alternatively, the impact of 'old' news on volatility. The necessary and sufficient conditions for the second moment to exist for the GARCH (1,1) process is given by the definition that coefficients of α and β need to be summed to less than unity in each case.

4.4 Markowitz efficient frontiers

To ascertain the optimal portfolio mix of the 12 countries, we calculate the Markowitz (1952) efficient frontier pre- and post-EU joining. This frontier represents the combination of assets which give the lowest risk as measured by volatility (standard deviation) for any selected level of return and is obtained by minimising

$$\sigma_p = \sqrt{\sum_{i=1}^{n} w_i^2 \sigma_{i=1}^2 + \sum_{i=1}^{n} \sum_{j=1}^{n} w_i w_j Cov_{ij}} \tag{4.4}$$

where: σ_p is the portfolio standard deviation, w_i – the weights of the individual assets in the portfolio, σ_i^2 – the variance of rates of return for asset I and Cov_{ij} – the covariance between the asset returns (R) in the portfolio.

This optimisation is repeated for various levels of R to minimise σ (or various levels of σ to maximise R). Using matrix multiplication, we calculate a variance-covariance matrix from the correlations shown in Tables 4.2 and 4.3 and the standard deviations in Table 4.1. The two endpoints of the frontier are the maximum mean return as per Table 4.1 and its associated return, and the minimum portfolio risk and its associated return obtained from the above optimisation function.

5 Empirical results

5.1 Descriptive statistics

Table 4.1 presents descriptive statistics for the daily returns for the pre- and post-EU periods. Daily returns are defined as logarithmic price relatives: $R_t = \ln(P_t / P_{t-1}) \times 100$. In every case the return series has a mean value close to zero and a distribution characterised by non-normality (Jarque-Bera statistics). The highest mean of returns in pre-EU period can be observed in the stock markets in Bulgaria (0.086) and Romania (0.155), countries which joined the EU at the latest expansion. Those two countries, however, have the lowest and negative return in the post-EU period of –0.083 for Romania and –0.128 for Bulgaria. Next are Slovenia (–0.003), Latvia (–0.004), also negative. The highest mean return is assigned to Cyprus (0.053). If the data is normally distributed, then the mean and variance would completely describe the distribution of the data and the higher moments of skewness and kurtosis would provide no additional information about that distribution. However, the data contains positive skewness for two markets for the pre-EU period and on six occasions in the post-EU period. The skewness is greater than zero in all cases but one, post-EU Cyprus, where skewness is very close to zero (0.001). All other values for skewness are negative which implies that the distribution has a long left tail, whereas the relevant Jarque-Bera statistics indicate rejection of the normality hypothesis. All markets generate kurtosis statistics more than 3 (which is the benchmark for a normal distribution) which indicates the series is characterised by leptokurtosis. This means that the distribution of the data contains a greater number of observations in the tails than that found in a normal distribution. Whilst it is possible to individually test the significance of the skewness and kurtosis, the more common approach is the joint test based on calculation of Jarque-Bera statistics with comparison to critical values, as shown in Table 4.1.

5.2 Non-stationarity of the levels prices time series

In order to test for the presence of stochastic non-stationarity in the return series data; two unit root tests: the ADF and the PP tests have been applied. Table 4.2 presents results from both tests. The customary finding, consistent with work on market efficiency, is that price level series should contain a unit root; suggesting a lack of predictability. If there is a rejection of unit roots in the price level series, this may be

Table 4.1 Stock market descriptive statistics

	Mean	Median	Max	Min	St Dev	Skew	Kurtos	Jarque-Bera	Normalityp-value
Pre-EU period									
Bulgaria	0.155	0.044	21.073	–20.899	1.857	–0.447	38.678	85710.45	0.000
Czech Rep	0.005	0.000	5.819	–7.077	1.187	–0.154	5.225	527.48	0.000
Cyprus	N/A	N/A	N/A	N/A	N/A	N/A	N/A	N/A	N/A
Estonia	0.077	0.076	7.352	–5.874	1.102	–0.086	6.969	742.47	0.000
Hungary	0.081	0.025	13.616	–18.034	1.789	–0.847	16.502	16.50	0.000
Latvia	0.103	0.039	9.461	–14.705	1.831	–1.249	20.157	14141.68	0.000
Lithuania	0.070	0.038	4.580	–10.216	0.889	–1.168	20.895	15321.54	0.000
Malta	0.057	0.000	9.573	–7.589	0.920	2.244	26.658	37570.67	0.000
Poland	0.037	0.000	7.893	–10.286	1.710	–0.077	6.053	973.45	0.000
Romania	0.086	0.000	11.544	–11.901	1.717	–0.012	9.731	4568.78	0.000
Slovakia	0.018	0.000	27.554	–12.452	1.734	2.185	40.294	161795.5	0.000
Slovenia	0.048	0.000	11.012	–11.344	1.255	–0.306	15.629	17951.95	0.000
Post-EU period									
Bulgaria	–0.128	0.000	7.292	–11.359	1.911	–0.832	8.154	887.682	0.000
Czech Rep	0.026	0.056	12.264	–16.185	1.762	–0.593	16.897	11518.66	0.000
Cyprus	0.053	0.000	12.124	–10.881	2.203	0.001	7.302	1026.47	0.000
Estonia	0.015	0.023	12.094	–7.045	1.192	0.196	16.261	10238.40	0.000
Hungary	0.043	0.028	13.177	–12.649	1.816	–0.184	9.927	2849.37	0.000
Latvia	–0.004	0.000	9.156	–7.414	1.331	0.011	9.329	2330.35	0.000
Lithuania	0.021	0.005	11.001	–9.111	1.301	0.123	17.468	12180.26	0.000
Malta	0.013	0.000	4.736	–4.536	0.813	0.067	8.937	2088.20	0.000
Poland	0.032	0.017	6.083	–8.288	1.433	–0.429	6.236	664.05	0.000
Romania	–0.083	0.000	10.091	–13.117	2.328	–0.492	6.604	422.33	0.000
Slovakia	0.032	0.014	11.880	–9.577	1.105	0.111	20.206	17532.81	0.000
Slovenia	–0.003	0.001	7.681	–8.299	1.147	–0.771	13.842	7101.94	0.000

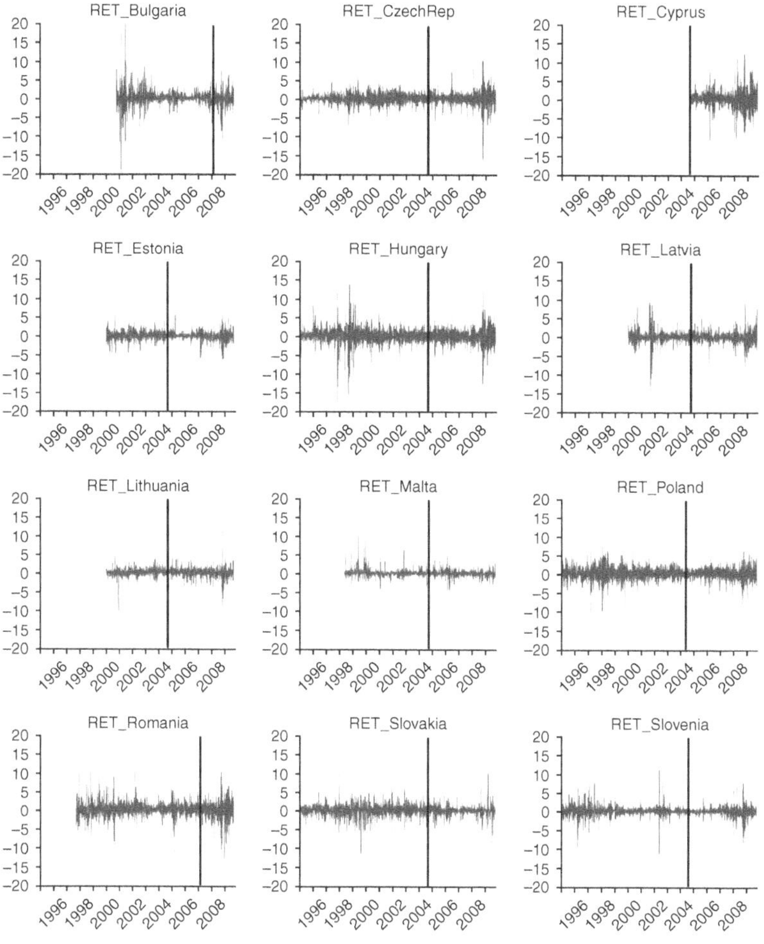

Figure 4.1 Daily returns series

Note: Graphs have been divided by a vertical line into two phases showing pre- and post-EU periods.

Table 4.2 Unit root tests on price levels and first differences

	ADF test				PP test			
	v_t		Δv_t		v_t		Δv_t	
	Without trend	**With trend**	**Without trend**	**With trend**	**Without trend**	**With trend**	**Without trend**	**With trend**
Pre-EU period								
Bulgaria	4.258	−1.653	−23.077***	−23.654***	4.145	−1.691	−34.258***	−33.927***
CzechRep	0.073	−1.478	−43.322***	−43.471***	0.061	−1.474	−43.544***	−43.451***
Cyprus	N/A	N/A	N/A	N/A	N/A	N/A	N/A	N/A
Estonia	2.538	−1.052	−26.295***	−26.559***	2.963	−0.687	−26.111***	−26.334***
Hungary	1.100	−1.970	−50.964***	−50.997***	1.062	−2.008	−50.974***	−51.009***
Latvia	1.840	−2.126	−17.577***	−17.721***	1.773	−2.270	−27.277***	−27.640***
Lithuania	3.469	0.541	−19.567***	−20.356***	3.693	0.787	−29.888***	−29.872***
Malta	0.541	−1.389	−25.065***	−25.111***	0.650	−1.352	−24.745***	−24.744***
Poland	0.802	−1.872	−45.637***	−45.649***	0.864	−1.795	−45.586***	−45.607***
Romania	2.456	−1.414	−15.456***	−15.812***	2.759	−1.352	−42.318***	−42.116***
Slovakia	−0.761	−3.128*	−15.433***	−15.429***	−0.768	−3.128*	−57.090***	−57.073***
Slovenia	2.574	−0.136	−35.807***	−35.963***	2.224	−0.518	−43.832***	−43.714***
Post-EU period								
Bulgaria	−1.143	−1.788	−12.529***	−12.609***	−1.103	−1.841	−24.338***	−24.278***
CzechRep	0.074	−1.397	−35.398***	−35.426***	0.065	−1.413	−35.341***	−35.366***
Cyprus	−0.119	−0.848	−33.630***	−33.684***	−0.100	−0.831	−33.742***	−33.790***
Estonia	−0.139	−1.268	−16.991***	−17.126***	−0.184	−1.289	−33.004***	−32.878***
Hungary	0.287	−1.664	−27.313***	−27.342***	0.277	−1.674	−34.281***	−34.249***
Latvia	−0.269	−1.009	−35.599***	−35.754***	−0.313	−1.114	−36.564***	−36.435***
Lithuania	0.026	−1.283	−31.159***	−31.251***	−0.141	−1.409	−34.261***	−34.127***
Malta	0.073	−1.100	−20.623***	−20.860***	−0.444	−1.100	−26.967***	−27.084***
Poland	0.241	−0.928	−35.366***	−35.387***	0.159	−1.017	−35.448***	−35.418***
Romania	−1.158	−1.506	−24.421***	−24.424***	−1.182	−1.392	−24.443***	−24.438***
Slovakia	0.286	−1.931	−36.578***	−36.861***	0.131	−1.994	−37.632***	−37.439***
Slovenia	−0.302	−0.294	−26.478***	−26.531***	−0.301	−0.303	−27.917***	−27.792***

Notes: v_t: variable in levels; Δv_t: variable in first difference; Critical values/without trend: −2.566 at the 1% level; −1.941 at the 5% level; −1.617 at 10% level; Critical values/with trend: −3.962 at the 1% level; −3.412 at the 5% level; −3.128 at 10% level; MacKinnon (1996) one-sided p-value; Significance levels: *** 0.01%, ** 0.05%, * 0.10.

consistent with the existence of price trends and the ability to predict prices. However, in only one case, that of Slovakia in the pre-EU period, do we reject the unit root in the price level series when we add a trend to the model. This result is consistent for both the ADF and the PP tests. However, it vanishes in the post-EU period. The evidence for the price level series is consistent with the existence of competitive markets.

For the returns, or differenced series, we find evidence strongly suggesting the existence of stationarity. Each of the test scores are below the critical value at the 5% level, and this result is not sensitive to the presence of an intercept term and trend. Both tests were performed using the maximum lag length in each case. The ADF and PP test statistics have a probability value of 0.01 for all markets, providing evidence that we may reject the null hypothesis of the existence of unit roots for the return series. Hence, the ADF and PP tests clearly indicate that the return data is stationary. We may conclude that if the price index series had not rejected the hypothesis of unit root existence then the stock markets' price series could display trend behaviour. However, our results suggest the contrary.

5.3 Pairwise correlation

The prior expectation of this analysis, based on previous research, is one of weak co-movements between the countries studied (Scheicher, 2001; Syriopoulos, 2007); however, some of the cross-country correlations may be found to be significant. In our data, the pre-EU period shows correlations on most occasions to be weak, and the correlation coefficients do not exceed a value of 0.1 (Table 4.3). It is observable that Slovakia's stock market remains isolated from all others; it demonstrates negative correlation with most of the other countries except Latvia, Malta, and Poland, where the value of the correlation coefficient is positive but still very small: 0.014, 0.010, and 0.032, respectively. The other market showing negative correlation is Bulgaria. This market is inversely correlated with Poland, Romania, and Slovakia and is very lowly correlated with all other CEE countries. On the other hand, the markets of the Czech Republic, Hungary, and Poland are reasonably highly correlated with each other, showing average correlations of 0.452. Estonia's stock market is different from all the other weakly correlated markets with an average correlation of 0.233 with Hungary, Lithuania, and Poland. The post-EU period shows an increase in stock market inter-relations, with stronger correlations between countries. Consequently, we can see that the values of the correlation coefficients increased significantly after all the countries concerned had joined the EU. Table 4.4 demonstrates

Table 4.3 Correlation coefficient matrix for pre-EU period, 1995–2004

	Bulgaria	**CzechR**	**Estonia**	**Hungary**	**Latvia**	**Lithuan**	**Malta**	**Poland**	**Romania**	**Slovakia**	**Slovenia**
Bulgaria	1										
CzechR	0.035	1									
Estonia	0.094	0.277	1								
Hungary	0.044	0.474	0.251	1							
Latvia	0.021	0.043	0.074	–0.007	1						
Lithuania	0.030	0.075	0.229	0.057	0.039	1					
Malta	0.050	0.014	0.020	0.060	0.001	0.003	1				
Poland	–0.042	0.425	0.219	0.456	–0.002	0.072	0.021	1			
Romania	–0.037	0.074	0.036	0.083	0.036	0.035	0.034	0.043	1		
Slovakia	–0.009	–0.026	–0.054	–0.028	0.014	–0.033	0.010	0.032	–0.028	1	
Slovenia	0.012	0.059	0.065	0.080	0.019	–0.039	0.008	0.007	0.066	0.047	1

Table 4.4 Correlation coefficient matrix for post-EU period, 2004–2009

	Bulgaria	CzechR	Cyprus	Estonia	Hungary	Latvia	Lithuan	Malta	Poland	Romania	Slovakia	Slovenia
Bulgaria	1											
CzechR	0.230	1										
Cyprus	0.325	0.511	1									
Estonia	0.351	0.289	0.379	1								
Hungary	0.187	0.403	0.612	0.285	1							
Latvia	0.274	0.207	0.249	0.325	0.175	1						
Lithuania	0.394	0.294	0.406	0.549	0.292	0.409	1					
Malta	0.097	0.059	0.023	0.074	0.033	0.080	0.087	1				
Poland	0.261	0.482	0.685	0.305	0.618	0.177	0.308	0.035	1			
Romania	0.319	0.408	0.500	0.328	0.359	0.238	0.363	0.065	0.414	1		
Slovakia	0.100	0.016	0.029	0.091	0.009	0.014	0.092	0.008	–0.023	0.046	1	
Slovenia	0.380	0.297	0.375	0.379	0.255	0.301	0.414	0.061	0.265	0.376	0.027	1

these correlation coefficients and, as previously, we can see a very strong relationship between three countries: the Czech Republic, Hungary, and Poland. However, the stock markets of Romania and Cyprus should be emphasised here as well (Cyprus has not been mentioned in the pre-EU discussion as data for this market is only available for the post-EU phase). Again we can see that the stock markets of Slovakia and Malta are different to all others stock market. Both of them show very weak correlations to all the other countries.

Overall, the correlation coefficients between the CEE stock markets are found to be relatively low and on some occasions negative in the pre-EU period. In the post-EU period, the correlation coefficients between the CEE markets are higher which indicates strengthening. This period also demonstrates that pre-EU negative correlations turn positive in the post-EU period. The stock markets of the Czech Republic, Hungary, and Poland have high and positive pairwise correlation, whereas the smaller markets of Malta and Slovakia remain isolated compared to their peers.

The increase in correlations in the post-EU period means that the scope for investors diversifying into these new markets has been diminished. Capiello et al. (2006) find much higher correlations amongst bond indices across EU member states than is the case with equity indices. This is perhaps not surprising given the influence of common monetary policies. Jorion and Goetzemann (1999) undertake simulations of the characteristics of emerging markets and suggest that high returns and low covariances with developed markets are characteristics of 'emergence', but not necessarily long-term characteristics. They also point out that many of today's emerging markets are 're-emerging' markets that had previously been prominent but had, for various reasons, sunk from the sight of international investors. They include Poland, Romania, and Czechoslovakia in this category, noting that they had active equity markets in the 1920s.

5.4 Volatility measures

For the GARCH process to be stationary, the parameters in the variance equation must sum to less than one (for GARCH (1,1) model $\alpha + \beta < 1$). The closer the sum to one, the less stable the variance will be in the long run, and the more permanent will be changes in the level of volatility as a consequence of 'volatility shocks'. Conversely, the smaller this sum relative to one, the more transient will be the effect of the volatility shocks, and the less of an adjustment there will be to expected returns. To test ARCH and GARCH coefficients values we again run the test for all twelve CEE stock markets in two time periods: pre- and post-EU.

Table 4.5 Estimated GARCH (1,1) model on return series data

	ω		α		β		
	Coef	SE	Coef	SE	Coef	SE	$\sum(\alpha+\beta)$
Pre-EU period							
Bulgaria	0.005	0.004	0.102	0.024	0.897	0.015	0.999
Czech Rep	0.027	0.008	0.105	0.016	0.879	0.014	0.984
Cyprus	N/A	N/A	N/A	N/A	N/A	N/A	N/A
Estonia	0.061	0.022	0.101	0.023	0.852	0.035	0.953
Hungary	0.179	0.056	0.215	0.074	0.742	0.066	0.957
Latvia	0.102	0.036	0.228	0.061	0.747	0.052	0.975
Lithuania	0.310	0.159	0.220	0.084	0.403	0.117	0.623
Malta	0.048	0.026	0.235	0.075	0.745	0.089	0.980
Poland	0.109	0.030	0.110	0.023	0.851	0.026	0.961
Romania	0.149	0.041	0.203	0.034	0.759	0.035	0.962
Slovakia	0.063	0.030	0.089	0.026	0.890	0.032	0.979
Slovenia	0.022	0.006	0.204	0.039	0.795	0.034	0.999
Post-EU period							
Bulgaria	0.166	0.061	0.269	0.067	0.685	0.065	0.954
Czech Rep	0.041	0.012	0.151	0.027	0.840	0.021	0.991
Cyprus	0.026	0.013	0.099	0.018	0.900	0.016	0.999
Estonia	0.004	0.003	0.153	0.029	0.846	0.023	0.999
Hungary	0.047	0.018	0.109	0.020	0.876	0.021	0.985
Latvia	0.079	0.021	0.199	0.039	0.759	0.039	0.958
Lithuania	0.070	0.035	0.171	0.029	0.792	0.053	0.963
Malta	0.093	0.029	0.291	0.052	0.590	0.068	0.881
Poland	0.014	0.007	0.072	0.016	0.923	0.015	0.995
Romania	0.313	0.114	0.289	0.082	0.681	0.073	0.970
Slovakia	0.034	0.017	0.098	0.030	0.880	0.032	0.978
Slovenia	0.032	0.009	0.237	0.050	0.748	0.039	0.985

Table 4.5 presents details of the GARCH model. The α and β coefficients are positive, significant, and summed to less than one for each stock market.

Volatility persistence in the CEE countries is generally very high. Overall, Hungary, Poland, Czech Republic, Romania, and Slovakia show similar volatility through the whole testing period with no dramatic changes through accession to the EU. The pre-EU period seems to be less volatile for Estonia and Lithuania. On the other hand, the post-EU period is less volatile for Bulgaria, Latvia, Malta, and Slovenia. The sum of ARCH and GARCH coefficients ($\alpha + \beta$) is very close to one, indicating that volatility shocks are quite persistent, which is often observed in high-frequency financial data and is a characteristic of emerging markets. Overall, the dynamics of volatility in the post-EU period seem to be more stable for all the stock markets as the standard deviation for this period is 0.032 (mean α+β = 0.972), as compared to the pre-EU period where the standard deviation is 3.3 times larger (0.107), with a mean of 0.943.

The conditional variance of the GARCH (1,1) model presented in Figure 4.2 shows a great deal of volatility over the defined time period

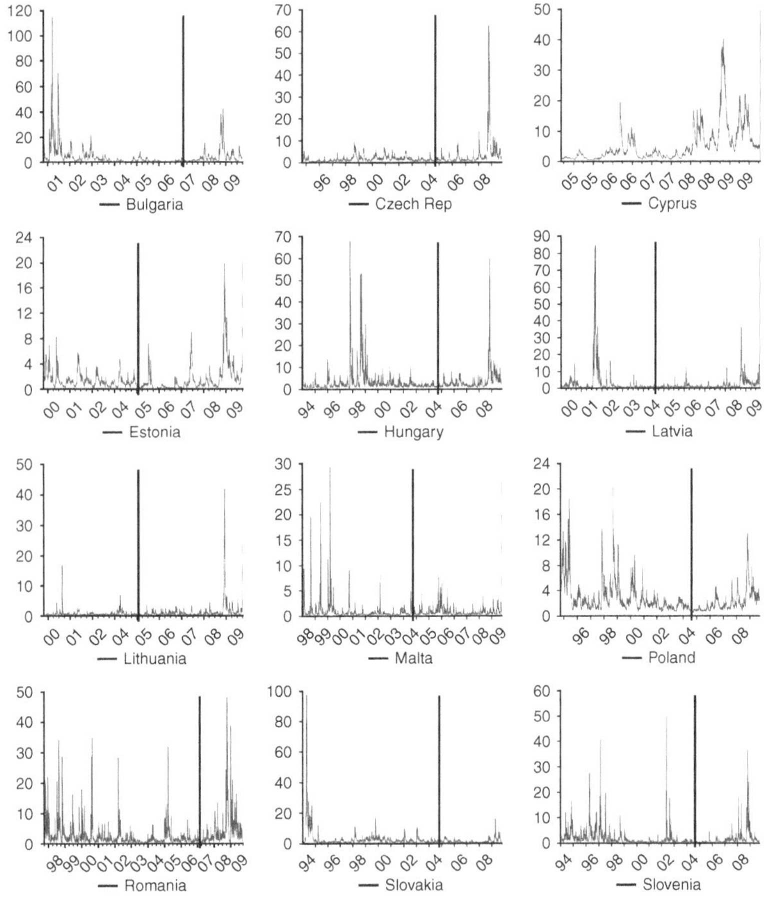

Figure 4.2 Conditional variance of GARCH (1,1) model

Note: Graphs have been divided by a vertical line into two phases showing pre- and post-EU periods.

with a number of fairly large spikes. Such spikes are normally associated with the arrival of major news to the market which has an influence on price adjustment. The last high spike visible in almost all the countries and observed in Figure 4.2 is at the end of 2008, during the global financial crisis. The evidence of volatility justifies the modelling of time varying conditional variances as opposed to the standard assumption of homoscedasticity.

5.5 Markowitz efficient frontier analysis

To calculate the Markowitz efficient frontiers for these markets pre- and post-EU expansion, as shown in Figure 4.3 below and summarised in Table 4.6, we use the correlations shown in Tables 4.3 and 4.4 and the standard deviations in Table 4.1. The two endpoints of the frontier are the maximum mean return as per Table 4.1 and its associated return, and the minimum portfolio risk and its associated return obtained from the above optimisation function. Using these highest and lowest return points, we calculate equidistant intervening return points to obtain a total of ten return scenarios. We minimise σ for each of these return scenarios to obtain pre- and post-EU efficient frontiers as shown in the following Figure 4.3.

The frontier shows a downward shift post-EU incorporation, meaning lower available returns for any given level of risk. Our concern is not so much with the levels of the frontier as these are influenced by global market events such as the Global Financial Crisis in the post-EU period, but rather with the optimal risk-return combination of assets that make up the frontier. These are shown in Table 4.6.

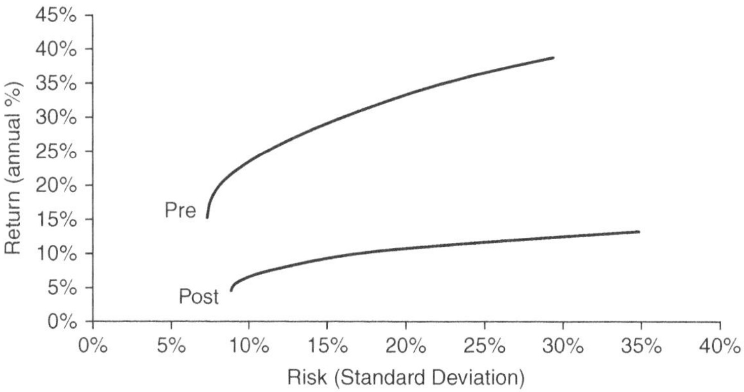

Figure 4.3 Efficient frontier

Table 4.6 Optimal asset allocation

Pre-EU period										
Return	38.8%	36.1%	33.5%	30.9%	28.3%	25.7%	23.1%	20.5%	17.9%	15.3%
Stdev	29.4%	24.3%	20.3%	17.1%	14.2%	11.7%	9.8%	8.3%	7.5%	7.3%
Optimal portfolio mix for each return level:										
Bulgaria	100.0%	80.4%	64.6%	51.4%	40.0%	30.0%	21.4%	14.1%	8.3%	4.8%
CzechR	0.0%	0.0%	0.0%	0.0%	0.0%	0.0%	0.0%	0.0%	1.0%	8.6%
Estonia	0.0%	0.0%	0.0%	4.5%	8.5%	10.6%	10.9%	10.7%	9.7%	7.6%
Hungary	0.0%	0.0%	1.6%	5.5%	5.9%	5.7%	4.9%	4.0%	2.0%	0.0%
Latvia	0.0%	18.0%	21.6%	20.5%	17.6%	14.6%	11.7%	8.9%	6.5%	4.8%
Lithuania	0.0%	0.0%	0.0%	3.6%	14.2%	20.6%	23.3%	24.5%	24.5%	23.7%
Malta	0.0%	0.0%	0.0%	0.0%	0.0%	6.1%	14.0%	19.2%	22.5%	23.6%
Poland	0.0%	0.0%	0.0%	0.0%	0.0%	0.0%	0.0%	0.0%	2.3%	2.2%
Romania	0.0%	1.5%	12.2%	14.5%	13.8%	12.4%	10.4%	8.4%	6.7%	5.3%
Slovakia	0.0%	0.0%	0.0%	0.0%	0.0%	0.0%	0.0%	2.3%	5.7%	7.4%
Slovenia	0.0%	0.0%	0.0%	0.0%	0.0%	0.0%	3.6%	7.9%	10.9%	11.9%
Post -EU period										
return	13.3%	12.3%	11.3%	10.4%	9.4%	8.4%	7.5%	6.5%	5.6%	4.6%
stdev	34.8%	28.6%	22.9%	18.2%	15.2%	13.1%	11.3%	9.9%	9.1%	8.9%
Optimal portfolio mix for each return level:										
Bulgaria	0.0%	0.0%	0.0%	0.0%	0.0%	0.0%	0.0%	0.0%	0.0%	0.0%
CzechR	0.0%	0.0%	0.0%	0.0%	0.0%	0.0%	0.0%	0.5%	1.3%	1.1%
Cyprus	100.0%	76.9%	56.7%	36.4%	19.9%	14.3%	8.6%	2.8%	0.0%	0.0%
Estonia	0.0%	0.0%	0.0%	0.0%	0.0%	0.0%	0.0%	1.2%	6.5%	9.1%
Hungary	0.0%	9.1%	12.7%	16.4%	18.3%	14.8%	11.3%	7.9%	4.0%	0.3%
Latvia	0.0%	0.0%	0.0%	0.0%	0.0%	0.0%	0.0%	0.0%	2.3%	9.7%
Lithuania	0.0%	0.0%	0.0%	0.0%	0.0%	0.0%	1.8%	5.4%	4.7%	1.8%
Malta	0.0%	0.0%	0.0%	0.0%	3.1%	15.1%	26.0%	34.5%	40.5%	44.0%
Poland	0.0%	0.0%	0.0%	0.0%	0.9%	4.8%	8.4%	11.0%	10.9%	9.5%
Romania	0.0%	0.0%	0.0%	0.0%	0.0%	0.0%	0.0%	0.0%	0.0%	0.0%
Slovakia	0.0%	14.0%	30.6%	47.1%	57.8%	50.9%	43.9%	36.7%	29.8%	24.4%
Slovenia	0.0%	0.0%	0.0%	0.0%	0.0%	0.0%	0.0%	0.0%	0.0%	0.0%

This table considers 10 return scenarios as shown in the top row of the table. The σ for each of these scenarios, as calculated by the optimisation function, is shown in row 2. The ensuing section of the table shows the portfolio mix from which these risk-return combinations are calculated. For example, in the post-EU period, to obtain a return of 13.3% with σ of 34.8%, the required investment is 100% in Cyprus. To obtain a post-EU return of 11.3% with an associated minimised σ of 22.9%, the optimal investment is 56.7% in Cyprus, with the balance in Slovakia and Hungary.

Investors seeking to maximise returns on this portfolio would invest all their funds in Bulgaria pre-EU incorporation. Investors seeking to minimise their risk pre-EU would invest just under half their funds in Lithuania and Malta, with the other half spread across portfolio assets, mainly Slovenia, Czech Republic, Estonia, and Slovakia. Post-EU, risk would be minimised by investing in Malta followed by Slovakia, Latvia, Poland, and Estonia. We can use the above to compare investment in the 'advanced emerging' markets of Poland, Hungary, and Czech Republic with 'other emerging markets'. If we classify the returns of the first three columns above as high-return scenarios, with low-return based on the last three columns, and mid-return based on the columns in between, then optimal investment in advanced emerging markets pre-EU would be below 6% for the high- and medium-return periods and 11% for the low-return scenarios. Post-EU optimal investment in advanced emerging markets would be up to 13% for the high scenario, and up to 20% during the mid- and lower-case scenarios. In summary, the 'other' emerging markets dominate for all pre- and post-EU scenarios.

6 Conclusions

In this chapter we analysed the relationships between the 12 CEE countries' emerging markets, their fundamental statistical and diagnostics tests, pairwise correlation, and volatility. The tests were conducted on data collected from January 1995 to September 2009, with the data divided into two groups representing pre- and post-EU periods according to accession to the EU by the named counties. Firstly, we provided descriptive statistics and applied unit root tests which suggested that the data behaves like typical price and return series. We examined pairwise correlations showing the relationship between the 12 stock markets pre- and post-EU. A GARCH (1,1) volatility model was adopted to assess dynamic volatility behaviour, and finally we applied a Markowitz efficient frontier analysis for both pre- and post-EU joining data periods.

It is not a surprise that the significant role of the Czech Republic, Hungarian, and Polish markets was evident. This confirms the finding in the Campos and Horvath (2012) and Horvath and Petrovski (2013) publications of successful and strong European integration after the fall of communism. Authors agree that these countries are experiencing solid growth and slowly but consistently creating a market-orientated economy. As a result, these markets have already been recognised by the FTSE and MSCI groups as advanced emerging markets. Furthermore, Estonia has developed into a strong international player through its membership in the EU. On the other hand, the Maltese and Slovakian stock markets appear to display more self-directed independent behaviour than their peers.

For an EU-based investor, the findings are not all good as revealed in our Markowitz analysis. Ideally, an investor based in the more developed markets of the EU would like to be able to invest in these Euro-denominated 'emerging markets' and benefit from risk diversification. Paradoxically, the diversification benefits appear to be reduced in terms of the findings of increased correlations. On the other hand, there is also evidence of a lowering of average risk in terms of variance-based measures post-joining the EU. The efficient frontier analysis suggests the 'other' emerging markets dominate for all pre- and post-EU scenarios.

These emerging markets are progressing very rapidly in their reforms and stability in domestic economies while in the process of becoming members of the EU. It is to be borne in mind that the aim and the greatest achievement of the creation of the EU is the development of a single market through a standardised system of laws which apply in all member states. Thus, restrictions between member countries on trade and free competition have gradually been eliminated. As an outcome of those reforms and expansion, the EU has more influence on the world stage when it speaks with a single voice in international affairs.

Note

1. SOFIX (Bulgaria), SEPX (Czech Republic), CYSE (Cyprus), OMX Tallinn Stock Exchange (Estonia), BUX (Hungary), OMX Riga Stock Exchange (Latvia), OMX Vilnius Stock Exchange (Lithuania), MSE (Malta), WIG (Poland), BET (Romania), SAX (Slovakia), and SBI (Slovenia).

References

Babetski, I, Komárek, L & Komárková, Z (2007), 'Financial Integration of Stock Markets Among New EU Member States and the Euro Area', *Czech Journal of Economics and Finance*, vol. 57, no. 7–8, pp. 341–362.

Bollerslev, T (1986), 'Generalized Autoregressive Conditional Heteroskedasticity', *Journal of Economics*, vol. 31, pp. 307–327.

Bruggemann, R & Trenkler, C (2007), 'Are Eastern European Countries Catching Up? Time Series Evidence for Czech Republic, Hungary and Poland', *Applied Economics Letters*, vol. 14, pp. 245–249.

Campos, N & Horvath, R (2012), 'Reform Redux: Measurement, Determinants and Growth Implications', *European Journal of Political Economy*, vol. 28, no. 2, pp. 227–237.

Capiello, L, Engle, R F & Sheppard, K (2006), 'Asymmetric Dynamics in the Correlations of Global Equity and Bond Returns', *Journal of Financial Econometrics*, vol. 4, no. 4, pp. 537–572.

Cuaresma, J C & Hlouskova, J (2005), 'Beating the Random Walk in Central and Eastern Europe', *Journal of Forecasting*, vol. 24, no. 3, pp. 189–201.

Dellas, H & Hess, M (2005), 'Financial Development and Stock Returns: A Cross-Country Analysis', *Journal of International Money and Finance*, vol. 24, no. 6, pp. 891–912.

Dickey, D A & Fuller, W A (1981), 'Likelihood Ration Statistics for Autoregressive Time Series with Unit Root', *Econometrica*, vol. 49, no. 4, pp. 1057–1072.

Egert, B & Kocenda, E (2007), 'Time-Varying Comovements in Developed and Emerging European Stock Markets: Evidence from Intraday Data', Working Paper WP 861, William Davidson Institute.

Engle, R (1982), 'Autoregressive Conditional Heteroscedasticity with Estimates of Variance of UK Inflation', *Econometrica*, vol. 50, no. 4, pp. 987–1008.

Engle, R F (2002), 'Dynamic Conditional Correlation: A Simple Class of Multivariate Generalized Autoregressive Conditional Heteroskedasticity Models', *Journal of Business & Economic Statistics*, vol. 20, no. 3, pp. 339–350.

Forbes, K J & Chinn, M D (2004), 'A Decomposition of Global Linkages in Financial Markets', *The Review of Economics and Statistics*, vol. 86, no. 3, pp. 705–722.

Hanousek, J & Kocenda, E (2011), 'Foreign News and Spillovers in Emerging European Stock Markets', *Review of International Economics*, vol. 19, no. 1, pp. 170–188.

Harrison, B & Moore, W (2009), 'Spillover Effects from London and Frankfurt to Central and Eastern European Stock Markets', *Applied Financial Economics*, vol. 19, no. 18, pp. 1509–1521.

Horvath, R & Petrovski, D (2013), 'International Stock Market Integrations: Central and South Eastern Europe Compared', *Economic Systems*, vol. 37, no. 1, pp. 81–91.

Hranaiova, J (1999), 'Price Behaviour in Emerging Stock Markets', *Working Paper Series*, WP 99–17.

Jorion, P & Goetzemann, W (1999), 'Re-emerging Markets', *Journal of Financial and Quantitative Analysis*, vol. 34, no. 1, pp. 1–32.

Kearney, C & Poti, V (2008), 'Have European Stocks Become More Volatile? An Empirical Investigation of Volatilities and Correlation in EMU Equity Markets at the Firm, Industry and Market Level', *European Financial Management*, vol. 14, no. 3, pp. 419–444.

Kocenda, E & Egert, R (2011), 'Time-varying Synchronization of European Stock Markets', *Empirical Economics*, vol. 40, no. 2, pp. 393–407.

Ling, S & McAleer, M (2002), 'Necessary and Sufficient Moment Conditions for the GARCH(r,s) and Asymmetric Power GARCH(r,s) Models', *Econometric Theory*, vol. 18, no. 3, pp. 722–729.

Phillips, P & Perron, P (1988), 'Testing for a Unit Root in Time Series Regression', *Biometrica*, vol. 75, pp. 335–346.

Samitas, A & Kenourgios, D (2011), 'Equity Market Integration in Emerging Balkan Markets', *Research in International Business and Finance*, vol. 25, no. 3, pp. 296–307.

Scheicher (2001), 'The Comovements of Stock Markets in Hungary, Poland and the Czech Republic', *International Journal of Finance and Economics*, vol. 6, no. 1, pp. 27–39.

Syriopoulos, T (2007), 'Dynamic Linkages Between Emerging European and Developed Stock Markets: Has the EMU Any Impact?' *International Review of Financial Analysis*, vol. 16, no. 1, pp. 41–60.

Walti, K (2005), 'The Macroeconomic Determinants of Stock Market Synchronisation', Working Paper, Trinity College, Department of Economics, Dublin.

Worthington, A & Higgs, H (2004), 'Transmission of Equity Returns and Volatility in Asian Developed and Emerging Markets: A Multivariate GARCH Analysis', *International Journal of Finance and Economics*, vol. 9, no. 1. pp. 71–80.

5 The Political Risk of Offshore Financial Centres: The Cyprus Bail-Out

David Chaikin

1 Overview

This chapter puts forward the idea that investors face a new type of political risk arising out of the increased international regulatory focus on financial crimes, such as money laundering, terrorist financing, foreign bribery, tax evasion, and financial sanctions. This political risk is manifested in the policies of international regulators towards offshore financial centres (OFCs), especially in emerging economies, and includes powerful policy making bodies, such as the Financial Action Task Force (money laundering, terrorist financing) and the Organisation of Economic Co-operation and Development (OECD) (foreign bribery, tax evasion), as well as the International Monetary Fund (IMF), the World Bank, and the Bank for International Settlements (financial stability). Both the G7 and G20 have drawn a link between systemic risk and weak anti-financial crime laws and practices, and have made the assumption that OFCs are more likely to present systemic risks arising from weak anti-financial crime laws.

The first part of the paper explores the meaning of political risk, which is a traditional category of risk faced by foreign investors. Political risk is sometimes described as part of country risk. Beginning with the rapid boom in transnational lending in the 1970s, followed by the dismantling of capital controls in the 1980s and the globalisation of the financial markets in the 1980s and beyond, political risk has become an even more important risk for investors. International institutions, credit rating institutions, and private consultancy firms monitor political risk for themselves and clients.

The second part of the paper explores the phenomenon of offshore financial centres in the context of a more expansive definition of political risk. The new political risk has been shaped by the 9/11 terrorist attacks in the United States and the Global Financial Crisis. It is argued that international institutions have redefined political risk by claiming that OFCs, particularly in emerging economies, impose higher financial crime risks. In order to understand this claim, OFCs are scrutinised by analysing their role in facilitating legitimate and illegitimate business activities. It is argued that the new political risks are a construct of powerful western countries and that this has influenced the viewpoint of international public institutions. Whether OFCs are more likely to be used for transnational criminal activity may be a matter of some importance to academic scholars, but what is more significant for international investors is their perception of financial crime risks. Given the viewpoint of supra-national public institutions concerning OFCs, global investors will need to pay special attention to the new type of political risk in making any investment decision.

The third part provides a case study of the financial crisis of Cyprus in 2012–2013 and its subsequent bail-out to illustrate the new form of political risk. The terms and conditions of the €10 billion bail-out by the Eurogroup (The European Commission, the European Central Bank, and the IMF) demonstrate the importance of the international financial crime agenda in shaping political risk. It was the branding of Cyprus as a Russian money-laundering haven that provided the justification for imposing harsh terms on bank depositors in Cyprus as part of the bail-out. The Cyprus case study provides a vehicle to explore the relationship between political risk and OFCs, and particularly the linkages between financial crime and financial stability. Although the collapse of the two leading banks in Cyprus was directly attributable to their losses from loans and investments in the Greek financial markets, the surplus monies would not have taken place on this scale without an oversized financial sector which was fuelled by non-transparent bank deposits.

Besides drawing some general lessons about political risk, the case study will also set out the implications for businesses that wish to invest in or through OFCs. The Cyprus case study demonstrates the risk of extreme financialisation of an OFC, which in turn is a feature of the globalisation of the world's financial markets over the past 30 years. It also explains that OFCs which have no significant natural political allies – Cyprus is a small island which was in effect 'punished' by its protector, the EU – and whose investments were sourced from unknown foreign persons may be subject to unsympathetic albeit legally permissible treatment, where the terms of the bail-out are influenced by an international financial crime agenda.

2 Political risk and financial globalisation

The economic literature provides numerous definitions of political risk, which is a traditional category of risk faced by foreign investors. Political risk is sometimes described as part of country risk, which has been defined as the risk that a borrower will be unable or unwilling to satisfy its financial obligations due to factors other than those that usually arise out of lending and investment decisions (Krayenbuehl, 1988: 3). There are two dimensions of country risk: the political willingness to honour financial obligations and the economic capability to honour financial obligations.

In a practical sense, the definition of political risk depends largely on the specific perspective of the observer, be it a multinational company, an international policy institution, individual investor, or insurance company (Leopold, 1998: 18–20). Consequently, there are a number of sources of information on political risk. International institutions, credit rating institutions, and private consultancy firms monitor political risk for themselves and clients.

Hitherto political risk has tended to be narrowly defined. For example, in the 1980s a leading authority defined political risk as the 'risk incurred by lenders and/or investment that the repatriation of their loans and investments in a particular country... is restricted by that country for political reasons only' (Ibid.). A more recent definition is the 'probability of disruption to operations of companies by political forces and events', irrespective of whether the source is in the host country or in the international environment (Multilateral Investment Guarantee Agency, 2011: 21).

The World Bank's Multilateral Investment Guarantee Agency's (MIGA, henceforth) definition is concerned with perceptions about the future in that political risk is the probability of the effect of political forces and events on business operations. Instead of a singular focus on political reasons for a decision, the MIGA view appears to embrace the notion that political and economic spaces are intertwined.

Beginning with the rapid boom in transnational lending in the 1970s, followed by the dismantling of capital controls in the 1980s, and the globalisation of the financial markets in the 1980s and beyond, political risk has become an even more important risk for investors. The collapse of the Soviet Union and Eastern European communist states, and the fall of authoritarian regimes and the emergence of democratic countries in Asia, together with the emergence of the tigers of Asia such as Taiwan and South Korea, have provided new investment opportunities in emerging economies. But at the same time these geo-political events have added new elements of complexity because of increased risks of political and economic uncertainty and instability.

According to the annual survey by the MIGA and the Economist Intelligence Unit (EIU), factors that are major constraints to foreign investment include 'lack of investment opportunities, poor infrastructure, the lack of qualified staff, the lack of financing for investments in these countries, political risk, macroeconomic instability, lack of information on the country's business environment, weak government institutions/red tape/corruption, and increased government regulation in the aftermath of the global financial crisis' (MIGA, 2013: 13).

The MIGA/EIU survey found that political risk was the second most significant factor in the decision-making process by investors in relation to making foreign direct investment (FDI) decisions in developing countries (MIGA, 2013: 14). The survey also found that in 2013, investors classified 'macroeconomic instability as the key constraint for investing into developing economies over the medium term' for the first time, reflecting both economic uncertainty and pessimism with the global economy (MIGA, 2013: 14, 18–22).

Traditionally, political risk concerned matters such as the risk of adverse regulatory change, breach of contract, transfer and convertibility restrictions, civil disturbances, non-honouring of financial obligations, and political expropriation of foreign assets without adequate compensation. A major impact of the 9/11 attacks on the United States has been a significant refocus on terrorism as a political risk but also money laundering and terrorist financing as political risks. This is illustrated by the work of the UN Security Council's

Counter-Terrorism Committee and the UN Security Council resolutions on terrorism.

The Global Financial Crisis has also impacted political risk in so far as there are perceived linkages between financial crime and financial instability. It is well-accepted that financial instability is a relevant factor for investing in emerging countries that are OFCs. More controversial has been the correlation of financial instability with financial crime, albeit there is a question whether the inadequate empirical evidence supporting this relationship. Nevertheless, by drawing a link between financial crimes generally and financial instability, political leaders in the G7 and G20 have created a strong perception that inadequate anti-financial crime laws increase the risk of financial instability.

My contention is that the notion of political risk has been expanded to include the perspective of international policy makers on financial crime matters in specific jurisdictions in so far as they may have a significant influence on the perceptions of foreign investors on political risk. The Cyprus case study will illustrate this idea, whereas in response to the financial crisis in Cyprus, the Eurogroup lenders justified the imposition of severe financial conditions on the government of Cyprus on the basis that Cyprus had failed to deal with money laundering by Russian investors.

There is a plethora of states that compete for international capital flows from investors in the developed world. At the same time, the BRIC countries – Brazil, Russia, India, and China – have also become a major source of capital for other developing or emerging markets. Investment from BRIC countries such as China may be influenced by political considerations, such as the need for Chinese State Owned Enterprises to secure foreign long-term energy and minerals supplies in developing countries. Whereas investors from BRIC countries may not be concerned about financial crimes because their governments are not so interested, investors from countries such as the United States must take financial crime risks into account because of the extraterritorial application of US laws.

According to a report by the Eurasia Group, which is among the leading political consultancy companies, economic risk rather than political risk has been the pre-eminent driver of investors' decisions in response to the Global Financial Crisis (GFC) (Eurasia, 2013). Although political risk has been a significant consideration in relation to specific jurisdictions, it has been the economic risk aversion of investors, following the GFC, that has been a major driver in investment decisions. The GFC resulted in a collapse of investor confidence, with investors becoming risk adverse about the 'quality of financial assets and the solvency of prominent banks' and fearing a financial implosion in a specific country or the contagion effects on other countries (Milesi-Ferretti, 2010). However, in its 2014 report on political risk, Eurasia predicted that investors' concern about financial implosion has subsided, that the 'big-picture economies' are now stable, and that political risk in emerging markets will be more important, as new political elections will take place in 2014 in a number of states (Eurasia, 2014).

3 Offshore financial centres

The phrase Offshore Financial Centres (OFCs) is of relatively recent origin, dating back to the early 1980s when major international policy-making bodies commenced studying the impact of offshore jurisdictions on national and international financial stability, international regulation, and international business.

It was the IMF which first understood the importance of OFCs in capturing a 'significant part of global financial flows' and the risks that OFCs' linkages with other financial centres might undermine global financial stability (IMF, 2013).

Since 2000 the IMF has carried out studies of OFCs so as to assess whether they comply with international standards on a range of matters. The international standards dealt with banking and payments systems, anti-money laundering/combating the financing of terrorism, accounting and auditing, corporate governance, securities market regulation, insurance regulation, and insolvency and creditors' rights, as well as fiscal transparency and monetary and financial transparency policies (IMF, 2013). The IMF sought to improve OFCs' regulatory structure by advising them on international best practices on compliance. Although in 2008 the IMF decided to integrate its OFC program with its Financial Sector Assistance program, it nevertheless continued to contribute to the on-going debate about the role of OFCs.

The failure of a country to comply with international standards or best practice in various regulatory matters is viewed as increasing regulatory risk. This has become significant for OFCs. For example, the Financial Action Task Force (FATF) and the OECD have focused on OFCs, with the FATF mandated to improve Anti-Money Laundering/Counter-Terrorism Financing (AML/CTF) laws and practices in OFCs, while the OECD has focused on tax evasion, aggressive tax planning, international tax co-operation, corporate and banking transparency, and foreign bribery.

There have been competing definitions of OFCs and consequently competing lists of jurisdictions that may be classified as OFCs. The definition of an OFC has been influenced by the regulatory agenda of international policy-making bodies, as well a set of assumptions, perceptions, and prejudices concerning jurisdictions that have sought to create financial centres servicing the demands of non-resident actors and institutions. The phrases OFC and tax haven have often been used in an interchangeable fashion (Antoine, 2005). Tax haven is the older term. It was defined by a series of characteristics, such as a low tax jurisdiction for non-residents, strict bank secrecy laws, and a lack of effective information exchange with other jurisdictions (Chaikin, 2009).

In contrast, the definition of OFC has become uni-polar with greater focus on financial stability, albeit with some reference to tax. For example, the IMF has defined OFCs as:

> Countries or jurisdictions with financial centres that contain financial institutions that deal primarily with non residents and/or in foreign currency on a scale out of proportion to the size of the host economy. Non resident-owned or -controlled institutions play a significant role within the centre. The institutions in the centre may well gain from tax benefits not available to those outside the centre. (IMF, 2003)

The IMF definition embraces the concern that jurisdictions with high levels of financialisation may impose external risks on the stability of the global financial system. There are many definitions of the phenomenon of financialisation, but one widely accepted definition refers to the significance of the financial sector in relation to the Gross Domestic Product of a nation state.

The IMF definition raises squarely the issue of whether there are increased risks and benefits from using OFCs from the viewpoint of international regulators. It also raises the question as to whether and how OFCs should be part of the calculus of decision-making by international investors. With the emergence of the GFC, the role of OFCs in cross border capital flows and in contributing to financial instability has been a major issue for international policy makers.

The IMF listed the following OFCs:

Table 5.1 OFCs with their principal international financial activity and Gross Domestic Product (GDP) per capita as per 2007

Country	GDP $/ capita	Internat'l banking	Insurance	Asset management	Mutual funds
Andorra	43,504	X	X	X	X
Anguilla	18,007	X			
Antigua	13,568	X		X	
Aruba	25,253	X		X	X
Bahamas	22,633	X	X	X	X
Bahrain	24,504	X	X	X	X
Barbados	11,599	X	X	X	X
Belize	4,438	X	X	X	X
Bermuda	90,698	X	X	X	X
British Virgin Islands	51,723	X			X
Caymans	57,222	X	X	X	X
Gibraltar	41,898	X	X	X	X
Grenada	5,753	X			
Guernsey	53,931	X			X
Isle of Man	44,773	X	X		X
Jersey	90,107	X		X	
Lebanon	6,110	X	X		X
Liechtenstein	118,040	X	X	X	X
Macao	39,731	X	X	X	
Mauritius	5,490	X	X	X	X
Monaco	40,090	X		X	X
Nauru	2,217	X			
Netherlands Antilles	18,078	X	X	X	
Panama	5,828	X	X		
Samoa	2,544	X	X		
Seychelles	–	X	X		X
St Kitts & Nevis	10,149	X	X	X	
St Lucia	5,820	X	X		
St Vincent & Grenadines	4,538	X	X		X
Turks & Caicos	29,706	X	X	X	X
Vanuatu	2,243	X	X		

Source: IMF (2013: 19–20).

This table demonstrates that there are significant differences in OFCs across a range of measures, as well as in terms of offshore financial activity. Firstly, the concept of small population in OFC ranges from micro-states such as the British Virgin Islands (22,545) to Lebanon (4.09 million), while GDP per capita ranges from $US 2,243 in Vanuatu to $US 118,040 in Liechtenstein. The table provides examples of less developed countries, such as Belize, St Lucia, St Vincent & Grenadines in the Americas, Lebanon in the Middle East, Mauritius and Seychelles in the Indian Ocean, as well as Nauru, Samoa, and Vanuatu in the Pacific.

The table demonstrates some of the legitimate uses of OFCs as servicing the global financial needs of Multinational Enterprises (MNEs), businesses, and high-net-worth individuals. There is a range of specialisations or niche markets, albeit that all the jurisdictions provide international banking services. The most diversified OFC is Cayman Islands, which has strengths in international banking and insurance, as well as being the market leader in offshore funds under management. In contrast to the other small OFCs, Cayman Islands is a significant player in the US securitisation market by providing structured finance expertise, professional services, and corporate vehicles (Ibid.). The British Virgin Islands has a more limited role, specialising in providing offshore companies and trusts, whereas Bermuda dominates the offshore captive insurance market, and Jersey has a strong reputation for both international banking and asset management (Chaikin, 2009).

Investors consider that OFCs may be attractive for tax planning and asset protection purposes. Indeed, as far back as 2000, the Financial Stability Forum Working Group on OFCs identified tax planning and asset protection as key reasons why investors may use OFCs. That is, OFCs provide important functions, such as maximising profits by international companies through low-tax regimes, income tax minimisation by investors, accumulation of reserves by insurance companies in low-tax regimes, and asset protection by individuals and companies for potential liabilities in onshore jurisdictions (Financial Stability Forum, 2000: 10).

4 Financial crime risks and offshore financial centres

Financial crime risk takes into account a number of considerations. There is a matrix of sub-components of financial crime risk that need to be fully addressed as part of the investment decision-making process in relation to political risk. The sub-component risks cover topics such as bribery and corruption, money laundering and terrorist financing, financial and political sanctions, and fraud. A description of those sub-risks, as well as the sources of information on those risks, is considered below.

4.1 Bribery and corruption risk

Bribery and corruption risk is frequently taken into account by international investors, including multinational enterprises in their decision to invest, expand or maintain their investment, or disinvest in a particular country. Corruption risk as a part of country risk has traditionally focused on supply-side corruption, whereby international investors make illicit payments to obtain or maintain business in developing countries. Under the OECD Convention on Foreign Bribery, which has been implemented in the national laws of the 40 participating countries, bribery of a public official is made a criminal offence. Enforcement of the Convention has become more marked, especially with the more aggressive extraterritorial enforcement of the US Foreign Corrupt Practices Act and the UK Bribery Act.

Investors in companies that engage in foreign bribery face the risk of losses arising out of the criminal prosecution of those companies, and huge fines and penalties arising out of criminal and civil proceedings. For example, the German company Siemens was subject to fines of over $800 million in 2008, whereas the US company Alcoa was fined $384 million in 2014. Enforcement actions also affect future business, in that companies involved in bribery may be suspended from tendering for government contracts and disbarred by international bodies, such as the World Bank. Given the importance of reputation for most lines of business, companies that are sanctioned for corruption face reputational losses resulting in a reduction in the value of the brand name, as well as decreased attractiveness to investors, future employees, and other stakeholders. More generally, corruption also endangers the success or otherwise of investment because it fuels social unrest, inequality, and political and economic instability.

OFCs have played important roles in the laundering of corrupt monies of Politically Exposed Persons (PEPs), such as President Marcos of the Philippines, General Sani Abacha of Nigeria, President Augusto Jose Ramon Pinochet Ugarte of Chile and President Alberto Fujimori of Peru. Grand corruption monies are frequently held in bank accounts in OFCs, where the true beneficial owner is concealed through international business companies based in OFCs such as Bahamas, Cayman Islands, British Virgin Islands and Hong Kong (Chaikin, 2010).

In assessing the bribery and corruption risk of a national jurisdiction, there are a number of useful sources of information. Transparency International's Annual Corruption Perceptions Index is the leading global barometer of public sector corruption by ranking 177 countries/territories by the perceived level of public sector corruption (Transparency International, 2013). Maplecroft Corruption Risk Index 'evaluates 197 countries on the reported prevalence and persistence of corruption in the public and private sectors, as well as the efficiency of governments in tackling the issue' (Maplecroft, 2013).

4.2 Money laundering/terrorist financing risk

There are a number of mechanisms for assessing the money laundering/terrorist financing risk of specific jurisdictions. The most authoritative source is the FATF (and regional FATFs) mutual evaluation reports of over 180 countries, which provide a rating of compliance with the International Standards on Combating Money Laundering and the Financing of Terrorism & Proliferation (the so-called FATF Recommendations) (FATF, 2013). Assessments of jurisdictions are made on an on-going basis, with the current schedule involving the fourth round of mutual evaluations. Investors must be careful in relying on the Mutual Evaluation Reports (MERs) in evaluating Money Laundering/Terrorism Financing (ML/TF) risk because many of these reports become out-of-date as countries implement action plans to remedy deficiencies identified in those reports, and there is no uniformity in the publication of these updated compliance reports.

The United States is a key jurisdiction that issues AML assessments in relation to specific jurisdictions. For example, the annual US State Department International Narcotics Control Strategy Report (INCSR) describes the efforts of countries to counter money laundering and financial crimes in relation to the international drug trade (US Department of State, 2013). Special attention should also be paid to the reports of various US House and Senate Committees, especially the US Senate Committee of Homeland Security and Governmental Affairs, Permanent Subcommittee on Investigations, which publishes details of its investigations into major financial crimes (US Senate, 2013).

Another source of information on money laundering risk is the Basel Institute on Governance. The Basel Institute has created the Basel AML index which measures 140 countries' risk levels in money laundering and terrorist financing based on public sources, especially the weighing of FATF reports, as well as various related topics, including 'banking secrecy, corruption, financial regulations, judicial strengths and civil rights' (Basel, 2013). The value of the Basel AML index is that it is independent and not influenced by wider political considerations.

Offshore financial centres have frequently featured in international reports because of their weakness in AML/CTF regulation. As far back as 1998, the United Nations identified OFCs as vulnerable to penetration by organised crime and money laundering (Blum, 1998). The attractiveness of OFCs to criminals was their lack of transparency and the refusal of OFCs to co-operate in transnational criminal investigations. Indeed, several studies by the United States Congress found that the lack of transparency of OFCs through banking, corporate, tax, and other commercial legislation was the single most important obstacle to international law and tax enforcement (Chaikin, 2013).

The position with most OFCs has considerably improved from 2001 when the FATF targeted mainly OFCs for blacklisting for their failure to implement international standards on money laundering and terrorist financing. The initial FATF black list consisted of 15 countries, with 12 OFCs (Bahamas, Cayman Islands, Cook Islands, Dominica, Lebanon, Liechtenstein, Marshall Islands, Nauru, Niue, Panama, St Kitts and Nevis, and St Vincent and the Grenadines) and three other jurisdictions (Israel, Philippines, and the Russian Federation). Eight jurisdictions were added in the 2001 FATF list, including the OFC of Grenada. The FATF lists' claim that the blacklisted jurisdictions were not co-operative in AML/CTF was not based on objective criteria, but appears to have been based on geo-political considerations in that it was a lack of resources and infrastructure that underlined their listing (Sharman, 2008). In any event, by 2006, all OFCs had been removed from the list because of significant changes to their legal and regulatory systems. Consequently, the OFCs' present-day compliance with AML standards is 'generally comparable to that of non-OFC jurisdictions' (IMF, 2008). However, there are variations in OFCs, with economically powerful OFCs such as the Cayman Islands and Jersey having relatively high levels of compliance, while small Pacific jurisdictions such as Vanuatu and Nauru having a relatively low level of compliance.

4.3 Offshore fraud risk

Investors face the risk of losing their investment through fraud. The risk of fraud is higher in offshore jurisdictions because investors do not have the same ability to carry out due diligence on offshore investments, are less familiar with the legal systems of offshore jurisdictions, and are vulnerable due to their desire for heightened financial secrecy

(Chaikin, 2011). There is also a higher fraud risk because regulators in offshore jurisdictions do not have the same incentive and do not have adequate resources to regulate financial institutions, corporate vehicles, or professions who service offshore clients, as compared to onshore clients.

During the 1980s to early 2000s, OFCs in the Caribbean, such as Antigua, Grenada, and Turks and Caicos, and OFCs in the South Pacific, such as Cook Islands, Nauru, and Vanuatu, provided fraudsters with the tools to carry out shell bank frauds. With lax bank licensing laws in OFCs, fraudsters could obtain a special banking license and use the paper/shell bank to carry out advanced fee frauds, balance sheet frauds, and tax evasion (United States Senate, 2000). But after 9/11, the US Patriot Act banned shell banks by excluding them from accessing the US financial system. Subsequently, nearly all OFCs have stopped issuing licenses for shell banks and most countries have implemented measures to prevent the misuse of their financial system by fraudsters, for example, requiring increased due diligence on correspondent banking.

The risk of foreign investors losing their investment from frauds in OFCs also came to the fore after the GFC exposed a series of long-running investment scams, particularly ponzi frauds. One of the most famous cases involved Sir Robert Allen Stanford, who ran an $8.2 billion ponzi scheme. Onshore investors based in Europe and Latin and South America deposited their monies in an Antiguan-based bank in return for receiving investors' certificates of deposit which proved to be worthless (Chaikin, 2011). The investors believed that their investment was conservative, safe and tax-effective, but instead lost their monies. Both offshore and onshore factors played a role in the fraud. The OFC of Antigua was very important in concealing the fraud because onshore victims were not aware that they were victims until it was too late, and corporate and financial secrecy posed an obstacle to carrying out an effective investigation. The lack of interest, skills, and resources of the Antiguan authorities, coupled with the excessive political influence of Sir Robert Stanford in Antigua, meant that the fraud continued for nearly 17 years, until the stock market boom collapsed. But it was not just the OFC that should be held responsible for the Stanford fraud. Onshore factors, such as the fact that the investment was sold through a US registered investment adviser and broker/dealer, and that a leading international bank provided correspondent banking facilities to the Antiguan bank, cloaked the investment scam in a sea of respectability and legitimacy.

4.4 Financial sanctions risk

Financial sanctions have been described as 'punitive measures used to support national security interests, advance foreign policy objectives, prompt a change in the behaviour of a country/regime, or suppress activities that threaten peace and security' (Lester, 2013). Sanctions may be imposed for a variety of reasons, including political (for example, US sanctions on Cuba because of its political regime), law and order (for example, US sanctions against international drug traffickers), or international peace (for example, UN sanctions against North Korea for violation of nuclear arms proliferation).

There is a variety of forms of sanctions, such as asset freezes and other financial restrictions, travel bans on designated individuals, and import/export restrictions on various commodities. The sanctions do not merely affect financial institutions but may affect investors of particular nationalities who are subject to the jurisdiction that imposes the sanction.

There are a number of international and national sanctions lists that should be taken into account in international investment. There are international sanctions, such as the UN Security Council's list; regional sanctions, as the framework of restrictions of the Common Foreign and Security Policy of the European Union; and national sanctions, most noticeably the US Treasury Office of Foreign Assets Control (United States Treasury, 2013). Given the aggression that US authorities apply in the enforcement of sanctions, the extraterritorial reach of those sanctions, and the very high penalties imposed on those corporations and individuals that violate those sanctions, it is vital that investors ensure that they give proper consideration to economic and political sanctions.

4.5 International tax evasion risk

From the investors' perspective, the use of OFCs to facilitate international tax evasion would not at first glance be a political risk; indeed, investors may well be seeking the tax benefits of using an OFC. But this traditional perspective ignores the increasingly aggressive enforcement of tax laws against financial institutions in OFCs which may have collateral consequences on investors.

Previously, OFCs did not co-operate in tax cases except in very limited circumstances, such as where there was clear evidence of tax fraud. The most significant development in this area has been the endorsement by major onshore and offshore financial centres of the OECD tax information exchange standard. Within a very short period of time, hundreds of bilateral tax information exchange agreements (TIEAs) have been entered into. It is too early to determine whether these agreements will be effective in combating international tax crimes; however, increased international co-operation is likely to result in OFCs being subject to greater scrutiny in relation to their role in illicit tax activities (Chaikin, 2009).

5 The financial crisis of Cyprus and the bail-out

Cyprus has been the 'poster boy' for globalisation. A small OFC with a highly educated and wealthy population of 862,000, strategically located in the Eastern Mediterranean, the economic future of Cyprus seemed assured when it joined the European Union in 2004 and the Eurozone in 2008. In 2011 the IMF designated Cyprus as an 'advanced economy'. The economic wealth of Cyprus depended on international trade (imports and exports) which was 100% of GDP for the first decade of the millennium, more than twice that of other Euro-member states. (European Commission, 2013: 18). The services sector contributed more than 80% of its Gross Domestic Product, with international banking, finance, and insurance, as well as legal and business consulting, shipping management, property investment, and travel playing a major role in wealth creation and employment (OECD, 2013: 7; European Commission, 2013: 14). However, a major banking crisis and subsequent bail-out in 2013 has caused significant losses to international investors which has reduced the attraction of Cyprus as an offshore financial centre.

The rapid growth of GDP in Cyprus from 2000 to 2010 was accompanied by a similar growth in credit and private and public sector indebtedness, resulting in 'unsustainable external and internal macroeconomic imbalances' (European Commission, 2013: 7). After joining the EU, there was a massive deposit inflow into banks in Cyprus, reaching a peak of 100% of GDP in 2008–2009 (Ibid.: 21). The externally sourced deposits (coupled with foreign direct investment which frequently turned into deposits held by 'shell companies') funded the continuing balance of trade deficits, and fuelled the credit expansion and asset price bubble in real estate. By the end of 2012 total assets of the financial sector was 718% of GDP (Ibid.: 11).

It was the business model of Cyprus as an OFC and the structure and regulation of its banking sector that explains in part the financial crisis in Cyprus. The business model made Cyprus a very attractive place for international banking deposits thereby fuelling excessive liquidity. Low corporate interest rates and relatively high deposit rates, coupled with a favourable business and tax environment, resulted in huge foreign non-resident deposits in the major banks in Cyprus. The network of 43 double taxation treaties also provided new opportunities for tax planning by foreign companies, for example, depositing excess reserves in banks in Cyprus.

The German government criticised the business model of Cyprus, accusing Russian companies of engaging in 'round tripping' whereby monies were channelled into Cyprus from Russia, and then routed back to Russia. Global Financial Integrity estimated that in 2011 alone foreign direct investment (FDI) from Russia into Cyprus was $121.6 Bn whereas FDI from Cyprus to Russia was $128.8 Bn, thereby taking advantage of the legal rights and taxation privileges of a foreign investor (Kar, 2013: 41–42). Global Financial Integrity hypothesised that given that the GDP of Cyprus was about $23 Bn, investments from Cyprus into Russia must be 'round-tripping of prior illicit depositors from Russia into Cyprus' (Ibid.: 42).

Similarly Nobel Prize winning laureate Professor Paul Krugman accused Cyprus of being both a tax haven and a money laundering haven (Krugman, 2013), albeit that Krugman's claims appear to be conflated. There is no issue that Cyprus had an attractive tax environment – a corporate tax rate of 10% (the lowest in the EU); tax exemptions for overseas permanent establishments; and no withholding tax on dividends, interest, and royalties paid from Cyprus – but this did not make it a tax haven (European Commission, 2013: 19). Although the taxation law of Cyprus complied with EU law and its Double Taxation Treaties complied with the OECD Model (including its tax information exchange provision), a 2013 OECD peer review report on Cyprus found that its implementation of the Transparency and Exchange of Information for Tax Purpose standards was generally non-compliant (OECD, 2013).

Nevertheless, it was the claims that Cypriot banks had facilitated Russian money laundering that influenced the terms of the Cypriot bail-out whereby large depositors were compelled to share in the burden of the losses of the Cypriot banks.

The banking market structure also contributed to the financial crisis. One feature of the banking structure of Cyprus was the oligopoly power of the two domestic banks, with the Bank of Cyprus and the Cyprus Popular Bank (Laiki Bank) controlling 40% of domestic deposits. Given the dominance of these banks in the economy of Cyprus, financial losses suffered by these banks had a disproportionate effect on the financial system of Cyprus.

Cyprus regulatory rules were also significant: under Cypriot banking law, banks were obliged to 'maintain a foreign currency deposit ratio of at least 70% and a euro liquidity ratio of at least 20%' (European Commission, 2013: 14). With excessive liquidity in the banking system, the major banks were incentivised by regulatory requirements to invest in sovereign loans, in particular €5.7 Bn of Greek euro-denominated sovereign bonds. It was the Cypriot bank's exposure to Greek sovereign debt which proved to be an overwhelming vulnerability during the Greek financial crisis, resulting in losses of €4.5 Bn and ultimately precipitating the financial crisis in Cyprus.

The first stage of the Greek financial crisis of 2009–2010 did not have an immediate adverse impact on Cyprus in that non-resident euro-area deposits increased from €2 Bn at the beginning of 2010 to €6.6 Bn in June 2012 (European Commission, 2013: 31). Many foreign (especially Russian) investors believed that the reputation of Cyprus as a respectable and successful offshore financial centre would protect their investments; they were not aware of the underlying exposure of Cypriot banks to the Greek capital markets. It was only at the second stage of the Greek financial crisis from 2011 onwards that Cypriot banks that operated in Greece experienced major liquidity outflows, with the Laiki Bank requiring emergency liquidity assistance from the Central Bank of Cyprus (Ibid.).

By the end of March 2012, the major banks in Cyprus took a 'haircut' of 74% of the nominal value of their Greek government bond holdings, and after another haircut in June 2012, the banks reduced their exposure to Greek government bonds to €1 Bn (European Commission, 2013: 31). Further, the Cyprus banks' non-performing loans in Greece reached 42% of total loans of €19 Bn by the end of September 2012 (Ibid.: 11). This highlighted the importance of 'concentration limits on security investments in prudential regulation' (Ibid.: 3). It also implied that investors should be cognisant of the concentration level in their investment decisions.

In June 2012, the Cypriot government applied for financial support under the European Stability Mechanism (ESM) in circumstances where as a euro area Member State it was suffering 'severe financial problems'. The negotiations for assistance were lengthy, complicated, and politically acrimonious. The delay in reaching an agreement and the rejection of the initial agreement by Cyprus resulted in a worsening of the financial position of Cyprus. In March 2013, the Troika (the European Central Bank, the European Commission, and the IMF), concluded agreements with Cyprus which was given a conditional loan of €9 Bn under the ESM and €1Bn from the IMF.

This was not the first time that a member of the euro currency zone had applied for financial assistance – Ireland, Greece, Portugal, and Spain had previously obtained loans under the ESM. There were significant differences in the macroeconomic adjustment programme in Cyprus as compared to other euro currency members. For the first time, the conditions for lender assistance required that depositors in financial institutions contribute to the financial package. Hitherto depositors in banks in the euro currency area believed that their deposits were 100% safe; bank losses would be financed by creditors, shareholders, and ultimately taxpayers. For example, in the case of the Greek bail-out, sovereign and junior and subordinate bond holders, and not depositors, were compelled to contribute to the losses (Das, 2013).

Under the Financial Assistance Facility Agreement between the ESM, the Republic of Cyprus, and the Central Bank of Cyprus, the two biggest banks (out of 46 banks in Cyprus) were restructured, with the Bank of Cyprus absorbing the Bank Laiki. The uninsured depositors at the Bank of Cyprus took an immediate haircut on uninsured deposits (over €100,000) in that 37.5% of deposits above €100,000 were converted into equity in the bank, 22.5% of deposits above €100,000 were frozen in non-interest bearing accounts subject to further write-offs, while the residual 40% attracted potential interest if the bank becomes profitable. Uninsured deposits in Bank Laiki faced higher potential losses in that they will be used to cover debts of Bank Laiki (Mendelson, 2013). Other financial institutions were recapitalised with the bail-out funds, for example, €1.5 Bn of the Cyprus bailout money was used to refinance the 93 co-operative credit institutions.

What was unprecedented in the Cyprus bailout was the political justification for refusing to bail out the depositors in the two major banks. Germany insisted that any bail-out funds not flow to foreign depositors who were characterised as largely corrupt Russian oligarchs and/or organised criminals. A report by the Bundesnachrichtendiendst (BND), Germany's foreign intelligence agency, claimed that 80 Russian oligarchs had obtained Cypriot (and hence EU) citizenship, that Russian investors held €20 Bn in Cypriot deposits, and that a large percentage of the Russian money was 'black money' (given that 40% of the money leaving Russia was 'black') (Volkery, 2012). A political campaign launched through national and international media characterised Cyprus as a Russian money-laundering haven, which did not deserve to be bailed out for the benefit of Russian oligarchs, criminals, and tax evaders.

Although there were sound economic reasons for insisting that depositors contribute to the bail-out, it was the political dimension of the bail-out that illustrated the political risk of investing in OFCs. Prior to the Cyprus bail-out, issues relating to international financial crime had never been explicitly used to influence the terms and conditions of an international debt adjustment programme. Cyprus has thus become a guinea pig whereby international financial crime agenda of powerful international policy-making institutions and governments has been used to attack the business model of an OFC.

That financial crime risks played a role in the Cyprus bail-out is evidenced by the terms of the macro-economic adjustment programme: Cyprus agreed to strengthen its anti-money laundering framework, increase financial transparency, and improve tax compliance and international tax co-operation (European Commission, 2013: 71–72, 87–89). The European Commission summarised the position (Ibid.: 46–47):

> Financial transparency will be enhanced by further strengthening the anti-money laundering framework. An independent audit was finalised by end of April 2013, the recommendations of which will be implemented without further delay as part of a comprehensive action plan, which should deal, *inter alia,* with improvements to the identification of the ultimate beneficial owners of Cypriot legal persons and arrangements, the reporting of suspicious transactions, the functioning of the Registrar of companies and other aspects of customer due diligence. The Cypriot authorities intend to establish trust registers with the supervisory authorities and launch a third-party assessment of the functioning of the Registrar of companies. Cooperation with foreign intelligence units will be strengthened, in particular in the area of timely identification of the ultimate beneficial owners of Cypriot legal persons and arrangements. Finally, by the end of 2013, the supervision department of the CBC will review its off-site and on-site supervisory procedures in order to further implement a risk-based approach to anti-money laundering supervision.

The significance of these measures is that OFCs with any weakness in AML and/or co-operation in international tax matters (not only in terms of law but also actual practice) may be treated differently by international credit-lending institutions in circumstances where the OFC is subject to financial stress. It does not matter that an OFC has a better compliance record under international AML or tax co-operation standards than other countries; Cyprus has a higher AML compliance record than other countries such as Germany.

Another dimension of the Cyprus bail-out was the imposition of capital controls to prevent debilitating flight of capital and the collapse of the financial sector in Cyprus. This was the first time that capital controls had been applied in the EU; there had been restrictions on money transfers of two institutions, the Franco-Belgium banking group Dexi, and Britain's bank and mortgage lender Northern Rock during the financial crisis, but this was not capital controls (Der Spiegel, 2013). Cyprus was allowed under its agreement with the Troika to impose 'administrative measures' restricting the movement of capital and payments so as to protect its financial sector. Such measures are permissible under European Union law on the ground of 'public policy or public security' – see articles 63 and 65 of the Treaty on the Function of the European Union (Sandbu, 2013). However, a number of legal commentators have suggested that these measures may not be legally justified or that they may violate bilateral investment treaties (Mendelson, 2013). Significantly, the capital controls enacted by Cyprus applied to all banks and financial institutions, as well as individuals and businesses. Whatever the legal aspect of the imposition of capital controls in the case of Cyprus, the impact of such controls on future decisions of investors is incalculable. There is little doubt that the capital controls in Cyprus has damaged its reputation as an OFC in relation to international banking, but it is not so clear whether the market for offshore trust and corporate entities in Cyprus has been permanently damaged.

6 Implications for investors

What is the implication for investors of the 'bail-in' procedure whereby wealthy bank depositors in the two biggest banks in Cyprus were required to contribute to the losses suffered by the banks? The most important lesson is that investors should be aware of the risk that monies in bank accounts which are greater than the statutory compensation levels may be lost if the depository institution is subject to financial stress and losses. Investors should examine the deposit insurance programmes of any country in which they have bank deposits since there are important differences between national schemes. Further, investors should no longer have any confidence in implied government guarantees of deposits even when given in advanced economies. Investors should not only be concerned about their own depositor risk but also the deposits of their business partners and other entities with whom they have a commercial relationship.

The Cyprus case study and the global financial crisis shows that it is unwise to assume the soundness of national banking systems and that it is prudent to be aware of the inter-connectedness of banking relationships which may result in unexpected financial losses. It was the Greek financial crisis that led directly to the losses of the banks in Cyprus and then contributed to the Cypriot financial crisis.

Countries that have higher levels of financialisation may face higher risks – they are more vulnerable to systemic financial instability and contagion risk merely because of the size of and dependence on the financial sector. This is because governments may not have the financial resources or be prepared politically to guarantee claims on the banking system in circumstances where the banking sector is larger than the GDP. As the Bank of England Chairman commented: 'The UK government cannot stand behind a banking system that is already many times the size of the economy' (Wolf, 2013). Some economists have gone further by arguing that increased financialisation, especially in emerging countries, undermines 'public sector borrowing capacity', thereby reducing policy options when facing financial instability (Grabel, 2013). Financialisation may also mean that investors are less 'sticky' with their investments in that they are more able to exit their investment at the first indication of financial trouble, thereby increasing the risk of a financial crisis (Ibid.).

Economists have noted the trend of increased financialisation in developed economies (Greenwood, 2013: 3), and that higher levels of financialisation are presented in OFCs. A major study showed that prior to its financial crisis the assets of the banking sector of Cyprus was 630% of GDP, as compared to the United States figure of 72%, or the average of the euro area of 270% (European Central Bank, 2013: 7, 30). Other OFCs such as Malta and Ireland had bank assets representing 789% and 609% of GDP respectively, while bank assets in Luxembourg constituted a massive 1666% of GDP (Ibid.).

What are the implications for investors of high levels of financialisation? First, there are a variety of meanings of financialisation (financial sector/GDP; bank assets/GDP; total size of market traded financial instruments/GDP), and major conceptual and practical difficulties in measurement (Burgess, 2011). Second, where a country with high levels of financialisation becomes ensnared in a financial crisis, one of the most likely remedies will be the deleveraging of the financial system. For example, the Cyprus financial system was deleveraged by 120% of GDP after the sale of the Greek operations of the Bank of Cyprus and Cyprus Popular Bank to the Greek bank, Piraeus. Subsequently these banks were restructured and consolidated under the 2013 adjustment programme, resulting in an additional 80% reduction in the size of the financial sector as a percentage of GDP (European Commission, 2013: 42). Thirdly, the significance of financialisation may vary between countries because of different bank business models and different niche markets with different risk implications. Investors need to ask some difficult questions. Is Luxembourg with bank assets totalling 1666% of GDP less risky than Cyprus because the great majority of those assets are held by subsidiaries and branches of foreign-controlled banks? Or does the answer to this question depend on the corporate governance standards, level of supervision, and culture of the foreign bank?

And do OFCs entail higher risks? The 'independent' Cypriot government report on the financial crisis in Cyprus did not consider that its status as an OFC and in particular its tax arrangements directly caused the crisis (Central Bank of Cyprus, 2013). It noted that 'large deposit balances that accumulated in the Cyprus-based accounts of offshore clients, many of them Russian, were remarkably stable well into the crisis period' (Ibid.: 5). The report did not consider that the OFC business model of Cyprus was the culprit, although it accepted that poorly-managed banks and an OFC that 'relies too much on tax appeal and poor supervision, and not enough on financial soundness and quality' undermined the effectiveness of Cyprus as an OFC (Ibid.: 7). The report also recognised the importance of the reputation of an OFC as servicing legitimate financial interests, and the impact of allegations of money laundering and financial crime. It observed that Cyprus did not adequately deal with the reputational risks in that it 'allowed it(self) to become associated with tax evasion and money of doubtful origin' (Ibid.: 7, 53), thereby weakening its negotiating position in concluding a debt adjustment programme.

7 Conclusions

Political risk is a well-known risk that investors take into account in their investment decisions. This chapter has explored the notion that there is a wider concept of political risk which takes into account the perceived financial crimes risk associated with a particular jurisdiction.

This expansive view of political risk is one of the most important new sovereign risks of the 21st century.

Claims that OFCs impose higher risks of money laundering, terrorist financing, and tax evasion have resulted in blacklisting threats, increased regulatory costs, and the undermining of the business model of OFCs. Although these political risks have been shaped by the 9/11 terrorist attacks and the GFC, they are likely to have a permanent influence on the investor environment. The international financial crime agenda promulgated by supra-national public institutions, powerful governments, non-governmental organisations, and the international media will have a direct impact on the reputation of OFCs as 'clean or dirty jurisdictions'.

The financial crisis of Cyprus and its subsequent bail-out provides a valuable case study to examine the political risks of OFCs. Cyprus demonstrates the risks of high levels of financialisation whereby bank deposits are sourced from unknown foreign persons, and where the terms of the bail-out are influenced by perceived financial crime risks. The Cyprus case has a wider significance not only for OFCs. Where a jurisdiction is branded as a money-laundering haven and/or tax haven, regardless of the validity of the claim, there is a risk that investors in that jurisdiction may suffer collateral damage.

References

Antoine, R B (2005), *Trusts and Related Tax Issues in Offshore Financial Law*, Oxford University Press.

Blum, J A, Levi, M, Naylor, R T, Williams, P (1998), *Financial Havens, Banking Secrecy and Money Laundering*, United Nations Office for Drug Control and Crime Prevention, December.

Burgess, S (2011), 'Measuring Financial Sector Output and Its Contribution to UK GDP', *Bank of England Quarterly Bulletin*, Q3, pp. 234–246.

Central Bank of Cyprus (2013), *Independent Commission on the Future of the Cyprus Banking Sector: Final Report and Recommendations — November*, viewed 16 April 2014 http://www.icfcbs.org/wp-content/uploads/2013/10/ICFCBS-Final-Report.pdf.

Chaikin, D (ed.) (2009), *Money Laundering, Tax Evasion and Tax Havens*, Australian Scholarly Publishing, Melbourne.

Chaikin, D (2010), 'International Anti-Money Laundering Laws: Improving External Accountability of Political Leaders', Briefing Paper No. 4, August, U4 Anti-Corruption Resources Centre, pp. 1–4.

Chaikin, D (2011) 'Corrupt Practices Involving Off-shore Financial Centres', Chapter 11 in *Handbook of Global Research and Practice in Corruption*, eds. Graycar, A & Smith, R G, Edward Elgar Publishing, pp 203–223

Chaikin, D (ed.) (2013), *Financial Crime Risks, Globalisation and the Professions*, Australian Scholarly Publishing, Melbourne.

Das, S (2013), *The Cyprus File – Why it Matters, Even to Americans!*, viewed 16 April 2014, http://www.ritholtz.com/blog/2013/03/the-cyprus-file-why-it-matters-even-to-americans.

Der Spiegel (2013), 'Search for a Solution: Troika Reportedly Rejects "Plan B" for Cyprus', *Der Spiegel*, March 22.

Eurasia (2013), *Political Risk Outlook.*

Eurasia (2014), *Top Risks for 2014.* http://www.eurasiagroup.net/pages/top-risks-2014.

European Central Bank (2013), *Banking Structures Report*, November.

European Commission (2013), *The Economic Adjustment Programme for Cyprus*, Occasional Paper 149, May.

Financial Assistance Facility Agreement between the European Stability Mechanism and the Republic of Cyprus and the Central Bank of Cyprus, 8 May 2013.

Financial Stability Forum (2000), *Report of the Working Group on Offshore Centres*, Bank for International Settlements, April 5 <http://www.financialstabilityboard.org/publications/r_0004b.pdf>

Grabel, I (2013), 'Book Review of *Financialization and Government Borrowing Capacity in Emerging Markets* by Iain Hardie', *Review of International Political Economy*, vol. 20, no. 5, pp. 1136–1139.

Greenwood, R & Scharfstein, D (2013), 'The Growth of Finance', *Journal of Economic Perspectives*, vol. 27, no. 2, pp. 3–28.

International Monetary Fund (IMF) (2003), *External Debt Statistics: Guide for Compilers and Users – Appendix III, Glossary*, Washington, DC.

International Monetary Fund (IMF) (2008), *Offshore Financial Centres: A Report on the Assessment Program and Proposal for Integration with the Financial Sector Assessment Program*, Washington, DC, May 8.

International Monetary Fund (IMF) (2013), *Offshore Financial Centres, IMF Staff Assessments*, Washington, DC.

Kar, D & Freitas, S (2013), *Russia: Illicit Financial Flows and the Underground Economy*, Global Financial Integrity, February.

Krayenbuehl, T E (1988) *Country Risk: Assessment and Monitoring*, Woodhead-Faulkner, 2nd edition.

Krugman, P (2013), 'Treasury Island Trauma', *New York Times*, 21 March, viewed 16 April 2014, http://www.nytimes.com/2013/03/22/opinion/krugman-treasure-island-trauma.html.

Leopold, G (1998), *Political Risk and Foreign Direct Investments*, Masters Thesis, Faculty of Economics and Statistics, University of Konstanz, Germany, viewed 16 April 2014, http://kops.ub.uni-konstanz.de/bitstream/handle/urn:nbn:de:bsz:352-opus-1612/161_1.pdf?sequence=1.

Lester, Z (2013), 'Impact of Sanction Laws on Banks and the Professions' in Chaikin, D (ed.), *Financial Crime Risks, Globalisation and the Professions*, Australian Scholarly Publishing, Melbourne, pp. 88–95.

Maplecroft (2013), *Corruption Risk Index reveals long-term lack of will to tackle corruption in BRICs*, September 24 <https://maplecroft.com>

Mendelson, M & Paparinskis, M (2013), 'Bail-ins and the International Investment Law of Expropriation: In and Beyond Cyprus', *Journal of International Banking and Financial Law*, vol. 28, no. 8, pp. 475–479.

Milesi-Ferretti, G M & Tille, C (2010), *The Great Retrenchment: International Capital Flows during the Global Financial Crisis*, IHEID Working Paper 18–2010, The Graduate Institute of International and Development Studies, Geneva, September.

Multilateral Investment Guarantee Agency (MIGA) (2011), *2011 World Investment and Political Risk*, World Bank.

Multilateral Investment Guarantee Agency (MIGA) (2013), *2013 World Investment and Political Risk*, World Bank, http://www.miga.org/documents/WIPR13.pdf.

Organisation of Economic Co-operation and Development (OECD) (2013), *Global Forum on Transparency and Exchange of Information for Tax Purposes Peer Reviews: Cyprus 2013. Phase 2: Implementation of the Standards in Practice*, November.

Sandbu, M (2013), 'Legal Debate Over Capital Controls', *Financial Times of London*, March 25.

Sharman, J C and Mistry, P S (2008), *Considering the Consequences; The Development Implications of Initiatives on Taxation, Anti-Money Laundering and the Combating of the Financing of Terrorism*, Commonwealth Secretariat.

Transparency International (2013), *2013 Corruption Perceptions Index*.

United States Senate (2000), *Correspondent Banking: A Gateway of Money Laundering*, US Permanent Subcommittee on Investigations Minority Staff Report, February 5.

United States Treasury (2013), *Office of Foreign Assets Control* <http://www.treasury.gov/about/organizational-structure/offices/Pages/Office-of-Foreign-Assets-Control.aspx>

Volkery, C 2012, 'Cyprus Bailout Talks Stalled: Money Laundering Accusations Could Delay Aid', *Der Spiegel*, November 6, viewed 16 April 2014, http://www.spiegel.de/international/europe/money-laundering-accusations-could-stall-aid-to-cyprus-a-865580.

Wolf, M (2013), 'Bank of England's Mark Carney Places a Bet on Big Finance', *Financial Times of London*, October 29, viewed 16 April 2014, http://www.ft.com/intl/cms/s/0/08dea9d4–4002–11e3–8882–00144feabdc0.html#axzz2qlq2lw8Y.

Part II

Rating Agencies and the Sovereign Rating Process

6

Travels in the Ratings Space: Developed and Developing Countries' Sovereign Ratings

Lúcio Vinhas de Souza

1 Introduction

Sovereign ratings, in short, are a *relative* measure of the creditworthiness of debt instruments issued by governments ('Sovereigns'): they therefore provide a comparative gauge of the risk associated in investing in those instruments. For fundamental reasons (their greater levels of wealth, more robust institutions, etc.), historically developed economies have been associated with higher average Sovereign ratings (i.e., less risk) than developing ones. However, the apparent structural break in terms of growth dynamics between developed and developing economies observed since the late 1990s has also been associated with, among other things, better external and fiscal positions. Without implying any mechanical causality, one could also expect a smaller ratings difference between developing and developed Sovereigns. This chapter assesses if this has indeed happened.

2 First things first: a brief history of Sovereign ratings

A gap between average Sovereign ratings for developed and developing economies has existed since the very beginning of Sovereign ratings history. While the first known publication of what can be called a sovereign risk report is John Moody's 1900 *Manual of Industrial and Miscellaneous Securities*, it did not have any actual Sovereign ratings.[1] Ratings proper, as synthetic measures of relative risk, would only appear in 1909, also a Moody's primer, but only for corporate debt instruments initially (see Sylla, 2002). Moody's starts rating foreign government bonds in its 'Moody's Analyses of Investments – Government and Municipal Securities of 1918', again becoming the first company in the world to engage in this activity (see Gaillard, 2011). This publication, albeit overwhelmingly covering US issuers (both Sovereign and Sub-Sovereign), also rated obligations issued by foreign government entities from ten non-US issuers (namely, Argentina, Canada, Cuba, Dominican Republic, France, Japan, Norway, Panama, Switzerland, and the UK: see Table 6.1 below).

As one can see from Table 6.1 above, from the very creation of the ratings system, developing economies had on average lower Sovereign ratings than developed ones: the Aaa-rated Sovereigns then were the US, UK, France, and Canada, while the highest-rated developing economies – Cuba and Panama – rated a notch below, had strong economic and institutional links with the US (in today's rating language, one could say that they benefit from a 'ratings uplift' arising from their relation with the US), while the other rated developing countries (Argentina and the Dominican Republic) had a two-notch differential.[2]

From those humble beginnings, the global economic recovery and the wave of financial innovation immediately after the First World War led to a fast, albeit brief, expansion of the global Sovereign ratings business:

Table 6.1 Early sovereign ratings

Country	Rating
Argentina	A
Canada	Aaa
Cuba*	Aa
Dominican Republic	A
France	Aaa
Japan	Aa
Norway	A
Panama**	Aa
Switzerland	A
UK	Aaa

Notes: *Cuba, granted as colony to the US after its victory in the 1898 Spanish-American war, became formally independent from the US in 1902, but under a constitution that granted the US significant intervention and supervision powers.
**Panama became independent in 1903, after a secession war from Colombia with US support, and under a treaty which granted US Sovereign rights upon part of the Panamanian territory, a situation that lasted until 1999. Also since 1903, Panama runs a hard-peg currency regime anchored in the US dollar.

Source: Moody's.

by the late 1920s, Moody's rated around 60% of the then-existing Sovereigns, and the gap between ratings of developed and developing economies was still present.[3]

However, the Great Depression (leading to a wave of Sovereign defaults in the early 1930s: almost a full third of rated countries were then in default at some point), financial re-regulation, and later Second World War swiftly rolled back that wave, with international Sovereign issuances almost fully ceasing: as a reflection of that, by the early 1940s several of the then-existing rating agencies effectively closed down their Sovereign businesses.[4]

Even after the end of that global conflict, a considerably more regulated global financial system and more restricted international capital flows[5] meant that as late as 1975, Moody's rated only *half a dozen* Sovereigns, including the US. Only with the (re)liberalisation of global capital flows (illustrated by the collapse in the first half of the 1970s of the Bretton Woods system of fixed exchange rates and restricted capital flows, and by the related repealing of the US's 'Interest Equalization Tax' in 1974) will international Sovereign debt issuance expand again, and with it the need for Sovereign ratings. Additionally, the Latin American debt crisis (started with the Mexican default of 1982[6]) delayed further a full renewed take-off of Sovereign ratings, namely until the so-called 'Brady Plan' in the second half of 1980s restructured Latin American Sovereign debt, while at the same time expanding the size of global Sovereign debt markets.[7]

3 The 1990s: structural breaks?

The 1990s witnessed another remarkable expansion of the universe of rated Sovereigns: between 1990 and 2000, their number *trebled*, increasing from around thirty to around a hundred (see Table 6.2). The collapse of communism and the break-ups of the Soviet Union, Federal Republic of Yugoslavia, and Czechoslovakia further increased the sheer number of Sovereigns and freed those economies to access international debt markets, at a moment in which international capital markets were expanding fast, making the advantages of having a Sovereign rating more apparent.

Since the early 1990s, developing economies in general (both those formerly centrally planned and the market ones) represent the fastest growing section of the Moody's rated universe: As one can also see in Table 6.2 below, they surpassed the total number of rated developed Sovereigns as early as 1997, reaching around 70% of the total rated

Table 6.2 Number of rated sovereigns, 1990–2013

	1990	**1991**	**1992**	**1993**	**1994**	**1995**	**1996**	**1997**	**1998**	**1999**	**2000**	**2001**
Total number of rated sovereigns	31	31	32	37	43	46	58	72	80	94	96	98
Total number of rated developed sovereigns	24	24	24	25	27	29	31	33	36	37	37	37
Total number of rated developing sovereigns	7	7	8	12	16	17	27	39	44	57	59	61
	2002	**2003**	**2004**	**2005**	**2006**	**2007**	**2008**	**2009**	**2010**	**2011**	**2012**	**2013**
Total number of rated sovereigns	97	97	99	101	103	107	108	107	111	113	118	122
Total number of rated developed sovereigns	37	37	37	37	37	37	37	37	37	37	37	37
Total number of rated developing sovereigns	60	60	62	64	66	70	71	70	74	76	81	85

Source: Moody's.

universe by 2013, a historically unprecedented situation.[8] Given that effectively all developed sovereigns were already rated by 1999, since the 1990s developing countries have been – and will remain being so – the drivers in terms of the increase in the number of rated sovereigns.

While this is happening, the growth rate of developing economies seemingly decouples from that in developed countries. Since 2000, the difference in annual GDP growth of developing and developed economies is around 4%, or around 2.4 times the historical average for the period 1960–2012.[9] Consequently, the share of developing economies in global GDP more than doubles during just the 20 years between 1992 and 2012, from less than 14% to over 31% (see Table 6.3).[10]

This 'growth gap' in favour of developing economies happened parallel to an improvement in several other areas related to the economic and fiscal sustainability of developing Sovereigns. For instance, between 2000 and 2012, using IMF data, their stock of government debt to GDP fell from 49% to less than 36% (while in developed countries, it increased from 71% to 108%); their budget deficit was roughly stable at around 1.7% of GDP (on the other hand, that in developed countries increased by *almost 15 times* during the same period, from 0.4% to 5.9% of GDP), their current account surplus averaged 2.2% of GDP p.a. during the same period (while developed countries registered a 0.7% of GDP deficit p.a.), leading developing economies to an astonishing accumulation of USD 6.5 trillion in hard currency reserves during those years. Those developments increased the fiscal buffers of developing economies and reduced their vulnerability to external liquidity shocks (arguably the

Table 6.3 Developed and developing countries' % share of world GDP (in nominal USD)

	1960	1965	1970	1975	1980	1985	1990
% Developed Economies in Global GDP	78.8	81.2	81.9	80.6	81.2	81.5	85.6
% Developing Economies in Global GDP	21.2	18.8	18.1	19.4	18.8	18.5	14.4
	1995	**2000**	**2005**	**2009**	**2010**	**2011**	**2012**
% Developed Economies in Global GDP	84.8	82.8	80.5	73.4	70.7	69.4	68.2
% Developing Economies in Global GDP	15.2	17.2	19.5	26.6	29.3	30.6	31.8

Source: World Bank.

Table 6.4 Average sovereign ratings, developed and developing economies

	2002	2003	2004	2005	2006	2007
Avg. Developed rating	Aa2	Aa2	Aa2	Aa2	Aa2	Aa1
Avg. Developing rating	Ba1	Ba1	Ba1	Ba1	Ba1	Ba1
	2008	2009	2010	2011	2012	2013
Avg. Developed rating	Aa2	Aa2	Aa2	Aa3	A1	A1
Avg. Developing rating	Ba1	Ba1	Ba1	Ba1	Ba1	Ba2

Source: Moody's.

most important underlying feature of the Latin American crisis in the 1980s, and of the Asian and Russian crises of the 1990s).

Of course, there is no mechanical relationship between any of those variables and their values and the Sovereign rating of any given country,[11] but intuitively one would expect those improvements in fiscal and external sustainability to be somewhat reflected at least in the relative difference between the Sovereign ratings of developing and developed economies. Indeed, this is the case, as one can see in Table 6.4 but not necessarily as one would expect.

Namely, albeit a decline in this difference since 2007, (a) the reduction is relatively small (slightly more than two rating 'notches', from over 9 to around 7) and (b) it has not come about via an improvement of developing economies' average rating (which has actually fallen, albeit slightly), but rather via *a worsening of the average rating of developed Sovereigns*, notably since the onset of the so called 'Sovereign debt crisis'. Why is this so?

4 The missing link: institutions

This persistent ratings difference is partially due to a 'mechanical' component: namely, the average *initial* rating of a developing sovereign is several 'notches' below that of a developed one (namely, Ba3, as opposed to A2, for the 1986–2013 period). The implication of this is that the large expansion of the developing Sovereigns rated universe since the 1990s *itself* has actually helped to keep their average ratings at a lower level. However, there is also more at play here.

Namely, Moody's definition of the creditworthiness of a Sovereign includes both the *ability* and the *willingness* to repay debt. While the ability may be at least partially captured by the macroeconomic variables described above, the willingness to pay refers to a more qualitative level

Table 6.5 Average 'rule of law' index, developed and developing economies

	1996	1998	2000	2002	2003	2004	2005
Developed economies	1.2	1.2	1.2	1.2	1.3	1.3	1.2
Developing economies	–0.4	–0.5	–0.4	–0.4	–0.5	–0.4	–0.4
Difference developed/ developing	1.6	1.7	1.6	1.7	1.7	1.7	1.6
	2006	**2007**	**2008**	**2009**	**2010**	**2011**	**2012**
Developed economies	1.2	1.2	1.3	1.3	1.3	1.3	1.3
Developing economies	–0.4	–0.4	–0.4	–0.4	–0.4	–0.4	–0.4
Difference developed/ developing	1.6	1.6	1.7	1.7	1.7	1.7	1.7

Source: World Bank.

of analysis that must also cover *institutional frameworks*, be those formal or informal. It is arguably in this area, and not in macro sustainability indicators, where developing countries now face the greater constraints. As an example of that, Table 6.5 shows the World Bank's 'Rule of Law' indicator.[12] As one can see, using this indicator, and in spite of the significantly improved macro picture during this period, not only has the 'institutional gap' between developed and developing countries not fallen, it has actually (albeit slightly) *increased*. Institutions, therefore, may be the real constraining factor for further 'upward ratings migration' for developing countries.

This is not necessarily surprising: a more robust macro picture, which may even be due to external and possibly temporary factors (for instance, the positive commodity price shock of the long 'commodity super cycle' caused by China's increased demand for commodities) does not automatically imply better institutions, albeit those are of fundamental importance for sustained improvements in competitiveness and creditworthiness.

5 Conclusion

This chapter aimed to address the following question: has the much improved macro performance of developing economies since the late

1990s resulted in a reduction of their long-standing (and fundamentals-based) lower average Sovereign ratings, when compared with developed countries?

The answer is largely no (or at least, not yet): the reduction has been relatively minor and fully accounted for by falls in developed Sovereigns ratings, not by improvements in developing ones.

A possible explanation for this is that developing countries, in spite of better macro-fundamentals, still have a long way to go in terms of institutional development. Institutions are a fundamental determinant of creditworthiness, and their advance (or even building) may require greater, more sustained and focused efforts than 'mere' macroeconomic improvements. However, they are well worth this effort.

Notes

1. Beyond the US, the other sovereigns with listed debt instruments in that publication were Argentina, Austria, Belgium, Brazil, Canada, Denmark, Germany, Mexico, the Netherlands, and the UK (see Moody, J., 1900).
2. The Sovereign rating system back then had much less 'granularity' than now: in the interwar period, the number of Moody's rating categories would grow to nine, compared to the current 21 (most of which are further refined by three 'outlook' qualifiers: negative, stable, and positive). Also, a formal division between 'investment' and 'speculative' grades will not be introduced by Moody's until 1931.
3. This percentage will only be reached again in the late 2000s, albeit at that time the number of existing Sovereigns, as an effect of decolonisation and the break-up of large Sovereign entities like the Soviet Union, was almost 150% bigger than that in the 1930s.
4. Of the three major international Sovereign ratings agencies, S&P, Moody's, and Fitch, Moody's was the only one that continued to publish regularly analytical reports covering Sovereigns (even if those were largely non-rated).
5. Not only all centrally planned economies were shut out of global capital flows until the collapse of communism in the late 1980s/early 1990s, but even among developed market economies international capital flows were largely controlled until at least the later part of the 1970s.
6. For Moody's definition of Sovereign default, see 'Moody's Default Definition and its Application to Sovereign Debt', 2013.
7. As recently as 1994, 'Brady Bonds' were estimated to represent over 60% of the negotiable stock of emerging Sovereign debt.
8. To produce this table the author used the IMF definition of what is a developed and what is a developing economy.
9. This chapter is not the place to discuss the reasons behind this development, but the opening up and integration of formerly closed planned economies (from the Soviet Union to China) into the global economy is likely the most important factor.

10. See Moody's Investors Service (2013), '2014 Outlook – Global Sovereigns: Credit Quality Stabilizing After Several Tumultuous Years'.
11. The methodology that Moody's currently uses as *part* of its Sovereign rating process is described in 'Refinements to the Sovereign Bond Methodology'(2013). However, it is necessary to stress that the methodology is just one of the tools used in the rating process, as the assessment of Sovereign risk is a very complex, multi-faceted, and multi-disciplinary process that cannot be reduced to the mechanics of any given model. Namely, the actual rating of any given Sovereign is always decided within the setting of the collective discussions of a 'rating committee', which uses the insights of the Sovereign methodology as one of the inputs that informs its discussions.
12. This is one of the measures that Moody's uses in its methodology as a proxy for institutional strength. The value of this normalised indicator ranges from –2.5 (weak rule of the law) to 2.5 (strong rule of the law).

References

Gaillard, N (2011), *A Century of Sovereign Ratings*, Springer, New York.

Moody, J (1900), *Manual of Industrial and Miscellaneous Securities*, New York.

Moody's Investors Service (2013), '2014 Outlook – Global Sovereigns: Credit Quality Stabilizing After Several Tumultuous Years (160671)'.

Moody's Investors Service (2013), 'Moody's Statistical Handbook: Country Credit (159963)', November 2013.

Moody's Investors Service (2013), 'Sovereign Defaults Series: Market Re-Access and Credit Standing After Sovereign Default (158940)'.

Moody's Investors Service (2013), 'Refinements to the Sovereign Bond Methodology (157246)'.

Moody's Investors Service (2013), 'Moody's Default Definition and Its Application to Sovereign Debt (152872)'.

Moody's Investors Service (several years), 'Moody's Manual of Investments – American and Foreign Government Securities', New York.

Sylla, R (2002), 'An Historical Primer on the Business of Credit Rating', in Levich, R, Majnoni, G & Reinhart, C (eds), *Ratings, Rating Agencies and the Global Financial System*, Kluwer Academic Publishers, Boston.

7
The Sovereign Rating Regulatory Dilemma

Jeffrey Manns

1 The reciprocal oversight problem

Rating agencies have long served as convenient scapegoats for sovereign downgrades that reflect years of fiscal mismanagement and growing economic and political risks.[1] The irony is that the existence of sovereign ratings reflects the need for external accountability of governments' fiscal management.[2] Politicians in both the developed and developing world have repeatedly demonstrated a remarkable ability to ignore fiscal realities and dissemble until a crisis is at their doorstep. For this reason markets value sovereign ratings both as proxies on how close governments are to the precipice of a default and as a tool of public pressure for fiscal restraint.[3]

Historically, emerging market nations have been the primary targets of sovereign downgrades. Emerging market development has often followed the pattern of heavily leveraged booms giving way to predictable busts, which reduces emerging market leaders to impotently condemning rating agencies for downgrades.[4] Emerging market leaders have few, if any, tools at their disposal to discipline or curb the leading rating agencies. Standard & Poor's (S&P), Moody's, and Fitch serve as the gold standard of the industry, yet are largely outside of the reach of emerging market nations. Standard & Poor's, Moody's, and Fitch are based in the United States (with Fitch partly based in the United Kingdom),[5] and emerging market countries lack the economic and regulatory clout to impose unilateral checks on rating agencies. In fact, developing nations' efforts to impose curbs on rating agencies would likely have the exact opposite of the intended effects by underscoring the gravity of the governments' fiscal problems and lack of credibility.[6] That may change in the future as countries such as the People's Republic of China seek to translate growing economic power into global regulatory influence. But that prospect remains in the distant future as the regulatory leverage and legitimacy of emerging market countries lag behind their economic progress.[7]

In contrast, what is striking about the most recent financial crisis is that the largest developed country and economic bloc – the United States and the European Union respectively – were subjected to sovereign ratings downgrades. As the two leading financial regulators, the United States and the European Union are better positioned than any other countries to use their economic power and regulatory sway to hold rating agencies accountable.[8] But downgrades of the United States and European Union countries starkly exposed the conflict of interest created by the reciprocal oversight of governments and rating agencies and undercut the potential for an overhaul of the industry.[9] Political backlashes to downgrades simultaneously led to calls for rating agency regulation and cast a pall over the reform process.[10] Both the United States and European Union are conflicted by their desire to downplay risks to state finances and the broader economy which dampened incentives to create a system of truly timely and accurate ratings. Rating agencies recognise they must tread carefully with sovereign ratings for fear of political backlashes and economic fall-out, yet sovereign ratings give rating agencies a trump card to push back against government regulation.

The financial crisis should have been a catalyst for comprehensive rating agency reforms given the role of rating agencies in understating risks in structured finance products which fuelled the financial crisis.[11] Governments on both sides of the Atlantic took steps to address the worst excesses of rating agencies in the run up to the financial crisis and took on the role of primary regulators of rating agencies. But reforms were watered down due in part to governments' conflicts of interest. While public pressure for rating agency accountability led to some reforms and litigation, it did not change the fact that governments have incentives to tolerate, if not embrace, systematically lax ratings to obscure their own fiscal shortcomings and their economies' broader issues.

The irony is that rating agencies generally have convergent incentives with governments to engage in deferential ratings to both public and private issuers, rather than to produce timely and accurate ratings. This strategy is designed to attract more business from issuers and to mitigate the risk of regulation as governments have little interest in interfering with financial markets during financial upswings. The financial crisis disturbed this equilibrium as public pressure for ratings reforms clashed with a deteriorating sovereign risk environment. Rating agencies could plausibly claim that sovereign downgrades were a response to pressure for more timely and accurate ratings, and the threat of further downgrades paradoxically both sparked outrage yet dampened incentives for governments to follow through on comprehensive rating agency reforms.

2 The inherent discretion in sovereign ratings

The irony of the reciprocal oversight dilemma is that it has long been overshadowed by the issuer-pays conflict of interest. An inherent conflict of interest exists from issuers hiring and paying rating agencies.[12] Rating agencies have incentives to 'tilt' ratings in favour of issuers for fear of biting the hands that feed. Rating agencies face reputational constraints, yet the pressure to woo and retain clients' business creates stronger incentives to defer to issuers.[13] This conflict increases the more opaque the financial instrument. The less transparency, the easier it is for issuers and rating agencies to water down standards without markets recognising the decline.[14] For example, empirical studies have documented that ratings inflation steadily increased as structured finance products became more complicated in the run up to the financial crisis.[15]

The issuer-pays conflict of interest does not literally apply for sovereign ratings because these ratings are frequently unsolicited and unpaid.[16] For example, rating agencies are not selected or paid by the US federal government to issue ratings on federal debt. Instead, they provide sovereign ratings as a public good which gives them a high profile accountability role that complements their profitable business for private issuers and state and local governments.[17] But a similar opaqueness problem that arises in the issuer-pays conflict of interest context manifests itself in sovereign ratings. Rating agencies enjoy great discretion in determining sovereign ratings because of the distinctive nature of the risks and strengths of sovereign states.[18] Part of this discretion is necessary given the nature of ratings as long-term assessments of credit risk.[19] It is one matter to predict the potential default rate of bundles of mortgages even if there are significant uncertainties about the quality of the underlying mortgages. It is another to capture precisely the complex web of interconnected risks that sovereign states face. Policymakers in the United States and European Union similarly failed to understand the scope of public risk during the financial crisis, so rating agencies can hardly be blamed for having significant wiggle room to grapple with these uncertainties.[20]

The danger is that rating agencies will exploit the ambiguity of sovereign ratings to stretch their power or to deter meaningful regulatory reforms. Rating agencies can leverage opaqueness to legitimise risk-taking during boom periods by understating risks or by threatening sovereign downgrades when busts occur and pressures for regulation rise.[21] S&P's sovereign rating methodology is indicative of the flexibility rating agencies enjoy in assessing sovereign ratings. S&P lends the appearance of mathematical precision to their method by translating qualitative criteria into quantitative metrics. Analysts compile five sets of scores that cover institutional and governance effectiveness, economic structure and growth prospects, external liquidity and international investments, fiscal performance and flexibility, and monetary flexibility.[22]

Each of these factors offers a legitimate lens to analyse the default risk of sovereign states. But the numerical scoring obscures the degree of discretion analysts have in establishing the scores. Determining factors such as political risk, economic growth prospects, and fiscal performance and flexibility entail exercises of extraordinary discretion and take place in the shadow of the need for sensitivity to the political and economic fall-out of downgrades. This discretion is all the more significant because rating agencies purport to focus on the long-term structural creditworthiness of sovereigns. Long-term assessments inevitably entail greater degrees of discretion and uncertainty than short-term determinations as part of the analysis is by definition at best informed conjecture.[23] For example, credit prospects for countries may be inherently more difficult to predict for countries compared to corporations because of the impact of elections in changing fiscal and economic policies.

Historically, analysts have used this discretion to tilt sovereign ratings in favour of governments, which reflects both the systematic advantages sovereigns have over private actors in meeting liquidity needs and the danger of provoking government regulation. For example, S&P's fundamental credit analysis is designed to provide a long-term assessment of risk and expressly prioritises sovereign rating stability over reactions to short-term market changes.[24] S&P's own data indicates that sovereigns enjoy systematically higher ratings than their private counterparts.[25] S&P's defence of its sovereign ratings lies in the low default rates compared to other types of issuers as in the past 40 years only a small percentage of investment-grade sovereigns have defaulted.[26]

Deferential sovereign ratings are partly understandable because of the unique ability of sovereigns to meet bond obligations by printing money or raising taxes. But the other part of the equation is that sovereign states enjoy the unique ability to push back at rating agencies through exercising regulatory powers. While emerging market countries may have limited ability to regulate rating agencies directly, even they can complicate the ability of rating agencies to do business in their countries. But the United States and the European Union are potentially more formidable foes because they can impose regulations that significantly affect rating agencies' business model and profitability. This fact raises the question of what changed during the financial crisis that unsettled a status quo in which rating agencies had incentives to be deferential to sovereigns.

3 The clashes between rating agencies and the United States and European Union

Rating agency and government recklessness unsettled the equilibrium of deferential ratings and set the leading rating agencies on a collision course with United States and European Union regulators. Many actors deserve blame for fuelling excessive risk-taking through the design of trillions of dollars of structured finance products that intentionally camouflaged substantial risks.[27] But rating agencies merit particular blame because a myriad of United States and European Union member statutes and regulations deputised rating agencies as gatekeepers of credit risk.[28] Rating agencies not only failed to identify financial risks in an accurate and timely way, but also legitimised the proliferation of deceptive financial instruments through issuing inflated ratings. As a result, rating agencies failed to identify increasing risks or to condition ratings on adequate diligence and disclosures by issuers.[29]

The enormity of the financial crisis, coupled with the degree of rating agencies' culpability,[30] made rating agency accountability a priority for American and European policymakers.[31] The problem is that government response to the financial crisis exposed the United States and European Union member states to potential sovereign rating downgrades which sparked clashes between governments and rating agencies. Governments on both sides of the Atlantic sought to mitigate the financial crisis by stabilising the banking sector through internalising the costs and risks of the financial sector's failures.[32] This nationalisation of financial risk-taking led to predictable results of governments' overstretching their balance sheets and facing sovereign rating downgrades.[33] This fact led to a stark illustration of the reciprocity of oversight conflict of interest. Governments grappled with the need to regulate rating agencies to avoid a repeat of the conditions that led to the financial crisis, while also seeking to deter rating agencies from issuing sovereign rating downgrades. Rating agencies tacitly leveraged their sovereign ratings power to push back at regulatory reforms.

4 Convergent, yet inadequate regulatory reforms

Both European Union and United States rating agency reforms occurred roughly contemporaneously with the Dodd-Frank Act of 2010 in the United States and a 2009 CRA Regulation in the European Union that was amended in 2011 and 2013.[34] Most rating agency reforms were broad in scope but limited in its impact. The defining theme of both American and European ratings reforms is their convergence on a set of conflicting, inadequate approaches. Both the American and European reforms centralised oversight in a federal regulator (the SEC and ESMA respectively) and laid out registration requirements to ensure the independence and integrity of the ratings process. But regulators spoke out of both sides of their mouths in trying to marginalise ratings by rolling back requirements for ratings,[35] while underscoring the importance of rating agencies by seeking to heighten transparency,[36] as well as asserting regulatory controls and private oversight to heighten accountability.[37] These strategies signalled regulators' determination to reign in the ratings industry, yet failed both individually and collectively to transform the industry.

The logic of rolling back government requirements for ratings was that governments had legitimised the reliance on ratings, and abolishing requirements would end the public endorsement of private proxies of credit risk.[38] American regulators replaced requirements for ratings with language requiring investors to consider the creditworthiness of securities independently from ratings.[39] Both European and American regulatory bodies were required to review and remove most references to rating agencies and to develop their own broader standards of creditworthiness to supplant the role of ratings.[40] But in spite of trans-Atlantic efforts to reduce reliance on ratings, markets and many government agencies have indicated that they will continue to rely on ratings as proxies for credit risk for the foreseeable future because of the absence of credible alternatives.[41] Decades of government requirements for ratings made ratings a virtual necessity, and market practices are now so deeply entrenched that the removal of government mandates has had little impact.[42]

Both governments also placed faith in a passive securities regulation approach which sought to use transparency and procedural requirements to facilitate public and private monitoring.[43] Statutes on both sides of the Atlantic expressly bar regulators from shaping the methodologies of rating agencies.[44] Instead, the focus on transparency is designed to ensure rating agencies consistently apply their methodologies. Both European Union and American regulators have demanded rating agencies issue annual reports detailing compliance with their own ratings methodologies, internal controls, and regulatory obligations.[45]

Rating agencies must publicly disclose the qualitative and quantitative methods for each rating, methodological changes, procedures for determining the likelihood of defaults, and significant errors.[46] Both American and European regulators created requirements for compliance with internal controls to ensure consistent application of ratings methodologies and rating symbols, as well as separation of the business and analyst spheres.[47]

Regulators also specified disclosures to make it easier for ratings users to gauge the performance of ratings as well as to understand the nature and limits of ratings. Rating agencies must disclose the initial ratings and changes in ratings for each rated security to facilitate comparisons across rating agencies.[48] In addition, rating agencies must periodically disclose information that indicates the degree of accuracy of past ratings.[49] For example, the European Union mandates semi-annual disclosure of rating performance by category compared to historical default rates.[50] In the European Union, this information must be disclosed to ESMA's centralised European Rating Platform to facilitate users' comparisons of ratings' accuracy over time.[51]

European regulators require disclosure of clients contributing 5% or more of revenue, their 20 largest clients, disclosure of fees and rating pricing, conflicts of interest, and compensation structures.[52] American rating agency reforms placed a greater emphasis on corporate governance controls. Half of the rating agency board of directors must consist of independent directors,[53] and boards are tasked with oversight of ratings methodologies, accuracy, internal controls and conflicts of interest.[54] While these strengthened internal controls and heightened transparency are all positive corporate governance steps, it is unclear whether any of these measures do much to address the challenges facing rating agencies.[55] The problem is that these reforms only skirt the deeper issues of rating agencies' incentives and ability to gauge risks in a timely and accurate way and the domination of the industry by three firms.

5 Resistance to transforming rating agencies into a regulated industry

In spite of efforts to rescind ratings requirements and rely on greater transparency, the primary impact of ratings reforms was to move the rating agency industry closer to becoming a regulated industry with centralised oversight by the SEC and ESMA respectively.[56] Most rating agency reforms were benign (if unlikely to have a significant impact) and excited little controversy from rating agencies or the general public. But the attempts to transform rating agencies into a regulated industry attracted significant opposition from rating agencies and sparked tit-for-tat clashes between rating agencies and the United States and the European Union. The irony is that both governments and rating agencies could plausibly claim to be doing their job and even performing duties that were long overdue. But the overlap of ratings reforms and sovereign downgrades highlighted the reciprocal oversight problem and ultimately exposed the lack of wherewithal for governments to follow through on the most significant reforms.[57]

In the United States the two most significant parts of rating agency reform elicited clashes from rating agencies, which led the federal government to back down. The first clash was the most visible and dramatic. Part of the Dodd-Frank Act called for exposing rating agencies to civil liability for fraud in securities lawsuits if their ratings were knowingly or recklessly inaccurate.[58] The leading rating agencies immediately struck back through blatant civil disobedience. To evade potential liability, they threatened to freeze the market for asset-backed securities by refusing to allow their ratings to be quoted in issuers' SEC filings. The SEC quickly caved and suspended the rule and stripped the one significant means of private accountability from the Dodd-Frank Act.[59]

Meanwhile, the leading rating agencies fought a guerrilla campaign of behind-the-scenes lobbying and more subtle public actions to weaken the SEC's efforts to implement the other significant part of the Dodd-Frank Act: the Franken Amendment. The Franken Amendment mandated that the SEC devise an alternative to the issuer-pays conflict of interest that incentivised deferential ratings for issuers.[60] The initial version of the Franken Amendment sought to transform rating agencies fully into a regulated industry by calling for the creation of an independent commission to select rating agencies for structured finance products using a lottery or random assignment system with an eventual transition to performance-based selection. But rating agency opposition led to a watering down of the proposal in the final legislation into a mandate that the Government Accountability Office (GAO) and the SEC conduct a series of studies over two years to consider the Franken Amendment and other alternatives for the current issuer-pays system.[61] The SEC had to implement the Franken Amendment's proposal 'unless the Commission determines that an alternative system would better serve the public interest and the protection of investors.'[62]

While the GAO and SEC conducted three studies and held a day of expert panels,[63] the resulting reports raised the pros and cons of the potential alternatives to the issuer-pays system, rather than recommended concrete action.[64] The SEC simply ignored the mandate to craft an alternative to the issuer-pays system.[65] While the SEC detailed some of the practical stumbling blocks to overhauling the issuer-pays system, part of the story of regulatory inaction appears due to the public and behind-the-scenes clash between rating agencies and the federal government.

The high-profile downgrade of the federal government's credit rating in August 2011 was the clearest example of the larger struggle between rating agencies and the federal government.[66] Standard & Poor's took advantage of a budget stalemate to downgrade the federal government, which led to an immediate market reaction. All three of the leading rating agencies engaged in muscle flexing by openly criticising the federal government's fiscal policies.[67] The increased scrutiny of the federal government's credit rating can be interpreted as a shot over the bow that underscored the ability of rating agencies to affect the United States and world markets. The brilliance of this strategy is that no one could fault rating agencies for being more proactive and timely in their ratings, as that was an objective of the Dodd-Frank Act.[68]

While there was no official retaliation, in February 2013 the Department of Justice singled S&P out in a lawsuit alleging fraud in asset-backed securities ratings based on a rarely-used anti-fraud provision of the Financial Institutions Reform, Recovery, and Enforcement Act of 1989 (FIRREA).[69] Applying a banking law statute to the securities context of rating agencies is a novel, yet untested approach, which seeks to bypass traditional barriers to suing rating agencies.[70] The inherent ambiguity of ratings will make it difficult for prosecutors to show that S&P's management knowingly committed fraud,[71] but the lawsuit has sent a clear message to the leading rating agencies that the federal government will seek to keep rating agencies in check.[72] In spite of this lawsuit no further concrete steps were taken to roll back the influence of rating agencies, and the SEC backed off from implementing the Franken Amendment.[73]

In contrast, the tit-for-tat between rating agencies and the European Union was more vitriolic in part because repeated sovereign downgrades exposed the weakness of the Eurozone and cast doubt on the viability of this feature of European integration.[74] The sovereign rating dominos fell in waves as fiscally weaker members of the Eurozone were downgraded from 2008 on, which led to a series of escalating financial guarantees by other Eurozone members that in turn led to further downgrades.[75] The outrage of Eurozone leaders was only equalled by their hypocrisy in seeking to find fault with the leading rating agencies for highlighting the fiscal vulnerability of Eurozone members.[76]

Eurozone regulatory leaders sought to 'tame' rating agencies by calling for the suspension of sovereign ratings 'in exceptional circumstances', creating a substitute European Union rating agency, regulators' requiring pre-approval of rating agency methods, marginalising the leading rating agencies by mandating issuers rotate rating agencies and employ smaller competitors, and exposing rating agencies to gross negligence liability.[77] With the notable exception of the call for gross negligence liability, these ideas underscored the European Union's weakness and appeared designed to attempt to paper over problems or to make rating agencies bend to the European Union's will and to inflate sovereign ratings.

The idea of banning sovereign ratings faltered because suppressing sovereign ratings would not only blatantly contradict the European Union's commitment to free speech, but also ironically serve as a red flag in underscoring the severity of member states' fiscal problems. For that reason, exercising a ban on sovereign ratings (ostensibly on 'prevention of disorder' grounds) would be far more significant than a ratings downgrade in provoking market panic at a potential cover up.[78] The logic behind politicians' calls for a European Union-controlled or -funded rating agency was that the leading rating agencies are so entrenched that the only way to foster viable competition is to create one out of whole cloth.[79] A government-owned or funded rating agency would be independent from issuers, but the 'solution' would simply replace one conflict of interest with another, more blatant conflict of interest. This idea faltered because of a recognition that markets would likely not trust ratings issued by a government-linked entity for fear that it would inflate the ratings of both sovereigns and companies who enjoy the government's favour.[80] Similarly, calls for regulators to pre-approve rating agency methodologies were abandoned swiftly because of concerns that regulators would abuse this power to undercut the independence of rating agencies.

The issuer rotation idea sought to erode the dominance of the leading rating agencies, yet suffered from practical shortcomings.[81] Mandating that issuers rotate rating agencies in three- to six-year intervals sought to foster greater competition and open up opportunities for smaller rating agencies and new entrants.[82] The problem with this approach is that small rating agencies are ill-equipped to fill this role as the three leading rating agencies account for 95% of the global market. As importantly, a rotation approach would not necessarily do anything to create incentives for rating agency accuracy. In the name of fostering the growth of smaller rating agencies, it could potentially amount to an entitlement system. In the face of a business and rating agency backlash, European leaders backed down and instead enacted a watered-down pilot program for rotation of rating agencies every four years for re-securitisations (which is a small fraction of the structured finance market).[83]

European leaders did implement timing and notice requirements for sovereign ratings and prohibited rating agencies from unveiling policy recommendations with sovereign rating watches or updates. Mandating one-day notice before sovereign rating changes may help to avoid errors, and requiring inclusion of a full research report justifying changes is valuable. But limiting sovereign ratings changes to three set times a year and barring 'direct or explicit requirements or recommendations from credit rating agencies' merely seek to postpone and cover up the European Union's fiscal weaknesses and will have little impact in dampening rating agencies' influence.[84]

Lastly, the European Union recently expanded opportunities for private oversight of rating agencies to allow private actors to take advantage of greater transparency.[85] Rating agencies are now exposed to private liability for intentional or grossly negligent infringement of the European Union's rating regulations, which strikes a balance between liability exposure and limits on frivolous litigation.[86] This approach may deter rating agencies from emulating the worst excesses in the run-up to the financial crisis, but by definition an extraordinary deviation from ordinary care means that the EU's gross negligence will do little to hold rating agencies accountable in the overwhelming majority of cases. Part of the problem is that the cause of action is based on non-compliance with EU regulations as this liability rule does not address rating agencies' deeper problems caused by the absence of competition and standards for defining rating accuracy.[87] While incentives for due diligence are positive, in the overwhelming majority of cases, rating agencies would face no accountability for the timeliness and accuracy of ratings.

These bold ideas largely fell to the wayside as rating agencies successfully fought most of these reforms behind the scenes and continued to highlight their relevance and impact by announcing changes in their risk assessments of European Union countries.[88] While European Union politicians were more vocal and potentially radical than their American counterparts, reforms on both sides of the Atlantic largely converged into watered-down measures that left the most important issues of rating agency competition and accountability unresolved. The irony is that the regulatory reforms that were implemented significantly raised the costs of being a rating agency and erected barriers to entry to the industry which may reinforce the leading rating agencies' dominance.

6 The challenges facing rating agency reform

American and European reforms left unresolved the difficult questions of how to foster rating agency accuracy and constructive competition. Both American and European politicians have embraced the rhetoric of promoting the selection of rating agencies based on performance, but the challenge is determining the benchmark for assessing rating agency performance. The danger is that performance standards may perversely distort ratings or accentuate herding effects. Similarly, reforms barely touched the question of how to lower barriers to entry for new rating agencies and facilitate competition.

Part of the challenge is that no clear consensus exists on what performance-based standards to use to assess rating agencies.[89] The SEC or ESMA is ill-equipped on its own to address these questions, yet there is no framework or organisation in place for securities industry participants to tackle this difficult, yet essential question. Proposals have suggested creating peer comparison models to examine whether rating agencies' percentage of predicted default of debt instruments deviated from that of their peers and whether annual yields of identically-rated debt securities from different asset classes varied in a significant way.[90] The dilemma of either of these performance-based metrics is that they may accentuate herding effects. Rating agencies would have greater incentives to engage in conscious parallelism to avoid liability, which could undercut the objectives of greater accuracy and accountability. Herding effects are already an issue in an oligopolistic industry,[91] and the solution could exacerbate the problem. An additional concern is that the benchmark would swiftly become the centrepiece of rating agencies' methodologies, regardless of whether the standards incentivise accuracy and timeliness.

Another important issue that industry participants need to resolve is gauging the merits of standardising ratings. In theory, standardising ratings will help facilitate comparability, and creating performance-based tests will foster accountability.[92] But the danger exists that these approaches may undercut rating agencies' incentives to create their own distinctive tests of risk and may leave all market participants worse off by forcing analyses through a single lens and thwarting innovation.[93]

Lastly, the stakeholders who purchase or rely on ratings for debt purchase decisions may better appreciate what smaller entrants or new competitors need to do to become credible alternatives to the leading rating agencies. The European Union's rotation pilot program would open up opportunities for small or new rating agencies. But regulators' low bar on who can qualify as a rating agency appears to be inadequate as few issuers or debt purchasers would want to rely on a 'reputational' intermediary that meets the current bare minimum requirements.[94] Instead of foisting smaller rating agencies on debt issuers, regulators would benefit from the development of professional standards for rating agencies by the spectrum of industry stakeholders.[95]

7 The case for a stakeholder regulatory organisation

Since sovereign ratings raise conflicts of interest that potentially compromise the integrity of both sovereign states and rating agencies, effective regulation requires moving beyond the false dichotomy of relying either on government or self-regulation.[96]

The role of rating agencies as monitors of sovereign risk casts a shadow over government regulation due to the reciprocal oversight problem. Government actors have incentives to exert power over rating agencies to dampen the influence of ratings and to deter rating agencies from highlighting sovereign weakness. Additionally, the questions of heightening rating agency accountability and competition have eluded regulators as rating agency reforms have not addressed these issues in any meaningful way.

The problem is that the reciprocal oversight problem has two sides to the coin. Just as governments may be suspect in their regulatory roles, private rating agencies may have perverse incentives to leverage sovereign ratings to their advantage. This fact makes self-regulation potentially problematic. Traditionally, a combination of self-regulation and market discipline was the answer to rating agency accountability. Policymakers assumed that the reputational concerns of rating agencies would provide strong incentives for their integrity and accuracy and eclipse any short-term gains from turning a blind eye to client misconduct.[97] Unfortunately, this assumption proved to be incorrect as reputational constraints waned amidst bubble markets and amidst increases in risk-seeking behaviour by participants in financial markets.[98] Part of the problem is both self-regulation and market discipline face limitations because of the nature of ratings. Rating agencies can hide behind their own approaches to assessing risk through a bucket system of categories and can use the opaqueness of ratings both to acknowledge the reality of uncertainties and as a cover for inaccuracy. Rating agencies can also elastically spin their failures as a product of the short-sightedness and knee-jerk reactions of markets, because ratings focus on structural, long-term concerns.[99]

For this reason reliance on self-regulation and market discipline appear to be inadequate. The question is whether the challenges facing rating agency accuracy and accountability could be better addressed at a collective level through a self-regulatory organisation. Self-regulatory organisations were created for a range of securities-related actors in the United States as a way to remedy the limits of government regulators.[100] The logic is simple that market participants are often better positioned to recognise and address emerging problems than regulators and have incentives to do so to avoid heavy-handed regulation.[101] Delegating a degree of self-regulation responsibilities to industry participants seeks to leverage self-interest in a constructive way through encouraging cooperation and collective action.[102] Self-regulatory organisations are designed to potentially craft solutions to pre-empt both potential disaster and the threat of government regulations in a more time- and cost-effective way. Industry participants would have incentives to design rules that can be practically implemented and to monitor one another for compliance in order to pre-empt government regulators stepping in.[103]

Reliance on self-regulation entails accepting as a necessary evil a degree of conflicts of interest from parties regulating themselves.[104] For example, industry participants may exploit the degree of deference to self-regulation to push for lax regulation. While self-regulatory organisations may more swiftly identify and address industry failures than regulators, their actions may come too late as industry participants face incentives not to admit their practices are potentially problematic.[105]

In theory a self-regulatory organisation approach would be appealing for rating agencies since the leading rating agencies are concentrated in the United States and the European Union, so either the SEC or ESMA (or both) could delegate rating agencies with this task. But the oligopolistic nature of the rating agency industry and the layers of conflicts of interest that exist make it likely that a pure self-regulatory organisation would serve to reinforce the status quo.[106] As noted earlier, rating agencies are generally selected and paid by debt issuers which incentivise deferential ratings for paying clients. This fact may give rating agencies incentives to craft rules that legitimise the regulatory tilt in favour of issuers or reinforce the ambiguity of ratings.[107]

This danger is accentuated by the fact that 95% of world-wide ratings are issued by three leading rating agencies which means that pure self-regulation could simply be a tool of entrenchment.[108] The leading rating agencies could use a self-regulatory organisation as a means of collusion to erect standards that would make it difficult for smaller rating agencies to compete. Rating agencies would have incentives to appear responsive to government demands for transparency, accuracy, and accountability, while crafting rules that do little to further these goals in substance.[109]

The distinctive challenges that a self-regulatory organisation would face cast doubt on the viability of this self-oversight strategy, but not on the desirability of collective action to enhance rating accuracy and industry accountability. One of the basic issues that has long plagued the rating agency industry is the question of who rating agencies are (and ought to be) accountable to. Government requirements for a broad range of actors – such as money market funds, banks, and regulators – to refer to ratings for risk assessments, effectively made ratings a public good and created widespread reliance that had survived the abolition of these requirements.[110] But rating agencies have repeatedly succumbed to temptations to tilt ratings towards issuers because issuers pay the bills. Additionally, the reciprocal oversight problem means that rating agencies also face pressure to defer to tilt ratings towards developed-world sovereigns as well because of the threat of regulations. In contrast, debt purchasers who rely on ratings as proxies of credit risk have no direct role in terms of accountability and oversight.

One answer to this problem is to create greater rating agency accountability to end users – debt purchasers who rely on ratings as proxies of the risk they are taking on. For example, strengthening private causes of action for debt purchasers by lowering pleading standards for rating agency fraud or exposing rating agencies to liability for negligence would give debt purchasers greater incentives to monitor ratings.[111] The resulting liability exposure could dampen rating agencies' incentives to tilt ratings in favour of issuers or sovereigns. The challenge is that it may be difficult to heighten rating agency accuracy by pulling rating agencies in multiple directions.[112]

Rather than replacing one market distortion with another, it would be desirable for the SEC or ESMA to create a broader system of rating agency accountability to the spectrum of stakeholders who rely on ratings. Creating a 'stakeholder regulatory organisation' would recognise the desirability of collective action and seek to temper the biases of the current system by giving representatives of debt issuers, debt purchasers, and rating agencies themselves a say in overseeing the rating agency industry and developing industry standards.[113] The underlying logic would be similar to a conventional self-regulatory organisation as the marketplace experience of stakeholders would make them far better informed than government actors about the strengths and weaknesses of the current ratings system and better positioned to develop industry standards.[114] But the stakeholder regulatory organisation would go a step further in bringing together representatives of the range of actors whose economic fortunes are directly affected by the timeliness and accuracy of ratings.

The danger is that self-interest could potentially place debt issuers and purchasers at loggerheads. Debt issuers would prefer the status quo of inflated ratings, while debt purchasers would advocate systematically conservative assessments of risk. For this reason achieving complete consensus among these divergent interests would be all but impossible as it would be difficult to get every single stakeholder representative to agree on reforms. Instead, stakeholder regulatory organisations would have the goal of having representatives of the different types of stakeholders and working towards forging consensus with a majority of representatives of each type of stakeholders. Regulators would still enjoy the ability to supersede the stakeholder regulatory organisation's decisions (because the power to regulate practically gives the SEC or ESMA the ability to have the final word on any issue within their jurisdiction).[115] But consensus within the stakeholder regulatory organisations would carry significant weight and legitimacy which would make it hard for regulators to dismiss their recommendations.[116]

One of the biggest challenges of a stakeholder regulatory organisation approach would be determining representatives of the spectrum of stakeholders and motivating consensus building. As the political class of Washington, DC knows all too well, putting adversaries at a negotiating table may lead to protracted stalemate and inaction. For example, the 2012 across-the-board sequestration cuts were designed as a default threat to bring the two American political parties together to forge a new budget because the default hurt each party's constituencies. But gridlock lasted for over two years before the two parties reached a budget deal.[117]

In contrast, the SEC or ESMA would have more potent regulatory tools to incentivise consensus building among private parties. Either agency or both in tandem could pressure parties to reach agreement on regulatory priorities or face the threat of unilateral government action which would heighten uncertainty and risk for all concerned. The repeat player nature of regulation means that regulators would have trump cards if particular stakeholders repeatedly appeared to be the stumbling blocks to consensus.[118] Not only could regulators supersede stalemates or agreements with their own policies, but they would also be able to take into account intransigence into shaping policies for rating agencies and other regulatory spheres affecting stakeholders. The threat of government action would not be a panacea, but it could make it more plausible for regulators to set the agenda for a stakeholder regulatory organisation by identifying issues they will act on if stakeholders cannot reach consensus.

Regulators could go a step further and employ a regulatory default approach in which they identify potential default rules to set a stakeholder regulatory organisation's agenda.[119] This approach would place the onus on industry stakeholders to agree on an alternative to forestall a default rule. For example, the SEC could enact a default recklessness liability rule on rating agencies that would come into effect if industry participants could not agree on a liability standard.[120] Rating agencies would plausibly respond by threatening to cover only well-known seasoned issuers and to raise the price of ratings to reflect this dramatic expansion of risk exposure. These changes would hurt debt markets in ways that would affect both issuers and debt purchasers and could spur these parties to work out a less disruptive standard of liability. The downside of a regulatory default rule approach is that stakeholders who stand to gain (or lose less) from the proposed default rule would have incentives to work to undermine compromises without blatantly opposing the process. For example, well-known seasoned issuers may believe they stand to gain market share if a recklessness standard makes ratings less widely available and regard that as well worth paying a higher price for ratings.

This holdout concern raises the related challenge of determining what actors are best positioned to represent the diverse array of ratings users. Part of the issue would be determining who chooses the representative stakeholders and what criterion is used to ensure that stakeholders are not rubber stamps for regulators or industry. The shortcomings of independent director requirements in the United States underscore this dilemma. Corporate boards of directors routinely nominate individuals who have no direct role in the company but who are part of overlapping circles in the business community. While independent directors are intended to serve as a check on management and as shareholder advocates, numerous scholars have documented how this role amounts to formalism in practice and has not transformed corporate governance.[121]

The lesson from the shortcomings of independent directors is the need to create a system in which a spectrum of stakeholder interests is genuinely represented. Trusting the government or a self-perpetuating independent board to select stakeholder representatives would ignore the incentives participants may have to tilt the system towards their interests. Instead, two suggestions merit consideration: committee representation similar to bankruptcy proceedings and enlistment of industry associations as representatives of stakeholders.

Part of the problem of rating agency accountability is the lack of any contractual relationship between rating agencies and the debt purchasers who rely on ratings which makes ex ante oversight difficult.[122] Giving debt purchaser representatives seats at the table of a stakeholder regulatory organisation would empower debt purchasers to play a role in advocating greater accuracy and accountability. But the diversity of debt purchaser interests would make it difficult to determine who should serve as representatives.

American bankruptcy law offers a framework for addressing diverse creditor interests that could be modified to apply to selecting representatives for a stakeholder regulatory organisation.[123] In bankruptcy the spectrum of stakeholders in the faltering company have a seat at the table to lay their claims to assets and must reach consensus to restructure debt. Interested creditors with the largest stakes for each class of secured debt are chosen to serve as creditor committee representatives,[124] and consensus is needed among each creditor committee for bankruptcy reorganisations to be approved. The logic is simple: the creditors with the most at stake safeguard the interest of those with similar types of claims, and agreement with each class of stakeholders is needed to change creditors' rights to enable bankrupt companies to restructure their debt.

Similar logic could guide the selection of debt purchaser representatives for a stakeholder regulatory organisation. Interested debt purchasers with the largest amount of investments for different classes of debt (such as sovereign and corporate debt) could serve as representatives to a stakeholder regulatory organisation. Since the initial purchasers of debt are likely repeat players with debt issuers (and therefore potentially more conflicted), it may make sense to break down debt purchasers based off of not only categories of debt, but also whether they are primary or secondary market purchasers since their interests may diverge. For example, primary market sovereign debt purchasers rely on ratings to ensure that they are buying a marketable product, but routinely sell out their stakes to secondary markets in rapid fashion. In contrast, secondary market purchasers are more likely to buy and hold debt issuances, and therefore the largest debt holders may have a stronger interest in the accuracy and timeliness of rating changes.

A similar principle could be applied to ensure adequate representation of debt issuers. Another key distinction would be to have stakeholder representation include not only well-known seasoned issuers, that is, established companies with a track record of issuing debt, but also representation of non-reporting and unseasoned issuers who would have divergent interests because they are new to the debt issuance process.[125] Ratings would matter far more to non-reporting and unseasoned issuers since markets would be less familiar with these companies and therefore more likely to rely on ratings as proxies for their risk exposure. Interested issuers with the largest issuances in the categories of well-known seasoned issuers and non-reporting and unseasoned issuers could serve as representatives of issuer perspectives on ratings.

Another alternative would be to rely on trade associations to represent the range of stakeholders. Either the SEC or ESMA or an independent board could award representation to trade associations that best reflect the spectrum of stakeholders. These groups would be the primary actors lobbying legislators and regulators behind the scenes to further the interests of issuers and debt purchasers in ratings reforms.[126] Expressly recognising their role in a stakeholder regulatory organisation would be a way of bringing their advocacy out of the shadows and into dialogue with one another. This approach would leverage existing private associations for a productive purpose. Associations may not always represent intra-industry interests which can diverge, but they may serve as the closest proxy for industry interests. But it is reasonable to believe that different trade associations would exist to represent divergent interests in the issuer and debt purchaser world as each faction would want its own interests represented in legislative and regulatory processes.

The downside of directly enlisting trade associations is that the government would be deputising lobbying organisations to perform a public function and give them an imprimatur of legitimacy. Enlisting private actors to perform public roles is far from new as that is the point of rating agencies as gatekeepers.[127] What is distinctive about this approach is that it calls for relying on private associations to act out of their self-interest rather than to put on a public hat (and relies on the virtues of Madisonian factionalism).[128] It is more realistic to think that industry advocates will represent their self-interest well and that the public benefit will be in the aggregate of each faction representing its interest and working on compromises that further their collective self-interest.

Another shortcoming of the approach is that some regulatory issues may not have a clear resolution. Regulation of rating agencies is fairly recent with much of the meaningful scope of regulation occurring in the wake of the financial crisis. The uncertainties of existing regulations may be a check on further rules and regulations until the implications and unintended consequences of the existing regulatory regimes are more evident. Similarly, some limitations on regulation may be due to genuine uncertainty or stark disagreement concerning how to gauge the accuracy of ratings. A stakeholder regulatory organisation could take the lead in trying to resolve this type of issue, but it is not clear that such an organisation could definitively resolve these types of concern or address it in a way that heightens understandings of risk in financial markets.

8 Conclusion

The clashes between Western countries and the leading rating agencies have underscored the conflicts of interest that exist in reciprocal oversight of countries and rating agencies. The countries best positioned to heighten rating agency accountability suffer from chronic deficits and unsustainable debt. This tension has given the United States and the European Union incentives not to pursue more sweeping rating agency reform for fear that a system of more timely and accurate ratings would expose sovereign weakness. On the other hand, systematically lax ratings that legitimised risk-taking in the run-up to the financial crisis demonstrated the limits of self-regulation and market discipline of rating agencies.

Instead of relying on government or self-regulation, American and European policymakers should seek to create a stakeholder regulatory organisation that brings together debt issuers, rating agencies, and debt purchasers to address rating agency reforms. The SEC and ESMA could use the threat of regulation or regulatory defaults to push stakeholders to chart out rating agency standards that are realistically achievable and more balanced than the current system. While significant stumbling blocks would remain for enhancing the quality of ratings, this framework could provide a path forward for reforms.

Notes

1. See, for example, Staikouras (2012: 71, 72–73) (discussing the temptation European politicians and policymakers faced in blaming rating agencies for European credit problems); see also Cunningham (2002: 1421, 1428–1429 & note 47) (discussing politicians' attempt to blame rating agencies for the Enron debacle).
2. See Afonso, Gomes, and Rother (2011: 1–2) (discussing how sovereign credit ratings serve as 'a condensed assessment of a government's ability and willingness to repay its public debt on time' and are pivotal for default probability analysis); Gulati and Triantis (2007: 977, 985) (discussing how markets use sovereign bond ratings as proxies of a country's financial stability).
3. See, for example, Mellios and Paget-Blanc (2006: 361–362) (describing how sovereign credit ratings affect financial markets); Oakley and Wise (2012) (discussing the market reaction to the downgrade of Portugal and Greece to junk bond status).
4. See Block and Valeer (2004: 917, 918–922) (discussing economic, political, and legal factors that shape sovereign risk in developing countries).
5. Fitch is technically based in both New York and London, but its roots are in the United States. See Fitch Ratings, *About Us*, <http://www.fitchratings.com/web/en/dynamic/about-us/about-us.jsp>.
6. See, for example, Warren (2012) (discussing the Argentine president's defiance in the face of sovereign rating downgrades).
7. Emerging markets account for only 18% of capital markets as of 2011, with China accounting for 7.6% of world markets. See Roxburgh, Lund, and Piotrowski (2011: 24, Exhibit 12).

8. The European Union and the United States remain the dominant economic powers with 2012 GDPs of $16.566 trillion and $15.685 trillion respectively, which account for 19.92% and 18.86% of the world economy. See IMF (2013). But the United States and European Union play a far larger role in capital markets and account for 31.8% and 30.8% of world markets respectively as of 2011. See Roxburgh, Lund, and Piotrowski 2011, supra note 7, p. 24, Exhibit 12).
9. An extensive literature has debated the scope and potential remedies for the shortcomings of the issuer-pays system for rating agencies. See, for example, Bai (2010: 47, 97–98) (arguing for the need for standardisation of rating agency performance statistics to facilitate comparability); Barnett (2012: 475, 501–502) (arguing in favour of greater regulatory oversight as preferable to potentially counter-productive efforts at fostering greater competition); Coffee (2011: 231, 233–236) (advocating the abolition of the issuer-pays system and analysing the merits of the potential alternatives for heightened public regulation); Gudzowski (2010: 245, 264–271) (advocating a government utility model for ratings); Listokin, and Taibleson (2010: 91, 94–95) (arguing that mandating that compensating rating agencies with the debt proceeds they rate would create greater incentives for rating accuracy); Manns (2009: 1011, 1015–1019) (calling for a user fee on investors to finance the creation of an independent board to select and compensate rating agencies based on a competitive bidding process). In contrast, this article is the first to identify and address the 'reciprocal oversight problem' for sovereign ratings. Sovereigns are conflicted in ratings reform because of their desire to downplay their financial imbalances, while rating agencies have incentives to leverage sovereign ratings to push back against ratings reforms. For this reason, this article advocates the creation of a 'stakeholder regulatory organisation' to work on establishing rating agency standards in a more effective way than either the government or rating agencies could on their own.
10. See, for example, Darbellay and Partnoy (2011: 1) (discussing how European Union leaders blamed rating agencies for exacerbating the debt crisis when Greek downgrades occurred before the unveiling of a bail-out plan).
11. See, for example, Goodhart (2009: 121–122) (discussing the role high fees for structured finance products played in inflating ratings).
12. *See* Coffee (2011, supra note 9, at 233–236) (advocating the abolition of the issuer-pays system).
13. *See* Manns (2009, supra note 9, at 1049) (discussing the shortcomings of reputational constraints).
14. *See* Bai (2010, supra note 9, at 63–66) (discussing how the degree of opaqueness of rated products can foster ratings inflation).
15. See, for example, Ashcraft, Goldsmith-Pinkham, and Vickery (2010: 23–24, table 3) (documenting a pattern of stability in high ratings in spite of declines in diligence of and asset quality in mortgage-backed securities from 2001 to 2008); Benmelech and Dlugosz (2009: 617, 624–628, 632–633) (criticising the lax process for credit rating of CDOs and the conflicts of interest created by the hiring of rating agencies by issuers); Bethel, Ferrell, and Hu (2008: 16–18, 21, 74) (documenting the stability of ratings in spite of marked decline in the extent of diligence into and quality of the underlying mortgages in mortgage-backed securities from 2001 to 2006).

16. See European Securities and Markets Authority (2013: 4).
17. See Bhatia (2002: 47) (discussing the publicity that rating agencies gain from sovereign ratings); Manns (2009, supra note 9, pp. 1056–1057) (discussing the role of ratings as public goods).
18. See Bruner (2008, pp. 125, 136–138) (discussing the 'lack of objective metrics of creditworthiness' for sovereign ratings).
19. See Cantor and Mann (2003: 7, 15) (discussing the emphasis on long-term concerns in determining ratings through the process of 'fundamental credit analysis').
20. See Gerding (2009: 127, 169) (discussing the failure of private and public risk models in failing to predict the scope and scale of the financial crisis).
21. See Manns (2011).
22. See Standard & Poor's (2013: 2–3) (hereinafter 'S&P Sovereign Rating').
23. See Muller and Watson (2013: 1–2) (discussing the challenges in quantifying the uncertainty in long-run predictions of economic variables).
24. See S&P Sovereign Rating (supra note 22, 5).
25. Ibid. at 4: 'Since 1975, 15-year cumulative default rates for sovereigns averaged 2.5% for investment-grade sovereigns and 24.8% for speculative-grade sovereigns.'
26. Ibid. at 4: 'At year-end 2012, almost 11% of our sovereign local- and foreign-currency ratings were "AAA" and roughly 15% were in the "AA" category, compared with about 0.3% and 5%, respectively, for private-sector issuers.'
27. Residential Mortgage Backed Securities (RMBS) and Mortgage-Based Collateralised Debt Obligations (CDO) are debt obligations based on large pools of mortgage loans whose cash flows derive from principal and interest payments from the underlying mortgages. See United States Securities and Exchange Commission, *Mortgage-Backed Securities*. Approximately $1.7 trillion in subprime RMBS were issued from 2001 to 2006. See Ashcraft and Schuermann (2008). JP Morgan has estimated that $500 to $600 billion in subprime CDOs were issued over this period. See Anderson and Timmons (2007); see also Crouhy, Jarrow, and Turnbull (2008: 8–19) (discussing the array of market participants who have potential culpability for the subprime mortgage crisis).
28. See, for example, Credit Rating Agency Reform Act of 2006, Pub. L. No. 109–291, §§ 4, 15E, 120 Stat. 1327, 1329–33 (codified at 15 U.S.C. § 78o–7 (2006)) (laying out the process for rating agencies to be certified as Nationally Recognized Statistical Rating Organizations (NRSRO)); Regulation S-K, 17 C.F.R. § 229.10(c) (2008) (mandating the inclusion of ongoing NRSRO ratings for issuers making filings under the Securities Act of 1933 and the Securities Exchange Act of 1934); see also Rating Agencies and the Use of Credit Ratings Under the Federal Securities Laws, 68 Fed. Reg. 35,258, 35,258 (June 12, 2003) [hereinafter SEC Concept Release] (discussing how since 1975 the SEC 'has relied on credit ratings from market-recognized credible rating agencies for distinguishing among grades of creditworthiness in various regulations under the federal securities laws).
29. See Manns (2013a: 749, 754–758).
30. See, for example, Bajaj and Landler (2007) (discussing the scale of subprime mortgage CDO exposure facing banks and other creditors); Shenn and Mildenberg (2008) (discussing how almost half the subprime bonds rated

by Standard & Poor's in 2006 and early 2007 were cut or placed on review for ratings downgrades in 2008, a fact which suggests rating agencies' lax approach).

31. See, for example, United States Securities and Exchange Commission (2008) (discussing the shortcomings of rating agencies' policies and procedures, internal audit processes, and surveillance of complex RMBS and CDOs); Staff of Securities Commission on Homeland Security & Governmental Affairs 2011, Subcommittee on Investigations, 112th Congress, p. 272 [hereinafter Wall Street Report] (discussing the 'fact that the rating agencies issued inaccurate ratings' and the role of 'conflicts of interest inherent in the "issuer-pays" model' in rating agencies' failures).
32. See Jensen (2012: 759, 761–763) (discussing the unsustainable debt Eurozone countries have taken on due to bailouts of its weaker members and their banking sectors).
33. See Panetta (2011: 20–23).
34. See Regulation (EC) No 1060/2009 of the European Parliament and of the Council of 16 September 2009 [hereinafter CRA Regulation I]; Regulation (EU) No 513/2011 of the European Parliament and of the Council of 11 May 2011 amending Regulation (EC) No 1060/2009 [hereinafter CRA Regulation II]; Regulation (EU) No 462/2013 of the European Parliament and of the Council of 21 May 2013 amending Regulation (EC) No 1060/2009 [hereinafter CRA Regulation III]; Dodd-Frank Wall Street Reform and Consumer Protection Act, Pub. L. No. 111–203, 124 Stat. 1376 (2010) [hereinafter Dodd-Frank Act].
35. See, for example, Flannery, Houston, and Partnoy (2010: 2085, 2086–2089) (arguing for a shift to reliance on credit default swap spreads to serve as a proxy of creditworthiness); Macey (2006, pp. 21–24) (advocating marginalising credit ratings because they provide 'no information of value to the investing public'); Partnoy (2009) (advocating the abolition of government-mandated requirements for rating because '[a] primary cause of the recent credit market turmoil was overdependence on credit ratings and credit rating agencies').
36. See, for example, Dennis (2009: 1111, 1144–1150) (arguing for greater rating agency disclosures and expanded SEC disciplinary and sanctions power).
37. See, for example, Bai (2010, supra note 9, pp. 97–98); Barnett (2012, supra note 9, pp. 501–502); Coffee (2011, supra note 9, pp. 233–236); Gudzowski (2010, supra note 9, pp. 264–271); Listokin and Taibleson (2010, supra note 9, pp. 94–95); Manns (2009, supra note 9, pp. 1015–1019).
38. U.S. regulators stated that the premise of these changes is to make clear that investors should not 'place undue reliance on the NRSRO ratings'. See References to Ratings of Nationally Recognized Statistical Rating Organizations, 73 Fed. Reg. 40,088, 40,088–89, 40,100 (proposed 11 July 2008) (to be codified at 17 C.F.R. pts. 240, 242, 249); CRA Regulation III, Art. 5b (making a similar point to justify European Union regulators' removal of requirement for ratings).
39. See Dodd-Frank Act § 939, 124 Stat. at 1885–86.
40. See Ibid. § 939A, 124 Stat. at 1887; CRA Regulation III, Art. 5b (mandating that European regulators 'all review and remove, where appropriate, all such references to credit ratings in existing guidelines and recommendations').

41. See, for example, Federal Deposit Insurance Corporation (2011: 3–4) (discussing how efforts to come up with alternatives for reliance on credit ratings is a work in progress because '[i]dentifying alternatives to credit ratings that are suitable for regulatory capital determinations is challenging and involves policy tradeoffs'); see also Basel Capital Accord III, 16 December 2010.
42. See Hilzenrath (2011).
43. See, for example, Dodd-Frank Act § 938, 124 Stat. at 1885–1887.
44. See CRA Regulation I, Article 23 (prohibiting member states and regulators from 'interfere[ing]with the content of credit ratings and methodologies'); Credit Rating Agency Reform Act of 2006, Pub. L. No. 109–291, 120 Stat. 1327, 1327–39 (codified at 15 U.S.C. § 78o–7 (2006)).
45. See PricewaterhouseCoopers LLP 2010; Dodd-Frank Wall Street Reform and Consumer Protection Act § 932(a), 124 Stat. at 1873.
46. See Dodd-Frank Act § 932, 124 Stat. at 1872–1883.
47. See Ibid. § 932, 124 Stat. at 1882–1883 (requiring board of director approval of the qualitative and quantitative approaches used in rating methodologies); CRA Regulation I, Part I, Annex I, Section D (detailing rating agency disclosures mandated by the European Union); CRA Regulation I, Part II, Annex I, Section D (detailing the additional information that rating agencies must disclose for structured finance products in the European Union).
48. See Dodd-Frank Act § 932, 124 Stat. at 1878.
49. Ibid.
50. See CRA Regulation I, Para 1, Part II, Annex I, Section E.
51. See CRA Regulation III, Art. 11a.
52. See CRA Regulation I, Art. II Para 1–2, Annex I, Section B, E; CRA Regulation III, Annex I, Section E.
53. See Dodd-Frank Act § 932, 124 Stat. at 1882.
54. See Ibid. § 932, 124 Stat. at 1882–1883.
55. See, for example, Fairfax (2010: 127, 131–132) (arguing that 'the independent director's value has been vastly overstated'); Sale (2006: 1375, 1378–1379) (questioning the efficacy of relying on independent directors to police corporate conduct because of the lack of SEC actions against independent directors).
56. See Ibid. § 932, 124 Stat. at 1877–1878 (centralising oversight in the SEC's Office of Credit Ratings).
57. The Dodd-Frank Act also lowered the pleading standards for Rule 10b-5 anti-fraud liability. While significant in theory, in practice the expanded pleading opportunities are unlikely to increase private litigation in any significant way because rating agencies effectively have a safe harbour of due diligence compliance. Compare 15 U.S.C. §§ 77k(b)(3)(C), 78j-1 (2006), *and* 17 C.F.R. § 240.10b-5 (2008), *with* Dodd-Frank Act § 933, 124 Stat. at 1883–84.
58. See Dodd-Frank Act § 939G, 124 Stat. at 1890.
59. See Morgenson (2011) (describing the rating agencies' reaction to the possible imposition of expert liability).
60. See Dodd-Frank Act § 939F, 124 Stat. at 1889–90.
61. Ibid. §§ 939D, 939F, 124 Stat. at 1888–90.
62. Ibid. § 939F, 124 Stat. at 1890.
63. See United States Government Accountability Office (2012: 8–14), United States Government Accountability Office (2010: 79–93).

64. See Securities & Exchange Commission (2012: 72–82).
65. See Dayen (2013).
66. See Paletta and Phillips (2011).
67. See, for example, Paletta (2011).
68. See Manns (2011).
69. See Viswanatha and Stempel (2013) (discussing how the lawsuit against S&P is the first enforcement action against a rating agency for its role in the financial crisis); Lazo and Tangel (2013) (discussing the potential implications of the lawsuit against S&P).
70. See Eaglesham, Neumann, and Perez (2013) (discussing how the legal strategy makes an end-run around traditional barriers to lawsuits).
71. See Manns (2013b).
72. For example, Moody's may also be the target of a FIRREA action as DOJ and the SEC have on-going probes concerning Moody's role in the financial crisis. See Neumann (2013).
73. More recently, Fitch reminded the federal government of the power of rating agencies by threatening to downgrade the federal government in response to the October 2013 government shutdown and debt ceiling stalemate. This pressure helped to foster a debt ceiling compromise and the reopening of the government, yet left unclear the future of both government and rating agency accountability in the United States. See Fitch Places United States 'AAA' Rating on Rating Watch Negative, Reuters, 15 October 2013, available at http://www.reuters.com/article/2013/10/15/fitch-places-united-states-aaa-on-rating-idUSFit67327220131015.
74. See, for example, Alessi, Wolverson, and Sergie (2013) (discussing how European leaders blamed rating agencies for exacerbating the Eurozone debt crisis).
75. For example, in the wake of the financial crisis, small Eurozone countries such as Portugal, Greece, and Cyprus were reduced to non-investment grade status by Standard & Poor's. Bailouts that sought to bolster these states and their banking sectors resulted in further downgrades for many of the stronger Eurozone countries. See Standard & Poor's (2012).
76. See, for example, Wise (2012) (criticising S&P's decision to treat Portugal's debt as non-investment grade as 'ill-founded' and 'seriously inconsistent').
77. See Barker (2011a) (discussing EU Internal Market Commissioner Barnier's controversial proposals to overhaul the rating agency industry).
78. Barker (2011b) (discussing EU Commissioner Barnier's swift retreat on a temporary ban on sovereign ratings in the face of an immediate backlash).
79. See Grundfest and Hochenberg (2009: 5–6).
80. See *Der Spiegel* (2012).
81. See Barker (2012).
82. See Brunsden (2012).
83. See CRA Regulation III, Art 14–18.
84. See CRA Regulation III, Art 42, 45.
85. See CRA Regulation III, Art 5a, 35a.
86. See CRA Regulation III, Art. 35a; Manns (2009, supra note 9, pp. 1076–1084) (proposing a gross negligence standard for rating agency liability similar to what the European Union embraced).
87. *Cf.* Fenster (2006: 885, 902–910) (discussing the limits of transparency).

88. See, for example, Standard & Poor's, *European Sovereign Ratings and Related Materials* (detailing S&P's sovereign rating changes for European Union countries); Jolly (2013), (discussing S&P's decision to downgrade the European Union's credit rating to one notch below AAA based on the weaker creditworthiness of the 28 member states).
89. See Coffee (2011, supra note 9, p. 258) (arguing that '[a] reliable track record for accuracy might take a decade or more to develop').
90. See Dombalagian (2012: 59, 78–79, 89).
91. See, for example, Piraino Jr. (2004: 9, 10–11) (discussing the pervasiveness of conscious parallelism in oligopolistic industries because the small number of players facilitates coordination without express communication).
92. See, for example, Bai (2010, supra note 9, pp. 96–97) (advocating the virtues of rating standardisation).
93. See, for example, Wall Street Report (supra note 31, p. 17).
94. See, for example, Credit Rating Agency Reform Act of 2006, Pub. L. No. 109–291, 120 Stat. 1327, 1327–1339 (codified at 15 U.S.C. § 78o–7 (2006)) (detailing the modest requirements to be a Nationally Recognized Statistical Rating Organization in the United States).
95. See Freeman (2003: 1285, 1328–1329) (discussing the virtues of industry self-regulation and professional-standard setting).
96. See Sinclair (1997: 529, 531) (discussing how academics and policymakers often falsely present a choice between the extremes of government control and complete self-regulation).
97. See Coffee Jr. (2002: 1403, 1406).
98. Ibid. at pp. 1412–1413.
99. See Cantor and Mann (2003, supra note 19) (discussing the emphasis on long-term concerns in determining ratings through the process of 'fundamental credit analysis').
100. See Birdthistle and Henderson (2013: 1, 4–5) (discussing the creeping federalisation of self-regulatory organisations); Karmel (2008: 151, 154–157) (providing an overview of securities self-regulatory organisations); Omarova (2011: 411, 419–425) (providing an overview of the academic literature on the role of self-regulatory organisations as a governance tool).
101. See Hu (1993: 1457, 1463–1464) (discussing the limitations of government regulators' ability to oversee complex financial risks).
102. See Michael (1995: 171, 181–186) (providing an overview of self-regulation's virtues, such as industry insiders' advantages in recognising and swiftly and cost-effectively addressing industry ills).
103. See Stefanadis (2003: 5, 6–8) (discussing how self-regulation facilitates the rapid development of industry-wide innovation and standards); Schulz and Held (2001) (discussing how self-regulation can facilitate more rapid decision-making and implementation than government rulemaking).
104. See Balleisen (2010: 443, 463–465) (discussing how self-regulation entails inherent tradeoffs, yet may be the only practical way to address cross-border challenges).
105. See Sinclair (1997, supra note 96, pp. 535–538) (discussing the limits of self-regulation and how self-regulated parties may exploit these shortcomings to thwart regulation and oversight).

106. See Macey and O'Hara (2005: 563, 565–567) (discussing the tension between the profit focus of the securities industry and incentives for effective self-regulation).
107. See Manns (2013a, supra note 29, pp. 757–760) (discussing the entrenchment of the ratings oligopoly and the impact of the issuer-pays conflict of interest).
108. See Rönsberg (2011) (discussing the market share of the leading rating agencies).
109. See Braithwaite (1993: 81, 93) (discussing the concern that self-regulation can be a façade designed to build false faith in industry and foster complacency about government inaction).
110. See Rating Agencies and the Use of Credit Ratings Under the Federal Securities Laws, 68 Fed. Reg. 35,258, 35,259 (June 12, 2003); Karp (2011).
111. *Cf.* CRA Regulation III, Art. 35a (imposing liability for intentional or grossly negligent infringement of the European Union's rating agency regulations).
112. See, for example, Haar (2013) (raising the danger that investors will try to leverage a lower pleading standard to seek compensation for their primary investment loss, regardless of rating agencies' culpability).
113. The academic debate on self-regulatory organisations has focused on the degree of government control versus the degree of industry control. See, for example, Black (2002: 103, 115–118) (discussing the spectrum of degrees of government and industry self-regulation); Gunningham and Rees (1997: 363, 391–392) (discussing the continuum of industry self-regulation from voluntary self-regulation to mandated partial self-regulation and full government control); Omarova (2011: 411, 438–439) (advocating embedded self-regulation consisting of an integration of government regulation and self-regulation). But no one has raised the idea of a 'stakeholder regulatory organisation' that incorporates the spectrum of stakeholders into industry regulation. This approach is designed to mitigate the shortcomings of the targeted industry's ability to regulate itself and to move out of the shadows the behind-the-scenes lobbying by stakeholders that takes place with government regulation.
114. While securities self-regulatory organisations frequently have an adjudicative role to resolve claims against its members, the focus of this article is on the potential role a stakeholder regulatory organisation could play in developing industry standards and engaging in rule-making. The conflicting interests of a spectrum of stakeholders may make it more difficult for the organisation to adjudicate claims between different factions of the stakeholder regulatory organisation's membership. See Birdthistle and Henderson (2013) (discussing the adjudicative role of US self-regulatory organisation FINRA).
115. See, for example, Registration, Responsibilities, and Oversight of Self-Regulatory Organization, 15 U.S.C. § 78s (2000) (detailing the SEC's ability to oversee and reject the decisions of financial self-regulatory organisations); Pildes (2009: 485, 524–525) (discussing the SEC's ability to reject or amend the decisions of securities' self-regulatory organisations).
116. See Moot (2010: 317, 325–326) (discussing the history of SEC deference to self-regulatory organisations).

117. See Weisman (2013).
118. See Freeman (2000: 543, 548–555) (discussing similar dynamics in 'negotiated rulemaking' between regulators and regulated industries).
119. The regulatory default concept has been used in the environmental law context to provide regulated parties with incentives to produce new information and make the case for alternatives. See, for example, Karkkainen (2006: 861, 869–870).
120. The SEC has twice considered and backed away from expert liability because of rating agency resistance. See Concept Release on Possible Rescission of Rule 436(g) Under the Securities Act of 1933, 74 Fed. Reg. 53,114, 53,114–15 (15 October 2009); Morgenson (2011) (describing the SEC's capitulation to rating agency resistance to expert liability).
121. See, for example, Fairfax (2010, supra note 55, pp. 131–132); Sale (2006, supra note 55, pp. 1378–1379).
122. Ex post accountability was recently introduced in the European Union for issuer or debt purchaser damages caused by intentional or grossly negligence violations of the CRA Regulation I and amendments (although gross negligence will still be a high bar for a successful suit). See CRA Regulation III, Art. 35a. But compliance with the EU ratings regulations is not tantamount to ex ante incentives for timely and accurate ratings.
123. See Bebchuk and Fried (1996: 857, 860–864) (discussing the conflicts of interest which may arise among creditors as issuers approach insolvency); Warren and Westbrook (2005: 1197, 1237–1238) (providing empirical data from the bankruptcy context which supports the concern about conflicts of interests among creditors).
124. See Title 11, Ch. 11(I) § 1102.
125. See Langevoort and Thompson (2013: 337, 379, & note 179) (discussing the distinguishing features of well-known seasoned issuers).
126. See, for example, Krawiec (2013: 53, 79–80) (detailing the role of trade associations in meetings with securities and financial regulators about implementation of the Dodd-Frank Act).
127. See, for example, Kraakman (1986: 53) (defining gatekeepers as 'private parties who are able to disrupt misconduct by withholding their cooperation from wrongdoers').
128. See Sunstein (1985: 29, 38–45) (providing an overview of Madison's constitutional vision of the productive role of faction offsetting faction).

References

Afonso, A, Gomes, P & Rother, P (2011), 'Short- and Long-Run Determinants of Sovereign Debt Credit Ratings', *International Journal of Finance and Economics*, vol. 16, no. 1, pp. 1–2.

Alessi, C, Wolverson, R & Sergie, M A (2013), The *Credit Rating Controversy*, Council on Foreign Relations, 22 October, http://www.cfr.org/financial-crises/credit-rating-controversy/p22328.

Anderson, J & Timmons, H (2007), 'Why a US Subprime Mortgage Crisis Is Felt Around the World', *New York Times*, 31 August, C1.

Ashcraft, A B & Schuermann, T (2008), 'Understanding the Securitization of Subprime Mortgage Credit', Staff Report No. 318, Federal Reserve Bank of New York.

Ashcraft, A, Goldsmith-Pinkham, P & Vickery, J (2010), *MBS Ratings and the Mortgage Credit Boom*, Staff Report No. 449, Federal Reserve Bank of New York, pp. 23–24, Table 3.

Bai, L (2010), 'The Performance Disclosures of Credit Rating Agencies: Are They Effective Reputational Sanctions?', *New York University Journal of Law & Business*, vol. 7, no. 1, pp. 47, 97–98.

Bajaj, V & Landler, M (2007), 'Mortgage Losses Echo in Europe and on Wall Street', *New York Times*, 10 August, A1, C7.

Balleisen, E J (2010), 'The Prospects for Effective "Coregulation" in the United States', in E J Balleisen & D A Moss (eds.), *Governments and Markets: Toward a New Theory of Regulation*, Cambridge University Press, New York, pp. 443, 463–465.

Barker, A (2011a), 'Barnier Backtracks on Ratings Reforms', *Financial Times*, 15 November.

Barker, A (2011b), 'Brussels to Unveil Curbs on Rating Agencies', *Financial Times*, 14 November.

Barker, A (2012), 'Move to Curb Rating Agencies Prompts Backlash', *Financial Times*, 29 March.

Barnett, J M (2012), 'Intermediaries Revisited: Is Efficient Certification Consistent with Profit Maximization?', *The Journal of Corporation Law*, vol. 37, no. 3, pp. 475, 501–502.

Basel Capital Accord III (16 December 2010), http://www.bis.org/bcbs/basel3.htm (retaining the use of ratings to assess credit and market risk).

Bhatia, A V (2002), 'Sovereign Credit Ratings Methodology: An Evaluation', Working Paper, International Monetary Fund, p. 47.

Bebchuk, L A & Fried, J M (1996), 'The Uneasy Case for the Priority of Secured Claims in Bankruptcy', *Yale Law Journal*, vol. 105, pp. 857, 860–864.

Benmelech, E & Dlugosz, J (2009), 'The Alchemy of CDO Credit Ratings', *Journal of Monetary Economics*, vol. 56, no. 5, pp. 617, 624–628, 632–633.

Bethel, J E, Ferrell, A & Hu, G (2008), 'Law and Economic Issues in Subprime Litigation', Discussion Paper No. 612, Harvard, John M. Olin Center for Law, Economics & Business, pp. 16–18, 21, 74.

Birdthistle, W A & Henderson, M T (2013), 'Becoming a Fifth Branch', *Cornell Law Review*, vol. 99, no. 1, pp. 1, 4–5.

Black, J (2002), 'Decentring Regulation: Understanding the Role of Regulation and Self-Regulation in a "Post-Regulatory" World', *Current Legal Problems*, vol. 54, no. 1, pp. 103, 115–118.

Block, S A & Valeer, P M (2004), 'The Price of Democracy: Sovereign Risk Ratings, Bond Spread, and Political Business Cycles in Developing Countries', *Journal of International Money & Finance*, vol. 23, no. 6, pp. 917, 918–922.

Braithwaite, J (1993), 'Responsive Regulation for Australia', in P Grabosky & J Braithwaite (eds), *Business Regulation and Australia's Future*, Australian Institute of Criminology, Canberra, pp. 81, 93.

Bruner, C M (2008), 'States, Markets, and Gatekeepers', *Michigan Journal of International Law*, vol. 30, pp. 125, 136–138.

Brunsden, J (2012), 'Credit Rating Firms in EU to Face Sovereign-Debt Limits', *Bloomberg*, 28 November, http://www.bloomberg.com/news/2012–11–27/credit-rating-companies-to-face-sovereign-debt-curbs-in-eu-plan.html.

Cantor, C & Mann, C (2003), *Measuring the Performance of Corporate Bond Ratings*, Moody's Investors Service, New York, pp. 7, 15.

Coffee, Jr, J C (2002), 'Understanding Enron: "It's About the Gatekeepers, Stupid"', *Business Lawyer*, vol. 57, no. 4, pp. 1403, 1406.

Coffee, Jr, J C (2011), 'Ratings Reform: The Good, the Bad, and the Ugly', *Harvard Business Law Review*, vol. 1, no. 1, pp. 231, 233–236

Crouhy, M G, Jarrow, R A & Turnbull, S M (2008), 'The Subprime Credit Crisis of 07', *The Journal of Derivatives*, vol. 16, no. 1, pp. 8–19.

Cunningham, L (2002), 'Sharing Accounting's Burden: Business Lawyers in Enron's Dark Shadow', *Business Lawyer*, vol. 57, no. 4, pp. 1421, 1428–1429 & note 47.

Darbellay, A & Partnoy, F (2011), 'Credit Rating Agencies Under the Dodd-Frank Act', *Banking & Financial Services Policy Report*, vol. 30, no. 12, p. 1

Dayen, D (2013), 'Financial Reform's Triple F Rating', *The American Prospect*, 21 February.

Dennis, K (2009), 'The Ratings Game: Explaining Rating Agency Failures in the Build Up to the Financial Crisis', *University of Miami Law Review*, vol. 63, pp. 1111, 1144–1150.

Der Spiegel (2012), 'Dearth of Investors: Plan to Set Up European Rating Agency Under Threat', 16 April.

Dombalagian, O H (2012), 'Regulating Informational Intermediation', *American University Business Law Review*, vol. 1, no. 1, pp. 59, 78–79, 89.

Eaglesham, J, Neumann, J & Perez, E (2013), 'US Sues S&P Over Ratings', *Wall Street Journal*, 5 February.

European Securities and Markets Authority (ESMA) (2013), 'Credit Rating Agencies: Sovereign Ratings Investigation', 2 December, ESMA/2013/1775, p. 4.

Fairfax, L M (2010), 'The Uneasy Case for the Inside Director', *Iowa Law Review*, vol. 96, no. 1, pp. 127, 131–132.

Federal Deposit Insurance Corporation (2011), *References to Credit Ratings in FDIC Regulations*, pp. 3–4, http://www.fdic.gov/regulations/reform/LA11-NI0117.pdf.

Fenster, M (2006), 'The Opacity of Transparency', *Iowa Law Review*, vol. 91, pp. 885, 902–910.

Fitch Ratings (2014), *About Us*, http://www.fitchratings.com/web/en/dynamic/about-us/about-us.jsp.

Flannery, M J, Houston, J F & Partnoy, F (2010), 'Credit Default Swap Spreads as Viable Substitutes for Credit Ratings', *University of Pennsylvania Law Review*, vol. 158, no. 7, pp. 2085, 2086–2089.

Freeman, J (2000), 'The Private Role in Public Governance', *New York University Law Review*, vol. 75, no. 3, pp. 543, 548–555.

Freeman, J (2003), 'Extending Public Law Norms through Privatization', *Harvard Law Review*, vol. 116, pp. 1285, 1328–1329.

Gerding, E (2009), 'Code, Crash, and Open Source: The Outsourcing of Financial Regulation to Risk Models and the Global Financial Crisis', *Washington Law Review*, vol. 84, pp. 127, 169.

Goodhart, C A E (2009), *The Regulatory Response to the Financial Crisis*, Edward Elgar Publishing, Cheltenham, United Kingdom.

Grundfest, J A & Hochenberg, E E (2009), 'Investor Owned and Controlled Rating Agencies: A Summary Introduction', Working Paper Series No. 66, Rock Center for Corporate Governance & Working Paper Series No. 391, Stanford University Law School Law & Economics Olin, pp. 5–6, http://www.ssrn.com/abstract=1494527.

Gudzowski, M (2010), 'Mortgage Credit Ratings and the Financial Crisis: The Need for a State-Run Mortgage Security Credit Rating Agency', *Columbia Business Law Review*, vol. 2010, no. 1, pp. 245, 264–271.

Gulati, M & Triantis, G (2007), 'Contracts without Law: Sovereign Versus Corporate Debt', *University of Cincinnati Law Review*, vol. 75, pp. 977, 985.

Gunningham, N & Rees, J (1997), 'Industry Self-Regulation: An Institutional Perspective', *Law & Policy*, vol. 19, no. 4, pp. 363, 391–392.

Haar, B (2013), 'Civil Liability of Credit Ratings Agencies after CRA3 – Regulatory All-or-Nothing Approaches between Immunity and Over-Deterrence', Research Paper No. 2013-02, University of Oslo Faculty of Law, http://ssrn.com/abstract=2198293.

Hilzenrath, D S (2011), 'SEC Poses Plan to Curb Reliance on Credit Ratings, but Regulators Cite Difficulties', *Washington Post*, 27 April.

Hu, H T C (1993), 'Misunderstood Derivatives: The Causes of Informal Failure and the Promise of Regulatory Incrementalism', *Yale Law Journal*, vol. 102, pp. 1457, 1463–1464.

International Monetary Fund (IMF) (2013), *World Economic Outlook*.

Jensen, C (2012), 'What Doesn't Kill Us Makes Us Stronger: But Can the Same Be Said of the Eurozone?', *International Lawyer*, vol. 46, no. 2, pp. 759, 761–763.

Jolly, D (2013), 'S&P Cuts European Union Credit Rating', *New York Times*, 20 December.

Karkkainen, B C (2006), 'Information-Forcing Environmental Regulation', *Florida State University Law Review*, vol. 33, no. 3, pp. 861, 869–870.

Karmel, R S (2008), 'Should Securities Self-Regulatory Organizations Be Considered Government Agencies?', *Stanford Journal of Law Business and Finance*, vol. 14, no. 1, pp. 151, 154–157.

Karp, G (2011), 'The Rise of Standard & Poor's', *Chicago Tribune*, 14 August, p.1.

Kraakman, R H 1986, 'Gatekeepers: The Anatomy of a Third-Party Enforcement Strategy', *Journal of Law, Economics & Organisation*, vol. 2, no. 1, pp. 53.

Krawiec, K D (2013), 'Don't "Screw Joe the Plumber": The Sausage-Making of Financial Reform', *Arizona Law Review*, vol. 55, no. 1, pp. 53, 79–80.

Langevoort, D C & Thompson, R B (2013), '"Publicness" in Contemporary Securities Regulation After the JOBS Act', *Georgetown Law Journal*, vol. 101, no. 2, pp. 337, 379 & n.179.

Lazo, A & Tangel, A (2013), 'Justice Department Sues S&P Over Mortgage Ratings', *LA Times*, 4 February.

Listokin, Y & Taibleson, B (2010), 'If You Misrate, Then You Lose: Improving Credit Rating Accuracy Through Incentive Compensation', *Yale Journal on Regulation*, vol. 27, pp. 91, 94–95.

Macey, J R & O'Hara, M (2005), 'From Markets to Venues: Securities Regulation in an Evolving World', *Stanford Law Review*, vol. 58, no. 2, pp. 563, 565–567.

Macey, J R (2006), 'The Politicization of American Corporate Governance', *Virginia Law & Business Review*, vol. 1, no. 1, pp. 21–24.
Manns, J (2009), 'Rating Risk after the Subprime Mortgage Crisis: A User Fee Approach for Rating Agency Accountability', *North Carolina Law Review*, vol. 87, pp. 1011, 1015–10.
Manns, J (2011), 'The Revenge of the Rating Agencies', *New York Times*, 10 August, A23.
Manns, J (2013a), 'Downgrading Rating Agency Reform', *George Washington Law Review*, vol. 81, April, pp. 749, 754–758.
Manns, J (2013b), 'Break up the Ratings Oligopoly', *Bloomberg*, 18 February.
Mellios, C & Paget-Blanc, E (2006), 'Which Factors Determine Sovereign Credit Ratings?', *The European Journal of Finance*, vol. 12, no. 4, pp. 361–362.
Michael, D C (1995), 'Federal Agency Use of Audited Self-Regulation as a Regulatory Technique', *Administrative Law Review*, vol. 47, pp. 171, 181–186.
Moot, J S (2010), 'When Should the FERC Defer to the NERC?', *Energy Law Journal*, vol. 31, no. 2, pp. 317, 325–326.
Morgenson, G (2011), 'Hey, S.E.C., That Escape Hatch Is Still Open', *New York Times*, 6 March, BU1.
Muller, U K & Watson, M W (2013), *Measuring Uncertainty About Long-Run Predictions*, http://www.princeton.edu/~umueller/longpred.pdf.
Neumann, J (2013), 'Two Firms, One Trail in Probe of Ratings', *Wall Street Journal*, 10 February.
Oakley, D & Wise, P (2012), 'Portuguese Bonds Hit as Traders Fear Default', *Financial Times*, 26 January.
Omarova, S T (2011), 'Wall Street as Community of Fate, Towards Financial Industry Self-Regulation', *University of Pennsylvania Law Review*, vol. 159, no. 2, pp. 411, 438–439.
Paletta, D & Phillips, M (2011), 'S&P Strips US of Top Credit Rating', *Wall Street Journal*, 6 August.
Paletta, D (2011), 'Rating Agencies Inch Closer to Historic Downgrade of US Debt', *Wall Street Journal*, 14 July.
Panetta, F (2011), 'The Impact of Sovereign Credit Risk on Bank Funding Conditions', Study Group for Committee on the Global Financial Settlement, Bank for International Settlements, CFGS Papers No. 43, pp. 20–23.
Partnoy, F (2009), 'Overdependence on Credit Ratings Was a Primary Cause of the Crisis', San Diego Legal Studies Paper No. 09–015, *Proceedings of the 2008 International Banking Conference, The First Credit Market Turmoil of the 21st Century*, World Scientific Publishers, pp. 1–2, http://papers.ssrn.com/sol3/papers.cfm?abstract_id=1430653.
Pildes, R H (2009), 'Separation of Powers, Independent Agencies and Financial Regulation: The Case of the Sarbanes-Oxley Act', *New York University Journal of Law & Business*, vol. 5, no. 2, pp. 485, 524–525.
Piraino Jr, T A (2004), 'Regulating Oligopoly Conduct Under the Antitrust Laws', *Minnesota Law Review*, vol. 89, pp. 9, 10–11.
PricewaterhouseCoopers LLP (2010), *A Closer Look: The Dodd-Frank Wall Street Reform and Consumer Protection Act: Impact on Credit Rating Agencies*.
Rönsberg, A (2011), 'S&P Warning Puts Damper on Eurogroup Plans', *Deutsche Welle*, 7 May.

Roxburgh, C, Lund, S & Piotrowski, J (2011), *Mapping Global Capital Markets 2011*, Report, McKinsey Global Institute, p. 24, Exhibit 12.

Sale, H A (2006), 'Independent Directors as Securities Monitors', *Business Lawyer*, vol. 61, no. 4, pp. 1375, 1378–1379.

Schulz, W & Held, T (2001), *Regulated Self-Regulation as a Form of Modern Government*, Hans Bredow Institute for Media Research at the University of Hamburg, B-12–B-13.

Securities & Exchange Commission (2012), *Report to Congress on Assigned Credit Ratings*, December, pp. 72–82, http://www.sec.gov/news/studies/2012/assigned-credit-ratings-study.pdf.

Shenn, J & Mildenberg, D (2008), 'Subprime, CDO Bank Losses May Exceed $265 Billion', *Bloomberg*, 31 January.

Sinclair, D (1997), 'Self-Regulation versus Command and Control? Beyond False Dichotomies', *Law & Policy*, vol. 19, no. 4, pp. 529, 531.

Staff of Securities Commission on Homeland Security & Governmental Affairs (2011), Subcommittee on Investigations, 112th Congress, (Wall Street Report) *Wall Street and the Financial Crisis: Anatomy of a Financial Collapse: Majority and Minority Staff* Report, p. 272.

Staikouras, P K (2012), 'A Theoretical and Empirical Review of the EU Regulation on Credit Rating Agencies: In Search of Truth, Not Scapegoats', *Financial Markets, Institutions and Instruments*, vol. 21, no. 2, pp. 71, 72–73.

Standard & Poor's (2012), *Standard & Poor's Takes Various Rating Actions on 16 Eurozone Sovereign Governments*, 13 January, http://www.standardandpoors.com/ratings/articles/en/us/?articleType=HTML&assetID=124532729476

Standard & Poor's (2013), *Credit FAQ: An Overview Of Standard & Poor's Sovereign Rating Criteria Update*, 26 June, http://www.standardandpoors.com/spf/upload/Ratings_US/SovereignGovernmentRatingMethodologyAndAssumptionsFAQ.pdf, pp. 2–3.

Standard & Poor's (2012), *European Sovereign Ratings and Related Materials*, http://www.standardandpoors.com/ratings/sovereign-actions/en/us.

Stefanadis, C (2003), 'Self-Regulation, Innovation, and the Financial Industry', *Journal of Regulatory Economics*, vol. 23, no. 1, pp. 5, 6–8.

Sunstein, C (1985), 'Interest Groups in American Public Law', *Stanford Law Review*, vol. 38, no. 1, pp. 29, 38–45.

United States Government Accountability Office (2010), *Securities and Exchange Commission: Action Needed to Improve Rating Agency Registration Program and Performance-Related Disclosures*, GAO-10–782, pp. 79–93, http://www.gao.gov/products/GAO-10–782.

United States Government Accountability Office (2012), *Credit Rating Agencies: Alternative Compensation Models for Nationally Recognized Statistical Rating Organizations*, GAO-12–240, pp. 8–14, http://www.gao.gov/products/GAO-12–240.

United States Securities and Exchange Commission (2008), *Summary Report of Issues Identified in the Commission Staff's Examinations of Select Credit Rating Agencies* (1–2 July).

United States Securities and Exchange Commission (2014), *Mortgage-Backed Securities*, http://www.sec.gov/answers/mortgagesecurities.htm.

Viswanatha, A & Stempel, J (2013), 'S&P Expects US Lawsuit Over Pre-Crisis Credit Ratings', *Reuters*, 4 February.

Warren, E & Westbrook, J L (2005), 'Contracting Out of Bankruptcy: An Empirical Intervention', *Harvard Law Review*, vol. 118, pp. 1197, 1237–1238.

Warren, M (2012), 'Argentine Leader Challenges Critics in US', *Businessweek*, September 24.

Weisman, J (2013), 'Senate Ends Budge Debate, Clearing Way to Passage', *New York Times*, 17 December.

Wise, P (2012), 'Portugal Condemns "Inconsistent" S&P Downgrade', *Financial Times*, 15 January.

8

A Framework for Understanding the Acceptability of Rating Agency Methodologies

Nigel Finch

Introduction

The objective of this paper is to explore the academic and other literature associated with the development and practices of international rating agencies and to develop a framework to understand the various rating agency methodologies.

These objectives are achieved in the chapter via three sections. Section 1 generally provides an introduction into international rating agencies and their historical development. From this, it is determined that the majority of international rating agencies are concerned with the financial markets, especially credit ratings. Also it is established that international rating agencies can affect behaviour in various ways including performance disclosure, changing general strategies, and financial strategies.

In Section 2, the academic literature relating to this topic is examined across five main areas: (1) the types of rating products; (2) identifying possible changes in company behaviour, especially disclosure, because of international rating agencies; (3) the motivations for companies to increase disclosure; (4) the independence of rating agencies; and (5) the independence of auditors in their role of issuing an opinion on company disclosures.

Section 3 examines the issues associated with independence for a rating agency and the acceptability of their ratings by using the auditor independence framework. The three rating methodologies (solicited, unsolicited, and co-operative) are also analysed to determine the acceptability of each method. This is done by examining the following: (1) the extent to which the rating agency is able to maintain independence;

(2) avoid conflict of interests; and (3) obtain reliable information to make an informed rating opinion. It finds that co-operative rating is the most acceptable rating methodology.

1 Introduction to international rating agencies

In the 1990s, the importance of international rating agencies became more pronounced among investors, creditors, regulators, and other stakeholders who were interested in screening companies based on specific financial criteria. In this period, rating agencies experienced growth and developed new ratings products (Cantor & Packer, 1996).

Worldwide, there are numerous rating agencies providing financial ratings; however, the rating industry counts only two major world players, both originating in the United States: Moody's Investor Services and Standard & Poor's (S&P). They have become global following the dramatic growth of international financial markets and an increasing reliance upon credit ratings (Cantor & Packer, 1994).

The six major financial rating types and the focus of these ratings are shown below in Table 8.1:

A brief description of each of the six rating types is provided below:

1.1 Life insurance ratings

Life insurance ratings rank the solvency of life insurance companies and for stakeholders, such as policy holders and life insurance agents, provide a convenient reference point for comparing insurers.

1.2 Credit ratings

Credit ratings are the most popular type of rating and rank the probability of default for a corporate issuer of debt, such as a private sector organisation or a public sector agency. Credit rating agencies are an

Table 8.1 Major financial rating types and their focus

Rating type	Focus of rating
Life Insurance	Solvency
Credit	Default Risk (corporation)
Mutual Fund	Performance
Sovereign	Default Risk (nation)
Corporate Governance	Performance
Sustainability	Performance

integral part of modern capital markets, and their ratings are used as benchmarks by regulators, lenders, and investors.

1.3 Mutual fund ratings

Mutual fund ratings rank the probability of excess investment performance of investment funds within the same asset class. For investors and their advisers, mutual fund ratings offer a way to monitor the performance of individual fund managers and asset classes within the growing managed investments market.

1.4 Sovereign ratings

Sovereign ratings rank the probability of risk of default of a sovereign country's obligation to repay its foreign debt. These ratings also set the maximum credit rating achievable for state and municipal agencies within that country's jurisdiction.

1.5 Corporate governance ratings

Corporate governance ratings rank the probity of information and decision-making systems within listed and multinational corporations. These ratings provide an assessment of an organisation's performance based on the effectiveness of its command and control systems.

1.6 Sustainability ratings

Sustainability ratings rank organisations' effectiveness at meeting the expectations of stakeholders while maintaining sustainable financial, environmental, and social performance. These ratings provide an assessment of an organisation's ability to deliver a sustainable future.

Currently, the ratings provided by international agencies such as Standard & Poor's and Moody's have become the default financial screening tools for rating risk and performance, and have become part of the essential lexicon of the corporate and investing community. As achieving and maintaining a favourable rating for a corporation is so important, ratings are seen as a key influencer in corporate behaviour (Dillemburg, Greene & Erekson, 2003). For example, the chief executive of the recently restructured Australian insurance company AMP announced that before the company embarked on any major acquisition strategy, the company wanted to improve its standing with international rating agencies (Barnett, 2004: 28). To achieve this improvement in standing, AMP plans to use surplus cash to pay down debt over the next 12 to 18 months. Lowering debt levels will affect its credit rating and AMP wants to achieve a minimum of an 'A' credit rating at a group level and an 'AA' rating at an AMP Life level. It is predicted that this will lower its cost of capital and improve its image for shareholders. Recently, part of AMP's corporate strategy was to achieve growth by acquisition. However, AMP is deferring the next step in rolling out its strategy until its debt levels are low enough to qualify for a higher credit rating and life rating (Barnett, 2004: 28). Part of the rating criteria used in these rating types is to factor into the rating a score based on debt levels (source: www.standardandpoors.com). The higher the debt levels, the lower the rating. In this example, the credit and insurance ratings are key influencers in AMP's corporate behaviour (i.e., its decision to defer acquisitions and instead focus on debt reduction).

Organisations in the 21st century are surrounded by ratings. An insurance company manages its activities carefully to maintain or improve its A.M. Best rating, as that rating significantly impacts its ability to sell insurance products to the market. A corporation with debt is extremely interested in the Standard & Poor's or Moody's rating it receives, as that rating affects the company's cost of capital. An investment manager of a mutual fund company manages its investment products to obtain the highest Morningstar ratings possible, as it will capture increased market share of the investment fund flows (Dillenburg, Greene, & Erekson, 2003: 172). Achieving a favourable rating is extremely important to companies because the ratings ultimately affect what products they can buy or sell, in what markets and at what prices (Cantor & Packer, 1995), which ultimately influences the profitability of the firm. All of these examples are of common rating schemes that measure financial ratings of companies and have an impact in influencing corporate behaviour.

2 Review of research relating to rating agencies

The aim of this section is to explore the academic and other literature associated with the development and practices of rating agencies. This section will briefly review prior research relating to rating agencies and examine auditor independence frameworks.

Historically, the majority of studies on rating agencies have tended to focus on the rating type, and how rating agencies rate firms differently around the world (e.g., Ferri, Lui, & Stiglitz, 1999; Monfort & Mulder, 2000; Cantor & Packer, 1994, 1996). Recently, new research has emerged that has looked at the influence ratings have on corporate behaviour. This area of research, and the literature explaining the contemporary trends in company disclosures, will now be examined.

Dillenburg et al. (2003: 171) state that financial ratings can affect corporate behaviour to the extent that they are subject to ratings, over time, changing their management practices and their level and type of disclosure in an attempt to better satisfy the rating criteria.

Ratings, especially insurance and credit ratings such as solvency and risk, are extremely important to companies because ultimately the ratings affect what products they can buy or sell, in what markets and at what prices (Cantor & Packer, 1995). For example, the credit rating that a company receives will determine which trading partners it will deal with, the cost of its capital, and ultimately the profitability and market value of the company. It should be no surprise that companies modify their behaviour to suit a higher score in these types of ratings.

Another factor that is affecting the behaviours of companies is the level of disclosure and transparency it makes to its stakeholders. This ultimately affects how the company is perceived in terms of economic and social metrics. Social metrics are how the stakeholders view the corporation's behaviour relative to acceptable standards regarding environmental, ethical, and social performance. This is often referred to as sustainability. Also, there has been a considerable amount of research undertaken into the correlation between the financial performance of a company and its disclosure regarding its CSR practices and the transparency of its corporate governance. While the conclusions of this research remain contested between business and academia, there is a growing body of credible evidence to suggest that there is a link between increased financial performance and increased levels of CSR disclosure and transparency (Bauer, Gunter, & Otten, 2003; Gompers, Ishii, & Metrick, 2003; Harrison & Freeman, 1999).

It is not just academics who are highlighting the link between disclosure and performance, but investors too. McKinsey's (2000) *Investor Opinion Survey on Corporate Governance* identified that three-quarters of investors believe that board practices are at least as important as financial performance when evaluating companies for investment. This McKinsey survey highlights that the majority of investors place Socially Responsible Investing (SRI) on par with or ahead of the financial performance of their investments.

With the changes in attitudes towards transparency and disclosure, especially from investors, and a greater appetite for socially responsible investing (Greene, 2003), companies are becoming more interested in these social metrics.

SRI in Australia continued to grow, rising to at least $21.3 billion in funds under management by 30 June 2003, an increase of 54% from

2002. The number of SRI managed funds has also increased substantially. In 1996, there were 10 SRI managed funds, and in 2003, this had grown to 63 managed funds (Greene, 2003).

In meeting this growing demand in SRI investment, new specialised products have been developed to track the performance of this new investment style. One of these is the Dow Jones Sustainability Index (DJSI), which has consistently outperformed the Dow Jones Industrial World Index (DJGI). For example, the total return on the index for the period December 1993 to February 2004 is 153% for DJSI and 108% for DJGI (*source*: www.sustainability-index.com). This is often cited as evidence that there is a link between increased financial performance of a firm and corporate social responsibility (Bauer et al., 2003; Brown & Caylor, 2004, Gompers et al., 2003; Hamid & Sandford, 2002; Harrison & Freeman, 1999; Pava & Krausz, 1996; Roman, Hayobor, & Agle, 1999; Waddock & Graves, 1997).

Internationally, companies are changing their behaviour and using disclosure and transparency as a strategy for gaining competitive advantage (Geld & Strawser, 2001; Fowler, 2002; Uren, 2003; Wilson, 2004). These companies are using their disclosure and reporting practices to differentiate their products and services, gain access to new markets, reduce their cost of capital, and improve their stock prices and their financial performance.

This change in corporate behaviour and reporting practices has been bought about by new economic and social disclosure frameworks, which focus around the voluntary disclosure of information by a company (Geld & Strawser, 2001). Frameworks such as Triple Bottom Line (TBL) and the Global Reporting Initiative (GRI) provide a means for a company to voluntarily disclose information to its stakeholders on a range of economic, environmental, and social metrics. Another catalyst for a change in corporate behaviour is the introduction of financial rating agencies specialising in measuring a company's performance against a range of social metrics.

Increasing stakeholder preferences for responsible and sustainable corporate behaviour (Greene, 2003) has spearheaded a new investment style, called Socially Responsible Investment (SRI), where investment is directed to those corporations who not only satisfy certain financial criteria, but also operate a business on a reliable, sustainable, and desirable basis that respects ethical values, people, communities, and the environment. SRI is slowly unfolding from a self-referential paradigm of screening to a comprehensive paradigm of seeking to modify corporate behaviour.

Another area in the literature that has received some attention has been the area of independence and rating methodologies. Rating methodologies can be classified as either paid (solicited) or unpaid (unsolicited or co-operative). The issue of a payment to a rating agency may: (1) create a conflict of interest between the rated company and the rating agency and (2) provide a less accurate rating.

Because the rating agency receives a payment from the rated company when a solicited rating methodology is used, there exists the possibility of a conflict of interest. This conflict of interest can create an upward bias in the rating result, hence providing a less accurate rating (Cantor & Packer, 1997; Winnie, 2003). This accuracy issue is not present in unsolicited or co-operative ratings.

Maintaining independence for a ratings agency is important as this will influence the acceptability of the rater's opinion in relation to a company's disclosures. Another area in the academic literature where the independence and acceptability of an opinion regarding company disclosures is vitally important is the area of audit independence.

2.1 The importance of auditor independence

The auditing of financial statements is an essential part of the framework, which supports capital markets and other activities. The auditor's opinion adds value to the financial statement disclosures provided by a company through the independent verification it provides (Johnstone, Sutton, & Warfield, 2001). If the auditor is not seen to act independently of the company, then the audit opinion loses its value to the stakeholders. They argue that auditor independence is fundamental to public confidence in the audit process and the acceptability by stakeholders of auditors' reports.

The collapse of Enron and the demise of Andersen have generally undermined confidence in the world's capital markets. Concern has focused on accounting and auditing practices, and particularly on the independence of auditors (Pound, Gay, & Simnett, 2002).

A significant and persistent criticism of auditors through the academic literature is that the provision by auditors of non-audit advisory services to companies undermines the independence of the audit. Four issues relating to the independence of the auditor have been identified (see Antle, 1984; ICAEW, 2000; Shockley, 1981; Pringle & Bushman, 1996). These four issues are: (1) the remuneration model of the audit firm; (2) the level of non-audit advisory services provided by the auditor to the company; (3) the procedures for issuing and varying an audit opinion; and (4) the existence of conflicts of interest between the two parties.

These audit independence issues are managed through both ethical codes of conduct and legislation. In Australia, for example, the CLERP 9 audit reform proposals are a legislative move designed to improve auditor independence. These reforms include a disclosure by the company in the annual report of non-audit advisory income, and a mandatory statement issued by the audit committee stating that they are satisfied that the provision of non-audit advisory services is compatible with auditor independence.

There are several similarities between the roles of auditors and financial rating agencies. Both issue opinions based on company disclosures; both are fundamental to the operation of financial markets; both have the capacity to affect the behaviour of a company; and both need to maintain independence to ensure acceptability of their opinions. It is for these reasons that this paper will, in Section 3, analyse the issues of independence in rating agencies from the framework of audit independence.

3 Independence in rating agencies

The aim of this section is to develop a framework to understand the various rating agency methodologies. This is achieved by focusing on the issues affecting the independence of rating agencies using an audit independence framework. We also analyse the three rating methodologies 'solicited', 'unsolicited', and 'co-operative'; compare their independence and acceptability; and summarise the acceptability of the rating methodologies before concluding:

> Maintaining independence for a rating agency is essential in protecting its credibility and ensuring that the objectivity of its judgment is not impaired because of its remuneration model, corporate relationships, conflicts of interest, or ownership.

Because a rated company may pay a fee to the rater, this does not in itself create an actual conflict of interest (i.e., a conflict that impairs the objectivity of the rater's judgment and is reflected in their rating). Rather, it is more appropriate to classify it as a potential conflict of interest (i.e., something that should be disclosed and managed to ensure that it does not become an actual conflict).

The revenue model common among many rating agencies comes from two principal sources: (a) the sale of subscriptions to their research and (b) fees paid by companies for the solicited ratings. This revenue model is analogous to members of the media that derive revenue from: (a) subscribers and (b) advertisers that include companies covered in their publications.

Take for example the issue of independence and conflict of interest in a media company that derives revenue from its subscribers and advertisers that include companies they cover. For a media company, maintaining independent, unbiased coverage of the companies they cover is important to subscribers and the marketplace in general.

Making opinions about the acceptability of financial statement disclosures is the role of the auditor, and audit independence is an area that has revived attention in the academic literature. For this reason, the audit independence framework will be used to identify issues of independence in rating agencies.

In determining if a ratings agency is independent of the company that it rates, four factors from the audit independence framework should be considered: (1) the remuneration model of the ratings agency; (2) the level of advisory services provided by the agency to the company; (3) the internal procedures of the ratings agency for issuing and varying a rating; and (4) the existence of conflicts of interest between the two parties. Each of these factors will be briefly described below:

3.1 Remuneration model of the rating agency

Many independent rating agencies manage potential conflict through their remuneration policies. For example, the revenue received by a ratings agency from a company that is rated by their analyst is not a factor in that analyst's compensation. Instead, an analyst's compensation is a function of performance metrics, such as the quality and timeliness of research.

3.2 Level of advisory services provided by the agency to the company

Rating agencies are seen as being independent where they do not have an advisory relationship with the companies they rate. This is similar to one of the principal requirements to protect the independence of auditor firms and their audit clients. This exclusion of an advisory relationship is a means by which the rating agency always maintains full independence, and its revenue model is not based on the success of, or tied to, the level of the rating issued, and the level of fee charged to a company is not dependent on the ratings assigned.

3.3 Procedures for issuing and varying a rating

Rating agencies maintain an independence from their clients where there are clear procedures for varying the rating where the circumstances of the rated company change. This ensures that the rating agency is at complete liberty to issue a different rating if circumstances change between, say, the issuance of the conditional rating and the final rating.

3.4 Existence of conflicts of interest

Conflicts of interest can arise from the remuneration model used by the rating agency (Cantor & Packer, 1997; Winnie, 2003), but they can also arise from the ownership structure. For example, the rating agency is owned or controlled by the company being rated. Rating agencies are seen as independent where there is no conflict of interest because of their ownership.

Next we will focus on the independence of rating agencies by using the framework developed in the audit independence literature to analyse their methodologies.

Ratings issued by a rating agency can generally be classified as solicited, unsolicited, or co-operative. This classification is used to distinguish the rating methodology upon three key attributes: (1) whether the company being rated has requested the rating; (2) whether the company being rated has paid the agency for the rating; and (3) whether the information source used by the rating agency relies on confidential and non-public information. The co-operative rating is a form of unsolicited rating where the rated organisation co-operates with the rating agency to provide additional sources of non-public information. This co-operation by the company to provide additional information helps to improve the reliability of the rating and therefore its acceptability to users.

Solicited ratings differ from unsolicited ratings in that the company seeking a rating requests the services of an agency to review its operations and issue a rating. An unrequested or unsolicited rating is where the rating agency issues a rating for a company, regardless of whether the company has requested the service or not. The co-operative rating is a form of unrequested or unsolicited rating. The compensation structure, hence agency framework, for unsolicited ratings differs markedly from solicited ratings in that the rating agency is not compensated by the firm for an unsolicited rating, whereas solicited ratings are almost entirely paid for by the rated organisation. As a co-operative rating is a form of unsolicited rating, the rating agency is not compensated for performing the rating service. The information source, hence rating methodologies, for unsolicited ratings differs markedly from solicited ratings in that an unsolicited rating is purely a statistical rating based on publicly available information published by the rated company (see Figure 8.1 below). With a co-operative rating, the rating agency relies on publicly available information as its primary source, plus supplementary information that may include surveys, interviews, and other types of specifically requested non-public data.

A comparison of the independence of rating methodologies is provided in Table 8.2 below.

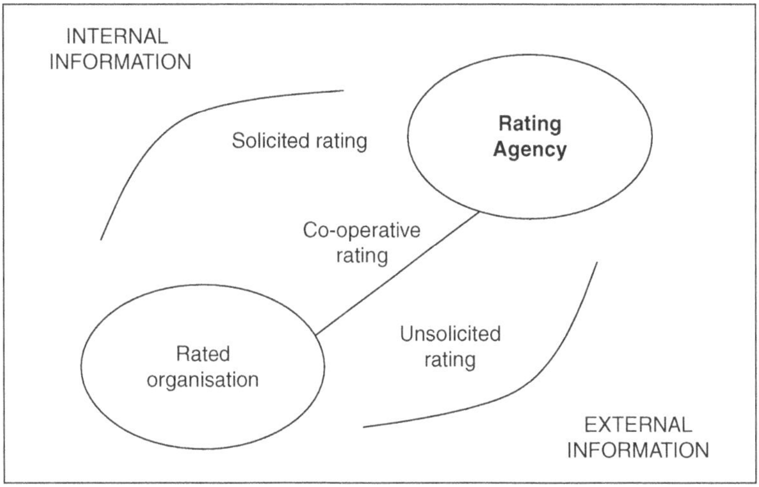

Figure 8.1 Information sources for solicited, unsolicited, and co-operative ratings

Table 8.2 Comparison of the independence of rating methodologies

	Solicited	**Unsolicited**	**Co-operative**
Requested by rated company	Yes	No	No
Payment to rating agency	Yes	No	No
Information source	Company confidential information	Public domain only	Public domain and company confidential
Maintained independence	No	Yes	Yes

Comparing the three different rating methodologies, it can be concluded that under the solicited rating method the rating agency has: (1) a more reliable information source to form an opinion; however, (2) it is unable to maintain its independence because of the existence of conflicts of interest, particularly in relation to the terms of its engagement and the payment it receives. These issues of independence are not typical under an unsolicited or co-operative rating methodology. Issues such as these will affect the acceptability of the rating method.

The acceptability of the rating is ultimately the measure of its success, and this will be influenced by two key factors. The first issue affecting the acceptability of the rating methodology is maintaining independence and avoiding conflicts of interest. This issue has already been examined above Section 3. The second issue that influences the acceptability of the rating methodology is the range of relevant information that is relied upon in forming the rating opinion.

Different rating methodologies rely on different information sources to determine the rating (see Table 8.3 below), and this source of information will ultimately determine the acceptability of the rating. Unsolicited ratings rely entirely on information in the public domain and, as such, the ability of the rating agency to issue an accurate rating is determined by the range of relevant information and the timeliness of the information that has been publicly disclosed by the company. Where a company does not disclose information into the public domain that is required by the rater's rating criteria, it is probable that any rating opinion that may be issued was not formed using all relevant information. This absence of information creates an acceptability issue for stakeholders relying on the rating. This acceptability issue is not present in solicited or co-operative ratings.

A summary of the acceptability of the rating methodologies is shown in Table 8.3 below:

Table 8.3 Comparison of acceptability of different rating methodologies

	Solicited	**Unsolicited**	**Co-operative**
Conflict of interest	Yes	No	No
Range of information	Yes	No	Yes
Acceptable methodology	No	No	Yes

In summary, the co-operative rating type can be seen as being a more acceptable methodology because this method avoids any potential conflict of interest while maintaining a high degree of reliability in the information source.

4 Conclusion

Rating agencies' methodologies are classified as solicited, unsolicited, or co-operative depending upon: (1) whether the rating has been requested; (2) whether the rating agency receives a payment; and (3) what information source the agency uses to form its opinion. These different methodologies will affect the level of independence the agency has in forming an unbiased and objective opinion, and ultimately this will affect the acceptability of the rating. The unsolicited and co-operative rating methods allow for independence to be maintained because independence is largely driven by agency remuneration. Ultimately, the most acceptable rating methodology is the co-operative rating method because of the greater reliability of the information source that is used in forming the rating opinion.

References

Antle, R (1984), 'Auditor Independence', *Journal of Accounting Research*, vol. 22, no. 1, pp. 1–20.

Barnett, D (2004), 'AMP to Work on Ratings', *Herald-Sun*, 8 March, News Ltd, p. 28.

Bauer R, Gunter N & Otten R (2003), 'Empirical Evidence on Corporate Governance in Europe: The Effect on Stock Returns, Firm Valuation and Performance', *Journal of Asset Management*, vol. 3, no. 4, pp. 296–314.

Brown, D L & Caylor M L (2004), *Corporate Governance Study: The Correlation between Corporate Governance and Company Performance*, Corporate Governance Study, Institutional Shareholder Services.

Cantor, R & Packer F (1994), 'The Credit Rating Industry', *Federal Reserve Bank of New York Quarterly Review*, Summer-Fall, vol. 19, no. 2, pp. 1–26.

Cantor, R & Packer F (1995), 'The Credit Rating Industry', *The Journal of Fixed Income*, vol. 5, no. 3 (December), pp. 10–34.

Cantor, R & Packer, F (1996), 'Determinants and Impacts of Sovereign Credit Ratings', *Economic Policy Review*, Federal Reserve Bank of New York, vol. 2, no. 2 (October), pp. 37–53.

Cantor, R & Packer, F (1997), 'Difference of Opinion and Selection Bias in the Credit Rating Industry, *Journal of Banking & Finance*, vol. 21, no. 10, pp. 1395–1417.

Dillenburg, S, Greene, T & Erekson, H (2003), 'Approaching Socially Responsible Investment with a Comprehensive Ratings Scheme: Total Social Impact', *Journal of Business Ethics*, vol. 43, no. 3, pp. 167–182.

Ferri, G, Liu L & Stiglitz, J (1999), 'The Procyclical Role of Rating Agencies: Evidence from the East Asian Crisis', *Economic Notes*, vol. 28, no. 3, pp. 335–356.

Fowler, G (2002), 'Sustainability Reporting — A Global Framework', *Company Director*, November, Sydney.

Geld, D S & Strawser, J A (2001), 'Corporate Social Responsibility and Financial Disclosures: An Alternative Explanation for Increased Disclosure', *Journal of Business Ethics*, vol. 1, no. 33, pp. 1–13.

Gompers, P A, Ishii, L J & Metrick, A (2003), 'Corporate Governance & Equity Prices', *Quarterly Journal Of Economics*, vol. 118, no. 1, pp. 107–158.

Greene, D (2003), *Socially Responsible Investment in Australia*, Ethical Investment Association, Sydney.

Hamid, N & Sandford, Y (2002), *Portfolio, Index & Futures Research: Are SRI Indices Responsible?*, European Equities Research, Deutsche Bank AG.

Harrison, J S & Freeman, R E (1999), 'Stakeholders, Social Responsibility and Performance: Empirical Evidence and Theoretical Perspectives', *Academy of Management Journal*, vol. 42, no. 5, pp. 479–486.

ICAEW (2000), *Review of Guidance on Auditor Independence*, Institute of Chartered Accountants in England & Wales, London.

Johnstone, K M, Sutton, M H & Warfield, T D (2001), 'Antecedents and Consequences of Independence Risk: Framework for Analysis', *Accounting Horizons*, vol. 15, no. 1 (March), pp.1–18.

McKinsey & Company (2000), *Investor Opinion Survey on Corporate Governance*, McKinsey & Company, London, UK.

Monfort, B & Mulder, C (2000), 'The Impact of Using Sovereign Ratings by Credit Rating Agencies on the Capital Requirements for Banks: A Study of Emerging Market Economies', IMF Working Paper, WP/00/69, March.

Pava, M L & Krausz, J (1996), 'The Association Between Corporate Social Responsibility and Financial Performance: The Paradox of Social Cost', *Journal of Business Ethics*, vol. 3, no. 15, pp. 321–357.

Pound, G, Gay, G & Simnett, R (2002), *Auditing Concepts and Methods*, McGraw-Hill, Sydney.

Pringle, L M & Bushman, T A (1996), 'An Examination of Independence in Fact when Auditors Perform Nonaudit Services for Audit Clients', *Accounting Enquiries*, vol. 6, no. 1 (August), pp. 91–120.

Roman, R M, Hayobor, S & Agle, B R (1999), 'The Relationship between Social and Financial Performance', *Business and Society*, vol. 38, no. 1, pp. 109–126.

Shockley, R A (1981), 'Perceptions of Auditors' Independence: An Empirical Analysis', *The Accounting Review*, vol. 56, no. 4 (October), pp. 785–800.

Uren, D (2003), *The Transparent Corporation: Managing Demands for Disclosure*, Allen & Unwin, Sydney.

Waddock, S & Graves, S (1997), 'The Corporate Social Performance–Financial Performance Link', *Strategic Management Journal*, vol. 18, no. 4, pp. 303–319.

Winnie, P H P (2003), 'Are Unsolicited Credit Ratings Biased Downwards?', *Journal of Banking & Finance*, vol. 27, no. 4, pp. 193–614.

Wilson, S (2004), 'In Good Governance, Westpac Lights the Way', *The Australian*, 17 February, p. 25.

9

Sovereign Wealth Funds and Investment Law

Mauro Megliani

1 Introduction

The term 'sovereign wealth fund' (SWF) covers a wide spectrum of State-owned investment vehicles which have in common to be funded from budget surpluses but which diverge in purposes, strategies, assets, investment choice, and legal form. As their investment strategies are mainly focused on foreign financial assets, this definition necessarily excludes those funds which invest solely in domestic assets. The investment in foreign assets may be distinguished in portfolio investment and in direct investment: the latter enables the investor to exert a certain influence on the target enterprise, where the former consists of purchasing bonds or equity for pure return purposes without the intention to influence the management of the enterprise.

Initially, SWFs merely sought profitable assets abroad in which to invest budget surpluses. This scenario evolved rapidly on the wave of the financial crisis, which made enterprises from Western nations crave fresh capital; consequently, SWFs have become ever more involved in direct investment. The trend is well-exemplified by the so-called Chinese 'Go Global Strategy'. In 2007, the Chinese Government incorporated the China Investment Corporation (CIC) to manage part of its massive foreign exchange reserves. CIC has since evolved from a traditional SWF into the centre of a web of investment, direct and indirect alike. This evolution has marked a change in investment strategies: on the one hand, CIC has moved progressively from investments in the financial sector to investments in natural resources; on the other hand, investments in large companies have been expanded from preferred stock to common stock which enables CIC to exert an influence on their management.[1]

It is self-evident that this tendency has raised some concerns. Fearing to see strategic sectors falling under foreign influence, host countries – mostly developed and industrialised ones – have adopted regulatory measures. Perhaps the most significant of these coincides with the Foreign Investment and National Securities Act (FINSA), enacted in 2007 by the US Congress,[2] whose operation is centred on the Committee on Foreign Investment in the United States (CFIUS), empowered to negotiate, impose, and enforce any agreement or condition with any party to a transaction potentially endangering US national security. Other governments have followed a similar route.[3]

From a substantive point of view, regulatory measures may be both preventive and repressive. The former usually consist of submitting to an authorisation process specific transactions such as the acquisition of a certain percentage of stock in a company, while the latter may amount to a freezing or divestiture order such as the limitation or prohibition of exerting voting rights in the acquired shares or the forced sale of the acquired shares.[4] The lawfulness of these measures at the international plane may be investigated against multilateral free trade treaties and bilateral investment treaties. As multilateral rules appear unsuited in relation to the phenomenon, the analysis will concentrate on the applicability of bilateral rules on expropriation to host States' repressive measures. In this connection the following issues will be examined: the capacity of SWFs to institute arbitral proceedings before the International Centre for the Settlement of Investment Dispute (ICSID), the evaluation of repressive measures in the light of the investment rules protecting foreign assets, and the subsumption of those measures under the emergency clause as Non-Precluded Measures.

2 The ICSID jurisdiction

Normally, Bilateral Investment Treaties (BITs) contain arbitration clauses for an *ad hoc* arbitration or the submission to the International Centre for the Settlement of Investment Dispute (ICSID). The majority of cases are settled under the ICSID framework.[5] The ICSID jurisdiction is based upon the fulfilment of three conditions: nationality of the parties, consent to submit, and investment disputes (Art. 25 ICSID Convention). With reference to the first condition, Article 25, para. 2 establishes that the dispute must involve a State party to the Convention and a national of another State. Juridical persons must possess the nationality of any contracting State other than the State party to the dispute on the date on which the parties have consented to submit to arbitration or, if having the nationality of the contracting State on that date, the parties have agreed to be treated as nationals of another contracting State because of foreign control.[6] The term 'juridical persons' may include even State-owned companies as long as they act in commercial capacity and not under governmental control.[7] In relation to SWFs, two problems arise: the legal framework and the governmental influence. As regards the legal framework, usually SWFs fall into one of the following typologies. (1) A separate legal entity with full capacity to act and governed by a specific constitutive law (e.g., Kuwait, Korea, Qatar, and the United Arab Emirates): generally, these SWFs are legal entities incorporated under public law. (2) A state-owned corporation (e.g., Singapore's Temasek and Government of Singapore Investment Corporation, or China's China Investment Corporation): although these corporations are typically governed by domestic company law, SWF-specific laws may also apply. (3) A pool of assets without a separate legal identity owned by the State or the central bank (e.g., Botswana, Canada (Alberta), Chile, and Norway):[8] as it is deprived of any separate personality, this third category does not satisfy the conditions of Article 25(2). In relation to governmental influence, the watershed is constituted by a clearly-defined policy purpose which would facilitate the formulation of appropriate investment strategies based on economic and financial objectives and would also ensure that the operational management of the SWF will conduct itself professionally and that SWFs will undertake investments without any intention or obligation to fulfil, directly or indirectly, any geopolitical agenda of the government. Public disclosure of the SWF's policy purpose would provide a better understanding of what SWFs seek to achieve and whether their behaviour is consistent with the specified purpose.[9] However, although SWFs generally base their operations on economic evaluation, it is impossible to exclude a political influence whose presence should be subject to a close case-by-case analysis.

With reference to the second condition, the consent to submit to the ICSID by the foreign State must be expressed in written form and formalised in an investment contract or a special *compromis* between the host State and foreign investors, or in an offer of the foreign State encapsulated in a host State legislation, a multilateral treaty, or a bilateral investment treaty (BIT).[10] In this connection, it is necessary to distinguish between 'treaty claims' and 'contract claims', with the former based on the violation of a BIT and the latter on a violation of the investment contract. In this respect, in *SGS v. Pakistan*, the arbitral Tribunal held that the presence of a domestic arbitral clause contained in investment contracts did not affect ICSID jurisdiction relating to a treaty claim,[11] while in *SGS v. Philippines*, the arbitral tribunal refused to exercise jurisdiction on contract claims in presence of an exclusive forum selection clause in the investment contract.[12]

With reference to the third condition, although neither the text of the Convention nor the Report of the Executive Directors contain a definition,[13] a notion of investment may be inferred from the preamble of the Convention where there is a clear reference to the need for international co-operation for economic development and to the role played by private investment in this respect. In *Fedax v. Venezuela*, the arbitral tribunal found that the basic features of an investment involve a certain duration, a certain regularity of profit and return, assumption of risk, a substantial commitment, and a significance for the host State's development.[14] As for shares in foreign companies, the ICSID tribunal case law has accepted shareholding as a form of investment in its various declinations: from minority shareholding,[15] to indirect shareholding through an intermediate company.[16] In this connection, it is to be emphasised that the investment requirement must satisfy a dual test: both under the ICSID Convention and under the BIT (or other instrument encapsulating the consent of the parties), where shares are usually enumerated as a form of protected investment.[17]

3 Repressive measures and their qualification

Once it has been established that ICSID tribunals have jurisdiction on the dispute, the question to ascertain is whether or not a repressive measure may amount to a form of expropriation.[18] Repressive measures are subsumable under the notion of indirect expropriation, that is, a form of expropriation which, although not substantiating in a physical taking, may still amount to a taking resulting in the effective loss of management, use, or control of the investment assets.[19] This type of expropriation is specifically addressed in the BITs which contain a reference to indirect expropriation or measures equivalent to expropriation or nationalisation.[20]

Indirect expropriation has two sub-species: creeping expropriation and regulatory takings. The former amounts to a slow and incremental interference with one or more of the ownership rights of a foreign investor who, although retaining the formal title, sees his rights of use of the property diminished as a result of the interference;[21] the latter embraces those takings of property that fall within the police powers of a State, or otherwise arise from State measures like those pertaining to the regulation of the environment, health, morals, culture, or economy of a host country.[22] Although as a matter of principle the distinction is clear, international law has yet to draw a clear line between non-compensable regulations expression of police powers and measures that have the effect of depriving foreign investors of their investment and are thus compensable.[23]

The point is well-captured in *Feldman v. Mexico*, where the arbitral tribunal, distinguishing between pure expropriatory measures and regulatory activity (under which governments are free to act in the broader public interest through protection of the environment, new or modified tax regimes, the granting or withdrawal of government subsidies, reductions or increases in tariff levels, the imposition of zoning restrictions, and the like), found that reasonable governmental regulations of this type cannot be achieved if any business that is adversely affected may seek compensation.[24] This holding is consonant with the customary international law rule pursuant to which 'a state is not responsible for loss of property or for other economic disadvantage resulting from bona fide general taxation, regulation, forfeiture for crime, or other action of the kind that is commonly accepted as within the police power of states'.[25] Nevertheless, in the field of investment law, arbitral tribunals are called to deal with many expropriatory measures disguised as regulation with the purpose of avoiding the obligation to compensate.[26] Facing this problem, ICSID tribunals, on the one hand, have found that regulatory measures – 'no matter how laudable and beneficial to the society as whole' – are tantamount to any other takings with the result that the State's obligation to pay remains unaffected,[27] while on the other hand, have given prevalence to BITs as treaty law on customary international law, confirming the obligation to compensate.[28]

This rigid line of reasoning has been recently tempered by a number of arbitral decisions introducing a sort of balance of interests between the right of the host state to enact regulatory measures and the right of investors to have their investment protected. As a matter of principle, in *Tecmed v. Mexico*, the arbitral tribunal, assuming that 'there must be a reasonable relationship of proportionality between the charge or weight imposed to the foreign investor and the aim sought to be realised by any expropriatory measure', found that 'to value such charge or weight, it is very important to measure the size of the ownership deprivation caused by the actions of the state and whether such deprivation was compensated or not'.[29] The issue of the balancing has been further developed in *LG & E v. Argentina*, where the arbitral tribunal took into consideration two competing interests: the degree of the interference with the right of ownership and the power of the State to regulate the matter. With reference to the first point, the arbitral tribunal examined the economic impact of the measure and its duration. In considering the severity of the economic impact, the tribunal focused its analysis on whether the economic impact of the measure was sufficiently severe as to generate the need for compensation, concluding that interference with the investment's ability to carry on its business is not satisfied where the investment continues to operate, even if profits are reduced. In considering duration, the tribunal found that an expropriation must be permanent, unless the investment's successful development depends on the realisation of certain activities at specific moments that may not bear temporary interferences. With reference to the second point, the arbitral tribunal, recognising that a State has the right to adopt measures having a social or general welfare purpose, held in principle that liability arises whenever the State's action is disproportionate to the need being addressed. In the instant case the arbitral tribunal came to the conclusion that the measure did not amount to expropriation as it did not deprive the investors of the right to enjoy the investment: on the one hand, although the value of the shares may have fluctuated during the economic crisis, the investors never lost control on their shares and were able to direct their business; on the other hand, the effects of the State action were not permanent and the investment continued to exist.[30]

The repressive measures applied to SWFs, consisting of forced sale of shares to the State, forced sales of shares on the market, and reduction of shares' voting rights, are to be assessed against this background. The first two measures are sufficiently severe and definitive to call for a compensation which may be escaped solely insofar as governmental acts are aimed at preserving the control on certain crucial sectors such as defence and certain utilities. Outside this scheme, compensation is due: in relation to forced sale of the shares to the State, as the State acts as a purchaser the shares are to be paid according to the fair market value;[31] in relation to forced sale of shares on the market, if the shares are transferred to a trustee to be sold on the market, the fair market value may be indicated by averaging out the market value of shares during a prolonged period before the market records reveal any substantial public awareness of the forced sale.[32] With reference to reduction of the shares' voting rights, the weak character of the measure does qualify as a regulatory measure, but an obligation to compensate may still arise under expropriation.

4 The BITs' Non-Precluded Measures

Most of the BITs contain a Non-Precluded Measure (NPM) clause capable of justifying an emergency measure in breach of the treaty as long as subsumable under its scope. If the repressive measure qualifies as a regulatory taking, the clause does not apply, while if the measure qualifies as expropriation, the clause may operate as an exemption.

NPM clauses were regularly inserted in the Friendship, Commerce, and Navigation (FCN) treaties stipulated by the United States after the Second World War. From the early FCN treaties, NPM clauses migrated into the international investment arena: the first known investment treaty containing a NPM clause was Germany's first BIT, which was concluded with Pakistan in 1959, while the first US BIT containing such a clause was the one concluded with Panama in 1982.[33] Although to this day NPM clauses appear in most of the BITs, their variegated formulation reflects the similar but not equal wording of the BITs.[34]

Generalising, the structure of the clause is articulated in three elements: the nexus requirements, the scope, and the permissible objectives. As to the nexus requirement, the measure is to be essential to one of the permissible objectives; as to the scope, the NMP clause may either apply to all the terms of the BIT or be confined to some specific provisions; as to the permissible objectives, the intent of the clause is to protect certain sensitive issues of public policy of the host States which could be affected by the obligations under the BITs. The indication of the permissible objectives is not homogeneous: for instance, under the US Model BIT (2012) a party is entitled to apply those measures that it considers necessary with respect to the 'maintenance or restoration of international peace or security, or the protection of its own essential security interests', while in the German Model BIT (2008) the reference is to those measures taken 'for reasons of public security and order'.[35]

Despite their recurrence in BITs, NPM clauses were not much object of an arbitral scrutiny until the investment disputes originated from the Argentine crisis. These controversies were all based upon Article XI of the US-Argentina BIT in whose words the treaty 'shall not preclude the application by either Party of measures necessary for the maintenance of public order, the fulfilment of its obligations with respect to the maintenance or restoration of international peace or security, or the protection of its own essential security interests'.[36] Ruling on this point, the ICSID tribunals rendered divergent decisions in relation to three crucial aspects: the self-judging character of the measure, the question of compensation, and the relationship with necessity under customary international law. As regards the self-judging character of the measure, in *CMS*, *Enron*, and *Sempra* the arbitral tribunals came to the conclusion that, although economic emergency may be covered by the essential security interests clause of the BIT, this determination is not self-judging;[37] although espousing the same view, in *LG&E* the arbitral tribunal held as a matter of principle that, even though the NPM clause were self-judging, Argentina's determination would be subject to a good faith review by the tribunal.[38] This approach, perfectly consistent with the implicitly self-judging nature of the clause in issue, may apply also in connection with explicitly self-judging NPM clauses[39] for at least three reasons: the political underpinnings of a subject matter does not bar international courts from execising jurisdiction; under the Vienna Convention on the Law of Treaties, States are expected to perform their obligations in good faith (Art. 26); and a good faith review may assure a balance of interests between host State power and foreign investors' protection.[40] As regards the question of compensation, most NPM clauses are drafted more as exceptions to BITs' provisions than as a mere justification for breach of obligation, with the result that the formulation of the clause precludes the application of BITs' obligations to measures which fall in the purview of the clause. In other words, the wrongfulness is precluded not so much because the violation of a BIT obligation is justified under certain circumstances, but rather because the very BIT obligation does not apply.[41] This view is coherent with Article 2 of the International Law Commission Articles on State Responsibility which clearly specifies that the wrongfulness does not arise as long as the conduct imputable to the State does not constitute a breach of international obligation.[42] The lack of wrongfulness in the host State's conduct eliminates the necessity to make reparation which is confined to injuries originated from internationally wrongful acts.[43] If the wording of the NMP clause can cover the expropriation clause of the BIT, the treaty obligation to make compensation is neutralised. However, it remains questionable whether or not it can prevail also on the parallel customary law rule to compensate:[44] with the NPM clause being an exceptional norm in the arena of investment law, its operation cannot impede the application of the customary rules.[45] As regards the question of the relationship with necessity under customary international law, the arbitral awards came to divergent conclusions in relation to the application of Article 25 of the International Law Commission's Articles on State Responsibility.[46] In *CMS*, *Enron*, and *Sempra* the arbitral tribunals substantively construed the treaty provision (Art. XI) in the light of the customary rule (Art. 25),[47] while in *LG&E* the arbitral tribunal maintained a distinction between the two levels.[48] This is far from being a theoretical issue. Assuming a contamination between treaty and custom, in the first three cases the arbitral tribunals found that the requirements encapsulated in Article 25 were not satisfied as, on the one hand, the measures adopted by Argentina were not the sole means to preserve an essential interest, and on the other hand, the respondent country had contributed to the economic crisis.[49] By contrast, in *LG&E* the arbitral tribunal concluded that although the analysis of Article 25 alone does not support Argentina's defence, the analysis of Article XI does.[50] The *LG&E* 'heretical' position was implicitly endorsed by the CMS Annulment Committee decision which found that the tribunal made an erroneous interpretation in placing on the same footing the treaty norm and the customary rule, as 'it did not examine whether the conditions laid down by Article XI were fulfilled and whether, as a consequence, the measures taken by Argentina were capable of constituting, even *prima facie*, a breach of the BIT'.[51] Article 25 may still come into play insofar as the emergency situation falls outside the scope of the BIT exception.[52]

Against this background, a repressive measure presenting certain regulatory features – although insufficient to qualify as a regulatory measure under the balancing of interests test – may still escape the BIT obligation to compensate as long as subsumable under a NPM clause. The permissible objectives are essential security measures and public order. The United States has sought to differentiate between essential security and public order under the BITs according to severity and scale. Whereas the 'public order' objective covers essentially law-enforcement related activities during peace time, 'essential security interests' are involved when the public order itself may be under severe stress due to armed hostilities or acute crises. Consonant to this reading, the latter instance embraces extraordinary measures adopted in connection with financial crises and the former includes less extraordinary measures in regular times.[53] To better understand the meaning of public order under which repressive measures normally fall, it is necessary to resort to the German BIT Model which, in turn distinguishes between 'public security' and 'public order', with the former including the integrity of the legal order in the form of all written laws and regulations, and the latter referring to the complementary category of all unwritten social, and thus extra-legal, norms that are nonetheless deemed necessary for a peaceful and harmonious coexistence of the community.[54] Repressive measures thus must pursue one of these scopes to be exempted from compensation.

5 Conclusion

Repressive measures against foreign investment are naturally assessed against the background of investment law. In this respect, these measures can escape the obligation of compensation in two moments. Not only when the measure is qualified as a regulatory taking but also when, in spite of its expropriatory characterisation, it can benefit from the presence of a NPM exception in the BIT. In both moments, the foreign investor may be frustrated in his expectation of being indemnified. To avoid this unfair outcome, a different and more equitable solution may be envisaged. In relation to regulatory measures, borrowing from the case law of the European Court of Human rights, the balancing test may be applied not only to establish the characterisation of the measure, but also to decide the quantification of the compensation: under this scheme, investors and regulatory State will not be obliged to bear alternatively, in its entirety, the burden of the measure. In relation to NPM clauses, the neutralisation of the BIT rule of compensation does not extend to the customary rule of indemnifying. As a result, the full compensation rule cedes to the appropriate compensation rule, which introduces a flexible and equitable element in the quantification of the due amount.

Notes

1. Cata Backer (2010: 120–123).
2. *Foreign Investment and National Security Act* (FINSA) of 2007, Pub. L. No. 110–49, 121 Stat. 246 (2007), codified at 50 U.S.C. app. § 2170.
3. Cata Backer (2010: 79–85).
4. Bassan (2010: 184).
5. The ICSID establishing Convention was drafted in 1965 by the International Bank for Reconstruction and Development (IBRD) in order to provide international methods of settlement to disputes on foreign investment, (1965) 4 ILM p. 532.
6. In this context the nationality is determined on the basis of the test of the incorporation or the seat of the person; still, many BITs combine the traditional criteria of incorporation and seat with those of controlling interests and substantial business activity. See Amerasinghe (1975: 259).

7. *Cekoslovenska Obchodni Banka A S v. The Slovak Republic* (decision on objections to jurisdiction, 24 May 1999), para. 16, available at http://www.italaw.com.
8. International Working Group of Sovereign Wealth Funds (IWG), 2008, GAPP 1. Principle.
9. IWG, 2008, GAPP 2. Sub-principle.
10. See Schreuer (2009: 192–217). The BITs refer to the ICSID as just one of the possibilities to settle the dispute; the other most resorted to alternative is the UNCITRAL Rules.
11. *SGS Société Générale de Surveillance SA v. Islamic Republic of Pakistan* (decision on objections to jurisdiction, 6 August 2003), paras 163–174, available at http://www.italaw.com.
12. *SGS Société Générale de Surveillance SA v. Republic of the Philippines* (decision on objections to jurisdiction, 29 January 2004), paras 130–144, available at http://www.italaw.com.
13. See the Report of the Executive Directors (1965) 4 ILM p. 524, para 27.
14. *Fedax N.V. v. The Republic of Venezuela* (decision on objection to jurisdiction, 11 July 1997), para 43, available at http://www.italaw.com.
15. 'There is indeed no requirement that an investment, in order to qualify, must necessarily be made by shareholders controlling a company or owning the majority of its shares', *CMS GAS Transmission Company v. The Republic of Argentina* (decision on objections to jurisdiction, 17 July 2003), para 51, available at http://www.italaw.com.
16. *Gas Natural v. The Argentine Republic*, Case No ARB/03/10 (decision on preliminary questions on jurisdiction, 17 June 2005), paras. 32–35, available at http://www.italaw.com.
17. See Schreuer (2009: 117–125).
18. BITs contain a clause pursuant to which expropriation against a foreign investment is permissible as far as it meets four conditions: public purpose, non-discrimination, due process, and compensation; the provision is substantively reproduced in all the BITs (Lowenfeld, 2008, p. 559).
19. Perhaps the first conceptualisation of the phenomenon goes back to Christie (1962: 309): the 'interference with an alien's property may amount to expropriation even when no explicit attempt is made to affect the legal title to the property, and even though the respondent State may specifically disclaim any such intention'. Cf. now Art. IV of the World Bank (1992) *Guidelines on the Treatment of Foreign Direct Investment*.
20. Dolzer & Schreuer (2012: 102–103).
21. UNCTAD (2000: 11–12).
22. UNCTAD (2000: 12).
23. *Saluka v. Czech Republic* (partial award of 17 March 2006), para 263, available at http://www.italaw.com.
24. *Feldman v. Mexico* (award 16 December 2002), para. 103, available at http://www.italaw.com.
25. American Law Institute (1987: § 712, comment sub g). '[T]he principle that a State does not commit an expropriation and is thus not liable to pay compensation to a dispossessed alien investor when it adopts general regulations that

are "commonly accepted as within the police power of States" forms part of customary international law today', *Saluka v. Czech Republic*, supra note 23, para 262.

26. '[A] blanket exception for regulatory measures would create a gaping loophole in international protections against expropriation', *Pope & Talbot v. Canada* (Interim award of 26 June 2000), para 99, available at http://www.italaw.com.
27. *Santa Elena v. Costa Rica* (award 17 February 2000), para 72, available at http://www.italaw.com.
28. '[W]hen a State enters into a bilateral investment treaty like the one in this case, it becomes bound by it and the investment-protection obligations it undertook therein must be honoured rather than be ignored by a later argument of the State's right to regulate', *ADC v. Hungary* (award of 2 October 2006), para 423, available at http://www.italaw.com.
29. *Tecmed v. Mexico* (award of 29 May 2003), para 122, available at http://www.italaw.com: the tribunal grounded its line of reasoning on a decision of the European Court of Human Rights, which, *inter alia*, emphasised that 'different considerations may apply to nationals and non-nationals and there may well be legitimate reason for requiring nationals to bear a greater burden in the public interest than non-nationals', *In the case of James and Others* (judgment of 21 February 1986), para 63, available at http://hudoc.echr.coe.int. These conclusions were subsequently acknowledged by the arbitral tribunal in *Azurix Corporation v. Argentina* (award of 14 July 2006), para 311, available at http://www.italaw.com.
30. *LG&E Energy Corp et al. v. Argentine Republic* (decision on liability 3 October 2006), paras 189–200, available at http://www.italaw.com. By contrast, in *Tecmed* (supra note 29, para 147), the arbitral tribunal found that '[t]he actions undertaken by the authorities to face these socio-political difficulties, where these difficulties do not have serious emergency or public hardship connotations, or wide-ranging and serious consequences, may not be considered from the standpoint of the Agreement or international law to be sufficient justification to deprive the foreign investor of its investment with no compensation'.
31. In *INA Corporation v. The Islamic Republic of Iran*, (1985) 8 Iran-US CTR, 373, 380, the Iran-US arbitral tribunal defined market value as 'the amount which a willing buyer would have paid a willing seller for the shares of a going concern, disregarding any diminution of value due to the nationalisation itself or the anticipation thereof, and excluding consideration of events thereafter that might have increased or decreased the value of the shares'.
32. See Wälde (2005: 419–420). If the outcome of the sale of the shares on the market does not meet this criterion, the State is called to compensate the difference.
33. Burke-White & von Staden (2008: 312–313).
34. See the relevant texts at http://www.unctad.org/sections/dite/iia/docs/bits.
35. Dolzer & Schreuer (2012: 391, 364).
36. United States – Argentina BIT of 14 November 1991, (1991) 31 ILM 124.

37. *CMS Gas Transmission Company v. The Argentine Republic* (award of 12 May 2005), para 373; *Enron Corporation Ponderosa Assets v. Argentine Republic* (award of 22 May 2007), para 332; *Sempra Energy v. Argentine Republic* (award of 28 September 2007), para 374; all available at http://www.italaw.com.
38. The arbitral tribunal started its reasoning from the premises that under the BIT, it was unclear who was entitled to decide what constituted an essential security measure, either Argentina itself or the tribunal. Based on the evidence regarding the understanding of the parties in 1991 at the time the BIT was signed, the tribunal ruled that the provision in issue was not self-judging (*LG&E v. Argentine Republic, supra* note 30, at paras 212–214).
39. The characterisation of a NPM clause as implicitly or explicitly self-judging depends upon the presence of the words 'it considers necessary'. The US Model BITs generally contain a self-judging version of the clause.
40. Burke-White & von Staden (2008: 377–378).
41. The non-applicability may cover the whole BIT or solely specific obligations, see Burke-White & von Staden (2008: 386–387).
42. Crawford (2002: 81–85).
43. See Article 31, *ILC Articles on State Responsibility*.
44. '[C]ustomary international law continues to exist and to apply separately from treaty law, even the two categories of law have an identical content', *Military and Paramilitary Activities In and Against Nicaragua (Nicaragua v. United States of America). Merits,* Judgment of 27 June 1986, (1986) *ICJ Rep.*, para. 179.
45. Art. XI of the United States-Argentina BIT reads as follows: 'the treaty shall not preclude the application of either party of measures (...)'; this formulation removes endogenous obstacles to the application of the NPM clause but does not extend its application beyond the framework of the BIT.
46. The norm reads as follows: 'Necessity may not be invoked by a State as a ground for precluding the wrongfulness of an act not in conformity with an international obligation of that State unless the act: (a) is the only way for the State to safeguard an essential interest against a grave and imminent peril; and (b) does not seriously impair an essential interest of the State or States towards which the obligation exists, or of the international community as a whole. In any case, necessity may not be invoked by a State as a ground for precluding wrongfulness if: (a) the international obligation in question excludes the possibility of invoking necessity; or (b) the State has contributed to the situation of necessity.' For a comment, Crawford (2002: 178–186).
47. *CMS Gas Transmission Company v. The Argentine Republic, supra* note 37, paras 353 *et seq.*; *Enron Corporation Ponderosa Assets v. Argentine Republic, supra* note 37, paras 333, 339; *Sempra Energy v. Argentine Republic, supra* note 37, paras 375–378.
48. *LG&E v. Argentine Republic, supra* note 30, at para 245.
49. *CMS Gas Transmission Company v. The Argentine Republic, supra* note 37, paras 324, 329; *Enron Corporation Ponderosa Assets v. Argentine Republic, supra* note 37, paras 308, 311–312; *Sempra Energy v. Argentine Republic, supra* note 37, paras 351, 354.

50. *LG&E v. Argentine Republic, supra* note 30, para 258.
51. 'Article XI and Article 25 are substantively different. The first covers measures necessary for the maintenance of public order or the protection of each Party's own essential security interests, without qualifying such measures. The second subordinates the state of necessity to four conditions'. However, given its limited powers, the *Ad Hoc* Committee did not annul the previous award. *CMS Gas Company v. Argentine Republic* (decision of the *ad hoc* Committee on the application for annulment of the Argentine Republic, 25 September 2007) paras 128–136, available at http://www.italaw.com.
52. Binder (2009: 625).
53. In case of exceptional circumstances, the obligation to compensate under the BIT resumes as far as a certain degree of stability has been re-established, *LG&E v. Argentine Republic,* supra note 30, para 261.
54. The wording of the NPM clause suggests a broad exception to the substantive protections of a BIT and a considerable risk-shifting from states to investors in exceptional situations that implicate public order. See Burke-White & von Staden (2008: 359–360).

References

Amerasinghe, C F (1975), 'Jurisdiction *Ratione Personae* under the Convention on the Settlement of Investment Disputes between States and Nationals of Other States', *British Yearbook of International Law,* vol. 47, no. 1, pp. 227–267.

American Law Institute (1987) *Restatement of the Law (Third): The Foreign Relations Law of the United States,* American Law Institute, St Paul

Binder C (2009), 'Changed Circumstances in Investment Law: Interfaces between the Law of Treaties and the Law of State Responsibility with a Special Focus on the Argentine Crisis' in Binder, C, Kriebaum, K, Reinisch, A & Witte, S (eds), *International Investment Law for the 21st Century,* Oxford University Press, Oxford, pp. 608–630.

Bassan, F (2010), 'Host States and Sovereign Wealth Funds, Between National Security and International Law', *European Business Law Review,* vol. 21, no. 2, pp. 165–201.

Burke-White, W W & von Staden, A (2008), 'Investment Protection in Extraordinary Times: The Interpretation of Non-Precluded Measures Provisions in Bilateral Investment Treaties', *Virginia Journal of International Law,* vol. 48, no. 2, pp. 307–410.

Cata Backer, L (2010), 'Sovereign Investing in Times of Crisis: Global Regulation of Sovereign Wealth Funds, State Owned Enterprises, and the Chinese Experience', *Transnational Law & Contemporary Problems,* vol. 19, no. 1, pp. 3–144.

Christie, G C (1962), 'What Constitutes a Taking of Property Under International Law?' *British Yearbook of International Law,* vol. 38, pp. 307–338.

Crawford, J (2002), *The International Law Commission's Articles on State Responsibility,* Cambridge University Press, Cambridge.

Dolzer, R & Schreuer, C (2012), *Principles of Investment Law,* Oxford University Press, Oxford.

International Working Group of Sovereign Wealth Funds (IWG) (2008), *Sovereign Wealth Funds Generally Accepted Principles and Practices: Santiago Principles*, avali-able at http://www.iwgswf.org/pubs/eng/santiagoprinciples.pdf.

Lowenfeld, A F (2008), *International Economic Law*, Oxford University Press, 2nd ed., Oxford.

Schreuer, C H (2009), *The ICSID Convention: A Commentary*, Cambridge University Press, 2nd ed., Cambridge.

United Nations Conference on Trade and Development (UNCTAD) (2000), *Taking of Property*, United Nations, New York /Geneva

Wälde, T (2005), 'The Serbian Loans Case: A Precedent for Investment Treaty Protection of Foreign Debt?' in T Weiler (ed.), *International Investment Law and Arbitration*, Cameron May, London, pp. 383–423.

World Bank (1992), *Legal Framework for the Treatment of Foreign Investment*, vol. II: *Guidelines*, World Bank, Washington, pp. 33–44.

10
Common Characteristics of Rated Sovereigns Prior to Default

Marie Cavanaugh, John B. Chambers, and Maximillian McGraw

1 Introduction

External imbalances and political issues are often the sovereign rating factors that best signal future default. External imbalances are associated with public or private sector excesses, and they generally have fiscal and monetary repercussions. In Standard & Poor's Ratings Services' view, no single measure consistently serves as a good leading indicator of sovereign default. Instead, a confluence of factors, including economic policy shortcomings, underlies most sovereign defaults.

Adding to the challenge of assessing creditworthiness is that some economic indicators improve prior to default, particularly fiscal and current account deficits, which may contract as access to funding is either curtailed or becomes much more expensive. Of course, stresses in any of these factors do not always lead to default. A sovereign is much less likely to default on debt obligations if public and private sector borrowings are invested in a way that is likely to boost production, particularly exports, and if policies are conducive to sustainable economic growth.

To identify and assess the common characteristics of sovereigns prior to default, we have done a study of rated sovereigns that have defaulted on their foreign currency debt. Fifteen sovereigns that Standard & Poor's rated prior to default have defaulted on foreign currency obligations (see Table 10.1). Four of these sovereigns use currencies that they do not control, and three of the remaining 11 sovereigns also defaulted on local currency obligations near the time of the foreign currency default.

We excluded Venezuela from this study because its 2005 default involved only oil-indexed obligations for which payments were triggered by rising oil prices after no payment had been necessary for many years. It took several months for the government to calculate the amounts

Table 10.1 Rated sovereigns that defaulted on foreign currency debt (as of 17 January 2014)

			Long-term foreign currency rating*		
Sovereign	**Date of default(s)**	**Local currency default as well**	**Three months prior to default**	**One year prior to default**	**Two years prior to default**
Argentina	Nov. 2001	Yes	B–/Negative	BB/Watch Neg	BB/Negative
Belize	Dec. 2006, Aug. 2012	No	CC/Negative	CCC–/Negative	B–/Negative
Cyprus	June 2013	Yes§	CCC/Negative	BB+/Negative	A–/Negative
Dominican Republic	Feb. 2005	No	CC/Negative	CCC/Negative	BB–/Stable
Ecuador	Dec. 2008	Yes§	B–/Stable	B–/Stable	CCC+/Stable
Greece	Feb. 2012, Dec. 2012	Yes§	CC/Negative	BB+/Watch Neg	BBB+/Watch Neg
Grenada	Dec. 2004, Oct. 2012, Mar. 2013	Yes§	B+/Watch Neg	BB–/Stable	BB–/Stable
Indonesia	Mar. 1999, Apr. 2000, Apr. 2002	No	CCC+/Negative	B–/Watch Neg	BBB/Stable
Jamaica	Jan. 2010, Feb. 2013	Yes	CCC+/Negative	B/Negative	B/Stable
Pakistan	Jan. 1999	No	CCC–/Negative	B+/Negative	B+/Stable
Paraguay	Feb. 2003	No	B/Negative	B/Negative	B/Negative
Russia	Jan. 1999	Yes	CCC–/Negative	BB–/Negative	BB–/Stable
Seychelles	Aug. 2008	No	B/Negative	B/Stable	N.R.
Uruguay	May 2003	No	CCC/Negative	BB–/Negative	BBB–/Stable
Venezuela	Jan. 2005	No	B/Stable	B–/Stable	CCC+/Negative

Note: *Prior to first listed default. §The distinction between foreign and local currencies is less meaningful because each country uses, as a local currency, a currency that the sovereign does not control. Ecuador uses the US dollar; Cyprus and Greece, as members of the European Economic and Monetary Union (EMU), use the euro; and Grenada, as a member of the Eastern Caribbean Currency Union (ECCU), uses the Eastern Caribbean dollar. Source: Standard & Poor's Ratings Direct, 'Sovereign Rating and Country T&C Assessment Histories', published monthly.

due, and it then made the late payments with interest. Also, the data for Belize, Greece, Grenada, Indonesia, and Jamaica pertain to their first defaults after we initially assigned sovereign ratings, not to their subsequent defaults.

2 External indebtedness and a weakening currency are common features of defaulting sovereigns

A net external liability position is a common denominator for all of the defaulting sovereigns. A net external liability position indicates that the combined public and private sectors have liabilities to non-residents that exceed assets invested by residents in other countries. This usually means that interest and dividend payments to non-residents exceed interest and dividends received from non-residents, which causes a net external outflow that weighs on the current account balance. In most cases, net external liability positions exceed current account receipts (see Figure 10.1), and the liability positions deteriorate prior to default. We identified three exceptions to this deteriorating trend: Belize, which had greatly diminished access to external financing as it struggled for several years to avoid default; Ecuador, which defaulted almost solely because of political factors; and Greece, which had received substantial official assistance and undertaken some reforms prior to default.

The improvements that occurred in the year after default (D+1 in Figure 10.1) generally resulted from either a weaker currency and an improvement in external performance because of reforms or a

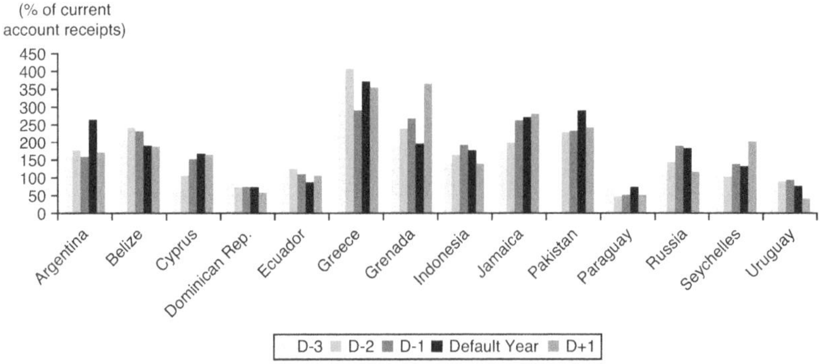

Figure 10.1 Net external liabilities

Source: Standard & Poor's and national sources.

reduction in the debt burden stemming from the debt rescheduling. However, interpretation of this and other figures is complicated by the fact that, in some instances, the default occurred early in the year and the statistics for the default year itself improved. In other cases, the default occurred late in the year, and some of the spill-over was in the following year.

In addition, all but the Dominican Republic, Ecuador, and Russia had current account deficits (see Figure 10.2 showing the current account deficit as a percent of current account receipts), which is consistent with the defaulted sovereigns' net external liability positions. Current account deficits reflect a country's shortfall in savings relative to investment and, thus, the need to fund investment externally. Reliance on external financing can become a source of pressure when investment returns disappoint or growth prospects dim and non-resident investors decide to disinvest. Equity investments are usually less burdensome in such situations because prices have fallen, but the foreign investors' repatriation of their equity investments may reduce a country's foreign exchange reserves substantially. This, along with a weakening currency, may raise the external debt service burden, particularly if it becomes more difficult or more expensive to roll over short-term cross-border interbank deposits or other short-term, or maturing long-term, external liabilities.

In seven of the countries, current account deficits regularly exceeded 20% of current account receipts prior to default. In Indonesia, Paraguay, and Uruguay, the relatively low average current account deficits mask a sharp reversal to surplus from deficit in the year prior to default as a

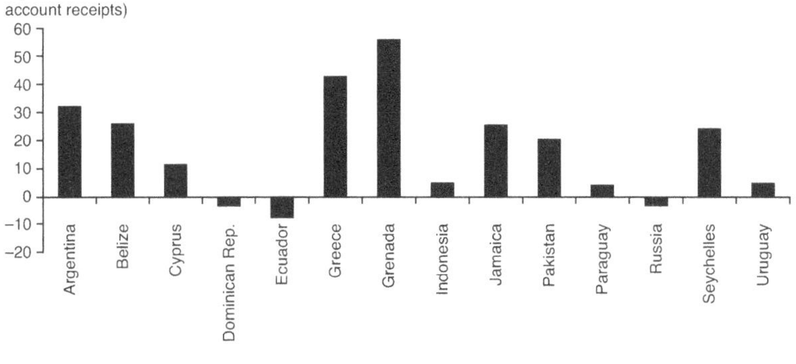

Figure 10.2 Average current account deficit in three years prior to default
Source: Standard & Poor's and national sources.

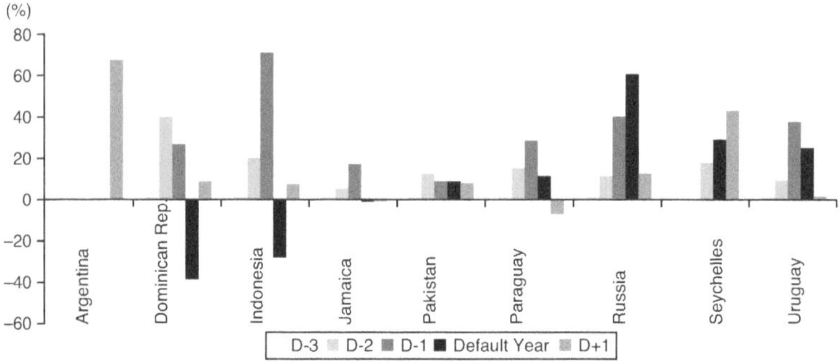

Figure 10.3 Depreciation of local currency against US dollar
Source: Standard & Poor's and national sources.

result of severe local currency depreciation (see Figure 10.3). Also, in many cases, such as Cyprus, short-term external liabilities or changes in investor sentiment-reducing equity flows were more important sources of pressure than the current account deficit. Among the surplus countries, Ecuador and Russia are both relatively undiversified, commodity-exporting countries, where political pressures often dominate economic matters. In the Dominican Republic, the default was, in part, related to bail-outs of the distressed electricity sector and a troubled bank that experienced governance issues.

Unsurprisingly, given the external imbalances, most sovereigns facing foreign currency default have external financing needs (defined as current account payments plus short-term external debt by remaining maturity) that exceed current account receipts and usable foreign exchange reserves. In Cyprus and Greece, the external financing needs were several multiples of resources.

Along with high external indebtedness, another feature of most of the defaulted sovereigns is a sharply depreciating currency (see Figure 10.3). The exceptions are countries with long-standing pegs to the US dollar (Belize and Grenada), sovereigns in a monetary union (Cyprus and Greece), and those that use the US dollar as their local currency (Ecuador); these sovereigns saw little, if any, currency movements. We have omitted these sovereigns from the figure. The sharp currency movements are partly a result of deteriorating political and economic fundamentals and partly a result of rising pressures on heavily managed currency regimes. The latter factor was sharpest in

Argentina, where the peso lost 67% of its value against the dollar after the country abandoned its link to the dollar in early 2002. (The default year is 2001 because of a distressed exchange in November.) This caused GDP per capita in dollar terms to fall by 63% in 2002. The appreciation in the default year for the Dominican Republic and Indonesia occurred after the distressed debt exchanges, when prospects looked somewhat better, and there was a partial reversal of the depreciation of prior years.

3 Real economy indicators are mixed for defaulting sovereigns

GDP per capita varies widely for the defaulting sovereigns in our study. GDP per capita in the year prior to a sovereign default was lowest in Pakistan, at US$400, and highest in Cyprus, at US$26,400 (see Figure 10.4). However, Cyprus and Greece are outliers, and the next-highest GDP per capita levels are $8,000–$11,000 (Argentina and the Seychelles). Aside from Argentina and Indonesia, which experienced 60–70% one-year declines in the value of their currencies, GDP per capita fell more moderately in percentage terms for the defaulting sovereigns, and in several cases did not drop in the default year or the years preceding or following.

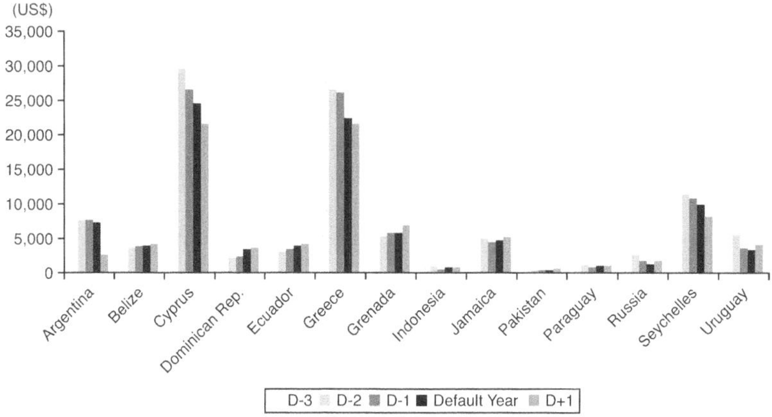

Figure 10.4 GDP per capita (US$)

Source: Standard & Poor's and national sources.

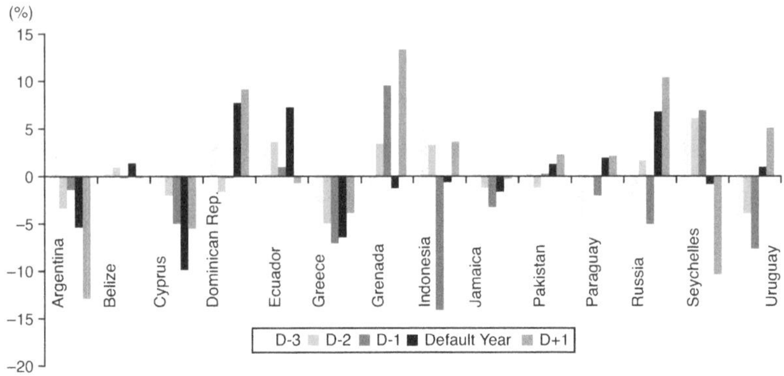

Figure 10.5 Real GDP per capita growth
Source: Standard & Poor's and national sources.

Real GDP per capita growth was negative in at least one year around the time of default for all defaulting sovereigns (see Figure 10.5), but the patterns varied widely. Ecuador, which defaulted primarily because of political issues; Grenada, which had problems stemming from a devastating hurricane; and the Seychelles all had no contraction in real GDP per capita growth in the two years prior to default. On the other hand, Cyprus, Greece, and Uruguay experienced persistent economic contraction in the years prior to default.

Following the turmoil resulting from sharp currency depreciation, a country is often in a much better position to increase export-driven growth. If monetary policy can limit the impact that depreciation has on domestic prices, this can be the beginning of economic recovery and the path back to an investment-grade rating, as has been the case for Russia and Uruguay. Recovery can be more difficult for sovereigns that need to absorb the full burden of an economic adjustment in lower wages and economic contraction, as in Cyprus, Greece, and Grenada.

4 Changes in government debt are a better indicator of deteriorating creditworthiness than headline deficits

Increasing government debt has been a better indicator of impending crisis than the headline deficit for defaulting sovereigns (see Figure 10.6). The change in general government debt was of double-digit size as a per cent of GDP around the time of default in all countries except Ecuador, where the default occurred mainly because of the government's view of

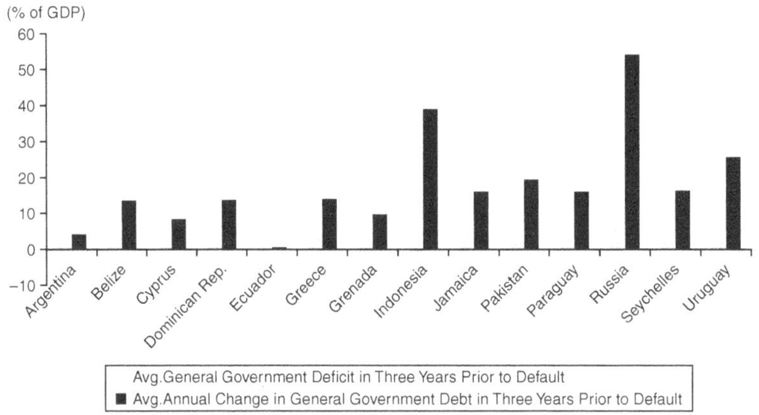

Figure 10.6 Change in general government debt exceeds headline deficit in years prior to default

Source: Standard & Poor's and national sources.

the legitimacy of some of the debt contracted by the prior administration. This is in sharp contrast to the far more modest headline deficits (see Figure 10.6). The large increase in debt did not occur in Argentina until it floated its currency, which was about two months after the distressed debt exchange, which led to the default rating. Although higher deficits diminish creditworthiness, their impact seems to be not as great as the shocks emanating from sharp currency movements and other balance-of-payment pressures, or from the transfer to the sovereign balance sheet of obligations previously recorded in the financial sector, the government-related entities (GRE) sector, or elsewhere.

After adjusting for non-cash items, debt forgiveness/restructuring, privatisation proceeds, and the use of cash balances, the increase in the stock of debt over the course of a year approximates the headline deficit. But, unlike the headline deficit, it also includes the impact of exchange-rate movements on the debt burden, the recognition of off-budget or contingent liabilities that need servicing, and possibly other quasi-fiscal factors. Another shortcoming of the headline, or reported, deficit is that it is sometimes targeted, by political and other attention, creating strong incentives to move some programs or functions to public-sector enterprises, where there may be less budgetary scrutiny.

For the 14 defaulting sovereigns in the study, headline general government deficits were rarely double-digit as a per cent of GDP and, in several cases, declined in either the year prior to default or the default year. Indonesia reported small general government surpluses over most of the period. In some cases, deeply negative real effective interest rates, the result of the sharply higher inflation that stemmed from the weakening currency, eased the interest burden on local currency-denominated debt, though the burden of servicing foreign currency-denominated debt rose.

Exchange rate movements, which typically affect the change in debt but not the headline deficit, are often an important part of the reason external pressures become fiscal problems. However, as we saw in the case of Cyprus, Greece, and several other defaulting sovereigns, balance-of-payment pressures may develop independently of exchange rate movements, when current account deficits are large and persistent and the country's net external liability position is large or widens sharply.

Similar to the change in debt, the general government debt burden tends to worsen around the time of default (see Figure 10.7). However, debt burdens in the year or two prior to default vary considerably, from less than 60% of GDP in Argentina, the Dominican Republic, Ecuador, Indonesia, Paraguay, Russia, and Uruguay to fairly consistently over 100% in Greece, Jamaica, and the Seychelles.

In contrast, many sovereigns that have never defaulted have long had general government debt burdens in excess of 60% of GDP. This is because taxation and monetary powers unique to sovereigns, as well

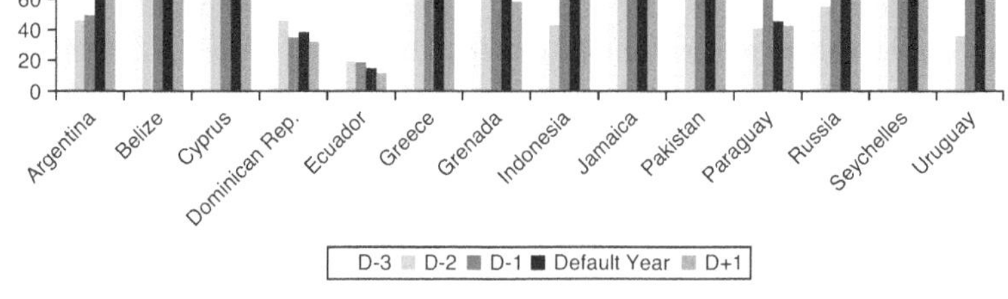

Figure 10.7 Net general government debt

Source: Standard & Poor's and national sources.

as domestic capital market characteristics, can permit governments to manage widely varying debt levels. This room to manoeuvre results, in part, from the credibility a government has established in past periods of stress. Thus, ratings tend not to be highly correlated with government debt burdens. A sovereign with an unblemished track record of honouring debt obligations and a strong domestic capital market providing long-term and fairly low-cost, market-based financing may have more fiscal flexibility than a sovereign with a lower debt-to-GDP ratio but a higher and more variable debt servicing burden. In addition, low debt burdens may reflect financing challenges and high interest costs, or, in some cases, recent debt relief, rather than fiscal flexibility.

5 Future sovereign foreign currency defaults would likely stem from a combination of political and economic factors

It seems likely that external imbalances and policy shortcomings will remain the leading indicators of sovereign foreign currency default. We believe external imbalances have been at the root of the problems in the Eurozone, though fiscal challenges have grown as a result. With larger financial sectors in many countries and more financial interconnectedness globally, we believe that sovereign decisions to support systemically important financial institutions may play a bigger role in sovereign creditworthiness than they did in these 14 defaults that we studied.

It is important to note that external and fiscal balances often improve in the year prior to default. One reason is that it may be increasingly difficult or costly to fund deficits, forcing cutbacks or arrears, which reduce recorded expenditures. Another reason is that rising inflation tends to boost revenues before expenditures, easing the fiscal deficit initially. In addition, higher inflation raises nominal GDP, which is the common denominator against which deficits and debt burdens are analysed, and this can lead to improvements in the ratios, which may not be sustainable.

Economic statistics may also be flattered by net inflows from abroad, particularly equity inflows. These provide an economic stimulus that boosts investment and growth and usually improves fiscal performance, but they can also affect inflation and may be devastating when they reverse. In all of these cases, an important part of analysing shifts in economic indicators is analysing their sustainability and their potential impact on other economic indicators.

Related Criteria and Research

Standard & Poor's RatingsDirect (2009), *Rating Implications of Exchange Offers and Similar Restructurings — Update.*

Standard & Poor's Ratings Direct (2011), *Distressed Sovereign Debt Exchanges: Examples from the Past and Lessons for the Future.*

Standard & Poor's RatingsDirect (2013a), *Sovereign Defaults and Rating Transition Data, 2012 Update.*

Standard & Poor's RatingsDirect (2013b), *Sovereign Government Rating Methodology and Assumptions.*

Standard & Poor's Ratings Direct (published monthly), *Sovereign Rating and Country T&C Assessment Histories.*

Part III

Management of Sovereign Risk and Ratings

11

Big Projects in Small Economies: The Determinants of Sovereign Risk and Its Control

Sean J. Hinton, Brian S. Fisher, and Anna M. Fisher

1 Introduction

In the search for untapped economically viable natural resources, the extractive industry is increasingly being forced to target larger, more capital-intensive projects in less developed countries. Such mega-projects can have a transformative impact, good or bad, on small host economies. The nature of such projects, and the way that they are typically structured and developed, unintentionally leads to specific economic problems that put pressure on host governments and project developers alike. Conventional approaches can lead to higher risk of expropriation, widespread and destructive rent-seeking behaviour, and intensified corruption. In projects of significant scale relative to the host economy, these unintended effects can lead to an increase in the overall level of sovereign risk in the territory.

Typically, the developers of multi-billion dollar natural resource projects have well-established processes for understanding and mitigating operational risk. Likewise they are keenly aware of the market risk associated with the particular commodities and industries concerned and, although such risks are difficult to mitigate at the project level, developers may pursue diversification strategies across geographies and commodities at the firm level.

Unlike market risk and operational risk, however, sovereign risk often receives less attention from project developers than it deserves. While it is usually reflected in capital allocation decision-making, the attention paid to managing and mitigating it is often relatively low despite the fact that its impact can, in the case of a full expropriation event, be in excess of the net present value (NPV) of the entire project.

These risks are not only significant in their impact but also quite frequent. In a 2009 analysis of the largest 190 oil and gas projects in the world, ERM, a sustainable development consultancy, found that 73% of projects experienced delays due to 'above ground' issues (such as geopolitical, political, or stakeholder pressure) versus 21% experiencing 'technical' delays (Cattaneo, 2009). Sovereign risk is usually considered to be exogenous, that is, outside the control of the project developer. As such, developers often fail to devote meaningful expenditure and resourcing to addressing it. However, in the case of a single project that contributes a significant percentage of the gross domestic product of the host country, sovereign risk is endogenous, and the operation of the project and the state of the economy are mutually interconnected. While much has been written in the literature on the policy choices facing governments, a deeper awareness of the nature of the impact such projects have on sovereign risk points the way to how developers can do their part to manage and mitigate such impacts and, in turn, sovereign risk itself.

2 Project characteristics that exacerbate friction between host governments and foreign developers

Three typical project characteristics exacerbate the probability of full or partial expropriation of a major project – or at least the generation of on-going friction between the project participants, the host government, and the foreign developer. These characteristics can be broadly specified as 'misaligned incentives', 'system shock', and share of benefits or 'fair share'.

2.1 Misaligned incentives: project ownership structures and the timing of benefits to project participants

In most jurisdictions the government effectively 'owns' the natural resource. Compensation for the transfer of ownership of the resource, or the right to exploit it, to a mineral developer can be achieved in many ways including agreements that specify both the form and amount of taxation payments, the development of infrastructure (that might be shared with other future producers) or deals in which the host government retains an equity interest in the project in addition to receiving taxation payments. Taxation arrangements can take many forms (see for example Otto et al., 2006), but typically maximum tax payments will not flow to the government until the mine is in full production. In some cases, a tax holiday for a given amount of time may be offered by the host government, and tax rates may be 'stabilised' (that is, set at specified levels) for an extended period.

Developing country governments rarely have the ability to raise development capital independently and as a result typically 'earn' any equity interest in the project by foregoing future dividend payments. The time path of such dividend payments will depend, among other factors, on uncertain future commodity prices, future mining costs (which in turn depend on global and local macroeconomic conditions as well as the characteristics of the particular mine) and the final capital cost of the project (which will depend on a great many variables from global industry cost escalation to project delays).

The result is that during the early years of a project, while the investor is making the up-front capital investments, the host government is receiving relatively modest tax revenue. And the time when the investor reaches its maximum capital exposure often coincides with the point at which the government receives the lowest proceeds, particularly if pre-payments of tax have been made. For example, at the Kumtor gold mine in the Kyrgyz Republic, five years passed between Cameco entering into an agreement with the government and commercial production commencing (Centerra Gold, 2013). In the case of the Oyu Tolgoi project in Mongolia, it is likely to be 12 to 14 years from the commencement of the project construction to the point of full production (see Fisher et al., 2011).

Given the size of the capital investment, it will be long after commencement of construction that dividends will flow from the project to the government, even though royalties will be paid from the start of production. In cases such as these, many years transpire before the domestic economy experiences the full economic benefits associated with resource production. It is understandable that the general public in host economies fails to understand either the magnitude of these time lags or the reasons for them. A domestic electorate, whose expectations have been inflated to expect instant transformation, may react to such conditions by putting intense political pressure on governments and investors alike. This risk can be most acute at precisely the moment when investors are most vulnerable to expropriation or aggressive renegotiation, with maximum capital exposed and projects that are newly operational.

2.2 System shock: the size of projects relative to the host economy and the speed with which they are developed relative to the maturation of local capacity

By definition, mega projects are large both in absolute terms and relative to the size of the host economy. Such a project may also be the first major investment in the country by a large foreign investor. As such, mega projects often herald significant follow-on foreign direct investment (FDI), which amplifies their impact. These projects are then developed at a speed that places strains on the capacity of government and, public private institutions to meet their needs. They also generate sudden flows of capital that are beyond the absorptive capacity of the economy and so lead to rent-seeking, misspending of public finances, and increased domestic consumption.

In any context the absolute size of these projects means they are complex to develop and require many, varied, and specialised resources to execute. In addition, they often represent a meaningful percentage of the country's gross domestic product (GDP) and a major source of government revenues. For example, at full production, Rio Tinto's Simandou iron ore mine is expected to contribute 2013US$7.7 billion to the Guinean economy (Rio Tinto, 2013b), which is greater than the estimated size of Guinean GDP in 2013 (2013US$6.3 billion) (IMF, 2013a). Another example is the Kumtor gold mine in the Kyrgyz Republic, which had a 5.5% share of the nation's GDP in 2012 and its share of total industrial output was 18.9% in the same year (Kumtor Operating Company, 2013). In the case of Mongolia, GDP is projected to be 36.4% higher in 2019, compared to what it otherwise would have been, as a result of the Oyu Tolgoi copper mine ramping up to full production (Fisher et al., 2011). Another way of expressing this is that Oyu Tolgoi's direct impact is projected to account for 25% of the increase in the size of the economy in 2020 and almost 50% of Mongolian exports at that time.

The impact of these projects due to their relative size is amplified by the fact that they are often the first significant foreign investments being made in these countries. The fact that they are breaking new ground makes these projects more difficult to negotiate, as they are setting legal and regulatory precedents, and there is often disproportionate media and public attention on them, both locally and internationally. This, and the fact that they are usually pursued by major mining/oil and gas companies with global reputations, means they are often viewed by the frontier investment community as 'gating events', legitimising the readiness of these countries to accept foreign investment and implicitly de-risking future investments in the country to some degree. Mongolia and Guinea are examples of countries that have experienced extreme jumps in foreign investment following a major commitment from an international investor to landmark projects. As a result of Oyu Tolgoi, Mongolia's FDI rose by 168% from 2009 to 2010 and then by another 173% between 2010 and 2011. In Guinea, preparations for the development of Vale and Rio Tinto's iron ore mines resulted in an FDI increase of 824% between 2010 and 2011 (World Bank, 2013). The completion of an investment agreement for a mega-project is therefore a strong signal to the market and almost inevitably triggers a significant wave of additional FDI, whether by those investing in infrastructure or supply-chain businesses to service the mega project, or by follow-on capital investment in smaller extractive projects in the same country. This amplifier effect of course operates in two directions, in that the mega project acts both as an enabler of initial investment flows but also as a litmus test for the continued attractiveness of the economy. Consequently, if the mega project falters or fails, the negative impact on the economy goes far beyond the direct activity of the project itself and the FDI tap can turn off as fast as it was turned on – as illustrated by the Oyu Tolgoi project in Mongolia. In July 2013, due to uncertainty surrounding the Mongolian Government's approval of project financing (Rio Tinto, 2013a), Rio Tinto, which holds the majority interest in the mine, delayed funding and work associated with the second underground development phase. By December 2012, US$6.5 billion had been spent on the Oyu Tolgoi project (Oyu Tolgoi, 2013), half the size of Mongolia's GDP in 2013. Delays in further expenditure could be expected to have a large negative impact on the Mongolian economy. And indeed the Mongolian Togrog (or Tugrik) depreciated against the US dollar by 15% between 30 June and mid-September 2013, making it one of the worst performing currencies in the world over that period. There was also a significant reduction in FDI in Mongolia. Between June 2012 and June 2013, FDI dropped by US$393 million.

Although these landmark projects typically take many years to negotiate, once begun they are usually developed as quickly as possible as both the market-driven investors and politically-driven government decision-makers are aligned in their need to deliver short-term results to their shareholders and electorates respectively. The explicit implication of the NPV-driven valuation models that are used by most financial and political stakeholders is: 'the quicker the better'. However, this fails to account for the stage of development of the economy, the changing and changeable levels of sovereign risk in general, and the specific possibility that the way in which the project is developed may itself have an impact on sovereign risk. In other words, a rush to deliver the project may lead to disputes with government that in turn lead to disagreements over the project agreements and destabilisation of the macro-economy of the host country. These unintended, potentially negative consequences come in two ways.

The first is by overwhelming the capacity of local individuals and institutions to manage and adapt to such sudden change. Mega projects are complex and technically difficult, making huge demands on domestic government and regulatory agencies, as well as on the private sector, placing significant pressure on local human resources and other domestic inputs.

Bureaucratic systems in developing countries are rarely capable of handling the intensity and technical complexities of major projects. To secure the project financing for the small 50MW Salkhit Wind Farm project in Mongolia the local company developing the project, Newcom LLC, reported having to secure 284 individual government signatures. Mega projects place exponentially greater demands on local systems. At the time the engineering drawings for the Oyu Tolgoi copper concentrator in Mongolia were submitted, the Ministry would have been required to review more than 13,000 documents in the space of a few months, more drawings than the Ministry had received in many years, and of a technical nature that very few personnel had previously experienced. There are numerous other areas where government decision-making at senior and junior levels, and regulatory capacity generally in Mongolia, has been tested by the development of the world-class Oyu Tolgoi project. One such is the specialised inspection agency established to handle environmental, social, and technical compliance – GASI (General Agency for Specialised Inspection) which is reported to have only one junior inspector in each province responsible for environmental inspections, and only nine qualified and experienced mining inspectors nationally.

Unintended negative consequences may also result when sudden development of large-scale projects brings rapid increases in government inflows. These come in three ways. First, they may come from negotiated up-front payments, as was the case for the Simandou iron ore development, where Rio Tinto paid the government $700 million to develop the mine as part of a Settlement Agreement signed between the two parties (Rio Tinto, 2013b). Second, new inflows can come from taxes associated with the construction phase of such projects. Third, they may come indirectly from the government's raising of sovereign debt made viable by the initiation of the mega project.

Faced with these sudden increases, government departments often do not have the capacity or motivation to spend such funds effectively. For example, long lead-time infrastructure and public works projects such as roads and power plants are not sufficiently advanced to be ready for financing. In Peru, local governments in some mining regions have not been able to keep up with the amount of incoming revenue, and in 2011 regional governments spent less than 60% of their resources. In some cases, rather than being allocated to infrastructure for health and education, revenues were used for new plazas or bull fighting rings (Calfucura, Ortiz, Sanborn, & Dammert, 2013). In addition to encouraging sub-optimal capital allocation to inefficient projects, such overwhelming revenue inflows can lead to leakage of funds in other ways – for example, through corruption or cash-hand-outs. From 2010 to August 2013, the Mongolian Government distributed 1,727.5 billion togrog (Mongolian National Statistics Office) in cash from the Human Development Fund to Mongolian citizens, about $US380 per person, which aroused criticism for fuelling inflation. Economic modelling has demonstrated that a policy such as distributing small amounts of cash to each citizen from the government proceeds from Oyu Tolgoi is not the most effective way to deploy the revenue from the project as it exacerbates structural adjustment pressures and precludes the opportunity of investing the funds in large infrastructure projects (Fisher et al., 2011). While rent-seeking behaviour in the context of natural resource development is present in some form in almost all economic settings, OECD and non-OECD alike, developing economies (and, perversely, developing democracies in particular (Collier & Hoeffler, 2007)) have fewer of the checks and balances, such as broad-based ownership of equity by citizens through developed capital markets, a free and responsible press, or a well-developed legal and regulatory infrastructure, that tend to moderate such behaviour in more developed economies.

The sudden increase in available capital in the economy not only overwhelms government institutions, but also causes challenges for the private sector. While advanced economies have the luxury of assuming market capacity will adjust along with supply and demand, less mature economies lack developed capital markets and often suffer from fragile or underdeveloped banking sectors. Further, entrepreneurs in the SME sector often lack the necessary training and capital to exploit new business opportunities. They may be structurally unable to learn and implement the technologies and associated practices of developed countries.

This set of factors lowers the national absorptive capacity of the economy and slows its ability to respond to the inflow of new money (Dahlman & Nelson, 1995). Consequently, the rate of new jobs growth is less than expected and new domestic investment also lags.

2.3 Fair share: the problem of inequitable distribution of benefits

Economic and social benefits are keenly anticipated throughout the host nation, whether they flow from the government's allocation of revenue, or from the company's allocation of procurement contracts, jobs, and infrastructure improvements. But big projects with a large national economic footprint often have only a small direct initial impact that usually benefits some groups far more than others. The problem of regional versus centralised distribution of extractive project benefits and the negative effect on the Gini coefficient is much discussed (Chupezi, Ingram, & Schure, 2009; Reeson, Measham, & Hosking, 2012; Grigoryan, 2013; Loayza, Mier y Teran, & Rigolini, 2013), but there are a number of other areas where appropriately balanced participation can be hard to manage, for example, the distribution of contracts and jobs among people from different ethnic/tribal groups or political factions. Yet failure to achieve this balance can be problematic and destabilising for both the project and the country.

A key challenge that developers of mega projects face is balancing the distribution of benefits of the project geographically – ensuring that they are neither too locally focused on the direct area around the project nor are they vulnerable to central government decision-makers appropriating the lion's share of the benefits for the capital, or other regions. The importance of benefit-distribution by governments being transparent and equitable is the focus of significant policy debate in the literature (International Council on Mining & Metals, 2008; De Castro, 2012; EI Source Book, 2013; Foreign Affairs, Trade and Development Canada, 2013). In addition, choices by the developer relating to the construction of project-related infrastructure, the distribution of procurement contracts to local and national suppliers, and the hiring of domestic human resources are only some of the ways in which projects can have significant impact on the host region.

To illustrate the problems of benefit distribution, the experience of Peru is useful. Peru's *Canon Minero*, a law establishing the distribution of mining revenues, has come under scrutiny as many non-mining regions see little or no benefit from the country's mineral wealth. Under the *Canon Minero*, whilst 50% of the income tax revenue collected by the revenue collection agency, SUNAT, is kept for the national government, the remaining 50% is redistributed to the three levels of subnational government, district, province, and region, through a complicated process that can result in the districts with active mines not only receiving their designated share of the revenue but also additional revenue that trickles down from the higher levels of government (Calfucura et al., 2013).

In 2011, *Canon Minero*'s largest beneficiary was the Ancash region, home to the Antamina copper mine, which received 582 million soles or US$227 million. At the other end of the spectrum, three of the 25 regional governments received between 2 and 7 million soles and six regions received no money from the *Canon Minero* (Calfucura et al., 2013). This results in economic development flowing to the local regions that have established mines at the expense of regions that do not. Attempts by government to re-balance distribution, however, can be met with hostility. In 2008, 20,000 protestors blocked the roads to the Monquegua region and took 48 police officers hostage in response to the government's decision to revise the *Canon Minero* in ways that would have resulted in reduced revenues for the region (Oxfam, 2009).

If benefits are too amply distributed in the local area, the 'honeypot' risk emerges, that is, the local area is disproportionately attractive, and this causes an influx of people into the mining region looking for work that may not exist. For example, during the planning phase of the Simandou iron ore development in Guinea, Rio Tinto's stakeholder engagement research showed that there was a perception within the community that a large quantity of jobs, goods, and services would become available because of the mine development. Surveys of the villages around the mine led to an estimate that between 2005 and 2011, 25 immigrants were attracted to the region per project worker. These people would have had to find alternative employment. An in-migration strategy was prepared to identify and mitigate the risks associated with the massive influx of job seekers and the unrealistic employment expectations. Some of the potential risks of the in-migration triggered by Simandou and other mega projects in emerging economies are the increased pressure on water resources and other local infrastructure such as sanitation due to the rise in solid waste and sewage; inflation in local prices, as demand for goods and services increases; and pressure on local people who are dependent on land-based incomes as land is used for in-migrant housing or uncontrolled squatter development (Rio Tinto,

2011). Tensions can arise due to these impacts, putting pressure on the mining company directly or via the local/national government.

Imbun (2013) outlines the impact of preferential labour arrangements for local people in Papua New Guinea and notes that, to date, excluded groups have passively accepted that local communities have the 'right' to dictate employment opportunities in mines in their local region. However, this practice has led to the development of squatter settlements around mining towns where the settlers have little to do legally. The influx of people into the Tabulil mining township is said to have had an adverse impact on the local Min culture and also led to growing demands for further compensation payments (Hyndman, 1995).

Other challenges all mega projects face are the assignment of contracts for construction and on-going procurement and the pressure to maximise national content. Assigning contracts to national suppliers can be difficult given the technical and financial disadvantages they suffer in comparison with international competitors. And yet, the advantages afforded by building a domestic supplier base are well worth pursuing. They include building support within the business community in the country, contributing to diversification in the national economy, and supporting development of sustainable national suppliers, all of which ultimately will also reduce costs for the developer.

Managing the equitable distribution of contracts within the pool of available national suppliers, however, remains a significant challenge. There is often only a small group of major suppliers initially capable of meeting tender criteria. So, there is a challenge in maintaining a diversity of supply from a wider range of suppliers of varying sizes and stages of development. Relying on only a few players can inadvertently create oligopolies. Suppliers can also be strongly identified with one or other elite (this may be a political faction or tribal group for example), and the assignment of contracts, either individually or collectively, can become fraught with unintended consequences and challenges. Distributing benefits amongst those groups, ensuring diversity without undermining the integrity of the tender process, can cause major problems for mineral developers.

Many companies and government agencies have undertaken efforts with some success to develop national suppliers so they are capable of providing services to the mining sector. Anglo American's Anglo Zimele fund and the Chilean Government agency CORFO are examples among many others. These policies, though well intended, do not always yield the hoped-for benefits and can sometimes have unintended negative consequences that exacerbate the problem. Programmes that assist the local area can limit the benefits seen by the rest of the population (World Bank, 2012), and programmes that promote suppliers, based on geography or nationality, can distort markets and perpetuate uncompetitive or sub-optimally productive practices (Hanlin, 2011).

The challenges associated with hiring personnel are similar to those confronting procurement. The aspiration to hire as many qualified local staff as possible in the face of skill gaps, and the inevitable salary inequalities created between foreign and local workers, can create inflationary pressure on local salaries within the economy and/or a brain drain away from government and other private sector jobs. Examples of salary disparity between foreign and local workers can be seen in Chinese construction companies operating in Angola. Despite both Chinese and Angolan construction workers receiving a wage above the country's minimum, the Angolans received 23–38% less than the Chinese employees, and their wages were half what the Chinese embassy recommended (Corkin, 2012). When the OK Tedi copper mine was being developed in Papua New Guinea during the 1980s, advisers stressed the potential for increased demand for skilled labour to drive wage rates higher, increasing the wage gap at a national level and in turn affecting government wage policy on the minimum wage (Imbun, 2011).

While developed economies' host governments might be expected to have the capacity, if not always the political will, to ameliorate these unequal distributions of benefits and take active management to ensure benefits are equally distributed, in the developing world, governments are often under intense pressure themselves from the same stakeholders as the project operators: political factions, ethnic/tribal groups, regional constituencies, etc. They are therefore not able or willing to enforce the benefit distribution that is so vital to future stability. All that remains is to wait for the trickle-down effects to work benefits slowly throughout the economy. The pace and demonstrable unreliability of that process means the unequal distribution of benefits creates intense and unintended pressure on local governments.

3 Unintended negative consequences for sovereign risk

The three project characteristics identified above, *'misaligned incentives'* created by the project structure, *'system shock'* flowing from project size and speed of implementation, and *'fair share'* – the problem of inequitable distribution of project benefits – each have their own impact on both the host government and the local community. These impacts are exacerbated, however, because of the gap between inflated expectations and the reality of the short-term impact. All three of the project effects detailed above cause structural problems for the local economy. As such, they increase sovereign risk by putting significant pressure on host governments to act in aggressive ways that are ultimately detrimental to the health of the economy and the project.

The advent of a major mineral development project in a developing economy is usually accompanied by the rise of inflated expectations among the local population. This 'expectation effect' is endemic as overpromising seems almost unavoidable in the process of negotiating a mega-project, with both sides, the investors and the host government, incentivised to play up the future benefits of the project to the broader population in order to curry popular opinion. Host governments are often negotiating these deals under intense domestic scrutiny and, given their landmark status, the handling of these projects and the terms of the deals are almost always the subject of populist resource-nationalist attacks, which give incumbent governments little choice but to inflate the future benefits of the deals in the public discourse. On the other side, the project developer is also often under pressure (from the markets, senior management, and boards) to close these deals as quickly as possible. Drumming up public support by highlighting the benefits of projects tends to be a feature of public awareness efforts. Whoever may be culpable of over-promising or responsible for under-delivering, it is the public who normally remains uninformed about the trade-offs and what is motivating the position of each side.

The frustration generated when these unrealistic expectations are inevitably unfulfilled is worsened when foreigners are perceived to be earning significant value from their local investments. Even when there is local (private or governmental) ownership of stakes in the mega project, that ownership is usually at the level of the privately held domestic entity. By contrast, in order to raise finance for these projects, foreign investors will often hold their stake in offshore-listed parent companies. This contrast in liquidity between domestic and foreign ownership, together with a poorly-developed understanding of capital markets in the host economy, can create popular backlash when the listed stock increases and foreigners are perceived to be making large capital gains on the back of domestic assets that have yet to create tangible local value. In the process of exploration, development, and financing of mega projects, there are often major transactions offshore, where early-stage junior companies may crystallise their gains by selling out to a major who then takes on the financing and management of the construction and operation of the project. Such transactions are an increasingly common feature in the ecosystem of the development of mega projects. While they generate returns for players in the early stages of the development process, they rarely benefit local stakeholders. In many cases the capital gains captured by the juniors are not subject to domestic tax laws, which compounds the problem and often exacerbates local resentment.

Disputes such as these have highlighted the importance of the clarity, stability, and enforceability of agreements made between host governments and companies wishing to invest prior to the acquisition of assets, as well as the cost of failing to ensure host economies share in the benefits throughout the lifecycle of such projects.

Finally, the timing of these three effects is problematic, as our research suggests that they can reach their maximum impact at the same point in the development of the project, creating a 'perfect storm' of unfulfilled public expectations, lack of visible economic impacts, overwhelmed bureaucratic systems, and dissatisfied stakeholders all creating significant pressure on the host government. As tensions mount, there is typically only one place to which governments can look to provide short-term relief: the investors behind the mega project who are perceived to have deep pockets. Compared to unpalatable domestic policy alternatives, the investors are an obvious and relatively easy short-term target for political opprobrium and/or a source of additional cash. And all this can happen at exactly the point at which project developers are most vulnerable with a newly-operational project and no real return on their investment to date.

4 Some options for investors to address these issues

Some options investors should consider to address the issues identified above include the following.

1. Careful choices about project ownership, corporate finance, and entity structure should align country and company interests and address the '*misaligned incentives*' problem. As early as possible in the negotiation of foundational agreements with host governments, choices around the location (onshore versus offshore) and form (listed versus private) of project vehicles, as well as the level and nature of host government participation (equity share or control or limiting returns to taxation) should be made. These must bear in mind the long-term sustainability of the relationship and the likelihood of an eventual rise in the voice of resource nationalism. One other feature of project structure that can have an impact on project stability is the

involvement of multiple parties. Bi-lateral arrangements involving a single project investor and a host government can be simpler to negotiate and manage, but ultimately place more pressure on the relationship. Some investors have successfully sought to share risk and spread engagement challenges by bringing other international participants, co-investors, and, in this context, especially looking to involve International Financial Institutions (for example EBRD, IFC), who are able to take commercial positions but can be viewed as 'honest broker', third-party participants.

2. The practical and economic realities of the geology and geography of the natural resource and its critical infrastructure will dictate a certain minimum level of up-front capital commitment that cannot be justified without a certain scale and speed of development. To mitigate the '*system shock*' problem detailed above, project designers should consider modular or staged approaches that attenuate up-front capital exposure and maximise optionality for future expansions as far as possible. Projects that ramp up over time can match project development to the host nation's development capacity and stage the growth of the project to local economic conditions. Doing this may require a change in approach to financial modelling. Traditional NPV calculations take a static view of the discount rate, accentuate scale, speed, and short-term cash flows, and focus on operational and financial inputs only. By contrast, capital allocation approaches more appropriate to multi-decade investment horizons should include assessment of risk-mitigation and value-preservation, should recognise the value of modular expansion optionality, and should assess inputs that include sustainability efforts and changing sovereign risk.
3. While a staged approach will not always be feasible or economic, all project developers should begin work, as early as possible in the project development cycle, to establish up-front, in the foundational co-operation and investment agreements with the host government, parameters and principles on the transparent and equitable distribution of proceeds. These will not be complete when the agreements are signed, but will require work to ensure implementation throughout the life of the project. Addressing the '*fair share*' problem only becomes harder once the project is up and running. So, investing the time to agree on these measures up-front is crucial.
4. Failure to ensure these principles are then implemented by the host government subsequently leads to increased costs and risk for investors as they are perceived to be accountable for resolving inequalities that emerge in practice. Therefore, investors must remain deeply

concerned with, and aware of, how these benefits are being distributed by governments throughout the life of the project and seek to be part of the national discourse on the subject. For example, to assist host governments and communities in understanding the impacts of mega projects, Rio Tinto has commenced detailed macroeconomic project impact assessments with follow-up studies including the modelling of impacts on regional communities (see, for example, Fisher et al., 2011; Rio Tinto, 2013a). The involvement of international institutional investors such as the IFC in the project is another way of spreading the burden of explaining the impacts of mega projects to host communities and governments.

5. All the problems identified above can be mitigated to some extent by focusing on the three key expenditure levers: procurement, people, and infrastructure. All three can be targeted at making the project's impact on the national economy both equitable and sustainable. Maximising local content in the short-term is a start, but it also requires careful consideration of the equitable allocation of benefits and the longer-term impact these will have on national development. For example, the project may consider enabling new, sustainable, and competitive sectors that deliver a more diversified national economy, supporting educational and capacity-building initiatives at a national scale, and collaboratively developing infrastructure in ways that enhance and enable national development plans.

5 Conclusion

Much has been written about a change in the mind-set of the extractive industry toward a greater recognition of the importance of safeguarding the social license to operate, and delivering the successful non-technical performance of major projects. It is fair to say, however, that the adoption of this new outlook is in its early stages when compared to the radical transformation of the industry's approach to environmental, health, and safety issues over the past 20 years. Few companies in the extractive industry assign sufficient resources or embed the necessary cultural and organisational changes to ensure that these issues continue to be addressed with sufficient scale or focus and over the necessary time-frame to achieve real impact.

However, there are major imperatives for the industry to pursue such change – a large share of the world's undeveloped mineral reserves are in emerging economies and since 2000 much of the growth in global mineral production has come from the developing world – so understanding how to operate effectively in such environments is necessary for those seeking to participate in such growth. Goldman Sachs research suggests that environmental, social, and governance (ESG) performance in companies in the oil and gas sector has some correlation to 'strong industry positioning…and high return on capital', as such companies are less vulnerable to costly delays that plague technically difficult projects in the developing (and developed) world.

Developers who seek to address these problems, mitigate these risks, and achieve healthy, sustainable, risk-adjusted returns on large-scale emerging market projects, must recognise and operationalise the insight that their projects have significant influence on, and are themselves deeply affected by, the overall health of the host economy and that they therefore have a crucial role to play outside the mine gate beyond just delivering a profitable operation.

As has been outlined above, the structure of the project's ownership and financing, the timing and design of the project's execution, and the equitable distribution of the project's benefits (the biggest levers for which are the core business areas of procurement, HR, and infrastructure) are all important ways that the developers of big projects in small economies can moderate sovereign risk and ultimately deliver benefits both to the host economy and to their own shareholders.

References

Calfucura, E, Ortiz, A M, Sanborn, C & Dammert, J L (2013), *Three Countries, Three Different Trajectories: Peru*, viewed 4 September 2013, <http://www.americasquarterly.org/charticles/natural-resource-extraction-chile-peru-colombia/pdf/PERU.pdf>.

Cattaneo, J (2009), *The New Politics of Natural Resources*, ERM Report, London.

Centerra Gold (2013), *Kumtor History*, viewed 19 September 2013, <http://www.centerragold.com/operations/kumtor-history>.

Chupezi, T J, Ingram, V & Schure, J (2009), 'Impacts of Artisanal Gold and Diamond Mining on Livelihoods and the Environment in the Sangha Tri-National Park landscape, viewed 19 September 2013, <http://www.cifor.org/publications/pdf_files/Books/BChupezi0901.pdf>.

Collier, P & Hoeffler, A (2007), *Testing the Neocon Agenda: Democracy in Resource-Rich Societies*, Department of Economics, University of Oxford, viewed 19 September 2013, <http://users.ox.ac.uk/~econpco/research/pdfs/TestingTheNeoconAgenda.pdf>.

Corkin, L (2012), 'Chinese Construction Companies in Angola: A Local Linkages Perspective', *Resources Policy*, vol. 37, no. 4, pp. 475–483.

Dahlman, C & Nelson, R (1995), 'Social Absorption Capability, National Innovation Systems and Economic Development', in Perkins, D H and Koo, B H (eds), *Social Capability and Long-term Growth*, Macmillan Press, Basingstoke.

De Castro, O (2012), 'Operational Aspects of Fiscal Policy in Resource-Rich Countries', *Proceedings of the Management of Natural Resources in Sub-Saharan Africa Kinshasa Conference*, viewed 14 October 2013, <http://www.imf.org/external/np/seminars/eng/2012/kinshasa/pdf/odc.pdf>.

EI Source Book (2013), *Revenue Management and Distribution*, viewed 14 October 2013, <http://www.eisourcebook.org/688_8RevenueManagementandDistribution.html>.

Fisher, B S, Batdelger, T, Gurney, A, Galindev, R, Begg, M, Buyantsogt, B, Lkhanaajav, E & Chadraaval, B (2011), *The Development of the Oyu Tolgoi Copper Mine: An Assessment of the Macroeconomic Consequences for Mongolia*, BAE Report, Canberra.

Foreign Affairs, Trade and Development Canada (2013), 'Natural Resources Management: Creating Jobs and Opportunities in Developing Countries', viewed 14 October 2013, <http://www.acdi-cida.gc.ca/acdi-cida/acdi-cida.nsf/eng/FRA-102311492-LK7>.

Grigoryan, A (2013), 'The Impact of Mining Sector on Growth, Inequality and Poverty: Evidence from Armenia', viewed 14 October 2013, <http://newsroom.aua.am/files/2013/04/mining_grigoryan.pdf>.

Hanlin, C (2011), *The Drive to Increase Local Procurement in the Mining Sector in Africa: Myth or Reality?* viewed 5 September 2013, <http://commodities.open.ac.uk/8025750500453F86/(httpAssets)/0DE9C320948C00538025787E003A5877/$file/The%20drive%20to%20increase%20local%20procurement%20in%20the%20Mining%20Sector%20in%20Africa%20Myth%20or%20reality.pdf>.

Hyndman, D (1995), 'Afek and Rebaibal: Ideologies of Social Protest and the Ok Tedi Mining Project', *Papua New Guinea Journal of the Polynesian Society*, vol. 104, no. 1, pp. 75–88.

Imbun, B Y (2010), *Anthropology of Mining in Papua New Guinea Greenfields*, Nova Science Publishers Inc., New York.

Imbun, B Y (2013), 'Maintaining Land Use Agreements in Papua New Guinea Mining: "Business as Usual"?', *Resources Policy*, vol. 38, no. 3, pp. 310–319.

IMF (2013a), *World Economic Outlook Database*, viewed 5 September 2013, <http://www.imf.org/external/pubs/ft/weo/2013/01/weodata/index.aspx>.

International Council on Mining & Metals (2008), *Resource Endowment Toolkit*, London.

Kumtor Operating Company (2013), *Contribution to the Economy*, viewed 10 October 2013, <http://www.kumtor.kg/en/media-relations/contribution-to-the-kyrgyz-economy/>.

Loayza, N, Mier y Teran, A & Rigolini, J (2013), Poverty, Inequality and the Local Natural Resource Curse, viewed 5 September 2013 <http://ftp.iza.org/dp7226.pdf>.

Otto, J, Andrews, C, Cawood, F, Doggett, M, Guj, P, Stermole, F, Stermole, J & Tilton, J (2006), *Mining Royalties: A Global Study of their Impact on Investors, Government, and Civil Society*, World Bank, Washington DC.

Oyu Tolgoi (2013), *Official Statement of Oyu Tolgoi LLC in Relation to Information, Data and Facts Related to Oyu Tolgoi Discussed During Open Session of the State Great Khural dated 1 February 2013*, viewed 19 September 2013, <http://ot.mn/en/node/3853>.

Oxfam (2009), *Mining Conflicts in Peru: Condition Critical*, viewed 4 September 2013, <http://www.oxfamamerica.org/articles/files/mining-conflicts-in-peru-condition-critical.pdf>.

Reeson, A F, Measham, T G & Hosking, K (2012), 'Mining Activity, Income Inequality and Gender in Australia', *Australian Journal of Agricultural and Resource Economics*, vol. 56, no. 2, pp. 302–313.

Rio Tinto (2011), *Simandou SEIA Volume 1 Mine, Chapter 18: In-Migration*, 19 September 2013, <http://www.riotintosimandou.com/documents/Mine/M_Ch18_InMigr_EN.pdf>.

Rio Tinto (2013a), *Development of Oyu Tolgoi Underground Mine Delayed*, 19 September 2013, <http://www.riotinto.com/documents/290713_Development_of_Oyu_TolgoI_underground_mine_delayed.pdf>.

Rio Tinto (2013b), *Simandou Economic Impact Report*, London.

World Bank (2012), *Increasing Local Procurement by the Mining Industry in West Africa*, viewed 5 September 2013, <http://siteresources.worldbank.org/INTENERGY2/Resources/8411-West_Africa.pdf>.

World Bank (2013), *Foreign Direct Investment, Net Inflows (BoP, current US$)*, viewed 19 September 2013, <http://data.worldbank.org/indicator/BX.KLT.DINV.CD.WD>.

12
Monetary Policy and International Reserves in Emerging Economies: Theory and Empirics

Prakash Kumar Shrestha and Willi Semmler

1 Introduction

One striking feature following the Asian economic crisis of 1997 is that many emerging economies have built up a large stock of international reserves (Aizenman & Marion, 2003; Aizenman & Lee, 2007; IMF, 2010). This reflects an important fact that sound macroeconomic management with low inflation may not insulate an economy from the likely adverse impact of volatile capital flows in the current international monetary system. The international monetary system has been observing global imbalances and unpredictable, volatile cross-border capital flows (IMF, 2010). A sharp accumulation of international reserves in many emerging countries in response to this has generated widespread concern among both policy makers and academic circles (Obstfeld, Shambaugh, & Taylor, 2010; IMF, 2010; Aizenman & Lee, 2007).

For most emerging countries, the reserve holdings have increased to high levels relative to traditional norms – almost 10 months of imports and 475% of short-term external debts in 2008 (IMF, 2010). The reserve accumulation beyond the traditional motives seems to be due to potential vulnerabilities and market imperfections in the international monetary and financial system (IMF, 2010). Many emerging and developing countries are facing an unstable international environment subject to a variety of shocks. Some events can lead to an outbreak of sudden and sharp reversals in the financial account, which is called a 'sudden stop'. The recent global financial and economic crisis of 2007 (which originated in the US, with the domino effects felt in emerging countries) has also sparked a renewed interest in the role of international reserves on macroeconomic and financial stability (IMF, 2010; Aizenman & Sun, 2009). Countries with a higher stock of foreign currency reserves, such as the East Asian countries and Central and Eastern European countries, weathered the adverse impact of sudden capital outflows and exchange rate depreciation emanating from the current global financial crisis to a large extent (Aizenman & Sun, 2009).

In this context, monetary policy should play an effective role in financial and external stability. The traditional role of price stability is insufficient in an era of growing trade and financial linkages among countries. There should be a new type of monetary policy rule. However, a Taylor-type monetary policy only focuses on inflation and output gap. Moreover, some inflation targeting countries only consider inflation as an objective for monetary policy. There is, therefore, an inadequate theoretical foundation linking monetary policy and international reserves in economic literature. In this context, this chapter attempts to provide a theoretical model and empirical evidence for a new type of monetary policy rule appropriate for emerging economies by considering international reserves as an important economic variable.

In developing a dynamic macro model for an open economy, this chapter incorporates some realistic and innovative features observed in emerging countries subject to speculative attacks and sudden capital outflows. In addition, this chapter examines empirically new monetary policy reaction function derived from the model by using the Auto Regressive Distributed Lag (ARDL) approach advanced by Pesaran, Shin, & Smith (2001). For empirical estimations, five emerging East Asian countries – Thailand, South Korea, Malaysia, Philippines, and Indonesia – are chosen. These countries were seriously affected by the 1997 financial crisis and have demonstrated a similar behaviour of accumulating international reserves in the post-crisis period and suffering from a similar type of shocks (Hsing, 2009).

2 Theoretical model

This section presents a dynamic open economy macro model that shows an interaction between the domestic macro economy, external sector, and monetary policy. The main purpose of this model is to analyse the process of international reserve accumulation and its relation to monetary policy actions by acknowledging the risk mitigation role of international reserves. For emerging economies with a managed floating exchange rate and imperfect capital mobility, international reserves are obviously important for domestic economy and have monetary implications. Since these countries need to pay attention to the external payment constraints because of the minor role of their currencies in international transactions, we propose that the central bank should have three target variables in its loss function: inflation, output gap, and international reserves. While the first two variables are traditionally considered for macroeconomic stability, the last one is necessary for financial and external stability. It is believed that with sufficient stock of international reserves, the central bank could defend the value of domestic currency and avoid a likely financial crisis. The Asian financial crisis of 1997 showed that sudden outflows of capital could trigger a currency crisis, and eventually a financial crisis.

Considering the important role of international reserves, we modify the central bank's loss function as follows (see also Svensson, 2000; Bar-Ilan & Lederman, 2007; Bar-Ilan & Marion, 2009).

$$L = \int_0^{\infty} e^{-rt} \left\{ \frac{\lambda_1}{2}(\pi_t - \pi^*)^2 + \frac{\lambda_2}{2}(y_t - y^*)^2 + \frac{\lambda_3}{2}(R_t - R^*)^2 \right\} dt \tag{12.1}$$

where π_t, y_t, and $\boldsymbol{R}_t$ represent the inflation, the log of actual output, and the log of international reserves, respectively, while π^*, y^*, and $\boldsymbol{R}^*$ are the targeted inflation, the potential output, and the targeted international reserve level, respectively. The parameters λ_1, λ_2, and λ_3 are the relative weights of the three variables in the objective function. Similar to the inflation and output gap, $\boldsymbol{R} > \boldsymbol{R}^*$ would imply costs to the country, for example social costs as in Rodrik (2006), while $\boldsymbol{R} < \boldsymbol{R}^*$ could entail capital flight and cause exchange rate depreciation and financial crisis by increasing the risk level of a country. Hence, our purposed loss function represents the current objective of many central banks of emerging and developing economies.

The objective of the central bank is to minimise the loss function through monetary policy instruments – by setting the short-term nominal interest rate. Monetary policy, in fact, needs to set the short-term interest rate for each period 't' to minimise the inter-temporal loss function, subject to the state of the economy (Svensson, 2003). We describe the state of the economy by the following simple but standard structure.

$$y_t = \alpha - \beta(i_t - \pi^e) + X_t(e), X'(e) > 0, \beta > 0 \tag{12.2}$$

$$\pi_t = \pi^e + \eta(y_t - y^*) + \theta e_t \tag{12.3}$$

Equation (12.2) represents an open economy IS curve, in which output (the log of real output, y_t) is assumed to depend on the real interest rate $(i_t - \pi^e)$ and the log of exchange rate, *e*. In this equation, i_t is the nominal interest rate, π^e is the expected inflation rate, and α and β are positive parameters. The last term is the net exports, which is assumed to be a positive function of the log of the exchange rate (*e*). On the other hand, Equation (12.3) represents an open economy Phillip curve, following the concept of Ball (1999) and Svensson (2000), where inflation is positively related to the output gap $(y_t - y^*)$, the expected inflation π^e, and the log of exchange rate (*e*).

In addition, we also have exchange rate and reserve accumulation dynamics for emerging economies, representing the law of motions for state variables. Equation (12.4) represents the exchange rate dynamics, where e is the log of exchange rate, and i and i^f are the domestic and the foreign interest rates. The degree of adjustment of exchange rate (a higher 'e' indicates a depreciation) depends on the speed of the capital mobility and the central bank's intervention in the foreign exchange markets, which is represented by α_1. Studies on exchange rates, such as Dornbusch (1976) and Svensson (2000), usually adopt the uncovered interest parity (UIP) theory to explain the exchange rate determination. However, several studies find weak empirical support for the UIP, for example, McCallum (1996), Flood and Rose (2001), and recently Engel (2011) and Baillie and Chang (2011). Hence, we depart from the UIP and presume that interest rate differences do not predict depreciation but an appreciation of the exchange rate. A rise in the domestic interest rate causes capital inflows. Baillie and Chang (2011) and Brunnermeier, Nagel, & Pedersen (2009) argue that carry trade and momentum trading tend to establish such a relationship. We thus postulate an exchange rate dynamic as:

$$\dot{e} = \alpha_1 \left\{ \frac{i_t^f - i_t}{\sigma} + \rho(i_t - i_t^f, R_t) \right\}, \rho_{i-i^f} > 0, \rho_R < 0 \tag{12.4}$$

The second part inside the bracket in Equation (12.4) represents the insurance premium for the country specific risk ρ, which is assumed to be a function of volatility of interest rate differential $i - i^f$ and the (log) level of international reserves R. This is the innovative part of our model. A currency of any country with a higher perception of risk should be weaker, *ceteris paribus* (Engel, 2011). Moreover, this equation further considers the volatility of returns (σ) which also affects the capital inflows; hence, the first term inside the bracket is a Sharpe ratio – excess return per unit of risk.

On the other hand, following the work of Bar-Ilan and Marion (2009) but considering capital inflows explicitly, Equation (12.5) shows the reserve accumulation dynamics in a small open economy. A country accumulates reserves through the current account and capital account transactions. The first term in Equation (12.5) represents the current account, while the second term denotes the net capital inflows. Since the capital account is open under financial liberalisation, both channels are important for changing international reserves in emerging countries. The first term, net exports, is assumed to be a function of the exchange rate, and the second term, $F(i_t - i_t^f, R_t)$, that is, net capital inflows is considered to be a function of interest rate differentials and the (log) level of international reserves.

$$\dot{R} = X(e_t) + F(i_t - i_t^f, R_t), F_{i-i^f} > 0, F_R > 0 \quad (12.5)$$

For simplifying the above model, we define some further auxiliary equations. Equation (12.6) represents the net export function which is a function of exchange rate, where ε represents the elasticity of exports to a change in exchange rate.

$$X_t(e) = \mathrm{m} + \varepsilon \mathrm{e}_t \quad (12.6)$$

Further, Equation (12.7) stands for the risk premium function for Equation (4), where the first term is a country risk associated with a currency run, which could be triggered by the (log) level of international reserves, and the second term is the exchange rate risk driven by the volatility of interest rate differentials. The terms $\boldsymbol{\sigma}_1$ and $\boldsymbol{\sigma}_2$ are coefficients. So, the risk premium is inversely related to the (log) level of international reserves and positively to the volatility of interest rate differential.

$$\rho(i_t - i_t^f, R_t) = \frac{\sigma_1}{R_t} + \frac{\sigma_2}{2}(i_t - i_t^f)^2 \quad (12.7)$$

$$F(i_t - i_t^f, R_t) = \beta_0 + \beta_1 \frac{i_t - i_t^f}{\sigma} + \beta_2 (R_t - R^*) + \frac{\beta_3}{e_t} \quad (12.8)$$

Moreover, we define Equation (12.8) as the net capital inflow dynamics for Equation (12.5). In Equation (12.8), the net capital flows depend positively on the interest rate differential, adjusted by the volatility, where $\boldsymbol{\sigma}$ represents the volatility of asset returns and $\boldsymbol{\beta}_0$, $\boldsymbol{\beta}_1$, and $\boldsymbol{\beta}_2$ are constant coefficients; here $\boldsymbol{\beta}_0$ represents an autonomous flow of foreign capital.

The third term of the Equation (12.8) indicates that the existing (log) level of international reserves relative to a certain target level, which also affects the capital flows by changing the perception of foreign investors in line with the 'sudden stop' literature. Technically, this can create a positive feedback loop for the reserve accumulation process. As such, a higher level of international reserves attracts more capital inflows on the belief that there would be no risks of repatriation of investments and vice versa. A country's risk premium may fall as international reserves increase (Levy-Yeyati, 2008). Risk will be low when there is an adequate level of international reserves, as it signals stability as well as credit-worthiness to foreign investors and international rating agencies. Finally, the last term shows the possible capital flows affected by the exchange rate movement. A continuous depreciation may cause capital outflows and vice versa. All of the above terms have been introduced to capture the realistic picture of the situation that emerging countries have been facing in the current state of the international monetary system.

By inserting Equations (12.2) and (12.3) into Equation (12.1) subject to the exchange rate Equation (12.4) and the reserve accumulation Equation (12.5), the problem of monetary policy is to set the interest rate to minimise the loss function as

$$\min_i L = \int_0^\infty e^{-rt}[\frac{\lambda_1}{2}\{\pi^e + \eta(\alpha - \beta(i_t - \pi^e\} + m + \varepsilon e_t - y^*) \\ + \theta e_t - \pi^*\}^2 + \ldots + \frac{\lambda_2}{2}\{(\alpha - \beta(i_t - \pi^e) + m + \varepsilon e_t - y^*\} \\ + \frac{\lambda_2}{2}(R_t - R^*)^2]dt \tag{12.9}$$

By replacing the auxiliary Equations (12.6)–(12.8) in Equations (12.2), (12.4), and (12.5) respectively, the associated current value Hamiltonian with the co-state variables q_1 and q_2 for the exchange rate and the level of international reserves is

$$H = -\frac{\lambda_1}{2}\{\pi^e + \eta(\alpha - \beta(i_t - \pi^e) + m + \varepsilon e_t - y^*) + \theta e_t - \pi^*\}^2 + \cdots \\ -\frac{\lambda_2}{2}\{\alpha - \beta(i_t - \pi^e) + m + \varepsilon e_t - y^*\}^2 - \frac{\lambda_3}{2}(R_t - R^*)^2 + \cdots \\ + q_1[\alpha_1\{\frac{i_t^f - i_t}{\sigma} + \frac{\sigma_1}{R_t} + \frac{\sigma_2}{2}(i_t - i_t^f)^2\}] + \cdots \\ + q_1\{m + \varepsilon e_t + \beta_0 + \beta_1\frac{i_t^f - i_t}{\sigma} + \beta_2(R_t - R^*) + \frac{\beta_3}{e_t}\} \tag{12.10}$$

The solution of this model gives us a monetary policy reaction function (a time path for policy instrument) to guide the policy decision amidst uncertain future from Equation (12.11). Such a reaction function includes three target variables: output gap, inflation, and international reserves. Detail derivation of such a rule is omitted here for lack of space and complexity.

3 Empirics

As per the theoretical framework discussed in Section 2, we set up the following monetary policy reaction function:

$$i_t = \alpha_0 + \alpha_R \log R_t + \alpha_\pi \pi_t + \alpha_y YG_t + \alpha_d D + \varepsilon_t \tag{12.11}$$

where i_t is the short-term interest rate, π_t the CPI-based inflation, YG_t the output gap, $\log R_t$ represents the (log) level of international reserves (in million US$), and D is the dummy variable for the crisis period since we have chosen five East Asian countries affected by the Asian crisis of 1997 for empirical estimation. The expected signs of the response parameters are $\alpha_R < 0$, $\alpha_\pi, \alpha_y > 0$.

Following Mohanty and Klau (2004) and taking into account the roles of exchange rate and foreign interest rate, we also estimate the following extended alternative monetary policy reaction function. This is also useful to examine the robustness of monetary policy reaction to the (log) level of international reserves.

$$i_t = \alpha_0 + \alpha_R \log R_t + \alpha_\pi \pi_t + \alpha_y YG_t + \alpha_d D + \alpha_e \Delta lreer + \alpha_i i^f + \varepsilon_t \tag{12.12}$$

where $\Delta lreer$ is the change in log of real exchange rate and i^f is the foreign interest rate, represented by the three-month US Treasury bill rate to examine the degree of capital market integration.

In our estimation, the inflation rate is the annual percentage change in the consumer price index, and the volume of international reserves are in million US$. The output gap is the percent deviation of the actual real output from potential output. The potential output is estimated by the HP filter process with a parameter of 1600 for the quarterly data. We use the short-term interest rate – the money market interest rate in most cases – as the relevant left-hand variable for the monetary policy reaction function. It is guided by the fact that many central banks until recently did not have an official policy rate, and it is obvious that monetary operating regimes varied considerably during the sample period. Hence, we consider short-term money market interest rate to be more appropriate in capturing the stance of monetary policy in a variety of operating procedures than the actual policy rate. In Malaysia and Thailand, the money market rates have tended to track their policy targets closely (McCauley, 2006). Moreover, we use the real effective exchange rate (REER) for Thailand, Korea, Malaysia, and Philippines, but the real exchange rate (RER) for Indonesia because of the unavailability of the REER. When the real exchange rate increases, it means real appreciation. We use a three-month US treasury bill rate as a proxy for the foreign interest rate.

We collect data from the IMF's International Financial Statistics online database. Depending on the availability of real sector data in quarterly frequency, different sample periods are chosen for each country as in Hsing (2009). For example, 1993:Q1 to 2010:Q2 for Thailand, 1984:Q1 to 2010:Q2 for South Korea, 1988:Q1 to 2010:Q2 for Malaysia, 1981:Q1 to 2010:Q2 for the Philippines, and 1997:Q1 to 2010:Q2 for Indonesia.

Table 12.1 presents the summary statistics of variables used in estimating the monetary reaction function and their correlations with the short-term interest rate. The average inflation and short-term interest rates are relatively high in Indonesia and the Philippines. In all sample countries, during the sample period, the average output gap remained negative and the REER undervalued. On an average, we observe a comparatively high volatility of short-term interest rate, inflation, and Δlreer in Indonesia, while Korea witnessed a higher volatility of the output gap and Δlreer. The (log) level of international reserves is negatively correlated with the short-term interest rate in all selected countries: –0.4 in Thailand to –0.7 in the Philippines. Moreover, the interest rates are found positively correlated with the inflation and the US Treasury bill rate, and negatively with the Δlreer as expected. However, the correlation coefficients with Δlreer are low, and correlations with the output gap are mixed and mostly low.

Much empirical estimation on monetary policy reactions relies on the simple ordinary least square (OLS) and the Generalised Method of Moments (GMM); for example, Mohanty and Klau (2004) use both the OLS and GMM, Clarida, Gali, & Gertler (1998) and Berument and Tasci (2004) use the GMM, and Hsing (2009) uses just the OLS. There are two major drawbacks on these methods: weak identification and spurious relation in a level form (Sutherland, 2010). Hence, we use the Auto Regressive Distributive Lag (ARDL), which is also called the bound test approach postulated by Pesaran et al. (2001). This approach is 'applicable irrespective of whether underlying regressors are purely

Table 12.1 Summary statistics of the variables used in the model

Countries	i	logR	π	YG	Δlreer	ustbill
			Mean			
Thailand	5.02	10.68	3.36	−0.08	−0.02	3.41
South Korea	8.74	10.53	4.19	−0.25	−0.12	4.47
Malaysia	4.53	10.28	2.79	−0.08	−0.28	4.03
Philippines	12.22	8.44	8.67	−0.21	−0.20	5.23
Indonesia	15.56	10.42	11.65	−0.18	−0.29	3.11
			Standard Deviation			
Thailand	4.92	0.50	2.51	4.51	4.65	1.86
South Korea	4.77	1.49	2.11	6.59	5.81	2.35
Malaysia	2.11	0.84	1.48	3.60	3.02	2.17
Philippines	5.37	1.38	7.93	6.07	4.55	3.12
Indonesia	16.42	0.36	12.36	3.47	13.91	1.90
			Correlation with short-term interest rate			
Thailand		−0.40	0.70	0.15	−0.21	0.54
South Korea		−0.66	0.71	−0.009	−0.20	0.56
Malaysia		−0.51	0.58	0.02	−0.10	0.39
Philippines		−0.70	0.74	0.08	−0.11	0.59
Indonesia		−0.68	0.82	−0.21	−0.18	0.41

Table 12.2 ADF test with constant (Lag length selected on the basis of AIC)

	Thailand	South Korea	Malaysia	Philippines	Indonesia
i_t	−2.24	−1.50	−1.96	−3.14**	−1.72
Δi_t	−6.60*	−8.65*	−6.59*		−3.15**
π_t	−1.67	−1.95	−2.56	−2.65***	−3.18**
$\Delta\pi_t$	−2.98**	−4.87*	3.59*		
YG_t	−3.14**	−6.70*	−3.54*	−4.93*	−5.72*
$\log(R)_t$	0.98	−1.26	−0.97	−0.57	0.03
$\Delta\log(R)_t$	−6.36*	−4.53*	−6.79*	−3.35**	−5.49*
$lreer_t$	−1.78	−3.05**	−1.84	−2.37	−2.38
$\Delta lreer_t$	−7.18*		−4.72*	−8.83*	−5.70*
$ustbill_t$	−2.68***	−1.92	−1.87	−2.45	−2.54
$\Delta ustbill_t$	−3.40*	−3.90*	−4.59*	−6.52*	−3.69*
Sample period	1993:1–2010:2	1984:1–2010:2	1988:1–2010:2	1981:1–2010:1	1997:1–2010:2

Note: * 1%significance level, ** 5% significance level and *** 10% significance level.

I(0), purely I(1) or mutually co-integrated' (Pesaran et al., 2001: 289). As shown in Table 12.2, some variables are stationary and the others are non-stationary. The inflation is I(0) in the Philippines and Indonesia, while I(1) in other countries; the short-term interest rate (i_t) is I(0) except in the Philippines. The output gap (YG_t) is I(0), and $\log(R_t)$ is I(1) in all sample countries. Moreover, the Δlreer is I(1) except in Korea, and the *ustbill* is also I(1) except in Thailand.

Although not appropriate when the variables are I(2), this approach is relatively more efficient in a small or finite sample (Fosu & Magnus, 2006). Our variables are not I(2) as seen in Table 12.2, hence we can apply the ARDL approach. Sutherland (2010) uses this method to estimate the monetary policy reaction function in the OECD countries, taking only inflation and output gap in a forward-looking framework. Yet, the application of this method in estimating monetary policy reaction function is quite new and an unexplored area. The basic set up for the estimation of the monetary reaction function according to the ARDL approach is as follows:

$$\Delta i_t = c_0 + \alpha_1 i_{t-1} + \alpha_x \times_{t-1} + \sum_{i=1}^{\rho-1} ø_i' Z_{t-i} + \delta' Ä\times_t + c_1 D + u_t \tag{12.13}$$

where X_t is a vector of independent variables such as inflation (π_t) output gap (YG_t), the log level of international reserves ($\log R_t$), Real Effective Exchange Rate ($REER_t$), and US Treasury bills ($ustbill_t$), that is, $X_t = (\log R_t, \pi_t, YG_t, REER_t, ustbill_t)$ and $Z_t = [i_t; X_t]$ and α_x is the vector of coefficients. D1 is dummy variable for the period of the Asian financial crisis. The bound testing approach is to estimate Equation (12.13) by the OLS estimation, in order to test for the existence of a long-run relationship among the variables by conducting an F-test for the joint significance of the coefficients of the lagged level of the variables, that is, H0: $\alpha_1 = \alpha_x = 0$ against the alternative hypothesis H1 = $\alpha_1 \neq \alpha_x \neq 0$. Pesaran et al. (2001) provide two asymptotic critical values, a lower value assuming the regressors are I(0) and an upper value assuming purely I(1) regressors. If F-statistic is above the upper critical value, we can reject the null hypothesis of no long-run relationship irrespective of the orders of integration of the time series (Fosu & Magnus, 2006). In addition, Pesaran et al. (2001) provide the bound test critical values for different numbers of independent variables. The disturbance u_t is assumed to be serially uncorrelated for which appropriate lag order ρ is selected.

The ARDL approach is first applied to the baseline specification in which $X_t = (\log R_t, \pi_t; YG_t)$. The appropriate lag length ρ for Equation (12.13) is selected by looking at AIC and SBC, and Lagrange Multiplier (LM) statistics for testing of no residual serial correlation against order 4 because of quarterly data. Table 12.3 shows the selection of lag

Table 12.3 Statistics for selecting lag orders

Countries	Statistics	Lag orders (1–7)						
Thailand	AIC	**3.98**	4.07	3.93	3.78	3.68		
	SIC	**4.41**	4.63	4.62	4.62	4.66		
	LM $\chi^2(4)$	**5.30**	4.63	8.35***	9.56**	24.99*		
South	AIC	3.48	3.37	3.31	3.29	3.27	3.32	**3.23**
Korea	SIC	**3.80**	3.80	3.84	3.92	4.00	4.15	4.16
	LM $\chi^2(4)$	7.01	12.0**	8.93***	21.84*	9.35***	9.05***	6.06
Malaysia	AIC	1.78	1.64	1.68	**1.65**	1.67		
	SIC	**2.15**	2.13	2.28	2.37	2.52		
	LM $\chi^2(4)$	4.52	9.51**	8.83***	3.6	8.38*		
Philippines	AIC	4.72	4.67	4.64	**4.64**	4.66	4.69	4.73
	SIC	5.03	**5.08**	5.15	5.24	5.37	5.50	5.64
	LM $\chi^2(4)$	14.7*	7.71	3.27	2.71	0.4	3.74	3.65
Indonesia	AIC	4.62	4.19	3.98	4.07	**3.75**		
	SIC	5.11	4.84	**4.79**	5.05	4.89		
	LM $\chi^2(4)$	14.4*	10.8*	3.02	3.69	5.73		

Note: * 1% significance level, ** 5% significance level, and *** 10% significance level.

orders – the lag order of 1 is selected for Thailand, 1 and 7 for Korea, 1 and 4 for Malaysia, 2 and 4 for the Philippines, and 3 and 5 for Indonesia to examine the level relationship.

Table 12.4 gives the values of F-statistics for testing the existence of a level relation. We compare this with the 0.05 critical value bounds for k = 3, that is, (3.25, 4.35) provided by Pesaran et al. (2001). Since F-statistics are outside the 0.05 critical value bounds except in the Philippines, we can conclusively reject the null hypothesis that there exists no level relationship. However, the test results remain inconclusive in the case of Philippines, where we do not accept the null hypothesis either. Despite inconclusive results in lag 2 and 3 for the Philippines, F-statistics for the level relation are higher than the upper critical bound when we take lag 1, although there is a serial correlation in error terms in this case.

After examining the existence of level relation, in the second step, we estimate the level relationship for the baseline model by the OLS, the error term of which will be used in the error correction estimation later. Table 12.5 depicts the estimation in the level form with p-value in parenthesis. The signs of coefficients are as theoretically expected. The response of the short-term interest rate to $\log R_t$ is negative, while to π_t and YG_t are positive. The level coefficient of $\log R_t$ and π_t are highly significant in all sample countries with the expected signs. The coefficients of $\log R_t$ are negative and statistically significant.

Table 12.4 Results from bound test for level relation

Countries	Lags	F-Stat	Critical bound values (0.05)
Thailand	1	6.51	3.25–4.35
South Korea	1	8.60	"
	7	6.69	"
Malaysia	1	4.39	"
	4	2.23	"
Philippines	1	5.77	"
	2	3.87	Inconclusive
	3	4.19	Inconclusive
Indonesia	3	8.07	3.25–4.35
	5	6.93	"

Table 12.5 Estimation of level relationship in baseline model

Countries	c	$LogR_t$	Π_t	YG_t	D1
Thailand	24.7 (0.00)	–2.25 (0.00)	1.2 (0.00)	0.10 (0.26)	3.06 (0.00)
South Korea	21.3 (0.00)	–1.66 (0.00)	1.1 (0.00)	0.03 (0.39)	7.46 (0.00)
Malaysia	13.0 (0.00)	–1.02 (0.00)	0.66 (0.00)	0.04 (0.33)	3.04 (0.00)
Philippines	24.15 (0.00)	–1.80 (0.00)	0.34 (0.00)	0.07 (0.10)	5.08 (0.00)
Indonesia	78.0 (0.00)	–7.02 (0.00)	0.67 (0.00)	–0.17 (0.31)	29.49 (0.00)

Note: p-value in parenthesis.

However, the coefficients of the output gap are not significantly different from zero in Thailand, Korea, and Malaysia, significant only in the Philippines and Indonesia. In this way, the evidence on the output stabilisation is mixed as in Mohanty and Klau (2004). This may be due to the fact that the estimates of the output gap may not adequately measure the gap, or a large chunk of real sector activities are out of the domain of monetary policy in these emerging economies. Moreover, estimating potential output is more difficult for emerging economies than for industrial economies, given the relative importance of supply shocks in the former (Mohanty & Klau, 2004). In addition, the real time output data may significantly differ from the ex-post data so that we get a biased picture in our estimation (Orphanides, 2001).

The significant negative response of the short-term interest rate to the (log) level of international reserves implies that when there is a rise in the level of international reserves, the central bank could get some leeway to reduce the short-term interest rate. On the other hand, while there is a fall in the level of international reserves, the central bank has to increase the interest rate to attract the capital inflows or to stop sudden capital outflows. However, there is a likely chance that one may interpret the coefficients of international reserves as a liquidity effect and similarly, the coefficients of inflation as a Fisher effect and the coefficients of output gap as a demand effect. Since we are assuming that the central bank exogenously determines the short-term interest rate, we can rule out such a possible interpretation by the assumption.

As we now have level relation, we can estimate the different orders of error correction form of ARDL (p, p1, p2, p3) models in four variables (i, logR, π, YG) that are selected by searching across the L^4 for each country, where L is number of lags in the error correction term specification with the estimates of the level relationship given as in Table 12.5. We take this as an equilibrium long-run relationship. We select the lag levels based on AIC criteria following the general to specific approach. Appendix 1 presents the conditional ECM regression associated with the above relationship, while Table 12.6 shows the coefficients of the error term only. In all sampled countries, the error correction term has been statistically significant with the expected sign, reflecting that any disequilibrium in the last period in the short-term interest rate is corrected in the current period. In other words, the short-term interest rate responds significantly to the disequilibrium of the previous period. The speed of adjustment of it is found to be high in Korea and the Philippines.

Empirical results presented in Appendix 1 of conditional ECM regression related to the above level relation provide further evidence of the complicated dynamics that seem to exist between the short-term interest and the major targeted variables. The regression for the ECM estimation fits well with relatively high adjusted R^2, ranging from 0.43 in Malaysia to 0.88 in Indonesia, and passes the diagnostic tests against the serial correlation. The LM statistics at lag 4 show that the null hypothesis

Table 12.6 Error correction form of ARDL (p, p_1, p_2, p_3) (Detail in Appendix 1)

Countries	ARDL(p, p1, p2, p3)	ecm(−1)	p-value
Thailand	ARDL(3, 4, 1, 5)	−0.21	0.01
South Korea	ARDL(5, 1, 1, 4)	−0.32	0.00
Malaysia	ARDL(4, 2, 3, 3)	−0.15	0.002
Philippines	ARDL(2, 4, 3, 0)	−0.41	0.00
Indonesia	ARDL(4, 2, 3, 3)	−0.16	0.00

of no serial correlation cannot be rejected in all cases at 5% level of significance. The coefficients of the change in international reserves are statistically significant with expected sign either at same period or a quarter lag. Except Malaysia, the short-term interest rates are also significantly responsive to change in inflation and the output gap (with lags in Thailand and Korea).

3.1 Robustness check with alternative and extending specification

In this section, we conduct the robustness check by extending the model to incorporate the REER and the foreign exchange rate, that is, estimating Equation (12.13) in the full form. We follow the same procedure as before. Table 12.7 presents the selection of lag order for (13), and Table 12.8 shows the bound test for level relation in the extended model. F-statistics clearly remain above the upper bound of critical values, reflecting the existence of level relation, except for Malaysia and the Philippines, where tests are inconclusive, but do not reject the null hypothesis of no level relation. Then, Table 12.9 presents the estimation of long-run level relationship which shows the long-run reaction coefficients of monetary policy to the target variables. Since we are not estimating an error correction version in the case, we added a dummy variable as well to account for the financial crisis.

The reaction of i_t to $\log R_t$ is still significant with the expected sign, except in Thailand. The reaction to inflation has also remained significant

Table 12.7 Selecting lag orders for the extended ARDL model

Countries	Statistics	Lag orders (1–5)				
Thailand	AIC	3.81	3.90	3.54	3.43	**2.75**
	SIC	4.43	4.73	4.58	4.68	**4.22**
	LM $\chi^2(4)$	5.11	16.2*	14.1*	18.2*	26.8*
South Korea	AIC	3.33	3.24	**3.15**	3.18	3.20
	SIC	**3.82**	3.88	3.96	4.14	4.33
	LM $\chi^2(4)$	8.3***	6.72	12.02**	5.58	5.09
Malaysia	AIC	1.78	1.56	**1.52**	1.56	1.61
	SIC	2.32	**2.28**	2.42	2.63	2.86
	LM $\chi^2(4)$	7.40	14.3*	10.3**	5.49	8.63***
Philippines	AIC	**4.44**	4.46	4.45	4.44	4.50
	SIC	**4.89**	5.06	5.20	5.34	5.55
	LM $\chi^2(4)$	1.69	1.25	4.92	2.24	2.59
Indonesia	AIC	4.03	3.71	3.58	**2.96**	
	SIC	4.76	4.67	4.79	**4.42**	
	LM $\chi^2(4)$	14.5*	7.81***	5.22	23.07*	

Note: * 1% significance level, ** 5% significance level, and *** 10% significance level.

Table 12.8 Bound test for level relation for the extended ARDL model Null hypothesis: no level relationship

Countries	Lags	F-Stat	Critical bound values (0.05) (2.62–3.79)
Thailand	1	9.43	Rejected
South Korea	1	5.31	"
	4	6.66	"
Malaysia	1	3.54	Inconclusive
	4	0.87	Rejected
Philippines	1	3.54	Inconclusive
Indonesia	3	7.80	Rejected

Table 12.9 Estimation of level relationship in the extended model

Countries	c	$LogR_t$	Π_t	YG_t	Δlreer	ustbil	D1
Thailand	1.83	−0.32	1.04	0.05	−0.15	0.76	3.56
	(0.86)	(0.73)	(0.00)	(0.57)	(0.06)	(0.00)	(0.00)
South Korea	15.87	−1.28	1.14	0.02	−0.05	0.32	6.68
	(0.00)	(0.00)	(0.00)	(0.50)	(0.21)	(0.02)	(0.00)
Malaysia	16.1	−1.27	0.64	0.07	0.10	−0.12	3.67
	(0.00)	(0.00)	(0.00)	(0.09)	(0.09)	(0.20)	(0.00)
Philippines	19.09	−1.34	0.38	0.05	−0.20	0.16	4.21
	(0.00)	(0.00)	(0.00)	(0.26)	(0.00)	(0.16)	(0.00)
Indonesia	71.75	−6.47	0.66	−0.17	0.02	0.17	30.11
	(0.00)	(0.00)	(0.00)	(0.33)	(0.66)	(0.54)	(0.00)

as before in all countries. The coefficient of output gap remains significant only in Malaysia, while the responses to change in Δlreer are only significant in Thailand and the Philippines, not in the other countries. Moreover, the response to the US Treasury bill, as a proxy for the foreign interest rate, is statistically significant only in Thailand and Korea. Hence, the final results show that monetary policy in open economy countries tends to respond to the inflation and the (log) level of international reserves more robustly than to the output gap, the REER, and the foreign interest rate. Obviously, there are some country-specific differences due to institutional factors.

4 Conclusions

Since international reserves play an important role in maintaining external and financial stability, conventional monetary policy rules need to be modified for emerging economies. We build an open economy dynamic macro model, which tends to capture economic structure and many policy behaviours of these economies. Our model provides a theoretical framework to derive the new monetary policy rule, which includes international reserves in addition to output gap and inflation in the monetary policy reaction function. In other words, optimal monetary policy rule should incorporate international reserves in addition to output gap and inflation.

Our empirical findings show that monetary policy has been reacting to the (log) level of international reserves in the selected East Asian countries. It shows that our theoretical model tends to reflect the real picture of emerging economies as regards to monetary policy reaction function. Our theoretical model and empirical findings therefore suggest that the conventional 'Taylor rule' focusing on the output gap and inflation is not fully appropriate for emerging countries because of a growing financial instability and external constraints in the current state of the international monetary system.

Appendix

Estimation of Error Correction Model

Regressors	Thailand	South Korea	Malaysia	Philippines	Indonesia
C	0.02(0.95)	−0.06(0.65)	0.07(0.28)	−0.20(0.35)	−0.40(0.33)
$\hat{e}_{t-1}$	−0.19(0.02)	−0.32(0.00)	−0.15(0.00)	−0.41(0.00)	−0.16(0.05)
Δi_{t-1}	0.2(0.18)	0.09(0.32)	0.23(0.00)	−0.04(0.67)	−0.03(0.77)
Δi_{t-2}	0.15(0.28)	−0.16(0.04)	0.08(0.45)	0.22(0.02)	0.24(0.01)
Δi_{t-3}	0.27(0.03)	−0.06(0.47)	0.15(0.14)		0.30(0.00)
Δi_{t-4}		0.14(0.08)	0.31(0.00)		0.14(0.11)
Δi_{t-5}		−0.08(0.31)			
$\Delta \log R_t$	−11.2(0.00)	−0.37(0.72)	−1.96(0.00)	−0.98(0.24)	−12.15(0.06)
$\Delta \log R_{t-1}$	−12.2(0.00)	−3.16(0.00)	0.51(0.44)	−3.20(0.00)	10.19(0.19)
$\Delta \log R_{t-2}$	3.87(0.36)		−2.07(0.00)	0.01(0.99)	−3.60(0.61)
$\Delta \log R_{t-3}$	2.67(0.54)		−0.07(0.92)	1.48(0.09)	
$\Delta \log R_{t-4}$	9.14(0.04)		1.59(0.02)		
$\Delta \pi_t$	0.50(0.01)	0.43(0.00)	0.10(0.13)	0.21(0.03)	0.61(0.00)
$\Delta \pi_{t-1}$	−0.67(0.00)	−0.44(0.00)	−0.01(0.86)	0.21(0.06)	−0.13(0.37)
$\Delta \pi_{t-2}$			−0.09(0.28)	0.10(0.33)	−0.16(0.20)
$\Delta \pi_{t-3}$			−0.24(0.00)	−0.25(0.01)	−0.23(0.06)
ΔYG_t	−0.04(0.67)	−0.03(0.67)	0.02(0.30)	0.07(0.00)	0.74(0.00)
ΔYG_{t-1}	0.45(0.00)	0.21(0.00)	0.02(0.34)		0.29(0.16)
ΔYG_{t-2}	−0.06(0.61)	0.20(0.00)	0.03(0.13)		0.69(0.00)
ΔYG_{t-3}	0.12(0.27)	0.21(0.00)	0.04(0.07)		0.85(0.00)
ΔYG_{t-4}	0.02(0.85)	0.24(0.00)			
ΔYG_{t-5}	−0.29(0.01)				
D1	0.65(0.35)	4.71(0.00)		2.18(0.03)	4.78(0.10)
$AdjR^2$	0.45	0.54	0.43	0.53	0.88
$\chi^2_{sc}(4)$	98(0.09)	7.67(0.10)	3.61(0.46)	3.27(0.51)	5.33(0.25)

Note: p-value in parenthesis.

References

Agu, C (2008), 'Does the Policy Reaction Function of the Central Bank of Nigeria Follow Any Benchmark?', *International Journal of Economic Perspectives*, vol. 2, no. 2, pp. 104–122.

Aizenman, J & Lee, J (2007), 'International Reserves: Precautionary versus Mercantilist Views, Theory and Evidence', *Open Economies Review*, vol. 18, no. 2, pp. 191–214.

Aizenman, J & Marion, N (2003), 'The High Demand for International Reserves in the Far East: What Is Going On?', *Journal of the Japanese and International Economies*, vol. 17, no. 3, pp. 370–400.

Aizenman, J & Sun, Y (2009), 'The Financial Crisis and Sizable International Reserves Depletion: From "Fear of Floating" to the "Fear of Losing" International Reserves?', NBER Working Paper Series, no. 15308.

Baillie, R T & Chang, S S (2011), 'Carry Trades, Momentum Trading and the Forward Premium Anomaly', *Journal of Financial Markets*, vol. 14, no. 3, pp. 441–464.

Ball, L (1999), 'Policy Rules for Open Economies' in Taylor, J B (ed.), *Monetary Policy Rules*, The University Chicago Press, Chicago.

Bar-Ilan, A & Lederman, D (2007), 'International Reserves and Monetary Policy', *Economics Letters*, vol. 97, no. 2, pp. 170–178.

Bar-Ilan, A & Marion, N P (2009), 'A Macroeconomic Perspective on Reserve Accumulation', *Review of International Economics*, vol. 17, no. 4, pp. 802–823.

Berument, H & Tasci, H (2004), 'Monetary Policy Rules in Practice: Evidence from Turkey', *International Journal of Finance and Economics*, vol. 9, no. 1, pp. 33–38.

Brunnermeier, M K, Nagel, S & Pedersen, L H (2009), 'Carry Trades and Currency Crashes', *NBER Macroeconomic Annual 2008*, vol. 23, pp. 313–347, University of Chicago Press.

Cecchetti, S G (2000), 'Making Monetary Policy: Objectives and Rules', *Oxford Review of Economic Policy*, vol. 16, no. 4, pp. 43–59.

Chang, H (2005), 'Estimating the Monetary Policy Reaction Function for Taiwan: A VAR Model', *International Journal of Applied Economics*, vol. 2, no. 1, pp. 50–61.

Clarida, R, Gali, J & Gertler, M (1998), 'Monetary Policy Rules in Practice: Some International Evidence', *European Economic Review*, vol. 42, no. 6, pp. 1033–1067.

Dornbusch, R (1976), 'Expectations and Exchange Rate Dynamics', *Journal of Political Economy*, vol. 84, no. 6, pp. 1161–1176.

Engel, C (2011), 'The Real Exchange Rate, Real Interest Rates and the Risk Premium', *NBER Working Paper*, no. 17116.

Flood, R P & Rose, A K (2001), 'Uncovered Interest Rate Parity in Crisis: The Interest Rate Defense in the 1990s', Working Paper, International Monetary Fund (IMF), no. WP/01/207.

Fosu, O A E & Magnus, F J (2006), 'Bound Testing Approach to Cointegration: An Examination of Foreign Direct Investment, Trade and Growth Relationship', *American Journal of Applied Sciences*, vol. 3, no. 11, pp. 2079–2085.

Genberg, H & He, D (2009), 'Monetary and Financial Cooperation Among Central Banks in East Asia and the Pacific', in Rajan, R S, Thangavelu, S & Parinduri, R A (eds), *Exchange Rate, Monetary and Financial Issues and Policies in Asia*, World Scientific, Singapore.

Hsing, Y (2009), 'Is the Monetary Policy Rule Responsive to Exchange Rate Changes? The Case of Indonesia, Malaysia, the Philippines and Thailand', *International Review of Economics*, vol. 56, no. 2, pp. 123–132.

Hsing, Y & Lee, S (2004). 'Estimating the Bank of Korea's Monetary Policy Reaction Function: New Evidence and Implications', *The Journal of the Korean Economy*, vol. 5, no. 1, pp. 1–16.

International Monetary Fund (IMF) (2010), *Reserve Accumulation and International Monetary Stability*.

Jeanne, O (2007), 'International Reserves in Emerging Market Countries: Too Much of a Good Thing', *Brookings Papers on Economic Activity*, vol. 1, pp. 56–79.

Jeanne, O & Ranciere, R (2006), 'The Optimal Level of International Reserves for Emerging Market Countries: Formulas and Applications', Working Paper, International Monetary Fund (IMF), No. WP/06/229.

Kim, S & Park, Y C (2006), 'Inflation Targeting in Korea: A Model of Success?', BIS Papers No. 31, Bank for International Settlements, pp. 140–164.

Lavoie, M (2006), *Introduction to Post Keynesian Economics*, Palgrave-Macmillan, New York.

Levy-Yeyati, E (2008), 'The Cost of Reserves', *Economics Letters*, vol. 100, no. 1, pp. 39–42.

McCallum, B T (1996), *International Monetary Economics*, Oxford University Press, New York.

McCauley, R N (2006), 'Understanding Monetary Policy in Malaysia and Thailand: Objectives, Instruments and Independence', BIS Papers No. 31, Bank of International Settlements, pp. 172–198.

Mohanty, M S & Klau, M, (2004), 'Monetary Policy Rules in Emerging Market Economies: Issues and Evidence', BIS Working Papers No. 149, <http://www.bis.org/publ/work149.pdf>.

Obstfeld, M, Shambaugh, J C & Taylor, A M (2010), 'Financial Stability, the Trilemma, and International Reserves', *Journal of Macroeconomics*, vol. 2, no. 2, pp. 57–94.

Orphanides, A (2001), 'Monetary Policy Rules Based on Real-Time Data', *American Economic Review*, vol. 91, no. 4, pp. 964–985.

Pesaran, H H, Shin, Y & Smith, R J (2001), 'Bound Testing Approaches to the Analysis of Level Relationship', *Journal of Applied Econometrics*, vol. 16, no. 3, pp. 289–326.

Rodrik, D (2006), 'The Social Cost of Foreign Exchange Reserves', *International Economic Journal*, vol. 20, no. 3, pp. 253–266.

Semmler, W, Griener, A & Zhang, W (2005), *Monetary and Fiscal Policies in the Euro Area: Macro Modeling, Learning and Empirics*, Elsevier, Amsterdam.

Sutherland, D (2010), 'Monetary Policy Reaction Functions in the OECD', Working Papers, No. 761, OECD Economics Department, viewed 18 June 2011 <http://dx.doi.org/10.1787/5kmfwj7z6d7j-en>.

Svensson, L E (2000), 'Open Economy Inflation Targeting', *Journal of International Economics*, vol. 50, no. 1, pp. 155–183.

Svensson, L E (2003), 'What Is Wrong with Taylor Rule? Using Judgement in Monetary Policy Through Targeting Rules', *Journal of Economic Literature*, vol. 41, no. 2, pp. 426–477.

Taylor, J B (1993), 'Discretion Versus Policy Rules in Practice', *Carnegie-Rochester Conferences Series on Public Policy*, vol. 39, pp. 195–214.

Taylor, J B (2001), 'The Role of the Exchange Rate in Monetary Policy Rules', *American Economic Review*, vol. 91, no. 2, pp. 263–267.

13

Stock Market Impact of Sovereign Rating Changes: Alternative Benchmark Models

Emawtee Bissoondoyal-Bheenick and Robert Brooks

1 Introduction

Given the current state of the world capital markets, more emphasis is being placed on the growing importance of credit rating agencies in providing standardised assessment of credit risk. One of the main applications of credit ratings is to assess the risk exposure of a national market. Sovereign credit ratings often serve as a ceiling for private sector ratings of any given country, which stretches their influence far beyond government securities. The change of sovereign ratings is one of the key factors that may trigger re-weighting of the portfolios held. One component of the literature assesses the national stock market impact of sovereign ratings changes (see for example Brooks, Faff, Hillier, & Hillier 2004; Pukthuanthong-Le, Elayan, & Rose 2007; Ferreira & Gama, 2007). Most of the studies in this area have used an event study methodology to assess the impact of sovereign ratings changes on stock market return. It should be noted though that most of these studies have used the conventional market model to calculate the abnormal return in the event study. The sovereign rating literature suggests that rating downgrades generally have a significant impact on the market, while rating upgrades do not have the same informative value. This study uses different benchmark models to test the validity of the results that are found in previous papers.

The key objective of this study is to provide an empirical comparison of the assessment of the impact of sovereign rating changes on national stock market returns by using different benchmark models of asset pricing. This study has a number of distinctive features. First, we assess the impact of sovereign rating changes on stock market returns using four different approaches, that is, the market model, the quadratic market model, the downside model, and the quadratic downside model. The major contribution is to assess whether the finding in the literature that, in general, rating downgrades have an impact on stock market returns while rating upgrades do not have the same informational value, are different when the four models are applied. The second key aspect of this analysis is that we include in our modelling the Fama-French factors. Hence the aim of this study is to make a comparison of the different methods of calculating abnormal returns to assess the impact of sovereign rating on the stock markets, that is, comparing the standard market model to the four variants of the Fama-French model: the standard three-factors model, a higher-order three-factor model, a downside version, and a higher-order downside model, and these models are then augmented with momentum factors. A test of the relationship of the credit risk and return using CAPM, Lintner (1965), Fama and French (1993), and Fama-French model augmented by momentum factor has been undertaken by Avramov, Chordia, Jostova, and Philipov (2009). However, their analysis is at a firm level and demonstrates that the credit risk effect is robust to adjustment of risk factors, as well as firm characteristics. In this chapter, we assess the impact on the overall stock market return and assess the impact of sovereign risk using alternative modelling techniques.

Empirical evidence on tests of asset pricing models suggests that multifactor models have some success in explaining the anomalies of the CAPM. To date, perhaps the most serious challenge to the validity of the CAPM has come from research by Fama and French (1992). There have been numerous studies which make use of the Fama-French factors for asset pricing and assess their relevance as compared to the CAPM. However, it should be highlighted that the Fama-French model has not been applied to test for the impact of sovereign rating changes on the market. A major debate in the asset pricing literature is whether the Fama-French factors might be substitutes for other factors. Two popular alternatives have been higher-order and downside factors. The Fama-French three-factor model may proxy for higher-order co-moments. For example, for the US, Chung, Johnson, and Schill (2006) find that Fama-French factors may proxy for higher-order co-moments. For the UK, Hung, Shackleton, and Xu (2004) find a similar effect. This suggests a need for consideration of such alternatives in the calculation of abnormal returns to provide a better insight on the impact of rating changes on stock markets.

Another criticism of the mean-variance CAPM, is that the model disregards the up and down movements of asset returns and the validity of the measure of risk, variance, is subject to the distribution of returns being symmetric and normal. There is argument in the literature that an alternate measure is to consider downside risk. In fact, Pettengill, Sundaram, and Mathur (1995) argue that appropriate allowance for up/down betas can overcome some aspects of the Fama-French critique of the CAPM. Estrada (2002) argues that the semi variance of return is a more plausible measure of risk and supports the D-CAPM (mean semi-variance) model, providing evidence of the significance of the model in the emerging markets context. Estrada and Serra (2005) and Estrada (2007) extend the findings on the significance of the downside model to the developed market setting.

While the application of the traditional CAPM is still being tested, another extension of the Fama-French factor model is to consider momentum factors. Jegadeesh and Titman (1993) report that stocks with higher returns in the previous 12 months tend to have higher future returns than stock with lower returns in the previous 12 months, that is, the momentum factor. In testing their three-factor model, Fama and French (1996) find that the model is able to capture the size and book to market effect, but not the momentum effect, which remains a challenge to their model. Carhart (1997) develops what is known as the four-factor model, which includes momentum.

Most of the studies in this area of sovereign ratings have used an event study methodology to assess the impact of sovereign ratings changes on stock market returns by using the market model as being the key model to calculate abnormal returns. Some of the most cited papers include Brooks et al. (2004), Reisen and von Maltzan (1999), Larrain, Reisen, and von Maltan (1997), Pukthuanthong-Le, Elayan, and Rose (2007), Ferreira and Gama (2007), and Gande and Parsley (2005). We therefore differentiate our study by undertaking this analysis using alternative benchmark models.

Our results reveal that consistent with the literature on the impact of sovereign ratings on stock market returns, we find a pre- as well as post-announcement effect on the stock market for a downgrade announcement, and in particular on day –3, day –1 and day 1 where the returns are significantly negative and an impact on the market following an upgrade announcement on the event day only with the returns being significant positive. Further, testing this impact using alternative benchmarks models suggests that the results are not sensitive to the multi-factor model specification. On average all the models, namely, the market model, the downside model, the Fama-French model, and the Fama-French model with the momentum factor, have consistent and similar results for both the upgrade and downgrade announcements. Contrary to the evidence from other models, the quadratic market model and the higher-order downside market model suggest that both upgrade and downgrade announcements have a significant impact on the market, and this is the case both pre- and post-announcement. The quadratic downside market model gives more plausible results in the case of upgrades, indicating that the rating announcements have a positive impact on the returns compared to the quadratic market model which provide some negative returns in this case. However, the overall results obtained in this study suggest that measuring abnormal returns using different benchmark models does not make a difference when assessing the impact of sovereign rating changes on national stock market returns. The remainder of the chapter is organised as follows. Section 2 explains the data and methodology used in the study. Section 3 discusses the results obtained, and Section 4 presents some concluding remarks.

2 Data and modelling framework

We investigate the impact of sovereign rating changes on the stock market return of countries using the population of all rating change announcements for the period 1 January 1975 through January 2010. We focus on the historical long-term foreign currency ratings for each country by Standard and Poor's. Standard and Poor's provides ratings in terms of foreign currency as well as local currency and is the earliest provider of ratings; thus, S&P has a well-established set of rating history. The initial sample of countries for which data could be available from S&P with a rating or a rating history from the year 1975 included 63 countries. This study focuses on the impact of a rating change, and there are nine countries for which there has been no rating change during this period. Following the inspection of the rating history for each country, daily market returns for each country were collected from *Datastream International*. The DataStream return index in USD for each country was used to proxy for the market return. The study included a final sample of 33 countries with rating changes.

To determine the impact of sovereign rating changes on stock market returns, an event study methodology is used. Following previous studies, we start our analysis with the conventional market model. In order to calculate the abnormal return that is the difference between the observed and predicted returns, we use the following equation.

$$AR_{it} = R_{it} - (\alpha_i + \beta_i R_{mt}) \tag{13.1}$$

Where R_{it} is the return on country i at day t, R_{mt} is the corresponding return on the world index at day t, and α_i and β_i are the market model parameters obtained from ordinary least squares regressions.

In this chapter, in addition to the conventional market model, we consider a different approach to the estimation of the abnormal returns. We consider the approach of specifying a quadratic market return term as an additional factor. The quadratic term is used to augment the traditional market model and produces a quadratic market model (QMM), and hence the abnormal returns are calculated as follows:

$$AR_{it} = R_{it} - (\alpha_i + \beta_i R_{mt} + \mu_i R_{mt}^2) \tag{13.2}$$

The QMM has been used in a number of previous studies. For example, Brooks and Faff (1998) perform tests of Barone-Adesi's (1985) two-factor APT against the unrestricted QMM using Morgan Stanley country index data; see also Lee and Rahman (1990) and Chen, Rahman, and Chan (1992). Kraus and Litzenberger (1976, 1983) proposed that the QMM is the returns-generating process consistent with the three-moment CAPM (or covariance-coskewness CAPM). A number of papers have since followed the Kraus and Litzenberger lead to examine higher moment asset pricing models using higher-order market models. Accordingly, the focus of this chapter is to analyse the impact of sovereign rating changes on stock market returns using the QMM framework for the estimation of the abnormal returns. Thus, our analysis extends the work in Mishra, Prakash, Karels, and Pactwa (2007) to the sovereign ratings case.

The CAPM is explained by an equilibrium in which investors maximise their utility function that depends on the mean and variance of returns of their portfolio. A criticism of the mean-variance CAPM is that the model disregards the up and down movements of asset returns and the validity of this measure of risk, variance, is subject to the distribution of returns being symmetric and normal. Hence, there is the argument in the literature that an alternate measure is to consider downside risk. Estrada (2002) argues that the semi variance of return is a more plausible measure of risk and supports the D-CAPM model. He argues that the semi variance of returns is a better measure because firstly, investors do not dislike volatility, but they do dislike downside volatility. Secondly, the semi variance is more useful than the variance when the underlying distribution of the security is asymmetric; see also Nantell and Price (1979). Thirdly, semi variance combines the information on both the variance and skewness. Hence, in this chapter, we extend our analysis to include the downside risk and hence estimate the following model to calculate abnormal returns.

$$AR_{it} = R_{it} - (\alpha_i + \beta_i \mathrm{R}_{mt} + \beta_i^{\mathrm{D}} D_{Down} R_{mt}), \quad \text{where } D_{Down} = 1 \text{ if } R_{mt} < 0 \qquad (13.3)$$

The issue of downside risk is also discussed by Galagedera and Brooks (2007), where they provide evidence that downside co-skewness is a better explanatory variable in emerging markets. If investors are more risk-averse to down markets, then assets that have high exposure to downside risk are unattractive and must command a risk premium. There are a number of proposed measures that have been provided in the literature as alternative measures of downside co-skewness; see for example, Hogan and Warren (1974) and Harlow and Rao (1989). In this chapter, we extend our analysis to estimate a different alternative to the CAPM by using a higher-order model in a downside framework. The following model has been used to calculate the abnormal returns.

$$\begin{aligned} AR_{it} = R_{it} - (\alpha_i + \beta_i R_{mt} + \beta_{2i}^{\mathrm{D}} D_{Down} R_{mt} + \mu_i R_{mt}^2 \\ + \mu_{2i}^{\mathrm{D}} D_{Down} R_{mt}^2), \quad \text{where } D_{Down} = 1 \text{ if } R_{mt} < 0 \end{aligned} \qquad (13.4)$$

Hence, this study assesses the impact of sovereign rating changes on stock market returns using four different approaches, that is, the market model, the quadratic market model, the downside model, and the quadratic downside model.

A further key contribution of this chapter is to test whether Fama-French factors are supplements or complements to the higher-order and downside models. Calculating abnormal returns using the Fama-French model has not been undertaken in the context of sovereign ratings. Hence we extend our models using the Fama-French factors. The Fama-French factors as well as the momentum factors, HML, SMB, and UMD, are available from the website of Kenneth French.

Even though these are US data, they have been used as a proxy to represent the world factors. There are some studies that explore the importance of US Fama-French factors in a local asset pricing setting, and the available evidence suggests that they may have a role as proxies for international factors of this type. In the context of explaining the returns on domestic portfolios and stocks, Griffin (2002) suggests that domestic factors are to be preferred. In contrast, Durand, Limkriangkrai, and Smith (2006), following the argument of Bekeart and Harvey (1995), support the use of US factors as global factors in the Australian market. The focus of our analysis is at the national market level, as such we make use of US factors as proxies for global factors. As highlighted, the abnormal returns will be calculated using different models, namely, the conventional Fama-French model, the higher-order Fama-French model, the downside Fama-French Model and the higher-order downside model. Hence the following equations are used to calculate the different abnormal returns (AR).

2.1 Fama-French three-factor model

$$AR_{it} = R_{it} - (\alpha_i + \beta i\ R_{world} + \beta_{2i}\ \text{HML} + \beta_{3i}\ \text{SMB}) \tag{13.5}$$

2.2 Higher-order Fama-French model

$$AR_{it} = R_{it} - (\alpha_i + \beta_i\ R_{world} + \beta_{2i}\ R_{world}^2 + \beta_{3i}\ \text{HML} + \beta_{4i}\ \text{SMB}) \tag{13.6}$$

2.3 Downside Fama-French model

$$AR_{it} = R_{it} - (\alpha_i + \beta_1\ R_{world} + \beta_{2i}^{D}\ D_{Down}\ R_{world} + \beta_{3i}\ \text{HML} + \beta_{4i}\ \text{SMB}), \quad \text{where } D_{Down} = 1 \text{ if } R_{world} < 0 \tag{13.7}$$

2.4 Higher-order downside Fama-French model

$$AR_{it} = R_{it} - (\alpha_i + \beta_i\ R_{world} + \beta_{2i}^{D}\ D_{Down}\ R_{world} + \beta_3\ R_{world}^2 + \beta_{4i}\ D_{Down}\ R_{world}^2 + \beta_{5i}\ \text{HML} + \beta_{6i}\ \text{SMB}, \quad \text{where } D_{Down} = 1 \text{ if } R_{world} < 0 \tag{13.8}$$

These multifactor models are then augmented to include the momentum factor, and the following models are estimated:

2.5 Fama-French four-factor model

$$AR_{it} = R_{it} - (\alpha_i + \beta_i\ R_{world} + \beta_{2i}\ \text{HML} + \beta_{3i}\ \text{SMB} + \beta_{4i}\ \text{UMD}) \tag{13.9}$$

2.6 Higher-order model momentum

$$AR_{it} = R_{it} - (\alpha_i + \beta_i\ R_{world} + \beta_{2i}\ R_{world}^2 + \beta_{3i}\ \text{HML} + \beta_{4i}\ \text{SMB} + \beta_{5i}\ \text{UMD}) \tag{13.10}$$

2.7 Downside Fama-French model with momentum

$$AR_{it} = R_{it} - (\alpha_i + \beta_1 R_{world} + \beta_{2i}{}^D D_{Down} R_{world} + \beta_{3i} HML + \beta_{4i} SMB + \beta_{5i} UMD), \quad \text{where } D_{Down} = 1 \text{ if } R_{world} < 0 \tag{13.11}$$

2.8 Higher-order downside Fama-French model with momentum

$$AR_{it} = Rit - (\alpha i + \beta_i R_{world} + \beta_{2i}{}^D D_{Down} R_{world} + \beta_3 R_{world}{}^2 + \beta_{4i} D_{Down} R_{world}{}^2 + \beta_{5i} HML + \beta_{6i} SMB + \beta_{7i} UMD), \quad \text{where } D_{Down} = 1 \text{ if } R_{world} < 0 \tag{13.12}$$

For all the different versions of the models, the parameters are estimated using approximately six months of daily return observations beginning 120 days through to 21 days before the sovereign rating change. The event period ranges from 10 days before to 10 days after the rating change. Averaging the abnormal returns over each day in the event period generates the average abnormal returns (AAR):

$$\overline{AAR} = 1/n \sum_{j=1}^{n} \text{ARjt} \tag{13.13}$$

Where N is the number of events for each day t in the event window

Abnormal return test statistics are calculated similar to Dodd (1980). In order to test whether the average abnormal returns are significantly different from zero, the following test statistic is calculated:

$$\text{t} = \overline{AAR_t} / \sigma_{ARt} \tag{13.14}$$

where AAR_t is the average abnormal returns for day t, and

$$\sigma_{ARt} = \left\langle 1/20 \left| \sum_{T=-10, T \neq t}^{+10} (ARt - AAR)2 \right| \right\rangle \tag{13.15}$$

with AAR the grand mean of the abnormal returns. The test statistics reported in the results section of the study have been calculated using the above equation over the entire event window and are the test statistics for the average abnormal return for each of the estimation techniques.

3 Results and discussion

3.1 Market model results

In order to determine the impact of foreign currency sovereign rating changes, an event study methodology is employed to detect the abnormal returns resulting from an upgrade or downgrade announcement. The results of our analysis are presented in Tables 13.1 through 13.3. The results in the tables are reported in two panels, with Panel A of each table reporting the results for ratings downgrades, while Panel B reports the results for ratings upgrades. We present the results for each model on an aggregate basis. The analysis includes 33 countries with 69 downgrades and 88 upgrades. The results for each model are reported over an event window of -10 days to 10 days after the announcement date.

Table 13.1 reports the results of the models estimated using the market model, higher-order market model, downside market model, and higher-order downside mode for all of the 33 countries on an aggregate basis. Analysis of Panel A indicates similar results across the market model and the downside model. The results from the market model which are reported over an event window of –10 days to 10 days after the announcement date indicates that for the downgrades there is strong negative tendency in the abnormal returns eight days prior to the announcement day with the abnormal returns being significantly negative at –0.09% three days prior to announcement and –1.24% one day prior to announcement day of the downgrade event. The results from the downside model indicate an average abnormal return of –0.07% three days prior and –1.27% one day prior to announcement. The average abnormal returns revert to positive after one day following the announcement for both the market model and the downside model. Similarly, the results following the higher-order downside model indicate a strong negative tendency in the returns 10 days prior to announcement, and we have a statistically significant result at four days prior to announcement at –0.3% and at –0.4% one day prior to announcement. The market seems to anticipate the downgrade announcement prior to the actual announcement day, indicating a pre-announcement effect, which does not support the efficient market hypothesis, if the rating change announcement is news. The results of the higher-order model, in contrast, indicates a very strong negative abnormal returns 10 days prior to announcement, and this tendency continues on announcement day as well two days following the announcement. The average abnormal return stands at –1.92% on the announcement day. The use of this model indicates analysing the impact of sovereign rating changes on stock market returns using the QMM framework for the estimation of the abnormal returns does provide some different results. The results of all four models in the case of downgrades are consistent with the literature, where downgrades are said to have a statistical impact on stock

Table 13.1 Average abnormal returns (AAR) and cumulative abnormal returns (CAR) as measures of the market reaction to Standard & Poor's (S&P) foreign currency rating changes All Countries- 33 Panel A: 69 downgrades

	OLS			Higher-order model			Downside model			Co-skewness-downside		
Day	AAR	CAR	TStats	AAR	CAR	TStats	AAR	CAR	TStats	AAR	CAR	TStats
−10	−0.002	−0.002	−0.38	−0.0181	−0.0181	−2.95**	−0.0011	−0.0011	−0.2	−0.0252	−0.0252	−1.58
−9	0.0016	−0.0004	0.3	−0.0123	−0.0304	−2.00**	0.0019	0.0008	0.35	−0.0072	−0.0324	−0.45
−8	−0.008	−0.0084	−1.56	−0.0201	−0.0506	−3.27**	−0.0044	−0.0036	−0.79	−0.0039	−0.0363	−0.24
−7	0.0014	−0.007	0.28	−0.0126	−0.0632	−2.05**	0.0025	−0.0011	0.45	−0.0027	−0.039	−0.17
−6	−0.0051	−0.0121	−0.99	−0.0177	−0.0809	−2.88**	−0.0008	−0.0019	−0.14	−0.0054	−0.0444	−0.34
−5	−0.0012	−0.0133	−0.24	−0.0157	−0.0967	−2.55**	0.0001	−0.0017	0.03	−0.0036	−0.048	−0.23
−4	−0.0025	−0.0158	−0.48	−0.0179	−0.1145	−2.90**	0.0016	−0.0001	0.29	−0.0315	−0.0795	−1.97*
−3	−0.0091	−0.0249	−1.77*	−0.0244	−0.1389	−3.97**	−0.0077	−0.0079	−1.69*	−0.0335	−0.113	−2.10**
−2	−0.0052	−0.0301	−1.01	−0.0224	−0.1614	−3.64**	−0.0053	−0.0132	−0.95	−0.0316	−0.1446	−1.98**
−1	−0.0124	−0.0425	−2.41**	−0.0302	−0.1915	−4.90**	−0.0127	−0.0259	−2.29**	−0.0415	−0.1861	−2.61**
0	−0.0039	−0.0463	−0.75	−0.0192	−0.2108	−3.12**	−0.0043	−0.0302	−0.77	−0.0118	−0.198	−0.74
1	−0.0052	−0.0516	−1.01	−0.019	−0.2298	−3.09**	−0.0005	−0.0307	−0.1	−0.0459	−0.2439	−2.88**
2	0.0037	−0.0478	0.73	−0.0115	−0.2413	−1.87**	0.0054	−0.0253	0.98	−0.0196	−0.2635	−1.23
3	0.0056	−0.0423	1.08	−0.0089	−0.2502	−1.44	0.0088	−0.0165	1.69*	−0.0177	−0.2813	−1.11
4	0.0055	−0.0367	1.08	−0.0056	−0.2558	−0.91	0.0064	−0.0101	1.15	0.0037	−0.2776	0.23
5	0.0024	−0.0343	0.48	−0.0106	−0.2664	−1.72*	0.0091	−0.001	1.67*	0.0036	−0.274	0.23
6	−0.0091	−0.0434	**−1.77***	−0.0237	−0.2901	−3.84**	−0.0035	−0.0044	−0.62	−0.0105	−0.2845	−0.66
7	0.0037	−0.0397	0.72	−0.0076	−0.2977	−1.24	0.0048	0.0004	0.87	0.0065	−0.278	0.4
8	−0.0015	−0.0412	−0.28	−0.0145	−0.3122	−2.36**	0.0024	0.0028	0.43	−0.0022	−0.2803	−0.14
9	−0.002	−0.0432	−0.4	−0.016	−0.3282	−2.60**	0.0022	0.0049	0.39	−0.0263	−0.3066	−1.65*
10	−0.0011	−0.0443	−0.22	−0.0164	−0.3446	−2.66**	0.0035	0.0085	0.64	−0.0269	−0.3334	−1.68*

Note: This table reports average abnormal returns (AAR) and cumulative abnormal returns (CAR) for **all countries** in the analysis as measures of the market reaction to Standard & Poor's (S&P) foreign currency rating changes. AAR and CAR are generated using a standard mean adjusted event study methodology. A rating change occurs when S&P announces a rating change. There are 88 upgrades and 69 downgrades for a sample of 33 countries. This table reports the results using the market model (Equation 13.1), higher-order model (Equation 13.2), downside market model (Equation 13.3), and higher-order downside model (Equation 13.4). The test statistics are calculated using Equation 13.15 and are the t stats for the AAR.

Panel B: 88 upgrades

	OLS			Higher-order model			Downside model			Co skewness-downside		
Day	AAR	CAR	TStats	AAR	CAR	TStats	AAR	CAR	TStats	AAR	CAR	TStats
–10	–0.0029	–0.0029	–1.4	–0.0274	–0.0274	–13.05**	–0.0031	–0.0031	–1.54	0.0038	0.0038	1.62
–9	–0.0018	–0.0046	–0.88	–0.0252	–0.0526	–11.96**	–0.0019	–0.005	–0.92	0.0056	0.0093	2.39**
–8	0.0019	–0.0027	0.95	–0.0211	0.9726	–10.02**	0.0018	–0.0032	0.87	0.0089	0.0183	3.83**
–7	–0.0003	–0.003	–0.12	–0.0249	0.9477	–11.82**	–0.0004	–0.0036	–0.21	0.0013	0.0196	0.56
–6	–0.0008	–0.0037	–0.38	–0.0245	1.9726	–11.66**	–0.0006	–0.0042	–0.29	0.0057	0.0253	2.45**
–5	–0.0011	–0.0048	–0.54	–0.0234	1.9492	–11.11**	–0.0012	–0.0054	–0.58	0.0051	0.0303	2.17**
–4	0.0032	–0.0016	1.59	–0.0196	2.9726	–9.32**	0.0033	–0.0021	1.63	0.0095	0.0398	4.08**
–3	0.002	0.0004	0.98	–0.0213	2.9513	–10.11**	0.0017	–0.0004	0.86	0.0077	0.0476	3.33**
–2	–0.0015	–0.0011	–0.73	–0.0254	3.9726	–12.07**	–0.0015	–0.0019	–0.77	0.0042	0.0518	1.82*
–1	0.0004	–0.0007	0.2	–0.0234	3.9492	–11.10**	0.0003	–0.0017	0.13	0.0065	0.0583	2.81**
0	0.0043	0.0037	2.13**	–0.02	4.9726	–9.53**	0.004	0.0023	1.97**	0.0106	0.0689	4.54**
1	0.0014	0.005	0.67	–0.0229	4.9496	–10.89**	0.001	0.0033	0.48	0.0086	0.0775	3.71**
2	–0.0026	0.0024	–1.3	–0.0253	5.9726	–12.01**	–0.0031	0.0001	–1.56	0.0039	0.0814	1.68*
3	0.0027	0.005	1.31	–0.0198	5.9528	–9.41**	0.0025	0.0026	1.22	0.0088	0.0902	3.76**
4	–0.0007	0.0043	–0.36	–0.0235	6.9726	–11.17**	–0.001	0.0016	–0.48	0.0052	0.0954	2.24**
5	–0.0018	0.0025	–0.87	–0.0238	6.9487	–11.33**	–0.0015	0.0001	–0.75	0.0056	0.101	2.41**
6	–0.0021	0.0005	–1.02	–0.024	7.9726	–11.41**	–0.0021	–0.002	–1.06	0.0035	0.1045	1.51
7	–0.0005	0	–0.23	–0.0249	7.9477	–11.81**	–0.0009	–0.0029	–0.44	0.006	0.1105	2.57**
8	0.0013	0.0013	0.66	–0.0218	8.9726	–10.37**	0.0013	–0.0017	0.62	0.0074	0.1179	3.18**
9	0	0.0013	0.01	–0.0232	8.9494	–11.02**	–0.0002	–0.0019	–0.11	0.0069	0.1248	2.95**
10	0.0007	0.0021	0.36	–0.0228	9.9726	–10.82**	0.0006	–0.0013	0.3	0.0073	0.132	3.12**

Note: * Denotes Statistical significance at 10%, ** Denotes statistical significance at 5%.

market returns (see Brooks et al., 2004). However, our results suggest a pre- and post-announcement effect on the market rather than an impact on the announcement day itself.

For upgrades reported in Panel B of Table 13.1, the market model and the downside model both find a strongly statistically significant reaction on the day of the ratings upgrade with the abnormal returns being positive at 0.43% for the market model and at 0.4% for the downside model. Once again the results from these two models are remarkably similar. The results from the market model and the downside model are consistent with the literature on ratings changes of individual companies, where upgrades do not have the same wealth impact on the market as downgrades (see, for example, Barron, Clare, & Thomas, 1997; Cornell, Landsman, & Shapiro, 1989; Ederington & Goh, 1998; Goh & Ederington, 1993, 1999; Zaima & McCarthy, 1988). The results from using the quadratic market model and the higher-order downside model are very different. For upgrades, all of the days in the event window show strongly statistically significant results. This suggests that allowance for higher-order moments might be important in assessing the national stock market impacts of sovereign rating changes. However, the results seems to be more plausible in the case of the higher-order downside model, given that the average abnormal returns are positive over the entire event window, which is what we will be expecting following an upgrade announcement, as compared to the negative returns reported for the quadratic model.

Overall, the results obtained from the analysis indicate that the market model and downside model seem to have the similar type of results in that the downgrades do have some impact on the market in particular prior to announcement days and the market reverts to normal following the announcement. For upgrades, the market tends to react only on the announcement day. These results are consistent with the general literature on the impact of sovereign rating changes on the stock market. However, the use of the quadratic models indicates that the market reacts to both upgrades and downgrades announcements, and it seems to have a reaction over a prolonged period of time.

3.2 Fama and French factors and momentum

The CAPM has been criticised because of empirical anomalies such as size, financial distress and momentum; see, for example, Banz (1981), Stattman (1980) and Rosenberg, Reid, and Lanstein (1985), Jegadeesh and Titman (1993). Previous studies have extended the CAPM to include factors that will correct for these anomalies. Empirical work by Fama and

French (1992, 1993) and Carhart (1997) have accounted for these factors and is commonly known as the three-factor model and the four-factor model respectively and reveals that these additional factor portfolios significantly improve the model's ability to capture the cross-sectional variation of stock returns, both within the US and internationally. In this study, we estimate the returns using the Fama-French three-factor model (Equation 13.5) and the Fama-French four-factor model (Equation 13.9) to assess if these different benchmark models have a significant impact on the abnormal returns following a rating change. In this section, we report the results of the abnormal returns estimated using the Fama-French model in Table 13.2 and the results using the four-factor model that is including momentum in Table 13.3. We augment the model to a quadratic version, a downside framework, and a higher-order downside model. The results are reported in Table 13.2 for the 33 countries with 88 upgrades and 69 downgrades. Rating agencies provide an independent assessment of the default probability. According to the private information hypothesis, equally known as the signalling or information asymmetry hypothesis (see, for example, Hsueh & Liu, 1992; Abad-Romero & Robles-Fernandez, 2006), in order for a rating agency to make a decision about rating changes, the agency has not only used public information, but it also has access to information which is only known by insiders. What is therefore expected is that announcements of a rating upgrade will have a positive impact on the market whilst a negative market reaction can be expected for a downgrade announcement. Panel A of Table 13.2 reports the downgrade announcement and Panel B, the impact on the returns following upgrade announcements. The results obtained using the Fama-French three-factor models are consistent with the information asymmetry hypothesis for downgrades and consistent with the efficient market hypothesis for upgrades. Including the Fama-French size and growth factors provide similar results to the results obtained from estimating the abnormal returns using the market model. Studies in the literature suggest that the three-factor model provides better results in stock pricing (see, for example, de Moor & Sercu, 2004); however, the results obtained in this study suggest that the three-factor model does not make a difference to the abnormal returns following a rating change. The results are reported over a window of –10 days to 10 days after the announcement. For the downgrades, the market tends to have a reaction on three days as well as one day prior to announcement. This result is consistent across all the versions of estimation used in this study and once again highlights the pre-announcement effect on day –3 and day –1, which is consistent to the previous results. The average abnormal

Table 13.2 Average abnormal returns (AAR) and cumulative abnormal returns (CAR) as measures of the market reaction to Standard & Poor's (S&P) foreign currency rating changes Panel A: 69 downgrades

	OLS			Higher-order model			Downside model			Co-skewness-downside		
Day	AAR	CAR	TStats	AAR	CAR	TStats	AAR	CAR	TStats	AAR	CAR	TStats
–10	0.0066	0.0066	1.09	0.003	0.003	0.50	0.001	0.001	0.18	–0.0019	–0.0019	0.07
–9	–0.0028	0.0038	–0.46	–0.0027	0.00028	–0.45	–0.0034	–0.0024	–0.63	–0.0026	–0.0045	–0.45
–8	0.0023	0.0062	0.38	0.00406	0.00434	0.67	0.0017	–0.0007	0.32	0.0026	–0.0019	0.45
–7	–0.0083	–0.0022	–1.38	–0.0041	0.00025	–0.68	–0.0059	–0.0066	–1.08	–0.0053	–0.0072	–0.92
–6	0.0027	0.0005	0.45	–7.00E–05	0.00018	–0.01	0.0016	–0.005	0.29	0.0001	–0.0071	0.01
–5	–0.0006	–0.0001	–0.1	–0.0027	–0.0025	–0.45	–0.0024	–0.0074	–0.44	–0.0007	–0.0079	–0.13
–4	0.0000	0.0000	0.00	0.00147	–0.0011	0.24	0.0012	–0.0062	0.23	0.0007	–0.0071	0.13
–3	–0.0118	–0.0119	–1.96**	–0.0122	–0.0133	–2.02**	–0.0116	–0.0177	–2.14**	–0.0134	–0.0206	–2.32**
–2	–0.0091	–0.021	–1.6	–0.0084	–0.0217	–1.59	–0.008	–0.0257	–1.48	–0.0071	–0.0277	–1.23
–1	–0.0096	–0.0306	–1.69*	–0.014	–0.0356	–2.31**	–0.0121	–0.0378	–2.23**	–0.0131	–0.0407	–2.25**
0	–0.0026	–0.0332	–0.44	–0.003	–0.0387	–0.50	–0.0046	–0.0424	–0.85	–0.0047	–0.0455	–0.81
1	–0.0064	–0.0397	–1.06	–0.0066	–0.0453	–1.09	–0.0049	–0.0473	–0.9	–0.0088	–0.0543	–1.52
2	0.0025	–0.0372	0.41	–0.0004	–0.0457	–0.07	0.0011	–0.0463	0.19	–0.0021	–0.0563	–0.35
3	0.0104	–0.0268	1.72*	0.01162	–0.0341	1.92*	0.0111	–0.0352	2.04**	0.0093	–0.047	1.66*
4	0.007	–0.0198	1.15	0.00266	–0.0315	0.44	0.0023	–0.0329	0.42	0.0022	–0.0449	0.38
5	–0.0042	–0.024	–0.69	–0.0025	–0.034	–0.42	–0.0019	–0.0348	–0.36	–0.0005	–0.0454	–0.09
6	0.0005	–0.0235	0.08	0.00214	–0.0318	0.35	0.0014	–0.0334	0.26	0.002	–0.0434	0.35
7	–0.0079	–0.0313	–1.3	–0.007	–0.0388	–1.15	–0.0052	–0.0387	–0.96	–0.0042	–0.0476	–0.73
8	–0.0041	–0.0355	–0.69	–0.005	–0.0437	–0.82	–0.0057	–0.04.44	–1.05	–0.005	–0.0526	–0.86
9	0	–0.0354	0.01	0.00421	–0.0395	0.70	0.0022	–0.0421	0.41	0.0068	–0.0458	1.17
10	–0.0003	–0.0357	–0.05	–0.0001	–0.0396	–0.02	–0.0012	–0.0433	–0.22	–0.0031	–0.0489	–0.54

Panel B: 88 upgrades

Day	OLS			Higher-order model			Downside model			Co-skewness-downside		
	AAR	CAR	TStats	AAR	CAR	TStats	AAR	CAR	TStats	AAR	CAR	TStats
−10	−0.0023	−0.0023	−1.08	−0.0019	−0.0019	−1.03	−0.0023	−0.0023	−1.17	−0.0019	−0.0019	−0.78
−9	−0.0011	−0.0034	−0.51	−0.0012	−0.0031	−0.61	−0.0012	−0.0035	−0.64	−0.0008	−0.0027	−0.34
−8	−0.001	−0.0043	−0.46	−0.0004	−0.0035	−0.21	−0.0011	−0.0046	−0.59	−0.0008	−0.0035	−0.35
−7	0.0019	−0.0024	0.89	0.0017	−0.0018	0.9	0.0013	−0.0034	0.65	0.0017	−0.0018	0.72
−6	0.0009	−0.0016	0.41	−0.0004	−0.0022	−0.21	−0.0004	−0.0037	−0.2	−0.0066	−0.0084	−2.76
−5	−0.0014	−0.0029	−0.64	−0.0008	−0.003	−0.43	−0.0011	−0.0049	−0.6	−0.0011	−0.0095	−0.47
−4	0.0022	−0.0007	0.17	0.00171	−0.0013	0.9	0.0019	−0.0029	1.01	0.0011	−0.0084	0.47
−3	0.0009	0.0002	0.41	0.00119	−0.0001	0.63	0.0015	−0.0015	0.78	0.0007	−0.0077	0.3
−2	−0.0006	−0.0004	−0.26	0.00027	0.00015	0.14	−0.0004	−0.0018	−0.2	−0.0008	−0.0085	−0.35
−1	0.0008	0.0004	0.39	0.00059	0.00074	0.31	0.0001	−0.0018	0.03	−0.0009	−0.0094	−0.37
0	0.0056	0.006	2.62**	0.00453	0.00527	2.40**	0.0044	0.0027	2.32**	0.0047	−0.0047	1.96**
1	0.0001	0.0061	0.07	0.0004	0.00567	0.21	0.0004	0.0031	0.22	0.0006	−0.0041	0.27
2	−0.0019	0.0042	−0.9	−0.003	0.00272	−1.56	−0.003	0.0001	−1.56	−0.0028	−0.0068	−1.17
3	0.0033	0.0075	1.56	0.00318	0.0059	1.68	0.0028	0.0029	1.46	0.0027	−0.0041	1.15
4	−0.0004	0.0071	−0.19	−0.0007	0.00517	−0.39	−0.0008	0.0021	−0.43	−0.0013	−0.0054	−0.56
5	−0.0017	0.0055	−0.78	−0.0016	0.00356	−0.85	−0.0016	0.0005	−0.81	−0.0008	−0.0063	−0.35
6	−0.0031	0.0024	−1.47	−0.0028	0.00073	−1.5	−0.0025	−0.002	−1.33	−0.0027	−0.009	−1.15
7	−0.0002	0.0021	−0.1	−0.0004	0.00036	−0.19	−0.0007	−0.0027	−0.36	−0.001	−0.01	−0.42
8	0.0026	0.0048	1.25	0.00138	0.00174	0.73	0.0019	−0.0008	0.99	0.0018	−0.0083	0.74
9	−0.001	0.0038	−0.46	−0.0011	0.00061	−0.6	−0.0015	−0.0024	−0.81	−0.0006	−0.0089	−0.25
10	0.0006	0.0044	0.26	0.00064	0.00125	0.34	0.0007	−0.0017	0.34	0.0017	−0.0072	0.71

Note: * Denotes Statistical significance at 10%, ** Denotes statistical significance at 5%.

returns are at –0.96% for the Fama-French three-factor model, –0.3% for the higher-order model, –1.21% for the downside model and –1.31% for the higher-order downside model one day prior to announcement. The market reverts back to normal following the announcement day. For the upgrades, across all the four estimation models, the market reacts only on the announcement day with the returns being positive and statistically significant over the event window.

Table 13.3 reports the results using the Fama-French four-factor models. We use the momentum factor in our analysis. Carhart (1997) develops what is known as the four-factor model, which includes momentum which we apply in the context of sovereign ratings. A very interesting finding is that the use of four factors in the estimation does not reveal any different results as compared to a three-factor model. Across all the four estimation techniques, Panel A indicates similar results to what was obtained in the three-factor analysis. The market seems to react three days as well as one day prior to announcement of the rating downgrade. There is a significant reaction on day three following the announcement of the downgrade, but the returns are positive which indicate that there could be other events affecting the stock market returns. Panel B reports the results following the upgrade announcement, and the results are similar to what was obtained using the three-factor models, that is, the market reacts to the upgrade on announcement day only and the market reverts to normal on the other days. This is consistent across the four estimation techniques.

While in the previous section under the market models estimation, the quadratic model provided different results, it seems that applying the Fama-French three factors and four factors does not provide significantly different abnormal returns in comparison to the use of market model in calculating the abnormal returns following a rating change announcement. The literature on the debate on the use of CAPM has been extensive and justifies the use of the alternative models. In this chapter we apply each of the different variations of the models to test if this is the case as we calculate the impact of sovereign rating changes on the stock market returns. Higher-order moments are an alternative response to the poor performance of the standard CAPM. It allows investors to have preference for higher moments in the return distribution beyond mean and variance. Kraus and Litzenberger (1976) develop the three-moment CAPM, where investors are concerned with the skewness in addition to the mean and variance (see also Harvey & Siddique, 2000).

Table 13.3 Average abnormal returns (AAR) and cumulative abnormal returns (CAR) as measures of the market reaction to Standard & Poor's (S&P) foreign currency rating changes Panel A: 69 downgrades

	FF model – 4 factor AAR			Higher-order model			Downside model			Co-skewness-downside AAR		
Day	AAR	CAR	T Stats	AAR	CAR	T Stats	AAR	CAR	T Stats	AAR	CAR	T Stats
−10	0.0005	0.0005	0.1	0.0028	0.0028	0.48	0.0008	0.0008	0.14	0.0013	0.0013	0.21
−9	−0.0038	−0.0033	−0.71	−0.0028	0.0001	−0.46	−0.0034	−0.0027	−0.64	−0.0034	−0.0021	−0.55
−8	0.0022	−0.0011	0.41	0.004	0.0041	0.67	0.0017	−0.001	0.3	0.0022	0	0.36
−7	−0.0056	−0.0067	−1.04	−0.004	0	−0.68	−0.0058	−0.0068	−1.07	−0.0051	−0.0051	−0.84
−6	0.0005	−0.0061	0.1	−0.0005	−0.0005	−0.08	0.0013	−0.0055	0.25	0	−0.0051	0
−5	−0.0026	−0.0088	−0.49	−0.0035	−0.0039	−0.58	−0.003	−0.0085	−0.55	−0.0034	−0.0084	−0.55
−4	0.0012	−0.0076	0.22	0.0014	−0.0025	0.24	0.0012	−0.0073	0.22	0.0013	−0.0071	0.22
−3	−0.0112	−0.0188	−2.07**	−0.0112	−0.0137	−1.88*	−0.0109	−0.0181	−2.01**	−0.0109	−0.018	−1.78*
−2	−0.0068	−0.0256	−1.26	−0.0086	−0.0223	−1.44	−0.0083	−0.0265	−1.54	−0.0077	−0.0257	−1.26
−1	−0.0118	−0.0374	−2.18**	−0.0138	−0.0361	−2.30**	−0.012	−0.0385	−2.22**	−0.0144	−0.0401	−2.36**
0	−0.0054	−0.0428	−1	−0.0029	−0.039	−0.49	−0.0047	−0.0432	−0.88	−0.0052	−0.0453	−0.85
1	−0.0069	−0.0496	−1.27	−0.007	−0.0461	−1.18	−0.0051	−0.0483	−0.94	−0.0123	−0.0576	−2.02
2	0.0009	−0.0488	0.16	−0.0004	−0.0465	−0.07	0.0012	−0.0472	0.21	−0.0001	−0.0577	−0.02
3	0.0111	−0.0377	2.05**	0.0118	−0.0347	1.98**	0.0113	−0.0358	2.09**	0.01	−0.0477	1.65*
4	0	−0.0377	0	0.0022	−0.0324	0.37	0.0017	−0.0341	0.32	0.0025	−0.0452	0.41
5	−0.0029	−0.0405	−0.53	−0.0025	−0.035	−0.43	−0.002	−0.0361	−0.37	−0.0014	−0.0465	−0.23
6	0.0036	−0.0369	0.67	0.0021	−0.0329	0.35	0.0016	−0.0346	0.29	0.0007	−0.0459	0.11
7	−0.0061	−0.043	−1.13	−0.007	−0.0399	−1.17	−0.0053	−0.0399	−0.98	−0.0045	−0.0504	−0.74
8	−0.0057	−0.0487	−1.06	−0.005	−0.0449	−0.83	−0.0059	−0.0458	−1.09	−0.0048	−0.0552	−0.78
9	0.0019	−0.0468	0.35	0.0045	−0.0404	0.76	0.0027	−0.0431	0.49	0.0071	−0.0481	1.17
10	−0.0022	−0.049	−0.4	−0.0002	−0.0406	−0.04	−0.0011	−0.0443	−0.21	−0.0022	−0.0503	−0.36

Note: This table reports average abnormal returns (AAR) and cumulative abnormal returns (CAR) for all countries in the analysis as measures of the market reaction to Standard & Poor's (S&P) foreign currency rating changes. AAR and CAR are generated using a standard mean adjusted event study methodology and the AR are calculated using **Fama-French four-factor model** (Equation 13.9), the higher-order Fama-French model (Equation 13.10), the Fama-French downside model (Equation 13.11), and the Fama-French higher-order downside model (Equation 13.12). Results are reported for 33 countries on an aggregate basis with 88 upgrades and 69 downgrades. The test statistics are calculated using Equation 13.15 and are the t stats for the AAR.

Panel B: 88 upgrades

	FF model – 4 factor AAR			Higher-order model			Downside model			Co-skewness-downside AAR		
Day	AAR	CAR	T Stats	AAR	CAR	T Stats	AAR	CAR	T Stats	AAR	CAR	T Stats
–10	–0.002	–0.002	–1.07	–0.0019	–0.0019	–0.98	–0.0021	–0.0021	–0.91	–0.0024	–0.0024	–0.96
–9	–0.0011	–0.0031	–0.57	–0.0013	–0.0031	–0.66	–0.0013	–0.0033	–0.56	–0.0011	–0.0035	–0.44
–8	–0.001	–0.0041	–0.53	–0.0013	–0.0045	–0.71	–0.0018	–0.0052	–0.82	–0.0016	–0.005	–0.64
–7	0.0009	–0.0033	0.45	0.0011	–0.0034	0.56	0.0004	–0.0048	0.16	0.001	–0.004	0.42
–6	–0.0003	–0.0036	–0.16	–0.0012	–0.0046	–0.63	–0.0009	–0.0057	–0.38	–0.0067	–0.0107	-2.71
–5	–0.0007	–0.0043	–0.38	–0.0005	–0.0051	–0.26	–0.0016	–0.0072	–0.7	–0.0008	–0.0115	–0.34
-4	0.0025	–0.0018	1.3	0.0022	–0.0029	1.13	0.003	–0.0042	1.35	0.0014	–0.0101	0.58
–3	0.0018	0	0.94	0.0017	–0.0013	0.87	0.0021	–0.0021	0.94	0.0011	–0.009	0.45
–2	–0.0004	–0.0004	–0.19	0.0004	–0.0009	0.19	0.0005	–0.0016	0.22	–0.0003	–0.0093	–0.14
–1	0.0002	–0.0002	0.09	0.0003	–0.0006	0.16	0	–0.0016	0	–0.001	–0.0104	–0.42
0	0.0043	0.0041	2.25**	0.004	0.0034	2.09**	0.0046	0.003	2.03**	0.0043	–0.0061	1.72*
1	0.0007	0.0048	0.38	0.0006	0.0039	0.3	0.0002	0.0031	0.08	0.0007	–0.0054	0.27
2	–0.002	0.0027	–1.08	–0.0025	0.0014	–1.34	–0.004	–0.0009	–1.78	–0.0029	–0.0084	–1.19
3	0.0032	0.006	1.7	0.0033	0.0047	1.76	0.0027	0.0018	1.19	0.0022	–0.0062	0.88
4	–0.0007	0.0052	–0.39	–0.0008	0.0039	–0.44	–0.0012	0.0006	–0.54	–0.0017	–0.0079	–0.69
5	–0.002	0.0032	–1.04	–0.0017	0.0022	–0.89	–0.0017	–0.0011	–0.74	–0.0017	–0.0096	–0.69
6	–0.0027	0.0006	–1.4	–0.0027	–0.0005	–1.43	–0.0034	–0.0045	–1.53	–0.004	–0.0136	–1.64
7	–0.0001	0.0005	–0.07	–0.0001	–0.0006	–0.04	0.0001	–0.0045	0.03	–0.0006	–0.0142	–0.23
8	0.0024	0.0028	1.23	0.0023	0.0017	1.2	0.0024	–0.002	1.08	0.0019	–0.0123	0.78
9	–0.0008	0.002	–0.41	–0.0009	0.0008	–0.48	–0.0016	–0.0036	–0.71	–0.0004	–0.0127	–0.16
10	0.0011	0.0031	0.56	0.001	0.0017	0.51	0.0012	–0.0025	0.52	0.0019	–0.0108	0.75

Similarly, in order to measure downside risk, we include a downside framework analysis. The CAPM model asserts that investors are rewarded only for systematic risk since unsystematic risk can be eliminated through diversification. Hence the expected return on a portfolio is the sum of the risk-free rate and a risk premium as measured by beta. Pettengill et al. (1995) test the relationship between portfolio beta and returns, which is modified to account for the conditional relationship between beta and realised returns. They argue that if the realised market return is above the risk-free return, portfolio betas and returns should be positively related, but if the realised market return is below the risk-free return, portfolio betas and returns should be inversely related. They therefore suggest that appropriate allowance for up/down betas can overcome some critiques of the CAPM. We equally test the models in a higher-order downside framework which has been applied by Galagedera and Brooks (2007), who investigate the issue of co-skewness as measure of risk in a downside framework.

The results obtained in our study suggest that the calculation of the abnormal return in the event study is not sensitive to the model specification. However, we still conclude that there is a stock market reaction for a rating downgrade and this does not seem to be the case when we have the upgrade announcement.

4 Conclusion

This chapter has analysed the national stock market impact of sovereign rating changes using different benchmark models for the calculation of abnormal returns, namely, the market model, the quadratic model, the downside model, and the higher-order downside model. We equally test whether Fama-French factors are complements or substitutes to higher-order model and downside models in assessing the impact of sovereign rating changes on national stock markets. We assess whether different benchmark models of asset pricing matter in testing the significance of sovereign rating changes using the population of all rating change announcements for the period 1 January 1975 through January 2010 from Standard and Poor's for a sample of 33 countries.

The results indicate that there is a stock market reaction following the announcement of a sovereign rating change. Upgrade announcements seem to have an impact on the market on the announcement day, which is consistent with the efficient market hypothesis, and there seems to be a market reaction for a downgrade both pre- and post-announcement day, in particular on day –3, day –1, and day +3. The returns are significantly negative on these days, which is consistent with the signalling hypothesis. As such our results are consistent with the general findings of the literature on sovereign ratings.

The aim of this chapter was to assess whether different benchmark models will provide alternative results to this test. The result shows that the market model and a downside model that allows for asymmetry in risk produce similar results for all countries and for the set of emerging markets. However, a quadratic market model and the higher-order downside model that allow for higher-order moments being important in the determination of risk produce very different results for the overall set of countries. This initially suggests that higher-order moments may play an important role in risk measurement for a subset of countries.

However, as we augment our model to use the Fama-French model and momentum, we find that the results are not sensitive to model specification. The key feature in the results is that these findings are robust across the different specification of the models, and hence it seems that assessment of the impact of sovereign rating changes is not sensitive to the model specification. While the literature highlights that the problems associated with the CAPM can be corrected by using different asset pricing models, our models suggest that the success of a multi-factor model depends substantially on the methodology and the data used in the analysis, a similar conclusion to that drawn by Harvey and Siddique (2000).

References

Abad-Romero, P & Robles-Fernandez, M D (2006), 'Risk and Return Around Bond Rating Changes: New Evidence From the Spanish Stock Market', *Journal of Business Finance and Accounting*, vol. 33, no. 5–6, pp. 885–908.

Avramov, D, Chordia, T, Jostova, G & Philipov, A (2009), 'Credit Ratings and the Cross-Section of Stock Returns', *Journal of Financial Markets*, vol. 12, no. 3, pp. 469–499.

Barron, M J, Clare, A D & Thomas, S H (1997), 'The Effect of Bond Rating Changes and New Ratings on UK Stock Returns', *Journal of Business Finance and Accounting*, vol. 24, no. 3, pp. 497–509.

Barone-Adesi, G (1985), 'Arbitrage Equilibrium with Skewed Asset Returns', *Journal of Financial and Quantitative Analysis*, vol. 20, no. 3, pp. 299–313.

Binder, J (1998), 'The Event Study Methodology Since 1969', *Review of Quantitative Finance and Accounting*, vol. 11, no. 2, pp. 111–137.

Bekeart, G & Harvey, C (1995), 'Time-Varying World Market Integration', *Journal of Finance*, vol. 50, no. 2, pp. 403–444.

Banz, R W (1981), 'The Relationship Between Return and Market Value of Common Stocks', *Journal of Financial Economics*, vol. 9, no. 1, pp. 3–18.

Brooks, R, Faff, R, Hillier, D & Hillier, J (2004), 'The National Market Impact of Sovereign Rating Changes', *Journal of Banking and Finance*, vol. 28, no. 1, pp. 233–250.

Carhart, M (1997), 'On Persistence of Mutual Fund Performance', *Journal of Finance*, vol. 52, no. 1, pp. 57–82.

Chung, Y, Johnson, H & Schill, M (2006), 'Asset Pricing When Returns Are Non-Normal: Fama-French Factors Versus Higher-Order Systematic Co-moments', *Journal of Business*, vol. 79, no. 2, pp. 923–940.

Cornell, B, Landsman, W & Shapiro, A C (1989), 'Cross-Sectional Regularities in the Response of Stock Prices to Bond Rating Changes', *Journal of Accounting, Auditing, and Finance*, vol. 4, no. 4, pp. 460–479.

De Moor, L & Sercu, P (2004), 'CAPM Tests and Alternative Factor Portfolio Composition: Getting the Alpha's Right', *Tijdschrift voor Economie en Management*, vol. 49, pp. 789–846.

Dodd, P (1980), 'Merger Proposals, Management Discretion and Stockholder Wealth', *Journal of Financial Economics*, vol. 8, no. 2, pp. 105–137.

Durand, R, Limkriangkrai, M & Smith, G (2006), 'In America's Thrall. The Effects of the US Market and US Security Characteristics on Australian Stock Returns', *Accounting and Finance*, vol. 46, no. 4, pp. 577–604.

Ederington, H L, Yawitz, B J & Roberts, B E (1987), 'The Informational Content of Bond Ratings', *The Journal of Financial Research*, vol. 10, pp. 211–227.

Estrada, J (2002), 'Systematic Risk in Emerging Markets: The D-CAPM', *Emerging Markets Review*, vol. 3, no. 4, pp. 365–379.

Estrada, J (2007), 'Mean-Semivariance Behavior: Downside Risk and Capital Asset Pricing', *International Review of Economics and Finance*, vol. 16, no. 2, pp. 169–185.

Estrada, J & Serra, P (2005), 'Risk and Return in Emerging Markets: Family Matters', *Journal of Multinational Financial Management*, vol. 15, no. 3, pp. 257–272.

Fama, E F & French, K R (1992), 'The Cross-Section of Expected Stock Returns', *Journal of Finance*, vol. 47, no. 1, pp. 27–65.

Fama, E F & French, K R (1993), 'Common Risk Factors in the Returns on Stocks and Bonds', *Journal of Financial Economics*, vol. 33, no. 1, pp. 3–56.

Fama, E F & French, K R (1996), 'Multifactor Explanations of Asset Pricing Anomalies', *Journal of Finance*, vol. 51, no. 1, pp. 55–84.

Ferreira, M & Gama, P (2007), 'Does Sovereign Debt Ratings News Spill Over to International Stock Markets?', *Journal of Banking and Finance*, vol. 31, no. 10, pp. 3162–3182.

Galagedera, D U A & Brooks, R (2007), 'Is Co-Skewness A Better Measure of Risk in the Downside Than Downside Beta? Evidence in Emerging Market Data', *Journal of Multinational Financial Management*, vol. 17, no. 3, pp. 214–230.

Gande, A & Parsley, D (2005), 'News Spillovers in the Sovereign Debt Market', *Journal of Financial Economics*, vol. 75, no. 3, pp. 691–734.

Goh, J C & Ederington, H (1993), 'Is a Bond Rating Downgrade Bad News, Good News or No News for Stockholders?', *Journal of Finance*, vol. 48, no. 5, pp. 2001–2008.

Goh, J C & Ederington, H (1999), 'Cross-Sectional Variation in the Stock Market Reaction to Bond Rating Changes', *Quarterly Review of Economics and Finance*, vol. 39, no. 1, pp. 101–112.

Griffin, J (2002), 'Are the Fama French Factors Global or Country Specific', *Review of Financial Studies*, vol. 15, no. 4, pp. 1121–1152.

Harlow, W V & Rao, R K S (1989), 'Asset Pricing in a Generalized Mean-Lower Partial Moment Framework: Theory and Evidence', *Journal of Financial and Quantitative Analysis*, vol. 24, pp. 285–311.

Harvey, C & Siddique, A (2000), 'Conditional Skewness in Asset Pricing Tests', *Journal of Finance*, vol. 55, no. 3, pp. 1263–1295.

Hogan, W & Warren, J (1974), 'Toward the Development of an Equilibrium Capital-Market Model Based on Semi-Variance', *Journal of Financial and Quantitative Analysis*, vol. 9, no. 1, pp. 1–11.

Hsueh, L P & Liu, Y A (1992), 'Market Anticipation and the Effect of Bond Rating Changes on Common Stock Prices', *Journal of Business Research*, vol. 24, no. 3, pp. 225–239.

Jegadeesh, N & Titman, S (1993). 'Returns to Buying Winners and Selling Losers: Implications for Stock Market Efficiency', *Journal of Finance*, vol. 48, no. 1, pp. 65–91.

Kraus, A & Litzenberger, R (1976), 'Skewness Preference and the Valuation of Risky Assets', *Journal of Finance*, vol. 31, no. 4, pp. 1085–1100.

Lintner, J (1965), 'The Valuation of Risk Assets and the Selection of Risky Investments in Stock Portfolios and Capital Budgets', *Review of Economics and Statistics*, vol. 47, pp. 13–37.

Mishra, S, Prakash, A, Karels, G & Pactwa, T (2007), 'Skewness Preference and the Measurement of Abnormal Returns', *Applied Economics*, vol. 39, no. 6, pp. 739–757.

Nguyen, P & Puri, T N (2009), 'Higher Order Systematic Co-moments and Asset Pricing: New Evidence', *The Financial Review*, vol. 44, no. 3, pp. 345–369.

Pettengill, G N, Sundaram, S & Mathur, I (1995), 'The Conditional Relation Between Beta and Returns', *Journal of Financial and Quantitative Analysis*, vol. 30, no. 1, pp. 101–116.

Price, K, Price, B & Nantell, T J (1982), 'Variance and Lower Partial Moment Measures of Systematic Risk: Some Analytical and Empirical Results', *Journal of Finance*, vol. 37, no. 3, pp. 843–855.

Pukthuanthong-Le, K, Elayan, F & Rose, L (2007), 'Equity and Debt Market Responses to Sovereign Credit Ratings Announcement', *Global Finance Journal*, vol. 18, no. 1, pp. 47–83.

Rosenberg, B, Reid, K & Lanstein, R (1985), 'Persuasive Evidence of Market Inefficiency', *The Journal of Portfolio Management*, vol. 11, no. 3,, pp. 9–16.

Stattman, D (1980), 'Book Values and Stock Returns', *The Chicago MBA: A Journal of Selected Papers*, vol. 4, pp. 25–45.

Zaima, J K & McCarthy, J (1988), 'The Impact of Bond Rating Changes on Common Stocks and Bonds: Tests of the Wealth Redistribution Hypothesis', *Financial Review*, vol. 23, no. 4, pp. 486–498.

14
Reserve Adequacy Measures for Emerging Market Economies

Willi Semmler and Lebogang Mateane

1 Introduction

The optimal level of reserves has been a controversial issue from the times of fixed exchange rate regimes to the recent times of exchange rate flexibility. Earlier literature such as that of Heller (1966) points out that reserve accumulation has been driven by a precautionary motive against balance of payments imbalances. Similarly, Clark (1970) notes that even in the presence of a temporary deterioration of the balance of payments, international reserves enable a country to follow its domestic policy goals and reserves are beneficial because they provide a country with leeway to adopt suitable policies in the event of a permanent deterioration. Amongst others in recent times, Lee (2004) mentions that international reserves may mitigate international liquidity constraints encountered by a country. Yet again in recent times, reserve accumulation has been considered to be motivated by a need to insure a country against balance of payments risks. This is evident in the view of using reserves as an insurance mechanism against sudden stops. For example, Jeanne and Ranciere (2006) argue that reserves can smooth domestic absorption in the event of a sudden stop when debt is not rolled over and instead reserves can be used to repay the debt. In a similar perspective, such a possibility and theoretical construct is outlined by Aizenman and Lee (2007) where long-term investment projects are financed using foreign assets and, in the event of sudden stops and capital flight, international reserves can help long-term investment projects to continue rather than be liquidated. Another view noted by Aizenman and Marion (2004) sees international reserves as an insurance against a threat of default on external debt that results in restricted or no access to international capital markets. Rather than generalising reserve accumulation to being motivated by self-insurance against sudden stops, Jeanne and Ranciere (2011) point out that reserve accumulation may be motivated by self-insurance against capital flow volatility. On the other hand, Aizenman (2007) emphasises that self-insurance against sudden stops and currency crises cannot fully account for the increase in reserve accumulation, especially for emerging market economies after the year 2000. Instead, he argues that reserve accumulation is an outcome of competitive hoarding and therefore self-insurance against latent domestic and external instability. Moreover, with increasing banking sector balance sheet fragility, there can be rapid exposure to instability which can filter throughout the whole economy. This type of outcome can be aggravated if a country and its banking sector is exposed to substantial amounts of debt denominated in a foreign currency. Reserve holdings and accumulation are also considered as an outcome of a mercantilist view of the economy. This view states that reserve accumulation is based on the objective of securing export competitiveness for a particular country. However, with respect to emerging markets, empirical findings by Aizenman and Lee (2007) show that the precautionary motive has more importance than the mercantilist motive for reserves.

Heller (1966) uses a framework in which he compares the actual level of reserves to the optimal level of reserves for both developed and less developed countries. His results suggest that developed countries are generally covered and have reserves beyond their optimal levels. On the other hand, less developed countries, especially in Latin America, Asia and Africa have reserves that are below their optimal levels.[1] This is in deep contrast with what evidence shows in recent times. According to Aizenman (2007), most, if not all, of the increase in the reserves-GDP ratio has taken place in emerging market economies, whereas the reserves-GDP ratio of developed economies has remained relatively constant. These substantial shifts in patterns indicate that reserve holdings and accumulation are a relevant issue for emerging market economies. In addition, policy authorities in emerging market economies are faced by issues such as which reserve adequacy measures are suitable for emerging market economies in general and which specific reserve adequacy measures are suitable for their own respective economies. Such issues are of relevance because, as noted by Feldstein (1999), Rodrik (2006), and the IMF (2011), holding reserves is costly. In addition, managing reserves with the inappropriate reserve adequacy measure may have severe consequences in the event a country experiences adverse economic outcomes.

This chapter provides an overview on some reasons for reserve accumulation and holdings, a survey on traditional reserve adequacy measures as well as an evaluation of the corresponding proposed reasons for traditional reserve adequacy measures. In addition, the chapter outlines critiques of traditional reserve adequacy measures, gives a brief outline on critiques surrounding frameworks used with respect to reserves and gives a brief outline on proposed alternative reserve adequacy measures. Furthermore, we empirically examine predominant traditional reserve adequacy measures with respect to a group of countries and analyse which ones may have been dominant after two major financial crises. We specifically focus on emerging market economies and outline other factors such as sovereign risk factors that may motivate reserve holdings and accumulation over and above the traditional reserve adequacy measures.

The rest of the chapter is structured as follows: Section 2 defines traditional reserve adequacy measures and outlines explanations and criticism surrounding the respective approaches. Section 3 outlines proposed alternative reserve adequacy measures and criticisms surrounding existing frameworks. Section 4 discusses sovereign risk factors that may influence reserve holdings, Section 5 provides a brief empirical analysis with reference to two major financial crises, and Section 6 concludes.

2 Traditional reserve adequacy measures: explanations and criticisms

In this section, we define three predominant traditional reserve adequacy measures as outlined in the literature. First, import cover or total reserves in the number of months of imports is based on the view that an adequate level of reserves should be able to cover three months of imports. As noted by the IMF (2011), this has been proposed as a procedure to safeguard the domestic economy in the event all inflows such as external financing and export revenue are no longer available. The second reserve adequacy measure is reserves as a cover for short-term external debt of a country[2] (which we refer to as short-term debt henceforth). In general, reserves are proposed to provide a hundred percent cover of short-term debt over a one-year period, and this is based on the Greenspan-Guidotti rule. The third reserve adequacy measure is broad money as a ratio of total reserves, where M2 is typically used as a proxy for broad money.[3] The motive for this coverage measure is so as to capture capital flight risk which is relevant because, as pointed out by the IMF (2011), recent capital account crises exhibit deposit outflows by domestic residents. Following on what we have noted so far, it is evident that there are many factors behind the precautionary motive of holding and accumulating reserves. For example, the precautionary motive for holding and accumulating reserves can be driven by an objective to mitigate current account vulnerability. In line with the IMF (2011) and in this context, factors such as import coverage and volatility of export receipts are typically used as determinants of reserve holdings and can motivate the accumulation of reserves. Furthermore, the precautionary motive for holding and accumulating reserves can be driven by an objective to mitigate capital account vulnerability. In this context, short-term external debt and broad money are typically used as determinants of reserve holdings and can motivate the accumulation of reserves. In their analysis, Aizenman and Marion (2003) outline and examine two factors that motivate such reserve holdings. First, in the context of conditional access to global capital markets and costly domestic tax collection, precautionary holdings are motivated by the need to smooth consumption and distortions over time. Secondly, following the 1997–1998 Asian financial crisis, precautionary holding of reserves are motivated by an increase in loss aversion and a desire to mitigate the increased volatility of shocks. With respect to current and past crises, the IMF (2011) points out that reserves as a liquidity buffer, along with sound policies, have enabled countries to avoid negative outcomes by smoothing consumption and managing capital outflows which would have had costly outcomes. Such a point has already been noted by the IMF (2001), where they make reference to international financial crises dating from years prior to 2001. They note countries have benefitted from reserves because they have been able to prevent and mitigate external crises, especially those that originate from the capital account, given that they have held and managed sufficient reserves and have been transparent to financial markets about their reserve holdings (specifically in providing timely and accurate information). In addition, they note that such procedures have provided policy authorities the ability to adjust policy much earlier and have provided markets enough time to assess any country risks.

Against this backdrop, Obstfeld, Shambaugh, and Taylor (2009) argue that reserve adequacy should not only be viewed for insuring against sudden stops but also in accounting for capital flight risk. Similarly, Obstfeld, Shambaugh, and Taylor (2008) bring to attention that, in general, governments do not take a passive stance to their respective exchange rate level, and with the possibility of a liberalised financial account generating more balance of payments instability, these are factors that can motivate reserve holding and accumulation. In this connection, greater exchange rate flexibility is also considered to be a factor that determines reserve holdings and accumulation because as noted by Aizenman and Marion (2004), in this context less reserves are needed to maintain a peg (and/or maintain the peg's credibility). Even with the points noted, it is also evident that reserves are not a solution to all macroeconomic problems; however, along with sound financial and macroeconomic policies, reserves may stabilise an economy that experiences adverse economic disturbances. Nevertheless, using a survey of reserve managers of emerging market economies, the IMF (2011) provides reasons documented for building reserves. These reasons are as follows: (i) buffer for liquidity needs, (ii) savings against income/ commodity price shocks, (iii) savings for future generations, (iv) management of exchange rate level, (v) smoothing of exchange rate volatility, (vi) bank recapitalisation costs, and (vii) other (e.g., currency boards). Furthermore, the dominant reason for building reserves based on the reserve manager's survey is the buffer for liquidity needs, followed by smoothing of exchange rate volatility, and finally management of the level of the exchange rate.

Although traditional reserve adequacy measures are widely cited in the literature, used in empirical analyses, and consistent with reasons provided by reserve managers in surveys, reserve adequacy measures are subject to criticism. For example, import cover or total reserves in the number of months of imports is considered by the IMF (2011) to be an arbitrary measure because empirical findings do not seem to suggest that three months or any number of months of import coverage is adequate. In addition, although reserves as a cover for short-term debt is widely used, the IMF (2011) points out that it is an arbitrary measure because the 12-month benchmark coverage is an outcome of how short-term debt levels are defined. The arbitrariness is problematic because as noted by the IMF (2011) the length of crises are generally not 12 months and interest rates associated with short-term debt do not generally reduce to zero during crises. Another factor that raises criticism is based on the events of the most recent financial crisis, where the IMF (2011) identifies that during the crisis, short-term debt and reserves did not exhibit a high degree of association. Moreover, a depletion of reserves was not necessarily due to short-term debt, and based on this experience, it has raised questions on the usage of short-term debt as an indicator and its associated duration. However, this is in contrast to an earlier analysis where the IMF (2001) had argued that, with respect to emerging market economies, reserves to short-term external debt by remaining maturity is the most relevant indicator for crisis prevention purposes.[4] The IMF (2011) also considers the third reserve coverage measure, namely broad money as a ratio of total reserves, problematic (where M2 is typically used as a proxy for broad money). They note that broad money as a ratio of total reserves is problematic because it may be relevant for domestic banks which have very large external exposure but this would already be captured by external debt indicators. In addition, with domestic resources available, the IMF (2011) identifies that there is no definite reason for needing highly liquid external resources more specifically for recapitalisation purposes. On the contrary, Obstfeld et al. (2008) provide a clear mechanism (and historical example using an emerging market economy) where domestic financial stability is configured with reserve management policy. They note that an internal and external drain can occur, which they refer to as a double drain, and the effects of a double drain risk may result in a collapse of M2. In this case, investors not only exchange domestic bank deposit balances for currency but they also exchange domestic bank deposits for foreign currency, foreign bank deposits, and foreign assets, and can also exchange domestic bank deposits for central bank reserves. This mechanism shows that investors can cause a collapse in M2 and deplete a central bank's reserves. Furthermore, Obstfeld et al. (2008) emphasise that another reason for evaluating broad money, as opposed to short-term debt only, is that evaluating short-term debt (as outlined in the Guidotti-Greenspan rule) concentrates on external drains and does not account for the role of domestic investors' financial decisions and the implications of these financial decisions. Nevertheless, expanding on the noted capital flight arguments, we would think that a central bank would probably prefer domestic balances to be exchanged for central bank's reserves. This would be a better outcome than having domestic currency flooding foreign exchange markets which may lead to further currency depreciation and possibly to a currency crisis that augments the on-going capital flight problem.

The criticisms and contrasting views surrounding reserve adequacy measures yet again highlight the conundrum faced by policy authorities in emerging market economies of which reserve adequacy measures are suitable for emerging market economies and which specific reserve adequacy measures are suitable for their own respective economy. In addition, with the recurrent frequency and severity of economic crises and economic disturbances (which can also vary), these raise the question of how policy should be configured towards appropriate reserve adequacy measures and optimal levels of reserve holdings. In this connection, the

IMF (2011) emphasises that the optimal level of reserve holding should depend on the type of shocks a country encounters. Furthermore, the IMF (2011) argues that sudden stops and currency crises which relate to the capital account may account for the shocks of emerging market economies because of their diversified exports and their degree of international market integration. This suggests reserve adequacy measures for emerging markets should be geared towards the capital account. Another factor highlighted by the IMF (2011) is that capital account crises that emerging markets encounter are interconnected with reserve holdings. This is evident because low reserve holdings may provide a negative signal to investors on the ability of a central bank to defend its currency. This in turn may have negative consequences such as a currency crisis, lowering the confidence in the domestic economy and restricting foreign borrowing. Based on the defined reserve adequacy measures, the reasons outlined for precautionary motives of accumulating reserves, and criticisms geared towards traditional reserve adequacy measures, it is clear and evident that a standard approach using a one-rule or one-size-fits-all quantitative measure for reserve coverage is inappropriate and may result in negative consequences in the event of economic disturbances.

3 Proposed alternative reserve adequacy measures

Next, we provide a brief outline on critiques surrounding frameworks used with respect to analysing reserves. In addition, this section outlines proposed alternative reserve adequacy measures. Firstly, the IMF (2011) argues that decisions relating to reserves should be motivated by evaluating the benefits relative to costs of reserves. This assertion is supported by a survey of reserve managers conducted by the IMF (2011), where 67% of countries document that they use a cost-benefit framework for their reserve strategies and to quantify costs associated with reserves. However, these types of cost-benefit frameworks have already been outlined in earlier literature. Heller (1966) considered the motives for reserves to be driven by an optimisation framework with an objective to balance benefits of reserves relative to the opportunity cost associated with reserves. However, explicit optimisation models are problematic because, as outlined by the IMF (2011), there is no consensus view on the form of utility and cost functions that would be used to evaluate such costs and benefits.[5] With respect to regression models, the IMF (2011) argues that they employ conduct assumptions on the part of the country and impose an assumption that reserve decisions are motivated by precautionary motives under which the reserve regression framework is considered to sufficiently characterise the precautionary motive. With respect to reserve adequacy measures, the IMF (2011) argues that these approaches put emphasis on adequate reserve levels given that there are potential balance of payments pressures. However, these approaches are associated with the extent to which a country is willing to insure itself, and this is contingent on the probability associated with potential shocks. As a result, with respect to emerging market economies, the IMF (2011) proposes a broader-based quantitative measure for adequate reserve levels. The reasoning behind these proposed measures is that balance of payments pressures have multiple sources in the current and capital accounts. Based on this, a risk-weighted measure is developed which accounts for the relative risk levels of different potential sources of balance of payments pressure, and it is also contingent on empirical capital outflows. In addition, the broader-based quantitative measure quantifies the level of reserves required relative to the risk-weighted measure.

In this connection, the IMF (2011) proposes an alternative approach to estimating outflows from two external liability variables, namely short-term debt and other portfolio liabilities. The new risk-weighted metric proposed by the IMF (2011) is with respect to two exchange regimes, where broad money and exports are included, and is defined as follows: For a fixed exchange rate regime, the risk-weighted metric is equal to 30% of short-term debt + 15% of other portfolio liabilities + 10% of M2 + 10% of exports. For a floating exchange rate regime, the risk-weighted metric is equal to 30% of short-term debt + 10% of other portfolio liabilities + 5% of M2 + 5% of exports. The proposed risk-weighted measure consists of two stages, where the first stage is the construction of the metric and the second stage is to consider the coverage against this metric a country should hold, and this is guided by factors such as crisis prevention, crisis mitigation, and observed reserve losses. We consider this to be a better reserve coverage measure because it accounts for different sources of risk and can address sovereign risk associated with specific countries rather than a standard approach using a one-rule or one-size-fits-all quantitative measure for reserve coverage. However, other literature emphasises that reserve adequacy measures should be aiming at a particular vulnerability. For example, Obstfeld et al. (2008) argue on the basis of reserve adequacy measures to address capital account vulnerability, and they emphasise on broad money as compared to short-term external debt.[6] In addition, Obstfeld et al. (2008) propose a new financial stability-based model of reserve accumulation and progress beyond traditional models of reserve accumulation which are based on buffer stock and mercantilist models of reserve accumulation. The most notable and different variable they use in their financial stability model is a measure of financial openness. In addition, they introduce two alternative debt measures, namely the fraction of internationally issued securities issued in foreign currency and the log of the ratio to GDP of all external liabilities in foreign currency. They generalise these variables and refer to them as the 'original sin' variables which they use to characterise their 'original sin' hypothesis. Nevertheless, following on the proposed alternatives, there may be other factors that may motivate reserve holdings and accumulation over and above what has been surveyed in the earlier parts of this chapter.

4 Sovereign risk factors: beyond traditional measures

In this section, we briefly cover other factors that may motivate reserve holdings and accumulation over and above what has been surveyed in the earlier parts of this chapter. As noted, holding reserves is costly, and with many emerging market economies holding reserve levels higher than the recommended levels, other factors may need to be taken into account. For example, Aizenman and Marion (2003) explain that advocates of large reserve holdings argue in their favour on the basis of the cost of holding reserves being insignificant as compared to the economic consequences of a crisis which is of relevance because of the frequency and severity of economic crises. In addition, Aizenman and Marion (2003) outline that increasing sovereign risk concerns may result in emerging market economies having limited or no access to international capital markets. In this connection, unlike advanced economies, not all emerging market economies are considered to have credible policies which are maintained with a high degree of certainty. Furthermore, Obstfeld et al. (2008) point out that emerging market economies may not have stable banking systems and may not be able to borrow in their own currency, and this can result in a greater demand for reserves. Moreover, not all emerging markets have better access to private credit and/or official swap lines. This is a point made by Obstfeld et al. (2009) which emphasises that emerging market economies will continue to accumulate reserves as long as they continue facing uncertainty with respect to access of large foreign exchange swaps whenever they are needed. Nevertheless, even with the other factors that may motivate reserves, more inclusive and country-specific factors need to be accounted for by policy authorities. Such a point is made by the IMF (2011) that other factors relevant to sovereign risk management should be considered and these factors (amongst others) can range from contingent financing mechanisms, country insurance and policies aiming towards financial and macroeconomic stability of each particular country rather than purely focusing on reserves.

5 Empirical analysis

The earlier sections of this chapter have provided an overview of reserve adequacy measures and the corresponding motivation for each respective reserve adequacy measure. In addition, the earlier sections have outlined some of the reasons for the precautionary motives for accumulating and holding reserves. In this section, we empirically examine predominant traditional reserve adequacy measures with respect to a group of emerging market economies and analyse which ones may have been important factors for reserve holdings and accumulation after two major financial crises. The two major financial crises we use are the 1997–1998 Asian financial crisis and the recent 2007–2009 global financial crisis. Other literature such as Aizenman and Marion (2003) and Obstfeld et al. (2008) group particular countries and use regression analysis on the grouped data to examine which factors may be motivating reserves. For example, the traditional regression model or estimating equation used by Aizenman and Marion (2003) is of the following representation:

$$\begin{aligned}\ln\left(\frac{R_{it}}{P_{it}}\right) &= \alpha_0 + \alpha_1 \ln(pop_{it}) + \alpha_2 \ln(gpc_{it}) + \alpha_3 \ln(exa_{it}) \\ &\quad + \alpha_4 \ln(imy_{it}) + \alpha_5 \ln(neer_{it}) + \varepsilon_t \end{aligned} \tag{1}$$

where R is actual holdings of reserves less gold valued in millions of US dollars and deflated by US GDP deflator P, *pop* is the total population of a country, *gpc* is real GDP per capita, *exa* is the volatility of real exports, *imy* is imports of goods and services as a share of GDP, and *neer* is the volatility of the nominal effective exchange rate. In addition, Aizenman and Marion (2003) account for political considerations in a second estimating equation. The second estimating equation uses the same variables as the traditional model but expands on these by including (i) an index of political corruption, which has a scale of 0–10 with 10 being the most corrupt and (ii) the probability of government change by constitutional means.[7]

In a similar manner to Aizenman and Marion (2003), the traditional regression model used by Obstfeld et al. (2008) is of the following representation:

$$\ln(\frac{R_{it}}{GDP_{it}}) = \beta_0 + \beta_1 \ln(pop_{it}) + \beta_2 \ln(imy_{it}) + \beta_3 exvol + \beta_4 \ln(gpc_{it}) + \upsilon_t \qquad (2)$$

Where R is actual holdings of reserves which are deflated by *GDP*, *pop* is the total population of a country, *imy* is imports of goods and services as a share of GDP, *exvol* is the exchange rate volatility and *gpc* is real GDP per capita converted at PPP exchange rates in current international dollars. Obstfeld et al. (2008) also propose a new financial stability-based model of reserve accumulation and progress beyond traditional models of reserve accumulation which are based on buffer stock and mercantilist models of reserve accumulation. Their financial stability model uses the log of the ratio of reserves to GDP as a dependent variable and uses the following as regressors: (i) the log of the ratio of M2 to GDP, (ii) a measure of financial openness, (iii) a pegged exchange rate dummy, (iv) a soft peg, (v) an advanced country dummy, and (vi) log of the ratio of foreign trade to GDP. In addition, Obstfeld et al. (2008) also include two alternative debt measures, namely the fraction of internationally-issued securities issued in foreign currency and the log of the ratio to GDP of all external liabilities in foreign currency along with the core variables in the financial stability model.

Our procedure is different to that of Aizenman and Marion (2003) and Obstfeld et al. (2008). We examine each individual country rather than group countries, and we conduct our analysis over shorter time spans which follow the 1997–1998 Asian financial crisis and the recent 2007–2009 global financial crisis. In addition, our procedure is simpler because we only evaluate either the year-on-year growth rate or the percentage point change or absolute change in the ratio of a relevant reserve adequacy measure. Our computations correspond to the periods 1999–2006, 2010–2012, and the average over 1999–2006 and 2010–2012. We use data on the variables as defined in the World Bank's World Development Indicators. The variables are as follows: (i) short-term debt as a percentage of total reserves, (ii) total reserves as a percentage of total external debt, (iii) money and quasi-money (M2) to total reserves ratio,[8] and (iv) total reserves in months of imports. We include one more reserve adequacy measure, namely total reserves as a percentage of total external debt rather than restricting our analysis to the three traditional reserve adequacy measures. We examine each of these reserve adequacy measures for the following 14 emerging market economies[9]: Bolivia, Brazil, China, Ecuador, Hong Kong, India, Indonesia, South Korea, Malaysia, Mexico, Russia, Singapore, South Africa, and Thailand. This procedure gives us an indication of which reserve adequacy measures may have been dominant after crisis outcomes and also provides an indication of the type of vulnerability that policy authorities set out to offset and possibly stabilise. In addition, based on the findings, we can also have an indication of which reserve adequacy is predominant amongst all the emerging market economies in our analysis and what seems to be the type of predominant vulnerability that policy authorities aim to mitigate.

Rather than evaluating full insurance of reserves to short-term debt as a mechanism of crisis prevention in a manner such as that proposed by the Greenspan-Guidotti rule, we focus on the percentage point change in short-term debt as a percentage of reserves. This procedure allows us to see after two major financial crises whether short-term debt as a percentage of reserves has been decreasing and could possibly imply policy authorities' objectives are to mitigate potential capital account vulnerability. Table 14.1 reports the percentage point change in short-term debt as a percentage of total reserves. On a year-on-year basis, most countries exhibit a negative percentage point change in short-term debt as a percentage of total reserves over the total sample. More importantly, after the 1997–1998 Asian financial crisis, all emerging market economies (precluding China) exhibited on average a negative average percentage point change in short-term debt as a percentage of total reserves over the period 1999–2006. This finding shows an increasing coverage of short-term debt by reserves. In addition, after the 1997–1998 Asian financial crisis and recent 2007–2009 global financial crisis, five out of the eleven emerging market economies exhibit on average a negative percentage point change in short-term debt as a percentage of total reserves. This also shows an increasing coverage of short-term debt by reserves after both financial crises in our analysis.

Similar patterns are exhibited in Table 14.1 with respect to total reserves as a percentage of total external debt. In this context, on a year-on-year basis, most countries exhibit a positive percentage point change in total reserves as a percentage of total external debt over the total sample. More importantly, after the 1997–1998 Asian financial crisis, all emerging market economies exhibit on average a positive average percentage point change in total reserves as a percentage of total external debt. This shows an increasing coverage with respect to a more

Table 14.1 Percentage point change in external debt measures relative to total reserves Panel A: Short-term debt as a percentage of total reserves

Post 1997–1998 Crisis	Bolivia	Brazil	China	Ecuador	India	Indonesia	Malaysia	Mexico	Russia	South Africa	Thailand
					–3.202	–12.845					
1999	–0.8439	12.34	–1.9406	–70.74	–11.9566	–7.0068	5.465	–63.50462	–33.086		
2000	0.94192	13.384	–1.7892	7.7204	–2.492	0.64149	–3.4743	–22.386	–71.23	–20.23213	–21.777
2001	–0.8283	–14.99	17.9692	61.2818	–2.842	–2.61152	6.65981	–20.725	–4.257	–14.48463	–5.5321
2002	8.28782	–16.99	–3.5248	101.54	0.126	–16.252	2.16693	14.7	–18.49	–6.512393	–9.3831
2003	–11.178	–11.93	–0.8935	–78.401	0.383	–1.30381	–5.3231	–8.4194	5.0763	–2.263172	–4.6519
2004	–8.843	–2.177	–2.5819	–22.569	–0.884	6.93448	–2.247	–7.1311	–17.9	–25.56753	–2.9389
2005	–11.299	–3.136	–0.751	–49.445	1.182	–28.9173	1.48139	–1.6809	–6.063	–5.984872	7.70463
2006	–3.2375	–20.92	–1.791	18.5997	7.699	–3.07699	–4.4586	4.444	–1.519	11.137656	–4.1693
Average 1999–2006	–3.3751	–5.552	0.58715	–4.0015	–0.004	–7.06778	–2.255	–6.0258	–13.61	–15.92646	–9.2292
Post 2007–2009 crisis											
2010	–0.1693	6.0163	2.1221	–5.9023	2.416	–2.02435	8.42439	4.7327	0.4898	–4.159185	5.80906
2011	–1.1551	–10.72	2.72592	–5.4665	7.341	0.31126	–0.207	2.0513	1.4847	–10.8971	–1.5317
Average 2010–2011	–0.6622	–2.354	2.42401	–5.6844	4.878	–0.85654	4.10869	3.392	0.9872	–7.52814	2.13868

Panel B: Total reserves as a percentage of total external debt post two crises

Post 1997–1998 Crisis	Bolivia	Brazil	China	Ecuador	India	Indonesia	Malaysia	Mexico	Russia	South Africa	Thailand
							11.8227				
1999	0.65086	−3.313	2.49518	0.49787	4.956	2.43042	−0.9707	−0.024	8.7049779	7.7461	
2000	−1.9674	−1.213	9.28088	−2.9033	4.618	2.41766	−5.3818	4.3285	12.026	−0.307192	5.01985
2001	3.82218	1.9829	1.62749	−1.2296	8.698	0.80185	−2.2121	3.6387	6.8538	0.7246535	8.17776
2002	−6.4353	0.714	41.2119	−1.4179	18.42	3.76902	3.74483	4.8088	9.1851	−6.12384	16.2918
2003	1.21515	4.585	40.7457	0.8031	19.54	2.09766	21.273	4.1527	7.2739	−2.93784	17.0646
2004	1.52448	3.0897	51.8081	1.21145	19.2	−0.6913	36.0059	1.9001	16.764	13.51664	18.1152
2005	5.53926	4.5756	40.1566	4.13249	7.262	−1.92081	8.24045	4.2609	14.012	7.1222155	11.4641
2006	28.7999	15.618	40.9976	−0.6915	−2.109	6.84136	13.5458	1.8776	25.406	2.7747368	33.5483
Average 1999–2006	4.14364	3.255	28.5404	0.05031	10.07	1.96823	10.8799	2.9996	11.437	2.934294	14.6785
Post 2007–2009 Crisis											
2010	18.4189	−2.814	−31.659	−11.064	−7.616	12.4387	−13.435	−0.5029	2.2235	−8.435042	−12.577
2011	24.444	5.1838	−47.004	0.40393	−14.13	2.28091	16.2527	2.5267	−2.329	0.1313217	4.9428
Average 2010–2011	21.4315	1.1848	−39.331	−5.3299	−10.88	7.35982	1.40907	1.0119	−0.053	−4.15186	−3.8169

comprehensive external debt measure. Furthermore, on average after the 1997–1998 and 2007–2009 crises, yet again five out of the eleven countries exhibit a positive percentage point change in total reserves as a percentage of external debt. The findings with respect to short-term debt as a percentage of total reserves and total reserves as a percentage of total external debt are similar and consistent.[10] This may mean that mitigating potential capital account vulnerability after crises may be a motivating factor for reserve holdings and accumulation for the emerging market economies in our analysis.

Table 14.2 reports the absolute change in the ratio of M2 to total reserves. On average after the 1997–1998 Asian financial crisis, most countries in our analysis exhibit a reduction in M2 as a ratio of reserves over the period 1999–2006 which shows an increased coverage of M2 by reserves. However, on average after the recent 2007–2009 global financial crisis, only Mexico and South Africa exhibit a reduction in M2 as a ratio of total reserves. The growth rate of total reserves in months of imports is reported in Panel B of Table 14.2. Data from the World Bank's World Development Indicators for total reserves in months of imports is only available from 2005–2011. As a result, we only report after the recent 2007–2009 global financial crisis. On a year-on-year basis, most countries exhibit a negative growth rate of total reserves in months of imports. Furthermore, all of the emerging market economies except for Mexico exhibit a negative growth rate of total reserves in months of imports. This implies reserve adequacy aiming at mitigating potential current account vulnerability may not be a motivating factor for reserve holdings and accumulation after crises for the emerging market economies in our analysis.

In the context of estimable equations or regression models and following on the above noted, Aizenman and Marion (2003) find that reserve holdings are an outcome of factors such as the size of international transactions, the volatility of international transactions, exchange rate arrangements of particular countries, and political considerations. Aizenman and Marion's (2003) findings show that an index of political corruption, using a scale of 0–10 with 10 being the worst corruption and the probability of government change by a constitutional procedure, are quantitatively and statistically significant factors of the determinants of reserve holdings. An increase in the index of political corruption significantly reduces reserves. Similarly, an increase in the probability of a government leadership change by constitutional means significantly reduces reserves, and both these factors improve the explanatory power of Aizenman and Marion's (2003) econometric model of reserves. Political

Table 14.2 Absolute change in ratio of M2 to total reserves and growth rate of total reserves in months of imports Panel A: Absolute change in ratio of M2 to total reserves

Post 1997–1998 Crisis	Bolivia	Brazil	China	Ecuador	India	Indonesia	Malaysia	Mexico	Russia	South Africa	Thailand
1999	–0.17	–0.68	0.716	–1.65114	0.026776	–0.22	0.569	0.197	–0.0621	–3.61831585	–0.1519333
2000	0.024	2.168	0.503	1.851939	–0.09506	–0.27	0.0399	0.057	0.63574	–0.82584721	0.21665994
2001	0.521	–1.67	–0.97	1.634817	–0.12935	–0.52	–0.1177	1.965	0.28785	–0.20157993	–0.2529406
2002	0.569	–1.24	–1.41	0.089086	–0.00419	–1.21	0.0373	–0.02	–0.3286	–0.52380585	–0.3578729
2003	–0.65	–0.75	–1.06	0.120565	0.021562	–0.8	0.1174	–0.89	–0.6851	4.424695855	0.34047214
2004	–0.95	0.793	–1.42	0.299066	0.097881	–0.22	0.119	–0.66	–0.8159	–3.57274238	–0.3192281
2005	–0.59	2.546	–0.55	–1.06116	0.110414	0.419	0.3831	0.552	0.07092	–1.08856205	0.05812809
2006	–0.78	–1.54	–0.14	0.853065	0.31495	–0.31	–0.0251	0.296	–0.0067	–0.60260564	–0.4064548
Average 1999–2006	–0.25	–0.05	–0.54	0.267031	0.042873	–0.39	0.1404	0.187	–0.113	–0.75109538	–0.1091462
Post 2007–2009 Crisis											
2010	0.017	0.413	0.037	3.174991	0.054264	0.604	–0.2916	0.379	0.19299	0.688213077	–0.0760755
2011	0.008	0.111	0.37	0.312195	0.089578	0.479	0.1531	0.232	–0.1169	–0.12134353	0.38138765
2012	0.061	–0.33	0.506	–	–0.07699	–0.13	0.1425	–0.18	0.09193	–0.67109238	0.11020112
Average 2010–2012	0.028	0.063	0.304	1.743593	0.022282	0.317	0.0013	0.145	0.056	–0.03474094	0.13850443

Panel B: Growth rate of total reserves in months of imports

Post 1997–1998 Crisis	Bolivia	Brazil	China	Ecuador	India	Indonesia	Malaysia	Mexico	Russia	South Africa	Thailand
2010	−3.46	−9.73	−13.7	−46.5652	−15.4278	−20.5	5.7807	−16.3	−15.787	−10.0631532	−7.2614899
2011	−11.3	−1.49	−12.1	−3.26683	−6.54985	−18.8	−11.596	−12	8.78045	−7.33683064	−15.354334
2012	0.354	9.047	−1.5	–	4.107396	–	−7.63	6.619	−0.8076	3.872348473	−3.1884921
Average 2010–2012	−4.79	−0.73	−9.09	−24.916	−5.95674	−19.7	−4.4819	−7.23	−2.6049	−4.50921177	−8.6014386

Notes: ** data for the respective country is only available up to the year 2011 and the average post 2007–2009 crisis only refers to average over 2010–2011. Data for total reserves in months of imports is only available from 2005–2011. As a result, we only report post the recent 2007–2009 global financial crisis.

factors also influence reserves in Aizenman and Marion (2004) where political uncertainty and corruption reduce reserves. Furthermore, using the 1997–1998 Asian financial crisis as a point of reference, Aizenman and Marion (2003) point out that holding large precautionary reserve balances has been an optimal strategy for countries facing sovereign risk. Using a model of the optimal level of reserves for emerging market economies, Jeanne and Ranciere (2006) find that reserves allow a country's government to smooth domestic absorption in crises. More specifically, the main benefit of reserves in their model is that reserves are geared towards crisis mitigation rather than crisis prevention. Using the degree of capital account liberalisation as an independent variable, Aizenman and Lee (2007) find that the more liberalised the capital account, the greater is the reserve accumulation. Although Obstfeld et al. (2008) use two alternative debt measures, they only find that the fraction of internationally-issued securities issued in foreign currency has a positive and statistically significant relationship with reserves. In addition, their financial stability model explains reserves well even when the fraction of internationally-issued securities issued in foreign currency is included along with the core variables. They argue that this finding implies that countries issuing more foreign currency denominated debt will have higher reserve holdings. However, they point out that a better specified framework would be required to provide a basis for a causal relationship between reserves and the proportion of foreign currency denominated debt. They argue that the proportion of foreign currency denominated debt may result in an increase in reserves because reserves may safeguard an economy in the event of a sudden stop. On the other hand, they also point out that with a currency peg to be maintained, large reserve holdings may provide a positive signal to investors that the currency peg may be maintained which in turn allows the possibility of issuing more foreign currency-denominated debt.

Nevertheless, in our analysis, after the 1997–1998 Asian financial crisis, most countries exhibit a reduction in M2 as a ratio of total reserves over the period 1999–2006, which shows an increased coverage of M2 by reserves. However, with respect to short-term debt as a percentage of total reserves and total reserves as a percentage of total external debt, the results are similar and more consistent over both financial crises. Although this may mean that mitigating potential capital account vulnerability after crises may be a motivating factor for reserve holdings, it seems that the procedure may be more configured towards external debt measures rather than towards M2 in an attempt to mitigate potential capital account vulnerability. This is in line with the argument by the IMF (2001), who note that capital account vulnerability is a feature generally specific to emerging market economies as compared to other types of markets and that is why reserve policy for emerging market economies should be aiming at stabilising potential capital account vulnerabilities. In addition, and to account for potential capital account vulnerabilities with respect to South Korea, Aizenman, Lee, & Rhee (2007) argue that following the 1997–1998 Asian financial crisis, monetary authorities should account for capital flows and configure reserves with short-term debt. Similarly, Obstfeld et al. (2008) argue on the basis of reserve adequacy measures to address capital account vulnerability. However, they emphasise on broad money as compared to short-term external debt.

On the other hand, our findings imply reserve adequacy aimed at mitigating potential current account vulnerability, may not be a motivating factor for reserve holdings and accumulation after crises for the emerging market economies in our analysis. However, this does not necessarily mean that current account variables are irrelevant. This is a point made by the IMF (2011), where they note that current account variables (e.g., import coverage and volatility of export receipts) are relevant because they have a significant impact in explaining the increase in reserves over the past decade. However, the IMF (2011) argue that reserve management should be aimed at capital account measures, and this is consistent with their view that emerging market economies are more susceptible to capital account shocks as compared to current account shocks. Furthermore, the IMF (2011) notes that capital account crises that emerging markets encounter are inter-connected with reserve holding. This is evident because low reserve holdings may provide a negative signal to investors on the ability of a central bank to defend its currency. This may in turn have negative consequences such as a currency crisis, lowering the confidence in the domestic economy and restricting foreign borrowing.

6 Conclusion

The frequency and severity of economic crises poses challenges for policy authorities across emerging market economies. In addition, the possibility of adverse economic consequences of a crisis poses policy challenges in emerging market economies with respect to issues such as which reserve adequacy measures are suitable for emerging market economies in general and which specific reserve adequacy measures are suitable for their own respective economy. This chapter provides an overview on some reasons for reserve accumulation and holdings, a survey on traditional reserve adequacy measures, as well as an evaluation of the corresponding proposed reasons for traditional reserve adequacy measures. Based on an empirical analysis, our findings suggest that after the 1997–1998 Asian financial crisis and the recent 2007–2009 global financial crisis, reserve adequacy measures suitable to mitigate capital account vulnerability seem to be dominant for a group of emerging market economies. In addition, our findings are consistent with findings and recommendations in other literature. However, this does not mean that reserve adequacy measures aiming at reducing current account vulnerability are irrelevant because in other analyses using regression models, variables such as import coverage and volatility of export receipts have a significant impact in explaining the increase in reserves.

Notes

1. We think that it is reasonable to consider some of the countries in Latin America and Asia (especially Asia) to have transformed from less developed countries to emerging market economies during the period 1966–2007.
2. Another comprehensive measure is the ratio of reserves to total external debt rather than short-term external debt.
3. Another measure instead of M2 as a ratio of total reserves may be used. For example, broad money to total reserves ratio may be used, where as defined in the World Bank's World Development Indicators, broad money is the sum of currency outside banks; demand deposits other than those of the central government; the time, savings, and foreign currency deposits of resident sectors other than the central government; bank and traveller's checks; and other securities such as certificates of deposit and commercial paper.
4. In fact the IMF (2001) explicitly states that reserves to short-term external debt ratio, as a predictor and an explanation of the depth of recent emerging market crises, has better empirical results as compared to reserves to imports ratio and reserves to broad money ratio.
5. With respect to applicable cost measures, the IMF (2011) notes that these costs usually range from sterilisation costs, actual or potential exchange rate valuation losses, the opportunity cost of foregone consumption or investment, and the cost from maturity mismatch between reserves and sovereign liabilities.
6. In a connected manner, based on outreach programs conducted by the IMF (2001), findings suggest that given there is uncertainty surrounding access to capital markets, reserve adequacy should be aiming at a framework that is based on capital account vulnerability. The IMF (2001) outlines that historical results, showing the benefits of reserves during periods of crises and as a mechanism to manage exchange rate volatility, have resulted in positive implications for reserve management policies.

7. Aizenman and Marion (2004) also use a similar estimating equation where in this context they also consider the probability of a government leadership change by unconstitutional means as compared to only using the probability of government leadership change by constitutional means. Similarly, Aizenman and Lee (2007) also have a similar estimating equation for reserves. However, they include some new variables; for example, to capture capital account liberalisation, they use an index of capital account liberalisation as a variable that determines the ratio of reserves to GDP. They also use residuals from a regression of the price level on relative income, a terms of trade index, and variants of crises dummy variables which are specific to particular crises and specific to particular regions.
8. As defined in the World Bank's World Development Indicators, money and quasi money comprise the sum of currency outside banks, demand deposits other than those of the central government, and the time, savings, and foreign currency deposits of resident sectors other than the central government. This definition is frequently called M2.
9. We examine the reserve adequacy measures wherever data is available for the respective countries.
10. Note: for short-term debt as a percentage of total reserves and total reserves as a percentage of total external debt, data is available until 2011. As a result, the year-on-year percentage point changes and average percentage point changes post the 2007–2009 crisis only correspond to the years 2010 and 2011.

References

Aizenman, J (2007), 'Large Hoarding of International Reserves and the Emerging Global Economic Architecture', Economics E2, UCSC and the NBER, Prepared for Growth and Business Cycles in Theory and Practice Conference, 12–13 July.

Aizenman, J & Lee, J (2007), 'International Reserves: Precautionary Versus Mercantilist Views, Theory and Evidence', *Open Economies Review*, vol. 18, no. 2, pp. 191–214.

Aizenman, J, Lee, Y & Rhee, Y (2007), 'International Reserves Management and Capital Mobility in a Volatile World: Policy Considerations and a Case Study of Korea', *Journal of the Japanese and International Economies*, vol. 21, no. 1, pp. 1–15.

Aizenman, J & Marion, N (2003), 'The High Demand for International Reserves in the Far East: What Is Going On?' *Journal of the Japanese and International Economies*, vol. 17, no. 3, pp. 370–400.

Aizenman, J & Marion, N (2004), 'International Reserve Holdings with Sovereign Risk and Costly Tax Collection', *The Economic Journal*, vol. 114, no. 497, pp. 569–591.

Clark, P B (1970), 'Optimum International Reserves and the Speed of Adjustment', *The Journal of Political Economy*, vol. 78, no. 2, (Mar–Apr), pp. 356–376.

Feldstein, M (1999), 'A Self-Help Guide for Emerging Markets', *Foreign Affairs*, vol. 78, no. 2 (Mar–Apr), pp. 93–109.

Heller, H R (1966), 'Optimal International Reserves', *The Economic Journal*, vol. 76, no. 302 (June), pp. 296–311.

International Monetary Fund (IMF) (2001), *Issues in Reserves Adequacy and Management*, Washington, DC.

International Monetary Fund (IMF) (2011), *Assessing Reserve Adequacy*, Washington, DC.

Jeanne, O & Ranciere, R (2006), 'The Optimal Level of International Reserves for Emerging Market Economies: Formulas and Applications', IMF Working Paper, WP/06/229.

Lee, J (2004), 'Insurance Value of International Reserves: An Option Pricing Approach', IMF Working Paper, WP/04/175.

Obstfeld, M, Shambaugh, J C & Taylor, A M (2008), 'Financial Stability, the Trilemma, and International Reserves', NBER Working Paper No. 14217, August 2008.

Obstfeld, M, Shambaugh, J C & Taylor, A M (2009), 'Financial Instability, Reserves and Central Bank Swap Lines in the Panic of 2008', NBER Working Paper No. 14826, March 2009.

Rodrik, D (2006), 'The Social Cost of Foreign Exchange Reserves', NBER Working Paper No. 11952, January 2006.

World Bank, *World Development Indicators 1960–2012*, <www.worldbank.org>.

15
The Price Impact of Sovereign Rating Announcements

Albert Metz and Merxe Tudela

1 Introduction

The impact of credit ratings on financial markets has gathered new interest in the wake of the European sovereign debt crisis. Some have suggested that credit rating agencies (CRAs) amplify contagious effects and create additional financial instability,[1] a charge which of course is at odds with another frequent complaint that rating agencies respond too slowly to new information and lag markets.[2] The current crisis has prompted some calls to limit the freedom of action of CRAs at least in the sovereign markets.[3]

In this chapter, we evaluate in a *mechanical* way the empirical impact of credit rating actions on sovereign emerging markets. By 'rating action' (the event) we mean upgrades and downgrades as well as outlook and watch list assignments which may anticipate rating changes. What this chapter does not do is to isolate the impact of the *news content* of the rating action itself on market prices.

Sovereign ratings are based on public information, and they are produced through public and transparent methodologies. In other words, sovereign ratings should be significantly predictable. All the factors which will move the rating, or even produce a new outlook, may already be incorporated into market prices well in advance of the actual rating action. Even in a world where credit ratings have a significant impact on funding costs and market credit perceptions, that impact may largely be discounted by the time a rating is actually changed or an outlook is announced.

In fact, the 'event' of a rating action may be that it was better than expected. For instance, suppose the fundamentals of a particular sovereign have deteriorated, and the market widely expects a downgrade of several notches. A rating agency does downgrade it, but only by one notch, and immediately puts the credit on stable outlook, signalling that further downgrades are not expected in the near term. The market may react favourably, in the sense that the rating actions were more generous than expected. An event study would find paradoxically that the negative rating action – a downgrade in this case – was associated with a *decrease* in Credit Default Swap (CDS) spreads or bond yields, not an increase. This might count as evidence against the relevance of ratings, when in fact it is precisely due to the very importance of ratings.

While studying the price impact of the news content of rating actions is an arguably more interesting question, it is not why CRAs have been under scrutiny lately and hence not the focus of our attention of this chapter. The recent criticism is that funding costs widen mechanically following CRA actions. This is the question we investigate.

Using a standard *event study* methodology, and focusing on the CDS market, we find that sovereign rating actions only have a marginally statistically significant effect on CDS returns of emerging markets if the action is credit negative, and none if it is credit positive. For a sample of countries that includes advanced economies only, rating actions, either positive or negative, have no effect on market prices. Even restricting the sample of countries to the EA-12, at the core of the criticisms, we do not find that rating actions impact market credit perceptions beyond what would be expected by chance. This would suggest that rating actions seem to marginally affect market perceptions of credit risk for the less developed economies in line with the traditional role of CRAs as *information providers*.

The remainder of the chapter is organised as follows. Section 2 briefly summarises previous research on the topic. Sections 3 and 4 describe the data and the methodology. The main results are presented in Section 5. We conclude in Section 6.

2 Related literature

Among the existing studies that address the impact of sovereign rating actions on market variables, Cantor and Packer (1996), for instance, study sovereign dollar bonds changes for a sample of 18 countries between 1987 and 1994. In particular, they examine the change in mean relative spreads over a two-day window, where relative yield spreads are defined as in ((sovereign bond yield – US Treasury rate)/US Treasury rate). The authors conclude that although agencies' ratings have a largely predictable component, they also appear to provide the market with information about non-investment-grade sovereigns that goes beyond that available in public data.

Kaminsky and Schmukler (2001) examine the impact of rating announcements on EMBI spreads (which reflect the difference between each country's sovereign bond yields relative to yields of benchmark instruments issued from developed countries) for 16 emerging markets in East Asia, Eastern Europe, and Latin America between 1990 and 2000. Using event study methods, the authors find that after an upgrade, bond spreads decline about 2% but increase by about 4% within ten days relative to the value ten days prior to the rating change. However, in the case of downgrades, while the contemporaneous reaction is similar to that of an upgrade (the spread changes about 2%), the bond markets do not recover following the downgrade.

Pukthuanthong-Le, Elayan, and Rose (2006) study the effect on rating events on stock and bond market returns for 34 countries between 1990 and 2000. Using an event study method, the authors find that downgrades have significant effects on market returns, but upgrades and affirmations do not have significant effects. Also, in contrast to the stock market, which reacts only to negative outlooks, bond markets also react to positive outlooks. Their multi-variate regression analysis shows that after controlling for country characteristics, positive rating events have no discernible impact on bond or stock markets and negative events have a significant impact on returns on those countries with less development and high inflation.

The IMF dedicated Chapter 3 of its World Economic Outlook in October 2010 to study how CRAs did their job and whether they inadvertently contributed to financial instability. The focus of the chapter is on sovereign ratings. The authors of the chapter analyse the impact of changes in sovereign ratings and credit warnings on CDS spreads for 72 sovereigns between January 2005 and July 2010. While they study the impact of rating announcements of the three major CRAs, they do so by examining the actions of each CRA individually, that is, the authors do not control for recent rating announcements by another rating agency. Changes in CDS spreads are considered within an event window of 41 days, from 20 days before to 20 days after the event, an unusually wide window. The chapter concludes that the agencies' traditional role as *information providers* is confirmed, as 'negative credit warning announcements are followed by statistically significant spread widening; 100bp for advanced economies and 160bp for emerging markets. The impact of positive rating changes is insignificant.' The authors also found that 'downgrades through the investment-grade threshold lead to statistically significant CDS spread widening of 38bp', providing evidence that some of the market impact of CRAs' actions is related to their *certification role*. But the authors found insufficient support for the *monitoring role* of CRAs as the market reaction to downgrades that follow negative credit watches, for example, was insignificant.

More recently, Arezki, Candelon, and Sy (2011) focus on whether sovereign rating news for European countries have spill-over effects both across countries and markets. Their sample study comprises the period January 2007–April 2010; however, most of the events occurred after July 2008 and the vast majority were downgrades or negative outlooks. The authors use a VAR model with four equations, each representing a given financial market (sovereign CDS spread, banking stock index, insurance stock index, and country stock market indices) and an event study technique in which the return on a given market is explained by a sequence of impulse dummies characterising the rating news. Such a specification relies on the assumptions that (1) markets are efficient as returns do not depend on past variables and (2) financial markets are not interrelated. The results are not conclusive: the sign and magnitude of the spill-over effect depends both on the type of announcements, the country experiencing the downgrade and the rating agency from which the announcements originate. The authors report that some rating changes, mostly downgrades, in a specific country are associated with positive spill-over in the other countries ('flight to safety') while outlook revisions are associated with negative spill-overs ('contagion'). They also find that downgrades to near speculative grade ratings for relatively large economies such as Greece have systematic spill-over effects across euro zone countries. According to the authors, this could be explained by rating-based rules such a as those in banking regulation, ECB collateral rules, 'credit events' in CDS contracts, or institutional investors' investment policies.

Afonso, Furceri, and Gomes (2011) conduct an event study analysis looking at the reaction of sovereign bond yield and CDS spreads to rating announcements in European Union countries from January 1995 until October 2010. The authors conclude that sovereign yield spreads respond negatively and weakly to positive events in the Economic and Monetary Union countries, but do not respond in countries outside the Economic and Monetary Union, while the response to negative announcements are similar across both sub-samples. However, they also find that there is evidence of bi-directional causality between sovereign ratings and spreads within a one–two week window.

Alsakka and Gwilym (2012) examine how the foreign exchange markets in 44 countries in Europe and Central Asia react to sovereign credit events before (2000–2006) and during (2006–2010) the recent financial crisis. The focus is on the response of bilateral exchange rates against the US dollar; during the study period there was no rating announcement involving the US, given the importance of the US dollar in global financial markets. Similar to the IMF study, the authors consider the effect of each rating agency separately and they do not control for other announcements either within the same rating agency or across rating agencies. To determine the impact of credit announcements on the own-country exchange rate, the authors regress the change in the exchange rate around the event date on changes in credit ratings (based on a logit-type transformation of a derived 58-point rating scale), initial rating, a set of country and year dummies, as well as the spread between yields on Baa and Aaa corporate bonds in the US as a proxy for the economic cycle. They allow for differential effects for positive and negative events, for rating changes and changes in the outlook/watch, and for announcements before and during the financial crisis. The results are a bit difficult to interpret as they vary substantially by CRA and by event window. During the pre-crisis period, positive signals are generally statistically insignificant in explaining movements in the exchange rate. However, there is evidence that negative signals, and specifically negative outlooks and watches, have a statistically (and also economically in the case of negative watches, as the exchange rate depreciates by around 15%) significant effect on exchange rates, although only if the rating announcements are made by S&P or Fitch. And in any case they tend to last only between three and seven days. During the crisis period, Moody's positive signals are found to move exchange rates between 2% and 3% for up to 14 days after the event, but positive signals by other rating agencies do not drive exchange rates. Negative announcements by any rating agency during the crisis are found to be statistically significant, again mostly driven by changes in outlook and watches. That said the economic impact appears much smaller than during the pre-crisis period: exchange rates depreciate between 1% and 3%.

While investigating the CDS market response to rating announcements, Galil and Soffer (2011) particularly address the challenge of differentiating 'between market responses to the various sources of information, such as rating announcements, news in the public media and private information'. Rating announcements by one rating agency are contaminated by similar announcements by other rating agencies or by the release of relevant information to the public. Hence 'the abnormal behavior of markets surrounding a rating announcement cannot be exclusively connected to the rating announcement itself'. The authors do not focus on sovereign ratings, though their database consists of 2152 firms from January 2002 and June 2006. However, their results indicate that the market response to negative news is overall stronger than to positive news. As negative news, including downgrades and negative reviews, tend to cluster, the residual contribution of a single negative rating announcement may be insignificant. While good news has a generally smaller effect on the market, it is also true that they are more infrequent than bad news, and therefore, the residual contribution of a single positive rating announcement is still significant.

This chapter complements previous research on credit rating announcements by being the first, to our knowledge, to examine the impact in the CDS market of sovereign rating actions of any type by any of the three major rating agencies for *all* rated sovereigns. It also controls for rating announcements by the same or another rating agency preceding the rating event in question. Previous studies have focused on a limited sample (by region, time period, or credit rating agency) of sovereign ratings and usually consider their impact on bond or equity markets where prices include other types of risk beyond credit risk. We also break from prior research which typically considers the rating actions of different agencies as separate events.

This chapter further offers two alternative characterisations of rating events we have not seen elsewhere. The first one constructs a new rating history for each country as the best (highest) outstanding rating on any day out of the three major rating agencies; it then associates the outlook and watch that corresponds to that rating. The second one similarly constructs a rating history for each country choosing the worst (lowest) rating out of the three outstanding. This permits us to study the impact of changes to the best and worst available major credit opinion. For instance, it is one thing to consider the impact of the first rating agency to downgrade a sovereign from Aaa to Aa; it may be a very different thing to consider the impact of the last agency to do so: is it more significant when the last Aaa opinion is taken away?

3 Data and descriptive statistics

3.1 Data

We define an *event* as a rating announcement by any of the three largest international rating agencies: Fitch Ratings (Fitch henceforth), Moody's

Investors Service (Moody's) and Standard & Poor's (S&P). The *event day* is the day when the rating announcement is made. All types of rating announcements except affirmations – that is, credit rating changes, rating reviews or watches, and rating outlooks – are considered in this study. A rating change signals a fundamental change in an issuer's creditworthiness as rating agencies 'rate through the cycle'; credit ratings are not typically influenced by events which only have a temporary effect on creditworthiness. Rating reviews and outlooks, on the other hand, indicate likely changes in creditworthiness. Credits are placed on review (for upgrade or downgrade) when a rating change is expected in the near term. The credit outlook (positive, negative, or stable) reflects the balance of credit risks over a longer horizon (Gupta, 2011). Reviews and outlooks are mutually exclusive events, with reviews superseding outlooks.

For each sovereign issuer, data on rating announcements were obtained from Reuters. We include all sovereigns rated by any of the three major rating agencies from the mid-2000s through early 2012. We selected the announcements relating to the most senior credit rating available, usually the long-term issuer rating. If both a local currency and a foreign currency long-term issuer rating for the same rating agency exist, we take the lower of the two. If more than one announcement is made on any given day concerning the same issuer (e.g., rating and outlook change), we consider the rating change over the review/outlook action.

In order to control for other events that might influence prices around the day of the rating announcement, and following Micu, Remolona, and Wooldridge (2006) and Pukthuanthong-Le, Elayan, and Rose (2007), among others, we control for foreshadowed announcements, that is, rating announcements which were preceded by another announcement on the same issuer, made either by the same rating agency or a different agency, within four weeks (20 business days).

The period over which we measure the effect of an announcement on prices is referred to as the *event window*. And by controlling for foreshadowed announcements we ensure that any event window spans only one event. If a rating announcement is thought to result in price pressures, then it should have a discernible price impact in the [0,+1] interval, where 0 is the event day and +1 is the day after the event. The justification for including a day after the event is that the announcement might have been made after the markets closed. For less liquid names one might want to consider a wider event window, for example [0,+15]. If rating announcements are irrelevant and are simply correlated with market movements, spreads should adjust ahead of the event day, for example, in intervals [–39,–21] or [–20,–1] or narrower windows.

The control or reference sample over which to evaluate the change in prices is referred to as the *estimation window*. Regardless of the event window the estimation window is the same and spans the interval [–81,–42], that is, 40 days (excluding weekends).

To examine how prices respond to credit announcements, we focus on excess CDS daily returns. We do so because changes in returns can result from any of: (1) a change in the risk-free rate, (2) a change in the market price of the risk of default, and (3) a change in the risk of default of the issuer (Ory & Raimbourg, 2008). Hence we consider excess returns, that is, relative to market-wide returns, and relative spreads rather than absolute changes in spreads. Data on CDS spreads are from MarkIt and restricted to the sample of five-year contracts as dealers update quotes for five-year maturities more frequently than those for other maturities.

3.2 Descriptive statistics

The unconditional sample of 642 events is broadly balanced across positive and negative events. Once we exclude those events that were preceded by another rating action in the four weeks prior to the event, the sample (uncontaminated sample) is not so well-balanced and shrinks by about 23% to 493. About 70% (348 actions) of those rating actions correspond to emerging markets, of which 16% are downgrades, 19% negative outlook or watch changes, 45% upgrades, and 20% positive outlook or watch changes.

Moreover, most of the actions, 85%, are on rating classes Baa to B.

In order to illustrate the correlation between CDS spreads and sovereign ratings, Exhibit 1 plots CDS average spreads by broad rating category for the sample of emerging markets. It is evident from the chart that spreads are increasing as we move down the rating scale, but it also reveals an exponential trend meaning that the relationship between ratings and spreads is not linear, just as the relationship between ratings and default rates is not linear. The regression shows that sovereign ratings account for 87% of the variation in spreads. This is not to say that we think ratings explain spreads, rather it is most likely indicative that both financial markets and credit rating agencies share the same pool of information. Cantor and Packer (1996) found a similar relationship between sovereign bond spreads and credit ratings.

Exhibit 2 plots mean CDS spreads by type of announcement around the event day for both emerging markets and advanced economies.

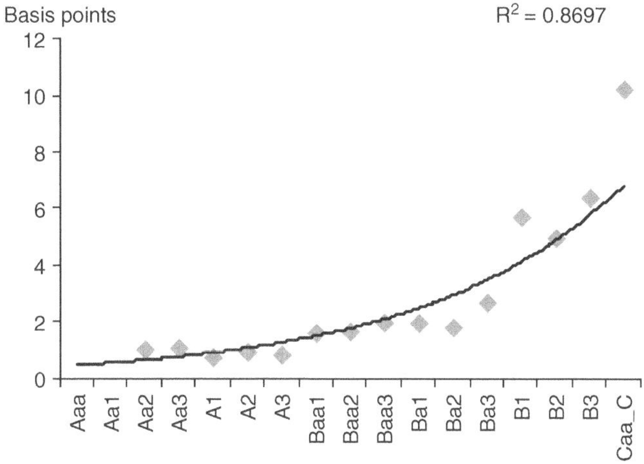

Figure 15.1 Sovereign CDS spreads by whole-letter rating; average spreads, emerging markets, 2005–February 2012

Source: MarkIt, Reuters, and Moody's calculations.

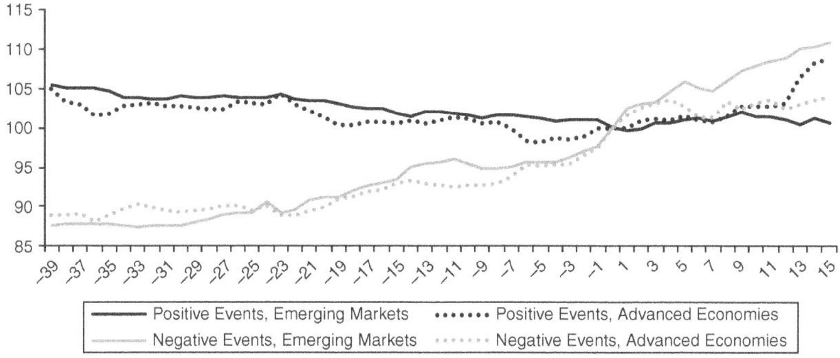

Figure 15.2 Mean spreads by type of rating announcement

Source: MarkIt, Reuters and Moody's calculations.

We normalised spreads to 100 at the day of the announcement. Rating agencies' changes in creditworthiness of emerging markets appear to be preceded by a similar evaluation by markets. During the 38 days preceding a negative (positive) announcement, mean spreads for emerging markets increased (decreased) by 11.6% (4.1%). At the day and the day after the announcement mean CDS spreads rise (fall) by a further 4.9% (1.5%).

The change in spreads before and after the rating event is smaller for advanced economies. During the 38 days prior to a negative (positive) rating announcement, mean spreads in advanced economies increase (decrease) by 9.6% (4.9%), while on the day and the day after the event the change in spreads are 4.1% for negative events and 0.1% for positive events. More importantly, after a few days following the rating event, the trend movement in spreads for advanced economies disappears and even starts to reverse.

4 Method

4.1 Excess returns

Following Micu, Remolona, and Woolddridge (2006) and others, we define CDS returns as the log change in CDS spreads. We then estimate excess returns as follows. For any given sample of N events, we have a vector of CDS daily returns $r_t = [r_{1t}, r_{2t}, \ldots, r_{Nt}]$ and a vector r_{kt} defined as the return of the market index k, which is set to the regional average CDS. We can calculate excess returns using the market model:

$$ar_{it} = r_{it} - \alpha_i - \beta_i r_{kt} \quad t \in \textit{event window} \tag{15.1}$$

The parameters α_i and β_i are estimated over the estimation window for each country and event separately.

We define the cumulative excess returns for each event as:

$$cer_i = \sum_{t=1}^{L} er_{it} \quad \textit{where L is the width of the event window}$$

with sample variance σ_i^2. If we think sovereign rating actions do not move sovereign spreads, we will expect excess returns, as defined above, to be not significantly different from zero.

4.2 Test statistics

Event-by-event tests

For each individual credit rating event, we test whether the cumulative excess return over the event window [0, +1] is statistically different from zero. To construct such a t-statistic we have to consider two sources of variation: (i) specification and innovation uncertainty, captured by the standard error of our regression model for excess returns (Equation 15.1), and (ii) parameter uncertainty, since the excess return over the event window is calculated using estimated parameters. We estimate the forecast error variance as follows:

$$\hat{Y}_0 = X_0\hat{\beta}$$
$$U = Y_0 - \hat{Y}_0$$
$$X_0\beta + X_0\hat{\beta}$$

$$V[U|X_0] = X_0\Sigma_\beta X_0' + \sigma_\varepsilon^2$$
$$\sigma_\varepsilon^2(X_0(X'X)^{-1}X_0' + 1)$$

Average excess returns

To test whether average excess CDS returns across all events of the same type (that is, negative events or positive events) is significantly different from zero, we employ a standardised cross-sectional t-test. The alternative hypothesis is that excess returns are greater than zero for negative rating announcements and less than zero for positive announcements. By assumption there is no correlation between excess returns across issuers and across time, so we can aggregate excess returns over a sub-sample of N events:

$$\overline{CER} = \frac{1}{N}\sum_{i=1}^{N} cer_i$$

But as Micu, Remolona, and Woolddridge (2006) note, rating announcements could also change the variance of CDS prices usually leading to the event window standard deviation being larger than the estimation window standard deviation. In which case the test statistic results in rejection of the null hypothesis more often than it should. To remedy this problem, we follow Daniels and Jensen (2004) and ignore the estimation window residual variance and use instead the cross-sectional variance in the event window itself to form the test statistic:

$$\bar{\sigma}^2 = \frac{1}{N^2}\sum_{i=1}^{N}\sigma_i^2$$

$$t_{N-1} = \frac{\overline{CER}}{\bar{\sigma}}$$

5 Results

Our first test is on individual announcements: we examine whether the cumulative excess returns over the day of the announcement and the day after the announcement are statistically different from zero. For the sample of emerging markets, we found that only 4% of rating announcements related to emerging markets have a statistically and economically (that is, the credit action should at least move spreads by six basis points) significant effect on excess CDS returns at the 5% level. That is well within the expected margin of error: in a random sample we would expect rating actions to have a statistically significant effect on prices 5% of the time at the 5% level of significance. Moreover, 32% of the time, excess returns move in the opposite direction as one would expect given the rating action.

However, once we divided the rating events between positive and negative, we found that while positive events do not have a statistically and economically significant effect on excess CDS returns at the 5% level, 8% of the negative announcements are found to have a statistically and economically significant effect on excess returns at the same 5% confidence. That is, there is some marginal evidence that negative rating events related to emerging markets might have some influence on credit spreads; in other words, negative rating actions seem to be informative for less developed countries in line with the traditional role of CRAs as *information providers*. One can argue that investors attach greater value to rating agencies' assessments of smaller/less developed countries on the basis that there is less and/or more costly information available about these countries, where problems of asymmetric information and transparency are more relevant, and where perhaps rating actions might unveil private information.

For the sample of advanced economies we found that 3.5% of all rating events have a significant association with CDS excess returns at the 5% significance level, which is perfectly consistent with the hypothesis that rating actions do not have a significant impact on CDS spreads beyond the margin of error. This is also the case when we further restrict the sample to the EA-12 countries where much of the criticism about CRAs determining market prices has centred recently.

Our second exercise focuses on the statistical significance of *average* excess returns. These results confirm our earlier results. While positive events have no statistically significant effect on average cumulative CDS excess returns over the day and the day after the announcement for emerging markets, negative events have some statistical significant effect on excess returns. That said, negative rating actions on less developed economies also had a significant effect on these sovereigns' CDS excess returns ahead of the announcement at the [–5,–1] window, that is, not all the impact is unanticipated.

For the advanced economies sample, we do not find any significant effect of average excess returns following any type of rating announcements.

5.1 Robustness Checks

Exhibit 3 shows how sensitive our results are to the definitions of rating event and estimation window. Our preferred specification is shown in the column labelled 'baseline'; the rest of the columns change either the gap between rating actions that defined an uncontaminated event (columns labelled 1 to 3) or the estimation window over which we estimated the market model as per Equation [1], and which helped us to define excess CDS returns (column 4), or the definition of the rating event per se (columns 5 and 6).

These robustness checks show that positive rating actions on emerging market sovereigns never move CDS spreads in any significant way across all specifications and that negative rating actions remain somewhat significant.

It is worth noting that once we include events that are contaminated by other rating announcements, by the same or other rating agency, the per cent of significant events increases to 13% (column 3), but in a contaminated sample, as explained earlier, we cannot isolate the impact of a particular rating action and hence its impact on CDS spreads.

For the last two robustness checks, we have constructed two alternative characterisations of rating events. The first one, column 5, constructs a new rating history for each country as the best outstanding rating at any day out of the three major rating agencies; we then associate the outlook and watch that corresponds to that rating. Similarly, in column 6, we construct a third rating history for each country, choosing the worst rating out of the three outstanding ratings by Moody's, S&P, and Fitch. Rating changes and changes in outlook/watch direction are defined, again, out of the new rating history. We still consider only uncontaminated events, that is, we only include those rating events that were not preceded by another event in the 20 days prior to the event. Comparing columns 5 and 6, it seems that markets are equally sensitive to the first or the last mover, that is, markets do not wait to react until the third rating agency moves its credit outlook

Table 15.1 Robustness tests, emerging markets

	Baseline	**1**	**2**	**3**	**4**	**5**	**6**
Estimation window	[−81,−42]	[−81,−42]	[−81,−42]	[−81,−42]	[−15,−1]	[−81,−42]	[−81,−42]
Gap between events	20	40	10	Contaminated sample	20	20	20
Event definition						Best of 3 ratings	Worst of 3 ratings
Percentage of events significant at the 5% level and with spreads moving by at least 6 basis points							
Positive events	2%	2%	1%	3%	2%	2%	2%
Negative events	8%	11%	8%	13%	8%	13%	14%
Percentage of events moving in the wrong direction	32%	31%	32%	33%	32%	37%	34%

Notes: Estimation window: Period over which the market equation is estimated. Gap between events: Number of days (excluding weekends) in between events to define the uncontaminated events sample.

Source: Moody's calculations.

for a particular sovereign closer to the assessment of the other two rating agencies.

6 Conclusion

Our study suggests that sovereign rating actions only have a marginally statistically significant effect on excess CDS returns for emerging markets if the action is credit negative. Positive events are found not to have any impact on excess returns for emerging markets. Moreover, 33% of the time, CDS returns move in the opposite direction as one would expect following a rating action.

If we restrict the sample to advanced economies, 2% and 4% of positive and negative credit events respectively have a significant impact on these countries' CDS excess returns at the 5% level. That is well within the expected margin of error: in a random sample, we would expect rating actions to have a statistically significant effect on prices 5% of the time at the 5% level of significance. And again in numerous occasions (about 38% of the time) spreads move in the opposite direction as one would presume following a rating action.

That is, we find that sovereign rating actions only have a statistically significant effect on spreads of small/less developed countries, and only if the action is credit negative in line with the traditional role of CRAs as *information providers*.

Of course, it is worth considering whether an event study is an appropriate method for addressing the question at hand, whether rating actions cause a change in credit risk perception in the sovereign market. It is certainly a standard method. Event studies are commonly employed to isolate the effect of news on a company's market value, for example. But in those cases, the release of the news *is* the event, so it seems reasonable to look at the company's excess equity return around the release of the news. But in the case of rating actions, the rating action itself is arguably *not* the event.

Why would we say that the rating action, even defined to include watch list and outlook announcements, might not be the event of interest? Sovereign ratings are based on public information, and they are produced through public and transparent methodologies. In other words, sovereign ratings should be significantly predictable. All the factors which will move the rating, or even produce a new outlook, may already be incorporated into market prices well in advance of the actual rating action. Even in a world where credit ratings have a significant impact on funding costs and market credit perceptions, that impact may largely be discounted by the time a rating is actually changed or an outlook is announced. This means that an event study, by its nature, will fail to detect the effect.

In fact, the 'event' of a rating action may be that it was better than expected. For instance, suppose the fundamentals of a particular sovereign have deteriorated, and the market widely expects a downgrade. A rating agency does downgrade it, but only by one notch, and immediately puts the credit on stable outlook, signalling that further downgrades are not expected in the near term. The market may react favourably, in the sense that the rating actions were far more generous than expected. An event study would find paradoxically that the negative rating action – a downgrade in this case – was associated with a *decrease* in CDS spreads or bond yields, not an increase. This might count as evidence against the relevance of ratings, when in fact it is precisely due to the very importance of ratings.

There are technical limits as well to the application of the event study methodology to rating actions. The difference in real, physical credit risk is really quite small among the higher rating categories. The difference in physical risk between Aaa and Aa1, for instance, will likely be lost in market prices compared to other concerns such as liquidity and risk premia. This is especially true in the sovereign market. During periods of general stress, when physical risk is increasing and rating actions may be more frequent, it could also be that risk aversion is increasing. Spreads will therefore be widening by much more than the change in physical risk. An event study might then attribute too much impact from rating actions on spreads. Of course, the event study methodology attempts to correct for such contemporaneous influences. But the concern remains that the correction may not be complete.

These concerns notwithstanding, an event study remains a common and natural approach to measuring the causal impact of ratings on market pricing. If a well-conducted study were to find significant effects, those may be hard to discount. But the absence of significant effects, as documented above, is not necessarily evidence that ratings are not relevant to market perceptions. Additional research may focus on first classifying rating actions as *unexpectedly* negative or positive. An event study around such surprising rating actions may well reveal an impact. We leave this to future research.

Appendix

Asia	Latin America &The Caribbean	Middle East & Africa	Euro area	Other advanced	Other
China	Argentina	Bahrain	Austria	Australia	Bulgarai
Hong Kong	Brazil	Egypt	Belgium	Denmark	Croatia
Indonesia	Chile	Lebanon	Cyprus	Finland	Czech Republic
Korea	Colombia	Morocco	Estonia	Iceland	Hungary
Malaysia	Costa Rica	Oman	France	Japan	Israel
Pakistan	Dominican Republic	Qatar	Germany	New Zealand	Kazakhstan
Philippines	Ecuador	Saudi Arabia	Greece	Norway	Latvia
Singapore	El Salvador	South Africa	Ireland	Sweden	Lithuania
Sri Lanka	Guatemala	Tunisia	Italy	UK	Poland
Thailand	Jamaica		Malta	USA	Romania
Vietnam	Mexico		Netherlands		Russia
	Panama		Portugal		Serbia
	Peru		Slovakia		Turkey
	Uruguay		Slovenia		Ukraine
	Venezuela		Spain		

Notes

1. For example, the chairman of the Treasury Committee in the UK accused rating agencies of acting like 'journalists looking for a splash' regarding the S&P downgrade of the US, see the FT Adviser article, April 2012 for a complete story; similarly, the Huffington Post in April 2011 wrote that the US congressional report found that the rating agencies 'triggered the worst financial crisis in decades when they were forced to downgrade the inflated ratings they slapped on complex mortgage-backed securities'.
2. During the 1997–1998 Asian crisis, credit rating agencies were also accused of first, being too slow to downgrade East Asian sovereigns, and second, of being procyclical and downgrading sovereigns by more than the worsening of the fundamentals would have justified (Kiff, Nowak, & Schumacher, 2012; Ferri, Liu, & Stiglitz, 1999).
3. See, for example, the European Parliament News, June 2012.

References

Afonso, A, Furceri, D & Gomes, P (2011), 'Sovereign Credit Ratings and Financial Market Linkages: Application to European Data', Working Paper Series No. 1347, European Central Bank.

Alsakka, R & Gwilym, O (2013), 'Rating Agencies' Signals During the European Sovereign Debt Crisis: Market Impact and Spillovers', *Journal of Economic Behavior & Organization*, vol. 85, pp. 144–162.

Arezki, R, Candelon, B & Sy, A (2011), 'Sovereign Rating News and Financial Markets Spillovers: Evidence from the European Debt Crisis', Working Paper Series No. 11/68, International Monetary Fund.

Daniels, K & Jensen, M S (2004), 'The Effect of Credit Ratings on Credit Default Swap Spreads and Credit Spreads', Working Paper Series No. 191, Centre for Analytical Finance, Aarhus School of Business, University of Aarhus.

Ferri, G, Liu, L & Stiglitz, J E (1999), 'The Procyclical Role of Rating Agencies: Evidence from the East Asian Crisis', *Economic Notes*, vol. 28, no. 3, pp. 335–355.

Galil, K & Soffer, G (2011), 'Good News, Bad News and Rating Announcements: An Empirical Investigation', *Journal of Banking & Finance*, vol. 35, pp. 3101–3119.

Gupta, V (2011), 'Effects of Watches, Outlooks and Previous Rating Actions on Rating Transitions and Default Rates', Moody's Special Comment, August, <https://www.moodys.com/researchdocumentcontentpage.aspx?docid=PBC_134938>.

IMF (2010), 'The Uses and Abuses of Sovereign Credit Ratings', *World Economic Outlook*, International Monetary Fund, Chapter 3, pp. 85–122.

Kaminsky, G & Schmukler, S (2001), 'Emerging Markets Instability: Do Sovereign Ratings Affect Country Risk and Stock Returns?' Working Paper, The World Bank Policy Research Working Paper Series.

Kiff, J, Nowak, S & Schumacher, L (2012), 'Are Rating Agencies Powerful? An Investigation into the Impact and Accuracy of Sovereign Ratings, Working Paper Series No. 12/23, World Bank.

Micu, M, Remolona, E & Woolddridge, P (2006), 'The Price Impact of Rating Announcements: Which Announcements Matter?', Working Paper No. 207, Bank of International Settlements (BIS).

Ory, J N & Raimbourg, P (2008), 'Credit Rating Agencies Function on Bond Markets: Price Stability vs. Information Transmission', 21st Australian Finance and Banking Conference 2008 Paper, <http://papers.ssrn.com/sol3/papers.cfm?abstract_id=1253043##>.

Pukthuanthong-Le, K, Elayan, F & Rose, L (2007), 'Equity and Debt Market Responses to Sovereign Credit Rating Announcement', *Global Finance Journal*, vol. 18, no. 1, pgs. 47–83.

Index

The manufacturer's authorised representative in the EU is Springer Nature Customer Service Centre GmbH, Europaplatz 3, 69115 Heidelberg, Germany. If you have any concerns regarding our products, please contact ProductSafety@springernature.com

Printed and bound by CPI Group (UK) Ltd, Croydon, CR0 4YY
14/10/2026
02233136-0014